Deploying Microsoft® SQL Server™ 7.0

Notes from the Field

PUBLISHED BY
Microsoft Press
A Division of Microsoft Corporation
One Microsoft Way
Redmond, Washington 98052-6399

Library of Congress Cataloging-in-Publication Data
Deploying Microsoft SQL Server 7.0 / Microsoft Corporation.
     p. cm.
   ISBN 0-7356-0726-5
   1. SQL Server. 2. Client/server computing.   I. Microsoft
Corporation.
   QA76.9.C55D46 1999
   005.75'85--DC21   99-23817
                                     CIP

Printed and bound in the United States of America.

1 2 3 4 5 6 7 8 9 QMQM 4 3 2 1 0 9

Distributed in Canada by Penguin Books Canada Limited.

A CIP catalogue record for this book is available from the British Library.

Microsoft Press books are available through booksellers and distributors worldwide. For further information about international editions, contact your local Microsoft Corporation office or contact Microsoft Press International directly at fax (425) 936-7329. Visit our Web site at mspress.microsoft.com.

Acquisitions Editor: Anne Hamilton
Project Editor: Thom Votteler

Contributors

We dedicate this volume to the authors, contributors, and reviewers who generously gave their time, experience, and vast knowledge to make this title a reality.

Program Manager
Michael Ohata

Senior Technical Editor
Bob Haynie

Group Program Manager
Per Vonge Nielsen

Project Managers—Consultants
Frank Abendroth, Abendroth Beratung, Westernohe Germany
Richard Graf, g&h Database Technologies GmbH
Christopher Etz, g&h Database Technologies GmbH

Contributors
Pat Amiot (Approach), Larry Barnes, Joyce Behrendt, Erin Blake, John Boen, Howard R. Burkett (James Martin + Company), Spencer Butt, Li-Wen Chen (MetaEdge Corporation), Susan Cushen, Christopher Etz (g&h Database Technologies GmbH), Tom Jamieson, Ann Jewett, Keith Klosterman, Manuel Martinez, Chris McKulka, Abu Moniruzzaman (Approach), Allen McDowell, Betsy Norton-Middaugh, David Morts, Tom Niccoli, Juan Jose Ortiz (MetaEdge Corporation), Lincoln Popp, Frank Rabeler (g&h Database Technologies GmbH), Jeffrey B. Rogers, Vijay Sankaran (James Martin + Company), Chris Stine, and Kathy Watanabe

Additional Contributors and Technical Review
Taime Amador, Ann Beebe, Chris Cale, Rolf Carlson (Approach), Gale Chock, Leslie Cole, Linda Comstock, Thomas Davidson, Nicholas Dritsas, Judy Dulcich, Denis Fuster (MetaEdge Corporation), Cynthia Givens, JeanAnn Bradley Honaker, Pat James, Douglas Leland, Fred Martin (Cotelligent), Larry Mascioli, Bryan McClain (Walklett Group), Greg McGuinness, John H. Miller, Ariel Netz, Axel Schwanke, Elizabeth J. Scott (Walklett Group), Carol Sells, Jeff Smith, Craig Snively, Ryan Trout, Tom Walklett (Walklett Group), and Daniel Zenzel

Indexer
Richard S. Shrout

Compositor
Barbara Norfleet

Project Editor
Thom Votteler

Contents

Part 2   Very Large Database Solutions

Part 3   Data Warehouse Scenarios

Introduction

Welcome to *Deploying Microsoft SQL Server 7.0,* fifth in the *Notes from the Field* series, featuring best practices from Microsoft Consulting Services, Microsoft Certified Solution Provider partners, and our own Information Technology Group. Designed for information technology (IT) and information systems (IS) professionals, this book condenses and organizes the broad expertise of consultants and support engineers, and offers you the benefit of their real-world experiences. Most of the chapters use fictitious customer names, but all of the case studies derive from customer scenarios or an amalgamation of several technical implementations where consultants and customers tested and proved their approaches and techniques.

You should use this book as a supplement to the Microsoft SQL Server 7.0 and product documentation, including the Microsoft SQL Server 7.0 Books Online and the *Microsoft SQL Server 7.0 Resource Guide* (part of the *Microsoft BackOffice 4.5 Resource Kit*). These resources contain a wealth of information, ranging from concept definition to details on Transact-SQL statement syntax. The book you are reading now often refers you to these resources for general and background information.

No single book can cover every deployment and implementation topic for a product as complex as SQL Server, especially one that requires solution development. This book doesn't try to. Instead, it focuses tightly on building the framework for identifying key issues in the design and development of your database solution. It is not a primer on good database design. Nor does it replace the expertise of partner companies or an extended team of designers, developers, and network and database administrators who will drive your project to completion.

What's in This Book

This book consists of four parts, each with several chapters.

Part 1: Deployment Strategy and Planning

Part 1 helps you understand how to approach and clear the first set of obstacles in designing and deploying an enterprise-scale distributed database applications. It looks at the core competencies needed in large database projects, a generic rollout plan for SQL Server 7.0, and best practices in formulating a deployment strategy and plan. Chapter 1 introduces you to a team structure based on the Microsoft Solutions Framework, describes basic competencies, and points you to readings and resources that can get the team going. Chapter 2 looks at SQL Server 7.0 in the context of how an organization develops its networking infrastructure over time, and reviews the strategy and path for upgrading from SQL Server 6.5. Chapter 3 highlights a datamart and data warehouse planning, development, and deployment process defined by industry leader James Martin + Co.

Part 2: Very Large Database Solutions

This section draws on the experience of enterprise customers who adopted SQL Server 7.0 early. The chapters walk you through the key issues in designing, building, tuning, and managing very large database (VLDB) systems. It arranges them topically, addresses them thoroughly, and offers lots of examples drawn from real-world cases. Because of its complexity, a VLDB project needs complete and accurate documentation to mitigate risk, and Chapter 4 describes how to organize and record each design and implementation step to ensure security, reliability, and expandability. Chapter 5 discusses basic hardware choices and SQL Server configuration issues. Chapter 6 surveys best practices for mapping your logical design in to a physical data model. Chapter 7 explains how to optimize queries and transactions. Chapter 8 describes how to plan and perform backups, reorganize indexes, and use the database consistency checker (DBCC) statements.

Part 3: Data Warehouse Scenarios

Data warehouse projects often demand joining forces with a partner company to gather requirements, design a solution, and manage the rollout. This part highlights several data warehouse (DW) case studies. Chapter 9 explores how Microsoft's human resources DW creates a single secure system for daily reporting. Chapter 10, on MS Sales, describes how the development team created a system to make timely, consistent, and accurate data available for users with divergent needs, *and* boost system performance. Chapter 11 looks at how MetaEdge uses metadata and components built on the Microsoft Repository to manage a data warehouse. And Chapter 12 showcases a simple but highly effective OLAP Services implementation used with a management reporting system.

Part 4: Replication Implementation

Replication is central to designing and deploying enterprise-scale distributed database applications. No doubt your organization will go into the twenty-first century striving to create and maximize a digital nervous system—using digital information to make better and faster business decisions—and whatever design you use, system availability will be crucial. This section examines the performance and reliability issues you need to consider when designing a replication infrastructure (Chapter 13) and best practices you can use to deploy it (Chapter 14).

Additional Information

The Appendix covers upgrading from Microsoft SQL Server 4.21 to version 6.5. If you are currently using SQL Server 4.21*x* and you want to upgrade to SQL Server 7.0, your options are somewhat limited. Because of the many database structural changes between SQL Server 4.21*x* and SQL Server 6.*x*, you cannot upgrade to SQL Server 7.0 directly from SQL Server 4.21*x*: you must first upgrade to SQL Server 6.5 and then to SQL Server 7.0. This section explains how.

Conventions Used

Convention	Description
ALL CAPITALS	Acronyms, filenames, and names of commands.
bold	Menus and menu commands, command buttons, property page and dialog box titles and options, command-line commands, options, and portions of syntax that must be typed exactly as shown. First occurrences of special terms, and book titles.
Initial Capitals	Names of applications, programs, servers, windows, directories, and paths.
Italic	Information you have to enter. Used also for emphasis as dictated by context.
`monospace type`	Sample command lines, program code, and program output.
Q123456, Title: How to Optimize Network Traffic over Windows NT	Knowledge Base article titles. Search for them on Microsoft TechNet or at http://support.microsoft.com/support/a.asp?M=F using the "Q" number (no spaces).

Icons That Highlight Text

These sidebar icons provide you with simple signposts:

Icon	Description
⚠	**Caution** or **Warning**. Advises you to take or avoid specific action to avoid potential damage.
	Note. Emphasizes, supplements, or qualifies points in the text.
	Best Practices or **Guidelines**. Highlights proven practices, techniques, or procedures from MCS real-world experiences.
	Tools. Indicates sample code or descriptions of utilities or tools provided in the text.

Some Important Business

The example companies, organizations, products, people, and events depicted in this book are fictitious. No association with any real company, organization, product, person, or event is intended or should be inferred.

Deployment Strategy and Planning

Enterprise resource planning, business operations, e-commerce, data warehousing—an intimidating list of database systems. Maybe your organization has already cleared a major hurdle by deciding that the time has come to plan for, design, and deploy this sort of technology. But there are plenty more hurdles before the first turn in the track: Where do you begin? What resources will you need? How do you allocate them for maximum efficiency? The complexity of enterprise-scale distributed database applications demands that you gather and assess requirements rigorously, that you create an architecture that meets current information technology needs and anticipates future ones, that you build a productive team out of people with diverse database development skills. Where do you *start*?

This section helps you understand how to approach and clear the first set of obstacles. It looks at the core competencies needed in large database projects, a generic rollout plan for Microsoft SQL Server 7.0, and best practices in formulating a deployment strategy and plan. Chapter 1 "The Right Team and the Right Skills" introduces you to a team structure based on the Microsoft Solutions Framework, describes basic competencies, and points you to readings and resources that can get the team going. Chapter 2 looks at SQL Server 7.0 in the context of how an organization develops its networking infrastructure over time, and reviews the strategy and path for upgrading from SQL Server 6.5. Chapter 3 highlights a datamart and data warehouse planning, development, and deployment process defined by industry leader James Martin + Co.

Based on extensive field experience, these chapters describe and explain the fundamental steps for getting any large database project moving forward.

C H A P T E R   1

The Right Team and the Right Skills

Deploying SQL Server 7.0 in your enterprise can involve several processes: upgrading to SQL Server 7.0 and converting databases and applications, creating a data warehouse or datamart, working with very large databases (VLDBs), and designing replication for a distributed computing environment. All these processes require planning, development, and testing. Obviously, a full deployment must involve numerous stages, during which teams pursue specific projects while coordinating in the overall process. To meet your business goals, you have to build teams so that they contain the right members with the right skills.

Infrastructure projects are constrained by budget, people, resources, and timelines. If the first step in your project is to identify the roles and responsibilities of members of the project team, you will be able to manage constraints effectively and, probably, save time and money. Using the Microsoft Solutions Framework (MSF) team model as a foundation, this chapter defines the team members needed and examines the skills they must bring to the project.

What You'll Find in This Chapter

- How to build the teams you will need to deploy SQL Server 7.0.

- A breakdown of the tasks involved in developing large database solutions.

- The core competencies team members need to complete these tasks.

- A survey of resources where you can learn more about individual skills and topics.

Building the Team

Although every project needs certain key team members, team composition also depends on *size*: of the project, the enterprise, the budget, and the available staff. Small organizations may use one person in several roles; large organizations may use several people in one role. Before you can plan hiring, allocation, or training needs, you have to identify roles and responsibilities.

The MSF team model provides a practical starting point from which to build out a project. The model creates a *team of peers*, working in interdependent and cooperating roles, without an established hierarchy (see http://www.microsoft.com/msf). This gives each team member a well-defined role focused on a specific mission, which encourages *ownership* and results in a better product. Team leaders focus on management, guidance, and coordination; team members focus on specific mission-critical tasks; everyone focuses on the defined business objectives.

The MSF model comprises six teams:

- **Product Management.** Identifies and sets priorities. Establishes and sustains the business case for the project.
- **Program Management.** Drives the project, overseeing planning, design, and implementation. Facilitates the day-to-day coordination required to meet organizational standards and interoperability goals.
- **Development.** Builds and implements products and services that meet the specification and user expectations. Evaluates technical solutions to be acquired, developed, and used.
- **Testing.** Finds, resolves, and documents all issues before release into production.
- **User Education.** Designs, develops, and publishes user performance solutions, online help, and training systems, including instructional materials that enable users to get the most out of the product or service. Packages the system so that it can be supported and used effectively.
- **Logistics Management.** Ensures smooth rollout, installation, and migration to the operations and support groups.

The MSF model offers these benefits:

- Gives each team member a stake in the project's success.
- Creates a culture that encourages clarity, efficiency, participation, commitment, and team spirit.
- Improves accountability for all roles.
- Results in a sustained focus on user needs and business goals.

Matching Skills to the Job

This section defines additional roles, responsibilities, and skills for team members for upgrading SQL Server, building a data warehouse, working with VLDBs, and replicating data across distributed applications. (Subsequent parts of this book—2, 3, and 4—provide in-depth discussions on implementation of VLDBs, data warehousing, and replication, respectively.) As previously mentioned, roles can be filled by one person or several people, depending on the size of the project, the enterprise, the budget, and the staff. A team can also be broken into smaller groups that concentrate on a specific area, such as planning, designing, and testing. Keep in mind that a data warehouse project is ongoing: after the warehouse is in place, there are continuing iterations and population projects. Some team members (as many as is practical, actually) will continue in their roles even after the first stage of the process is implemented.

Upgrade SQL Server project team.

Role	Responsibilities	Skills
Database Administrator	Technical configuration of all SQL Server 7.0 servers and databases. Helps with database conversion, backup planning, resolving keyword conflicts, back-out planning, and SQL Server database loading.	Database schema Backup/recovery strategies Data Transformation Services (DTS) Microsoft Repository English Query
Database Operations	Maintains, operates, monitors, and repairs the SQL Server 7.0 database environment after installation.	SQL Server services, management, and design
Developer	Modifies applications to be compatible with SQL Server 7.0 and communicates application issues to the development teams.	Knows existing applications Can build scaleable applications
Technical Consulting (third-level technical support)	Provides consulting services and problem resolution (including keyword, syntax, and semantic changes) for internal business units.	Database schema Data Transformation Services (DTS) Office and BackOffice Integration Upgrade/Conversion tools
Network Administrator	Maintains the Microsoft Windows NT Server 4.0 implementation	Office and BackOffice Integration
Marketing and Customer Relations	Develops and carries out the SQL Server rollout marketing program (product demonstrations, newsletters, and pilot site coordination). Acts as a client advocate in design meetings.	Familiar with business goals and objectives
Financial Control	Monitors project financial aspects. Tracks expenses against budget allocations.	Familiar with business goals and objectives

Data warehouse project team.

Role	Responsibility	Skills
Business Analyst, Technical Staff	Provides business objectives, critical success factors, and future development plans and the strategy for implementing them.	Knowledge of business goals and objectives
Decision Support System (DSS) Developers	Develops query grammar.	OLAP Services English Query
Network Administrator	Provides hardware and operating systems (OS) support.	Office and BackOffice Integration Administration of SQL Server (backup/restore, automation, performance)
Systems Engineer	Develops a data model for a data warehouse or datamart.	Database schema design Security (Windows NT and SQL Server)
Database Administrator	Transfers data from the operation database to OLAP Services, using Data Transformation Services (DTS).	Microsoft Repository Data Transformation Services (DTS) Replication
Developer	Develops project front-end applications.	Knows OLE DB for OLAP (OLAP API)
Data Steward	Oversees and tracks changes to specific data elements and their uses across systems	Database schema design Microsoft Repository Data Transformation Services (DTS)
Data Owner	Responsible for the data held in each business subject area	Database schema design Microsoft Repository Data Transformation Services (DTS)
Financial Control	Monitors financial aspects of the project. Tracks expenses against budget allocations.	Familiar with business goals and objectives

VLDB project team.

Role	Responsibility	Skills
System Administrator	Ensures high availability of VLDB environment.	Familiar with cluster software, such as Microsoft Cluster Server
		Microsoft Office and BackOffice integration
		Web fundamentals
		Enterprise versions of SQL Server and Windows NT
		Hot backup server
		Security (Windows NT and SQL Server)
		SQL Server administration (backup/restore, automation, performance)
		Replication
Database Administrator	Develops database structure.	Database schema design
		Microsoft Repository
		Data Transformation Services (DTS)
Developer	Responsible for optimizing application performance.	Familiar with network use
		OLE DB
		English Query

Replication project team.

Role	Responsibility	Skills
System Administrator	Designs replication project based on distributed computing environment.	Familiar with SQL Server 7.0 replication features
		Familiar with data warehousing strategies
		Can work with legacy systems and mobile applications
		Security (Windows NT and SQL Server)
		Administration of SQL Server (backup/restore, automation, performance)

The remaining sections break down the competencies associated with deploying SQL Server 7.0 in the enterprise: migrating applications and upgrading to SQL Server 7.0, designing a data warehouse, working with VLDBs, and applying a replication strategy. Use the resources listed for each competency to build team member skills.

Migrating/Upgrading

This scenario requires knowledge of existing applications, database schemas, competitors' features, and how to build scaleable applications.

Competency: Build Schemas and Migrate Applications

Because SQL Server's storage engine can address more data, building the schema to support performance in large databases is important. A large part of this competency is migrating applications to SQL Server from competitors' systems such as Oracle, Sybase, Informix, and Btrieve. This competency also requires rewriting or revising code for performance.

Build schemas and migrate applications.

Resource	Location
"Upgrading to Microsoft SQL Server 7.0"	http://www.microsoft.com/sql/migration.htm or Microsoft TechNet
"Migrating Your Microsoft Access Database to Microsoft SQL Server 7.0"	You can also find the TechNet CD online: http://www.microsoft.com/technet/
"Migrating Sybase Applications to Microsoft SQL Server"	
"Migrating Oracle Applications to Microsoft SQL Server"	
"Btrieve Migration Kit"	http://www.microsoft.com/sql/migration.htm
"Migrating Btrieve Applications to Microsoft SQL Server"	TechNet
SQL Server Training and Certification	http://www.microsoft.com/train_cert/resource/sql7.htm

Competency: Develop Management Systems

A new system requires a new management system. The capabilities of Query Analyzer, SQL Profiler, and SQL Server Enterprise Manager have been improved, so database administrators need to become familiar with these tools. System performance can be boosted by using files and filegroups for backup/restore and by segmenting data.

Develop management systems.

Resource	Location
Microsoft SQL Server 7.0 Reviewer's Guide	TechNet
	You can also find the TechNet CD online: http://www.microsoft.com/technet/
"Accessing Heterogeneous Data with Microsoft SQL Server 7.0"	http://www.microsoft.com/sql/70/gen/dw.htm or TechNet

Data Warehousing

Planning a datamart or data warehouse requires application development, data model design, data analysis, data loading and transformation, and query language development. See Part 3 "Data Warehouse Scenarios" for detailed implementation discussions.

Competency: Develop Applications Using OLAP

In certain situations, it may be necessary to develop front-end applications using the native online analytical processing application programming interface (OLAP API) or OLE DB for OLAP.

Develop applications using OLAP.

Resource	Location
"SQL Server OLAP Services"	http://www.microsoft.com/backoffice/sql/70/gen/olap.htm
"SQL Server 7.0 OLAP Services"	http://www.microsoft.com/sql/70/gen/dw.htm or TechNet
	You can also find the TechNet CD online: http://www.microsoft.com/technet/
"Microsoft SQL Server Scalability"	TechNet
"Semiadditive Measures with Microsoft SQL Server 7.0 OLAP Services"	http://www.microsoft.com/sql/70/whpprs/semiadd.htm

Competency: Integrate with English Query

English Query allows data warehouse users to get data with natural language queries rather than by using SQL queries. To implement this feature you have to develop query grammar.

Integrate with English Query.

Resource	Location
"Developing with Microsoft English Query in SQL Server 7.0"	http://www.microsoft.com/sql/70/gen/dw.htm or TechNet
	You can also find the TechNet CD online: http://www.microsoft.com/technet/
"Developing with Microsoft English Query"	TechNet

Competency: Microsoft Repository and Data Transformation Services

Microsoft Repository provides an infrastructure for shared metadata, providing the general object model (UML) with specialization for software development and data warehousing. Once the data model has been defined, and OLAP Services is set up, DTS is used to move the data from the operation database to an OLAP cube. This requires transforming the data from its current format into OLAP Services' format.

Microsoft Repository and Data Transformation Services.

Resource	Location
"The Data Warehousing Strategy"	http://msdn.microsoft.com or TechNet
	You can also find the TechNet CD online: http://www.microsoft.com/technet/
"Migrating Oracle Applications to Microsoft SQL Server"	http://www.microsoft.com/sql/migration.htm or TechNet
"Microsoft SQL Server 7.0 Data Warehouse Framework"	http://www.microsoft.com/sql/70/gen/dw.htm or TechNet
"Microsoft Repository in Data Warehousing"	
"Microsoft SQL Server 7.0 Decision Support Services"	TechNet
"Microsoft SQL Server 7.0 OLAP Services"	http://www.microsoft.com/sql/70/gen/olap.htm or TechNet

Competency: Apply Data Modeling Techniques

Developing a data model for a datamart or warehouse requires understanding logical and physical design, as well as data flow.

Apply data modeling techniques.

Resource	Location
"Microsoft SQL Server 7.0 Decision Support Services"	TechNet
	You can also find the TechNet CD online: http://www.microsoft.com/technet/
"Replication for SQL Server 7.0"	http://www.microsoft.com/sql/70/whpprs/repwp.htm
"Replication for Microsoft SQL Server Version 7.0"	TechNet
"Microsoft SQL Server 7.0 OLAP Services"	http://www.microsoft.com/sql/70/gen/olap.htm or TechNet
"Upgrading to Microsoft SQL Server 7.0"	http://www.microsoft.com/sql/migration.htm

Competency: SQL Server Architecture

Plan the migration of data from any online transaction processing (OLTP) data source (SQL Server, Oracle, DB/2, IMS) into the OLAP store, using DTS. Develop the scripts and the procedures to move the data from the operational stores into the appropriate store for OLAP Services, using multidimensional OLAP (MOLAP), relational OLAP (ROLAP), or hybrid OLAP (HOLAP) cubes. Tuning the server for optimal performance is key because of the large amounts of data handled in a data warehouse environment.

SQL Server architecture.

Resource	Location
"Microsoft SQL Server Architectural Planning and Design"	TechNet
	You can also find the TechNet CD online: http://www.microsoft.com/technet/
"Migrating Oracle Applications to Microsoft SQL Server"	http://www.microsoft.com/sql/migration.htm or TechNet
"Migrating Your Microsoft Access Database to Microsoft SQL Server 7.0"	
"Microsoft SQL Server Scalability"	TechNet
SQL Server 7.0 Query Processor"	http://www.microsoft.com/sql/70/whpprs/qp.htm or TechNet
"SQL Server 7.0 Storage Engine"	http://www.microsoft.com/sql/70/whpprs/storng.htm or TechNet
"Microsoft SQL Server Diagnostics"	TechNet
"Microsoft SQL Server 7.0 OLAP Services"	http://www.microsoft.com/sql/70/gen/dw.htm or TechNet
"SQL Server 7.0 Distributed Queries: OLE DB Connectivity"	http://www.microsoft.com/sql/70/gen/dw.htm
"Cluster Support for Microsoft SQL Server"	TechNet
"The Data Warehousing Strategy"	http://msdn.microsoft.com or TechNet

Competency: Develop with Microsoft Office and Visual Tools

Microsoft Office provides many of the tools needed to analyze the operational data: Excel has PivotTable Services and graphing capabilities, Access allows users to work directly with the data, and Word delivers reports. Visual Studio tools, such as Visual C++ and Visual Basic, are key to customizing the data warehouse.

Developing with Office and Visual Tools.

Resource	Location
"Microsoft SQL Server 7.0 OLAP Services"	http://www.microsoft.com/sql/70/gen/olap.htm or TechNet
	You can also find the TechNet CD online: http://www.microsoft.com/technet/
"Microsoft Access 2000 Data Engine Options"	http://www.microsoft.com/office/2000/Access/documents/MSDataEng.htm
"SQL Server 7.0 Distributed Queries: OLE DB Connectivity"	http://www.microsoft.com/sql/70/gen/dw.htm
"Microsoft SQL Server 7.0 Decision Support Services"	TechNet
SQL Server Reviewer's Guide	TechNet
"The Data Warehousing Strategy"	http://msdn.microsoft.com or TechNet

Competency: Integrate with Other Applications

If you have existing SAP, Baan, or PeopleSoft applications, you have to be able to use OLAP Services with them. The skills needed to integrate with other applications are found in other competencies; DTS, schema design, and SQL Server architecture.

Integrate with other applications.

Resource	Location
"Microsoft SQL Server 7.0 Data Warehouse Framework"	http://www.microsoft.com/sql/70/gen/dw.htm or TechNet
	You can also find the TechNet CD online: http://www.microsoft.com/technet/
"Accessing Heterogeneous Data with Microsoft SQL Server 7.0"	
"Microsoft SQL Server 7.0 OLAP Services"	
"Designing and Building the Database"	TechNet
"Migrating Oracle Applications to Microsoft SQL Server"	http://www.microsoft.com/sql or TechNet
"Btreive Migration Kit"	TechNet
"Microsoft SQL Server Scalability"	TechNet
"Microsoft Access 2000 Data Engine Options"	http://www.microsoft.com/office/2000/Access/documents/MSDataEng.htm

Competency: Integrate with BackOffice

Operational data from heterogeneous data sources such as DB2, Oracle, IMS, etc., may make up the input to the data warehouse. Such data needs to be brought into OLAP Services, via SNA Server, and other methods. Microsoft Internet Information Server provides services that can help deliver the data to the customers via a Web interface, and Exchange can provide notification services to alert users to key pieces of information.

Integrate with BackOffice.

Resource	Location
SQL Server security	SQL Server Resource Guide on TechNet
	You can also find the TechNet CD online: http://www.microsoft.com/technet/
"SQL Server 7.0 Distributed Queries: OLE DB Connectivity"	http://www.microsoft.com/sql/70/gen/dw.htm
"Textual Searches on Database Data Using Microsoft SQL Server 7.0"	

Competency: Using Third-Party Tools

Several independent software vendors (ISVs) provide OLAP tools with useful features and capabilities. Research tool vendors carefully. See "The Right Tool for the Right Job" in "The James Martin + Company Datamart/Data Warehouse Development and Deployment Process" (Chapter 3) for suggestions on how to research tools and how to evaluate and work with vendors.

Working with Very Large Databases

To implement VLDBs, you must design a high-availability system that is scalable. See Part 2 of this book, "Very Large Database Solutions," for detailed implementation information.

Competency: Design for High Availability Using MSCS or Hot Backups

To give acceptable performance, a VLDB system must be designed to meet high availability standards. These can usually be met by using the Enterprise versions of SQL Server and Windows NT, clustering, and hot backup servers.

Design for high availability using MSCS or hot backups.

Resource	Location
"Benchmark: High Performance Online Database Backup for Very Large Databases"	http://www.microsoft.com/sql/70/gen/perform.htm or TechNet
	You can also find the TechNet CD online: http://www.microsoft.com/technet/
"Microsoft SQL Server Scalability"	TechNet
"Microsoft SQL Server 7.0 Query Processor"	http://www.microsoft.com/sql/70/whpprs/qp.htm or TechNet
"SQL Server 7.0 Distributed Queries: OLE DB Connectivity"	http://www.microsoft.com/sql/70/gen/dw.htm
"Textual Searches on Database Data Using Microsoft SQL Server 7.0"	

Competency: Design the Hardware Infrastructure to Support Applications

Special hardware may be required to meet the demands of enterprise-scale applications. Before network designers can create the network architecture, they must know the needs of the applications to be implemented.

Design the hardware infrastructure.

Resource	Location:
"Benchmark: High Performance Online Database Backup for Very Large Databases"	http://www.microsoft.com/sql/70/gen/perform.htm or TechNet
	You can also find the TechNet CD online: http://www.microsoft.com/technet/
"Microsoft TerraServer"	http://www.microsoft.com/sql/70/gen/commerce.htm or TechNet

Competency: Design a Database Schema

Huge databases require a solid structure. Developers can use the Visual Database Tools application that comes with SQL Server to design an appropriate application schema that takes into consideration data type, server location, and usage patterns. Developers must also understand how to normalize and denormalize the structure for performance.

Design a database schema.

Resource	Location
SQL Server security	SQL Server Resource Guide on TechNet
	You can also find the TechNet CD online: http://www.microsoft.com/technet/
"Btreive Migration Kit"	http://www.microsoft.com/sql/migration.htm
"Microsoft TerraServer"	http://www.microsoft.com/sql/70/gen/commerce.htm or TechNet
"Microsoft SQL Server 7.0 Performance Tuning Guide"	TechNet
"Microsoft SQL Server 7.0 OLAP Services"	http://www.microsoft.com/sql/70/gen/olap.htm or TechNet
"Microsoft SQL Server 7.0 Storage Engine"	http://www.microsoft.com/sql/70/whpprs/storeng.htm
"The Data Warehousing Strategy"	http://msdn.microsoft.com or TechNet
SQL Server Reviewer's Guide	TechNet
"Microsoft SQL Server 7.0 Data Warehouse Framework"	http://www.microsoft.com/sql/70/gen/dw.htm
"Configuring OLE DB Providers for Distributed Queries"	TechNet
"Textual Searches on File Data Using Microsoft SQL Server 7.0"	TechNet

Competency: Develop Applications for Performance

After choosing a schema design suitable for large applications, developers must optimize the applications for the number of users, their location, LAN or WAN communications, network speed, remote hookups, average daily transaction levels, and so on. Other key factors include distribution of transactions or replication, backup/restore design and traffic, logging requirements, and the language used for application development.

Develop for performance.

Resource	Location
"Microsoft SQL Server Scalability"	TechNet
	You can also find the TechNet CD online: http://www.microsoft.com/technet/
"Benchmark: High Performance Online Database Backup for Very Large Databases"	http://www.microsoft.com/sql/70/gen/perform.htm or TechNet

Resource	Location
"Microsoft TerraServer"	http://www.microsoft.com/sql/70/gen/commerce.htm or TechNet
"Microsoft SQL Server 7.0 Performance Tuning Guide"	TechNet
Microsoft Reviewer's Guide	TechNet
Search for **query tuning** in *Microsoft SQL Server Diagnostics*	TechNet
"Microsoft SQL Server 7.0 Storage Engine"	http://www.microsoft.com/sql/70/whpprs/storeng.htm
"The Data Warehousing Strategy"	http://msdn.microsoft.com or TechNet
"SQL Server 7.0 Distributed Queries: OLE DB Connectivity"	http://www.microsoft.com/sql/70/gen/dw.htm
"Textual Searches on File Data Using Microsoft SQL Server 7.0"	TechNet

Design and Build Applications Using Replication

In a distributed computing environment, replication may be across a network, legacy mainframe systems, or mobile disconnected offices. The replication strategy must address this. Part 4 of this book, "Replication Implementation," examines design and deployment issues in depth.

Competency: Develop a Replication Strategy

Decide if the application requires replication, and, if it does, what type and how often. Consider network connectivity and a practical degree of automation.

Develop a replication strategy.

Resource	Location
"Migrating Your Microsoft Access Database to Microsoft SQL Server 7.0"	http://www.microsoft.com/sql/migration.htm and TechNet
"Migrating Oracle Applications to Microsoft SQL Server"	You can also find the TechNet CD online: http://www.microsoft.com/technet/
SQL Server 7.0 Upgrade—Knowledge Measure Enterprise and Support Training	http://estweb/SQL_Server_7_Upgrade
SQL Server 7.0 Reviewer's Guide	TechNet
"The Data Warehousing Strategy"	http://msdn.microsoft.com or TechNet

(continued)

Resource	Location
"SQL Server 7.0 Distributed Queries: OLE DB Connectivity"	http://www.microsoft.com/sql/70/gen/dw.htm
"Textual Searches on File Data Using Microsoft SQL Server 7.0"	TechNet
"Microsoft SQL Server 7.0 Data Warehousing Framework"	TechNet
"Replication for SQL Server 7.0"	http://www.microsoft.com/sql/70/whpprs/repwp.htm
"Replication for Microsoft SQL Server Version 7.0"	TechNet

Competency: Replicate Data from Legacy Systems

In a distributed environment, applications may draw data from many sources. If the environment includes mainframes or UNIX systems, developers need to know about these systems and their underlying schemas, security features, and connectivity issues (SNA, TCP/IP, etc.).

Replicate data from legacy systems.

Resource	Location
"Migrating Oracle Applications to Microsoft SQL Server"	http://www.microsoft.com/sql/migration.htm or TechNet
	You can also find the TechNet CD online: http://www.microsoft.com/technet/
"Btreive Migration Kit"	http://www.microsoft.com/sql/migration.htm
"The Data Warehousing Strategy"	http://msdn.microsoft.com or TechNet
"Configuring OLE DB Providers for Distributed Queries"	http://www.microsoft.com/sql/70/gen/dw.htm
"Textual Searches on File Data Using Microsoft SQL Server 7.0"	TechNet

Competency: Design a Mobile Disconnected Strategy

Because SQL Server runs on Windows 9x and Windows NT operating systems, most applications probably will be written for and ported to these platforms. Developers must take this preference into account when designing data replication.

Design a mobile disconnected strategy.

Resource	Found at:
"Microsoft Access 2000 Data Engine Options"	http://www.microsoft.com/office/2000/Access/documents/ MSDataEng.htm
"Developing Mobile Applications: Comparing Microsoft SQL Server 7.0 to Sybase Adaptive Server Anywhere 6.0"	http://www.microsoft.com/sql/migration.htm or TechNet You can also find the TechNet CD online: http://www.microsoft.com/technet/
SQL Server Reviewer's Guide	TechNet

CHAPTER 2

Mapping the IT Rollout Cycle

*By Abu
Moniruzzaman
and Pat Amiot,
Approach*

This chapter describes a generic SQL Server 7.0 rollout plan. It keeps an eye on the big picture, looking at how SQL Server can fit into the enterprise, from upgrading SQL Server 6.5 computers to building business intelligence (data warehousing) solutions, to how SQL Server supports distributed database applications that integrate with other products, eventually forming a knowledge management system. It also keeps your hands on the steering wheel, reviewing basic procedures and tools to navigate through the upgrade process.

What You'll Find in This Chapter

- How to move a standard SQL Server 7.0 installation up to the enterprise level.

- How to integrate SQL Server 7.0 with Other Microsoft products.

- SQL Server 7.0 installation methods.

- Basic considerations for deploying SQL Server 7.0.

- Methods for upgrading from earlier SQL Server versions.

- Methods for migrating to SQL Server 7.0 from other products.

SQL 7.0 Server: From Operations to Business Intelligence to Knowledge Management

Microsoft SQL Server is a relational database that runs on Windows 95, Windows 98, and Windows NT. SQL (Structured Query Language) is an industry standard for defining, changing, and managing data. It provides a scaleable database engine, a programming model for developers, tools for other complex operations, single-console management, integrated security, administrative scripting, automation of routine tasks, and event-based job execution and alerting. But as information systems (IS) managers and database administrators (DBA) know, rolling out new technology, even on an upgrade, requires detailed planning and design, coordination with other network administrators, *and* systematic sequencing of functionality over time.

Because many organizations do not have enough resources to add all SQL Server components and modules, the discussion begins with basic SQL Server functionality, which requires fewer resources. Later, it describes comprehensive data warehousing features (business intelligence) and data mining capabilities (business operations and knowledge management) that you can implement when resources permit. The focus is on upgrading to SQL Server 7.0 and the requirements for successful migration.

Initial Considerations

For any SQL Server 7.0 installation, begin by evaluating basic system requirements.

Hardware

Select hardware by evaluating your requirements against budget (and other constraints). For example, SQL Server scales very well across multiple processors. Symmetric multi-processing (SMP) configurations provide better performance. Clustering Windows NT servers can boost transaction rates by balancing load, but it requires more computers. And a local tape drive can simplify SQL Server backup and restore (see the section "Infrastructure Inventory and Requirements," below).

Security

SQL Server comes with two security modes: *Windows NT only* or *SQL Server and Windows NT*. Base your selection on application requirements. *Windows NT only* uses a single Windows NT domain logon, avoids using SQL Server-level security, and allows easier SQL Server account administration.

SQL Server Installation

OLAP Services, Microsoft English Query, and full-text search require additional system memory, and are not needed for a basic SQL Server installation. If you are focused on getting SQL Server operational, these services need not be part of your initial design; you can add them later. This option allows you to add functionality as the system grows and as users become more experienced and productive. In the early planning and design stages, you have to evaluate your goals and decide between SQL Server's Enterprise or Standard editions. (For more information on these options, see the section "Standard versus Enterprise Edition" later in this chapter.)

SQL Mail

If you have a messaging server compliant with Messaging Application Programming Interface (MAPI), you can configure SQL Server to take advantage of SQL Mail for alerts, notification, or paging support services. This provides "SQL Server Support" e-mail through the messaging server—a benefit if the support group changes often—and is easier than maintaining a list of pager e-mail addresses within SQL Server notification. This option requires a MAPI profile for a Windows NT account (the account for the MSSQLServer service) and requires that the MAPI client application be installed on the SQL Server computer.

Databases

You can generate application databases from schema(s) or by installing applications such as Microsoft Systems Management Server (SMS). Consider how you want to set up end-user access permission to the database. Per-logon permissions are based on roles such as "Database Owner," etc.

Maintenance

You can create tasks manually or use the SQL Server Database Maintenance Plan Wizard to create, sequence, and schedule a standard set of tasks for all databases. Sequencing ensures that tasks do not start until all prerequisite tasks are complete; scheduling helps you load-balance on the network. Backup and restore (for SQL Server and Windows NT) also come under maintenance. You need to consider network loading when devising a strategy. For instance, it is more efficient to install a local tape drive than to move files across a slow network connection.

Administration

Performance Monitor for SQL Server makes it possible to measure SQL Server performance by tracking counters, objects, page faults, cache hit ratio, etc. With SQL Server Profiler, you can trace SQL Server and rerun a saved trace even on another SQL Server. SQL Server Query Analyzer shows execution plans and index analyses, and is a tuning tool.

To the Enterprise Level

Once SQL Server has been implemented and used successfully in production, you can extend the design by taking it to the Enterprise level. An expanded design allows other applications to access a central operational database, keeping information consistent. The design can be further extended to include datamarts or data warehouses. Some *N*-tier applications use Microsoft Transaction Services (MTS) as a middle layer for applications with many end users (using SQL Server as the back-end layer). Some applications derive replication benefits by expanding the SQL Server to include other OLE databases.

Microsoft Transaction Service (MTS)

An *N*-tier design that uses MTS is approaching Enterprise level, if only because MTS can pool SQL Server connections for many end users and use the Microsoft Distributed Transaction Coordinator (MSDTC) to provide cross-server transactions. If you use MTS, you must use MSDTC services on any SQL Servers that MTS accesses for objects that support or require transactions. If you use MSDTC, you must configure SQL Server for the corresponding remote servers, which need to enable remote procedure calls (RPCs) for both servers, and map permissions for remote logons to a local logon on the server where the SQL command occurs.

Very Large Databases (VLDBs)

SQL Server has high-speed optimizations that support VLDB environments all the way to multiple-terabyte databases. The Transact-SQL BACKUP and RESTORE statements are optimized to read through a database serially and write in parallel to multiple backup devices. You can also reduce traffic by performing incremental backups or by backing up individual files or filegroups. You can speed data entry by performing multiple bulk-copy operations concurrently against a single table. Under SQL Server 7.0, operations that create multiple indexes on a table can create them concurrently. SQL Server databases now map directly to Windows files, simplifying database creation and administration. I/O rates are improved by the new 8-KB database page size (extendable to 64 KB).

See Part 2 of this book, "Very Large Database Solutions," for in-depth discussions on VLDB implementation.

Enterprise Resource Planning (ERP)

SQL Server integrates with the products of ERP vendors such as SAP, BAAN, and PeopleSoft. Its graphical user interface and environment simplify installation and administration of ERP software, and it provides tools for data retrieval and analysis and for running major third-part ERP products.

Replication

Replicating data between multiple SQL Servers and other OLE DB providers guarantees data consistency. When designing a replication strategy, consider the areas below. Replication is covered in more detail in Chapters 13 and 14. Part 4 of this book, "Replication Implementation," examines design and deployment of replication in depth.

Network Topology

Are the servers in the same LAN or across the WAN? This is important when setting up the servers for publishing, subscribing, and distribution. For an example, consider server A and server B, each of which can be used across the WAN. Server A has a huge load on it from Web users; server B needs server A data for analysis. Periodic data updates are made on server B, and these must be updated on server A. What is the best way to configure replication? First, both servers should have local distribution databases, because they are used over the WAN. Second, you should try to put the entire load of replication on server B, because server A already carries a large load. To do this, configure replication so that publications on B are pushed to A, and publications on A are pulled by B.

Replication Data

Decide which data needs to be replicated and which filters (horizontal and vertical) can be placed on replication. Not all data needs to be replicated from a given table, and data can be merged from multiple tables before replication. Base the design on data requirements.

Implementation

The next step is to implement replication. SQL Server has wizards to help you specify servers for distribution, publication, and subscription. You can also do this manually. As the enterprise grows, SQL Server scalability allows you to add subscribing or publishing servers.

Security

The SQL Server Agent service is used for replication, and the account under which it runs (which should be a domain-level account) must be granted permissions to carry out the replication (whether a push or pull) on the given server. Use the Publication Access List (PAL) to assign permissions.

Mobile Computers

Mobile users can also take advantage of replication, especially with SQL Server Desktop version, which reduces maintenance by allowing the same code base to be used on both server and client computers. You can set up replication so that mobile users can update when they get back to the office or by dialing in to the network.

Solving More Complex Problems with Business Intelligence

Technology makes it possible to capture and store more data, sometimes so much data that it becomes difficult to manage and use. One solution for this problem is a data warehouse—an integrated store of information collected from other systems that becomes the foundation for decision support and data analysis. You can use SQL Server 7.0, with Data Transformation Services (DTS), OLAP Services, PivotTable Service, and English Query, to design and build cost-effective data warehousing solutions.

Data Transformation Services

DTS facilitates the import, export, and transformation of heterogeneous data. It supports transformations between source and target data using an OLE DB-based architecture. For example, consider a training company with four regional offices, each responsible for a predefined geographical region. The company uses a central SQL Server to store sales data. At the beginning of each quarter, each regional manager populates a Microsoft Excel spreadsheet with sales targets for each salesperson, and uses DTS Import Wizard to import the spreadsheets to the central database. At the end of each quarter, the manager uses the DTS Export Wizard to create a regional spreadsheet that compares target and actual sales figures for each region.

The DTS package concept performs a series of tasks as part of a transformation. DTS has its own in-process component object model (COM) server engine that can be used independently of SQL Server and that supports scripting for each column using Visual Basic and Java Script development software. Each transformation can include data quality checks and validation, aggregation, and duplicate elimination. You can also combine multiple columns into a single column or build multiple rows from a single input. Once the package is executed, DTS checks to see if the destination table already exists and then gives you the option of dropping and recreating the destination table.

Metadata

A software system design defines the kinds of data that populate the system. After the system is in production, users add data. There is a distinction between *kinds of data* and *data*. This is often called the type/instance distinction, because designers deal in types (such as classes or properties) and users deal in instances (such as objects or property values). These are also called *metadata* and *data*.

If you save package information to Microsoft Repository, you can save metadata about the databases referenced in the package, such as:

- Primary and foreign keys
- Column type, size, precision, scale, and nullability information
- Indexes

You can import metadata to Microsoft Repository through SQL Server Enterprise Manager, or by using the DTS Designer scanning options (also available in the DTS Import and Export wizards). When you use SQL Server Enterprise Manager to import metadata you can read the metadata from only one database (catalog). When you use DTS Designer (or the DTS Import and Export wizards) you can read the metadata from all referenced databases in a package by selecting **Scan all referenced catalogs** in the **Scanning Options** dialog box. For the metadata to work, the data provider specified must support OLE DB schema rowsets.

See Chapter 11 for a discussion of an implementation of the Microsoft Repository.

Microsoft Repository

DTS Designer provides features for saving package metadata and data lineage information to Microsoft Repository, and linking those types of information. You can store catalog metadata for databases referenced in a package, and accounting information about the package version history of a particular row of data for the datamart or data warehouse. DTS Designer uses its own information model for structuring package metadata and data lineage information and saving it to Microsoft Repository. To browse this information, you can:

- Use the DTS repository browser and viewing tools found in SQL Server Enterprise Manager (available through the console tree, under Data Transformation Services, Metadata). These are basic tools for exploring a package's metadata and version history, and for looking up the specific package version that generated a row of data.

- Write an external repository tool capable of viewing package version data and metadata. This requires familiarity with repository information models and programming. For more information, see the repository documentation supplied with Microsoft SQL Server, and the Microsoft Repository Software Development Kit.

- Use the DTS Wizard to:
  - Specify any custom settings used by the OLD DB provider to connect to the data source or destination.
  - Copy an entire table, or the results of an SQL query, such as those involving joins of multiple tables or distributed queries. DTS can copy schema and data between relational databases, but it does not copy indexes, stored procedures, or referential integrity constraints.
  - Build a query using the DTS Query Builder Wizard. This allows users inexperienced with the SQL language to build queries interactively.
  - Change the name, data type, size, precision, scale, and nullability of a column when copying from the source to the destination, where a valid data-type conversion applies.
  - Specify transformation rules that govern how data is copied between columns of different data types, sizes, precision, scales, and nullabilities.
  - Execute a Microsoft ActiveX script (Microsoft Visual Basic or JScript) that can modify (transform) the data when it is copied from the source to the destination. Or you can perform any operation supported by Visual Basic or JScript development software.
  - Save the DTS package to the SQL Server **msdb** database, Microsoft Repository, or a COM-structured storage file.
  - Schedule the DTS package for later execution.

OLAP

SQL Server supports online analytical processing (OLAP), which performs tasks from corporate reporting and analysis to data modeling and decision support. It improves performance by creating intelligent aggregations that reduce database size and initial or incremental load times. SQL Server's storage architecture supports various OLAP implementations:

- MOLAP (multidimensional OLAP storage) uses a multidimensional structure to contain aggregations and a copy of the base data.
- ROLAP (relational OLAP storage) uses tables in the data warehouse relational database to store a cube's aggregations.
- HOLAP (hybrid OLAP storage) combines attributes of both MOLAP and ROLAP. Aggregation data is stored in MOLAP structures and the base data is left in the data warehouse's relational database.

Numerous analysis functions provide comprehensive data modeling and decision support. OLAP Services incorporates intelligent aggregation selection, automatically choosing a subset of all possible aggregations from which the remaining aggregations can be quickly calculated when they are needed. Cube designers can use the Aggregation Design Wizard to specify the tradeoff between disk storage requirements and the amount of precalculated aggregation, and to partition cubes to spread data across several servers even though it is presented to users as if it were stored in one place.

PivotTable Service

Microsoft PivotTable Service provides client-side access to OLAP data for custom applications, uses a client-side cache to improve performance, accelerates dynamic views, and supports mobile and disconnected analysis.

The service runs on client workstations. With it, you can use Visual Basic or other languages to develop custom applications that make use of data taken from OLAP or taken directly from relational databases via Microsoft OLE DB technology. It can also store cubes locally on a client machine, making it possible for remote users to analyze data without connecting to OLAP Services.

Microsoft Office 2000

Office 2000 provides support for SQL Server 7.0 OLAP Services, allowing Microsoft Excel 2000 users, for instance, to analyze gigabytes and terabytes of data. With an Excel 2000 PivotTable dynamic view, you can use OLAP Services to create persistent local cubes of data from an SQL Server. Office 2000 Web Components also support OLAP for browsing and charting.

SQL Server English Query

The Microsoft English Query environment allows developers to convert relational databases into English Query applications, allowing users to query in natural language instead of SQL statements. Setting this up requires creating a second logical schema to the physical schema, but once the mapping is complete the benefits of being able to query in plain language can be significant. It is a good example of features that can be deployed after the system has been in production for a while, to extend functionality and create greater usefulness for more users.

Integration with Other Microsoft Products and Knowledge Management

Integrating data is not enough to produce a business intelligence solution: systems must be integrated as well.

SQL Server integrates tightly with Microsoft Site Server. With Site Server, users can search Web sites, file servers, public folders, and data stored in any ODBC data source, and can create "search catalogs" from all of these sources—manually or dynamically through Site Server scheduling—that Site Server can use in

Knowledge Manager (KM) pages. Users can search catalogs for information in particular categories, and share search results within the company through "shared briefs." Users can receive automatic brief updates through e-mail or channels (including particular pages generated by SQL Server Web Server Assistant).

Workflow applications using Microsoft Exchange Server can be integrated with SQL Server databases. You can create a solution that allows users to receive e-mail, retrieve or create a client record in SQL Server using a Visual Basic application, then enter or modify basic information about the sender—name, company name, subject, etc. You can also design a billing and time-tracking application using the Outlook Contacts and Tasks folders.

Microsoft SNA Server can be integrated with SQL Server in many ways. Once Windows NT Server and Microsoft SQL Server are adopted by an organization that also uses host-based database technology, there are several strong arguments for database integration:

- Data warehousing or data mining. Integrating the data in distributed SQL Server databases with host-based databases provides access to large applications or specific query engines that can analyze the data from a variety of perspectives.

- Web enablement for Internet or intranet applications. The Windows NT Server Web server integrates with SQL Server. It can be used to provide data to customers' individual queries to host data.

- You can access data remotely from a Windows NT application using SQL Server and SNA Server. A system can have a back-end that uses SNA Server as a gateway to access the legacy databases, SQL Server to replicate network data, and a front-end application to consolidate user tasks.

From SQL Server 6.5 to 7.0

SQL 7.0 Server's redesigned architecture simplifies the development, deployment, maintenance, and management of database applications. Databases no longer reside on SQL Server logical devices, but on operating-system files; database devices and segments no longer reside on top of operating-system files, but consist of two or more Windows files. A database can grow and shrink within configurable limits—the database administrator (DBA) does not have to change its size, pre-allocate space, or manage data structures.

Space is managed more efficiently. SQL Server 7.0 has 8-KB page size (instead of 2 KB), 64-KB I/O, 8060 bytes/row, no column limit, variable-length character fields (up to a KB), and the ability to add and delete columns from existing tables without unloading and reloading data. Redesigned utilities support terabyte-size databases. The new page and row formats support row-level locking, are extensible for future requirements, and improve performance when large blocks of data are accessed, because each I/O operation retrieves more data.

New indexing strategies improve performance: the use of multiple indexes in a single table or multiple tables, multi-covered and join indexes, parallel index creation on the same table, and automatic statistics maintenance by default. Parallel execution of a single query across multiple processors improves performance.

The query processor has been redesigned to better support the large databases and complex queries found in decision support, data warehousing, and OLAP applications.

Full row-level locking is implemented for both data rows and index entries. Dynamic locking automatically chooses the optimal level (row, page, multiple page, and table) for each database operation, improving concurrency without tuning. The database also supports the use of hints to force a particular level of locking.

SQL Server 7.0 Enterprise Edition supports memory addressing greater than 4 GB, in conjunction with Windows 2000 Server, Alpha processor-based systems, and other techniques.

And there are new advanced profiling and tuning tools:

- Profiling improves debugging by allowing the capture and replay of server activity
- Index tuning wizard steps you through the index tuning process
- Graphical query analyzer allows in-depth query analysis
- SQL Server 7.0 supports a linguistic search of character data stored in the database, which operates on words and phrases, not just character patterns

Standard versus Enterprise Edition

SQL Server 7.0 Standard Edition is intended for small enterprises, where memory or processor demands are small. It can run on Windows NT Small Business Server, Windows NT Standard, or Windows NT Enterprise Edition. It can support up to a 4-processor SMP system and up to 4 GB of physical memory. It can be upgraded to the Enterprise Edition.

The Enterprise Edition is intended for large enterprises. It runs only on Windows NT Enterprise Edition and supports up to an 8-processor SMP system—32 processors with OEM-modified HALs (hardware abstraction layers). It can support up to 8 GB of physical memory for a system with Intel EMA.

Infrastructure Inventory and Requirements

For day-to-day operations, start with:

- DEC Alpha and compatible systems, Intel or compatible (Pentium 166 MHz or higher, Pentium PRO, or Pentium II)
- 64 MB of RAM (minimum for Enterprise Edition) or 32 MB of RAM (minimum for other editions)
- 180 MB for full installation
- Microsoft Windows NT Server Enterprise Edition version 4.0 or later with SP4 or later, or Windows NT Server Standard Edition version 4.0 or later with SP4 or later.
- Microsoft Internet Explorer version 4.01 with SP1 or later
- SQL Server Enterprise Edition or SQL Server Standard Edition

To take the advantage of data warehousing, you can later add:

- OLAP Services with 50 MB
- English Query with 12 MB

RAID (redundant array of independent disks) implementation on hard disks can directly affect SQL Server's performance. RAID levels 0, 1, and 5 are typically used with SQL Server. For recoverability, you should place data and log files on separate RAID drives. Place the transaction log on the mirrored drive (RAID 1). SQL Server is designed to create heavy loads when reading the transaction log, and RAID 1 increases this performance because data can be read independently from each drive (although it must be written simultaneously to both drives in the mirror). Each mirrored drive can seek and read different data simultaneously. Read bandwidth is almost doubled in mirroring.

For data, use either RAID 0 or 5. RAID 5 provides better reliability and recovery but somewhat slower performance. It permits simultaneous write and read operations, which is preferred when setting up fault tolerance in Windows NT Server, and if there is a single drive failure, the parity information can be used to reconstruct the lost data. The extra overhead associated with collecting parity information creates the performance difference between RAID 5 and 0.

RAID 0 (striping without parity) provides better performance but lower reliability and slower recovery. It can increase performance significantly, particularly for multi-user and single-user systems, by allowing simultaneous operation of drives in the array. It is, however, *anti-fault-tolerant*: if any drive in the array fails, the entire array fails, and the data cannot be recovered.

For higher backup/restore throughput, use a computer with a local tape unit directly connected with an expansion bus via SCSI adapter to the system bus. Remote tape backup/restore is slower because it is limited to the LAN speed.

Test Lab

For deployment, upgrading, or migration you need a lab to test replication, applications, MS DTC distributed transactions, and executive tasks. Ideally, the lab environment should allow you to test all applications (all features, functionality) against SQL Server 7.0. You also need to test custom-designed tasks to make sure they function properly in the SQL Server 7.0 environment with the changes in the Transact-SQL syntax. Document any problems found and resolve them before deployment.

The strategy for creating the computing environment is determined by your plans for the test lab. If you are going to roll the test lab into the production environment, the hardware should be the same as the planned production environment. If you are going to dedicate the hardware for testing you should make sure that the resulting lab will, at a minimum, be able to accommodate the required functionality and scale of the production system (see the "Infrastructure Inventory and Requirements" section, above).

Create a testing environment that closely reflects the production environment—an exact copy is the best, but often this is not feasible due to cost. The applications that will be running in production will determine the degree to which the test lab needs to mimic the production environment. The test lab should be able to accommodate the minimum requirements of the production environment. When you create the test lab consider:

- Network topology
- Hard drive configuration (capacity, fault tolerance method, etc.)
- RAM
- Configuration of server settings
- Number of CPUs
- Number of users and user load
- Other application servers, operating systems, and software (service packs, mail clients, MTS, MSMQ, IIS, Site Server, etc.)

When testing is complete, you can roll some of this hardware into the production, but you should seriously consider holding back as much as possible for a permanent test lab. You can use it to recreate problems for troubleshooting, to study performance and integration issues, and to test future software. Since many companies set up SQL Server first, then later add OLAP applications, English

Query, Data Transformation Services, Office 2000, or other Microsoft BackOffice systems, a test lab is an asset that continues to be useful.

New Installation of SQL Server

Once you have the right hardware and software (see the "Infrastructure Inventory and Requirements" section, above), install the prerequisites, and then run the SQL Server Setup program from the SQL Server compact disc or off the network (copy the contents of the compact disc to a shared network directory). The program presents the main SQL Server 7.0 installation screen. If it is not presented, browse the CD and double-click the file AUTORUN.EXE; with it you can read the release notes, browse Books Online, connect to the Microsoft SQL Server Web site, or install the prerequisites and SQL Server.

Attended Installation

To install SQL Server:

1. Back up the current SQL Server version 6.*x* installation if you are installing SQL Server 7.0 on the same computer.

2. Stop all SQL Server-related services before beginning SQL Server 7.0 setup. Setup checks to see if the ODBC files are available for updating. If they are in use a dialog box is displayed showing the services or applications you need to stop before Setup continues. Use the *retry* option to see if the ODBC files are "unlocked."

3. Shut down Microsoft Windows NT Event Viewer.

4. Review the hardware and software requirements for installing SQL Server.

5. Create a domain user account (recommended, but not required) to which you can assign the MSSQLServer and SQLServerAgent services

6. Log on to the system under a user account with administrative privileges.

7. Select a character set, sort order, and Unicode collation.

Note   You should develop a standard within your organization for these options during the planning phases. Many server-to-server activities can fail if the character set, sort order, and Unicode collation are not consistent across servers. If you need to change the character set later, for instance, you must rebuild the databases and reload the data.

8. Review all other SQL Server installation options and be prepared to make the appropriate selections when you run Setup.

You can install SQL Server 7.0 on a server that already has SQL Server 6.*x* installed on a different directory. Both versions contain their own database files. SQL Server 7.0 adds a version switch, which you can use to switch between SQL Server 6.*x* and SQL Server 7.0.

Unattended Installation

To invoke an unattended installation, you must first generate an InstallShield .ISS file. Start SQL Server Setup with the **k=Rc** switch and proceed through the dialog boxes to install SQL Server as normal. With this switch set, Setup records your dialog box choices in a Windows directory file named SETUP.ISS, but does not install SQL Server on the local computer. When you have completed the installation process, you can move the file or copy it to another location for use on other servers. For subsequent automated installations, start Setup and specify a previously generated .ISS file as input by using the **-f1** setup command-line option. The syntax is:

```
Setupsql.exe -f1 <full path to ISS file> -SMS -s
```

If you don't specify the **-SMS** switch, the underlying InstallShield setup process, SQLSTP.EXE, starts a process to perform the setup and immediately returns control to you. The **-s** switch causes Setup to run in silent mode.

Remote setup is supported only between Windows NT computers of the same processor type. All prerequisites must first be installed on the remote computer. Remote setup is not supported on a clustered Windows NT Server, and can be used only for a new installation, not for upgrades, maintenance mode, or build-to-build upgrades. It installs the same version of SQL Server 7.0 on the remote computer as is being run on the source computer. So, for example, if you are running the SQL Server 7.0 standard edition on a Windows NT *Server* computer, you cannot remote install to a Windows NT *Workstation* computer. You have to use the same version of SQL Server on the local computer and on remote computers.

Upgrade to SQL Server 7.0 from Earlier Versions (4.21, 6.0, or 6.5)

You can use the SQL Server Upgrade Wizard to upgrade from SQL Server 6.*x*, but you must follow these steps:

- If you are running SQL Server version 4.21a (or earlier) you must first upgrade to SQL Server 6.0 or 6.5, and then upgrade to SQL Server 7.0. (See Appendix A for more details.)
- Before upgrading from SQL Server 6.0, you must have installed Service Pack 3 for SQL Server 6.0.

- Before upgrading from SQL Server 6.5, you must have installed Service Pack 3 for SQL Server 6.5 (or a later service pack).

For basic computer-to-computer upgrade, SQL Server 7.0 requires a Pentium 166 with at least 32 MB of RAM. You can perform a side-by-side upgrade if the SQL Server 6.x computer also has free space equal to at least 1.5 times the amount of space used by the SQL Server 6.x data files.

Once you have SQL Server 7.0 installed, you can use its fully automated upgrade utility to transfer in version 6.x databases. Many factors affect the amount of time needed to complete the conversion. Each object in the SQL Server 6.x database must be rebuilt in the SQL Server 7.0 database, and every row must be transferred. Depending on the complexity of each database, the length of time needed to convert two 10-GB databases with differing numbers of rows and objects can vary widely. Hardware platform, number of processors, disk subsystem, and amount of RAM also determine the time required. Selecting "data validation" during setup doubles the time required.

Rough estimates of conversion times.

Database size	Estimated time to convert
400 MB	Less than 20 minutes
1 GB	Less than 1 hour
10 GB	Less than 4 hours
50 GB	Less than 12 hours
100 GB	Less than 24 hours

The scenarios below illustrate upgrade methods. Depending on how you set up servers, you may have to borrow elements from more than one scenario.

Upgrade Scenarios

After SQL Server 7.0 is installed, you can use its Upgrade Wizard to complete the upgrade. There are three SQL Server 6.x-to-7.0 upgrade methods: from one computer to another computer, from hard disk to hard disk in the same computer, and from tape unit to hard disk in the same computer. All methods require that all prerequisites be installed first, that SQL Server 7.0 be installed next, and that the SQL Server 6.x to SQL Server 7.0 upgrade be performed last. SQL Server 6.x is unavailable during the installation of SQL Server 7.0. You may also have to schedule time to prevent production users from accessing the SQL Server 6.x, because you will likely have to reboot the computer after installing each of the software packages.

Computer-to-Computer, Two Computers

Install SQL Server 7.0 on one computer and then connect to the computer where the existing SQL Server 6.x is installed. In addition to the space needed for installing SQL Server 7.0, the computer must have at least 1.5 times the amount of space used by the SQL Server 6.x data files. In most cases, the transfer will use less space than the SQL Server 6.x data uses, but extra space is required for the upgrade. When the upgrade is complete, SQL Server 7.0 immediately takes over as the production server.

Side-by-Side, One Computer

There are two ways to install SQL Server 7.0 on a computer that is currently running SQL Server 6.x.

Hard Disk to Hard Disk

If after installing SQL Server 7.0, the computer has free space equal to at least 1.5 times the amount of space used by the SQL Server 6.x data files, you can perform the upgrade over a direct pipeline.

Tape Unit to Hard Disk

If the required space is not available on your hard disks, but you would still like to perform a side-by-side upgrade, you must use the tape option in the SQL Server Upgrade Wizard. The tape drive must be installed on the local computer. During the upgrade process (and after copying the SQL Server 6.x data files to tape), you must delete the 6.x device files to create the disk space for the SQL Server 7.0 data files. The speed of this method is limited by the tape media and may be substantially slower than upgrading over a direct pipeline. When the upgrade is complete, SQL Server 7.0 immediately takes over as the production server.

SQL Server Security Issues

Back Up the SQL Server 6.x Installation

Before upgrading databases check them for errors that can prevent a successful upgrade. You should run database integrity checks against *all* the databases with the DBCC CHECKDB, DBCC CHECKCATALOG, DBCC NEWALLOC, and DBCC TEXTALL commands.

CHECKDB spends most of its time checking things within pages: the page chain, index sorting order, data "reasonableness," page offset "reasonableness," correctness of table **sysindexes** entries, and data row count (which should equal the leaf row count for non-clustered indexes). Running time depends largely on the number of indexes in the database and number of rows per table, and cannot be predicted by database size alone.

CHECKCATALOG checks the consistency of system tables and relationships between system tables for the database. It makes sure that every type in **syscolumns** has a matching entry in **systypes**, that every table and view in **sysobjects** has at least one column in **syscolumns**, and that the last checkpoint in **syslogs** is valid. It also reports on any segments that have been defined.

NEWALLOC checks data and index pages against corresponding extent structures, details all table information, and provides the same summary information provided by CHECKALLOC, which is retained for compatibility. It returns a listing for each allocation unit of the number of extents currently reserved for use by objects, the number of pages marked as being used by objects, and the actual number of pages being used by objects.

TEXTALL selects tables in the database that have **text** or **image** columns and checks the allocation of **text** or **image** columns for one table.

If database inconsistencies are found, you must repair the database or restore to a clean one before you begin the upgrade process. You should then back up the SQL Server 6.*x* installation, including the **master**, **model**, and **msdb** databases, as well as all the user-defined databases. You may also want to back up the actual data and log files (Windows NT files).

Measure the Success of the Upgrade

You must check database consistency to ensure that the data brought over from the SQL Server 6.*x* databases matches the data in the SQL Server 7.0 database. This includes counting table rows and checking for the existence of all user-defined objects in the database, including stored procedures, triggers, defaults, views, and keys.

To ensure proper consistency checking during migration, the first step is to run the SQL Server DBCC CHECKDB procedure. It checks and updates indexes, row counts, and other database information in the system tables. You must check system table accuracy: they provide system stored procedures with the requested information.

Next, collect all the user-defined tables, views, stored procedures, keys, triggers, and defaults in the database from the **sysobjects** system table. This is simple for SQL 6.5 databases, because system tables and procedures and views are kept separate from the user-defined counterparts. In SQL Server 7.0 it is a little more difficult, because system objects are kept within the database, and tables, views, and procedures exist in the **sysobjects** table generated by SQL Server 7.0. To work around this, look at the **status** column in **sysobjects** along with the type: all user-defined stored procedures and views have a status of 0 and user-defined tables have a status of 0 or higher.

Next, get the row counts and references for each table. The row count is easy to retrieve with the system procedure **sp_spaceused**, which captures each table's **rows** column. Use the **sp_fkeys** stored procedure to get references and keys. It provides you with all foreign keys referencing a table and the table's primary key. Compare the references on each database to see if the references were created successfully. Comparing the objects in both databases along with row counts and references gives a good indication of database consistency.

Replication

You can't take advantage of new replication features until all publisher, distributor, and subscriber servers needed for replication have been upgraded to SQL Server 7.0. However, you do not have to disable replication in the SQL Server 6.5 environment to upgrade: SQL Server 7.0 can replicate to SQL Server 6.*x*.

There are other limitations. You can upgrade replication only if you are upgrading from SQL Server 6.*x* with a one-computer upgrade. Otherwise, you must upgrade your databases, then manually re-establish replication with SQL Server 7.0. You must upgrade the distributor server first. Before beginning the upgrade from SQL Server 6.*x*, make sure that if any new subscribers have been added they have completed initial synchronization. Make sure that no updates are occurring to the publishing server(s) that correspond to the distributor server you are about to upgrade. Run the log reader task for the production server to make sure all transactions have been copied from the transaction log of the publisher to the distribution database. Finally, run the distribution task to make sure that all transactions have been distributed to subscribers before you begin upgrading the SQL Server containing the distribution database.

Correlation Between SQL Server 6.5 and SQL Server 7.0 After the Upgrade

Once you have upgraded to SQL Server 7.0, there is no correlation, data mapping, or data sharing with your previous installation of SQL Server 6.*x*. If you have chosen not to delete the SQL Server 6.*x* data files, you will have two full copies of the data on disk, one for each SQL Server installation. When you are satisfied with the upgrade, use the custom uninstaller for SQL Server 6.*x* from the **Microsoft: Switch** menu to delete the SQL Server 6.*x* data files.

Plans to Go Back to SQL 6.*x* from Production 7.0

Before beginning an upgrade, create a fall-back plan. Sometimes problems force a retreat during deployment, but they can also arise after the upgrade is complete and the SQL Server 7.0 environment has run in production for a few days, by which time data most likely has been updated, modified, deleted, or inserted; so how do you go back to the SQL Server 6.*x* environment? What happens to the new data that is out of sync with the older SQL Server 6.*x* version? There are a number of strategies that ensure a smooth back-out from SQL 7.0 to SQL 6.x. These include:

- Setting up replication to copy all data from SQL Server 7.0 to 6.*x* databases just for a short time until the new environment has been verified.

- Using Data Transformation Services to import/export all data from SQL Server 7.0 to 6.*x* databases at the time of retreat.

- Using BCP in character type to import/export (via text file or Microsoft Access) all data from SQL Server 7.0 to 6.*x* databases.

How New Transact-SQL Commands Affect the Upgrade

Transact-SQL contains queries, updates, definition statements, procedure calls, and more. You must complete a thorough code review to make sure it will upgrade to SQL Server 7.0 without problems. Although SQL Server 7.0 currently comes with a SQL Server 6.5 compatibility mode to assure that existing code will not need to be migrated, SQL Server 6.5 compatibility mode cannot exploit all the new SQL Server 7.0 features. And this mode may not be offered in future releases.

Code searching helps identify all the places where Transact-SQL statements can reside, such as in the database itself, in dynamic SQL in user applications, in reports, and in other sources. Carefully identifying which SQL statements are being used assures a smooth migration. Once you identify the code sources, analyze it for potential upgrade problems. To identify codes, make a chart of all the sources of SQL Server script that access the server being migrated. They can reside in:

- Stored procedures that are already in the database

- Applications that call stored procedures

- Applications that create dynamic SQL

- Report generation tools that make SQL queries

- Microsoft Office products, such as Word, Excel, Access, etc.

To search, use the **sysprocesses** system table. It contains information about the real-time connections to the server, particularly the calling application column, which shows who is calling the server and can help identify a source of SQL Server script.

Check out the SQL Server Profiler, which traps application information such as the source name. Also examine the various versions of the applications: different versions may have been introduced during iterations of the database.

Once you have identified the codes, export them to a text file and examine them to evaluate changes. You can easily sort the output file to gather information on compatibility level, file location, etc., and then decide what issues need to be fixed and when. Move all dynamic SQL into stored procedures; this forces all future SQL changes to reside in the database and protects you from having to revisit applications next time. If test scripts are available for the Transact-SQL code, you should rerun the code in the SQL Server 7.0 environment to ensure its correctness and performance.

Application Compatibility

User applications (desktop, system services, Web applications, report generation tools, etc.) access the SQL Server database, so you need to make sure they will still work correctly and effectively after the upgrade.

Identification

First you need to find which applications use the database in question. Use these sources:

- **Management.** Speak to managers, project leads, DBAs, etc., about which applications are in effect.
- **SQL Trace (SQL Server Profiler).** This can show which applications currently access the database.
- **Sysprocesses.** This table contains information about which applications access a database.
- **Versions.** Several versions of the same application may access a database.
- **Web applications.** Check the IIS logs to see which applications are active. Make sure the database back-ends are available for these applications.
- **Reporting tools.** All reporting tools use a database access method.
- **Microsoft Office.** Don't overlook Word, Excel, and Access.

Database Access Mechanisms

Next, you need to see *how* the applications access the database. In a well-designed application, the locations within the code for database access should be centralized. Check these APIs:

DB-Library

In SQL Server 7.0, some DB-Library functions have been removed or changed. For more information, check the SQL Server Books Online for SQL Server 7.0: Installing SQL Server; Upgrading from an Earlier Version of SQL Server; Backwards Compatibility; SQL Server Backward Compatibility Details.

ODBC

Some ODBC library functions have been removed, others changed. For more information, check the SQL Server Books Online for SQL Server 7.0: Installing SQL Server; Upgrading from an Earlier Version of SQL Server; Backwards Compatibility; SQL Server Backward Compatibility Details.

Database Access Objects (DAO)

Applications that still involve DAO should be migrated to ADO. If this is not possible, check that the data sources for the DAO objects (ODBC, Access, SQL Server, etc.) are still running.

Remote Data Objects (RDO)

Applications that still involve RDO should be migrated to ADO. If this is not possible, check that the data sources for the RDO objects (ODBC, Access, SQL Server, etc.) are still running.

OLE-DB

There should be no changes necessary for OLE-DB.

SQL DMO

Applications developed using SQL Distributed Management Objects (DMO) will need to be replaced. The SQL Server 7.0 layout has changed completely from the SQL Server 6.5 layout.

Open Data Services

Extended stored procedures may have to be rewritten. Several source code changes within the ODS API are no longer used by SQL Server 7.0.

Testing

Test each application thoroughly. Applications built in-house should already have test plans associated with them. If source code is not available, use tools such as ListDLLs or DependencyWalker (Microsoft Visual Studio 6.0) to find out which data access libraries the application loads.

Performance

Collect performance information before and after the migration.

Security

Check the application's security mechanism performance before and after the migration.

It is recommended that you migrate to an up-to-date database access mechanism such as ADO, and that you limit mechanisms to one or two. ODBC and ADO should be sufficient for most organizations.

Migrate to SQL Server 7.0 from Other Products

Over time, organizations often acquire a heterogeneous collection of computers, networks and databases, yet they still need access to information and data from diverse applications, if possible in ways that are transparent to users. SQL Server 7.0 provides tools for working with data in a heterogeneous environment:

- **Data Transformation Services (DTS).** DTS imports, exports, and transforms data from heterogeneous data sources. Any OLE DB product can use DTS, including Oracle, Informix, and Microsoft Excel.

- **Support for distributed queries.** SQL Server 7.0 allows linking remote servers (using any OLE DB provider) and using data in queries that come from heterogeneous sources. This action is transparent to the client program, which sees the tables as if they were native SQL Server tables, and it reduces network traffic because the query engine tries to execute as much work as possible at the remote machine. Data does not need to be moved; it can be left in its native store.

- **Heterogeneous replication.** Any open database connectivity (ODBC) driver or OLE DB data product can participate in SQL Server 7.0 replication.

- **Integrated support for data warehousing.** You can create data warehouses or datamarts from a variety of relational databases, including SQL Server, Oracle, and Informix. SQL Server can coexist with other systems.

Over time, consistency may prove more desirable than coexistence, in which case migration to SQL Server 7.0 can provide:

- **Single, scalable codebase.** You can use the same source code across all platforms.

- **Ease of use.** It includes graphical tools, task pads, and more than 30 wizards to help DBAs automate and schedule routine tasks.

- **Dynamic self-management.** This helps reduce the frequency and severity of disk and memory allocation errors.

- **Outstanding performance on the Windows NT platform.**

- **VLDB scalability and performance.**

- **Accessible business intelligence.** Data warehousing capabilities such as integrated data transformation services, Microsoft SQL Server OLAP Services, and graphical modeling tools.

■ **Integration with Windows NT, Office, and BackOffice.** Integration allows cross-system use of management tools such as the Microsoft Windows NT Event Viewer, which provides automated alerts (over pagers or e-mail) of database issues. Excel 2000 users can analyze gigabytes and terabytes of data with OLAP Services. SQL Server 7.0 integrates fully with Windows NT security and systems management, Exchange Server, Systems Management Server, and SNA Server.

To plan a migration to SQL Server from a third-party product, you must consider:

■ Data and object definitions

■ Changes in Transact-SQL and in the language of system-stored procedures

■ Administrative changes.

The steps of the migration process are:

■ Review architectural differences that require changes to administrative procedures.

■ Migrate data and objects using SQL Server Data Transformation Services (DTS).

■ Review the other products' stored procedures, triggers, SQL scripts, and applications for necessary language changes.

■ Change client code as necessary. SQL statements issued by third-party applications must reflect changes to object names forced by keyword conflicts. The applications' SQL syntax must comply with Microsoft Transact-SQL syntax.

■ Test the client code.

■ Make required changes to the customer's administrative procedures.

■ Review the new features available in Microsoft SQL Server and make changes to take advantage of these features.

SQL Server Tools Used in Migrations

SQL Server has tools for migrating data and applications from other products.

SQL Server Enterprise Manager

■ Manages logons and user permissions.

■ Creates scripts

■ Manages backup of SQL Server objects

■ Backs up databases and transaction logs

- Manages tables, views, stored procedures, triggers, indexes, rules, defaults, and user-defined data types
- Creates full-text indexes, database diagrams, and database maintenance plans
- Imports and exports data with Data Transformation Services
- Transforms data
- Performs Web administration tasks

SQL Server Query Analyzer

SQL Server Query Analyzer is a graphical query tool that helps you see how to analyze a query plan, execute multiple queries simultaneously, view data, and obtain index recommendations. The **Showplan** option reports data retrieval methods chosen by the SQL Server query optimizer.

SQL Server Profiler

This captures a continuous record of real-time server activity, allowing you to monitor events produced through SQL Server, filter events based on user-specified criteria, and direct the trace output to the screen, a file, or a table. You can also use it to replay previously captured traces. Application developers can use it to identify transactions that might be slowing an application's performance, which can be particularly useful when migrating an application from file-based to client-server architecture and optimizing the application for its new environment.

Conclusion

When you plan a migration, you must address changes in administrative procedures, migrating object definitions and data, and resolving differences in Transact-SQL statements and system stored procedures.

Microsoft provides data warehousing, VLDB, and ERP features in SQL Server 7.0 that are built on the architecture of the Microsoft Data Warehousing Framework. An upgrade wizard simplifies moving from SQL Server 6.5 to SQL Server version 7.0. These features and products such as Microsoft SQL Server OLAP Services should lower the cost and complexity of data warehousing functionality. The OLAP browsing capabilities planned for Office 2000 should further increase the toolbox for designers of data warehousing and decision-support applications.

C H A P T E R   3

The James Martin + Company Datamart/Data Warehouse Development and Deployment Process

By Howard R. Burkett and Vijay Sankaran, James Martin + Company

Effective data warehouse design, construction, and maintenance are sophisticated and complicated endeavors. Tools such as Microsoft SQL Server 7.0 reduce cost and complexity, but even with the best of tools and intentions you can still fail—and the odds are steeper if you are trying data warehousing for the first time.

This observation is true of any large project, but it doesn't mean you shouldn't try: it just means you should pay more attention. A data warehouse can significantly boost productivity, if it is designed to meet business needs, and it can provide a solid platform for expansion and improvement. Complexity can be dealt with (sometimes easily) if you are willing to plan thoroughly and proceed carefully.

This chapter can help you select and evaluate a basic approach for a data warehouse (or datamart) project. It doesn't provide all the procedures, steps, and details that you'll need, but it does discuss all the areas that you should address. It works through every phase from business needs assessment to delivery and sign-off. At every step, it offers recommendations and alternatives. It clearly shows tasks, their average durations, and how to divide and assign responsibilities.

What You'll Find in This Chapter

- How to identify the business reasons for creating a data warehouse (DW).

- How to use the PACE concept: Plan, Activate, Control, End.

- How to develop the business case: strategic visioning, enterprise engineering assessment, business process reengineering, and value stream assessment.

- How to carry out the Business Question Assessment.

- How to carry out the architecture review and design.

- How to choose the tools needed to create and operate the DW.

- How to execute the details of design: the physical model and operating plans.

- How to implement planning, move into production, and turn the new DW over to management, support, and maintenance.

The approach described here is based on a detailed data warehouse project development process designed, tested, and used successfully by James Martin + Company (jm+co—a Microsoft Certified Solutions Provider). During the long effort to develop this process, mistakes were made, lessons were learned, and procedures were perfected—or at least refined and improved. The result has been extensively field tested and has improved the quality and efficiency of jm+co efforts. There are many ways to go about a task this complex, so this is a long chapter. But the process is logical and sequential, and once you get into its rationale you will see that it provides a simple, step-by-step roadmap that can guide you through a maze of possibilities and hazards.

The complexity and special challenges of designing a data warehouse are really the only things that set it apart from any large project—but these are significant. The bad news is that mistakes are easy to make; the good news is that many of them have been made already. This chapter can help you avoid them.

Step 1: Understand the Business Driver

To be successful, a project needs a set of repeatable tasks that can be clearly and logically applied to achieve a specific goal. This chapter demonstrates how to break out, assign, and schedule tasks, but to be effective they must be directed by an understanding of the project's business driver.

What makes a successful data warehouse project? The first part of the answer is easy: stay on schedule and within budget. The second part is harder: the data warehouse you create must be what you need it to be and it must allow its users to do what they need to do. That is why you need to understand the business driver. The DW must satisfy the business need, and to do that it must have the necessary capabilities and logic built into it. When it is completed, it must transfer smoothly into production and become useful quickly.

Step 2: Follow a Proven Plan

There are numerous DW design plans available. The process described in this chapter is based on a set of tasks developed and refined by many people, in numerous engagements, over several years.

Figure 3.1 shows the process. Building a data warehouse is an iterative process; so some processes repeat. Where to begin? You can start in any of several places.

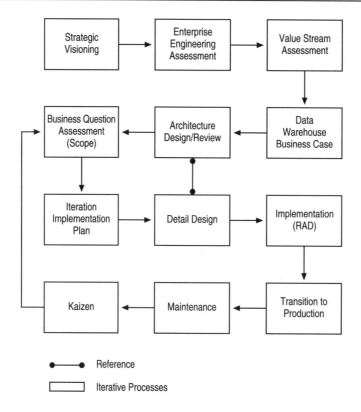

Figure 3.1   Process road map.

Setting the PACE

The Microsoft Data Warehousing strategy is designed to make data warehousing easier by creating consistency, enhancing scalability, and facilitating integration. Like most projects, a data warehouse project has a core group of common tasks. Further, it is iterative, so a solid plan can help by creating stability and repeatability based on standards. The **PACE** concept can help provide these standards.

Pace Overview

PACE covers the four areas common to any project:

- **P**lan
- **A**ctivate
- **C**ontrol
- **E**nd

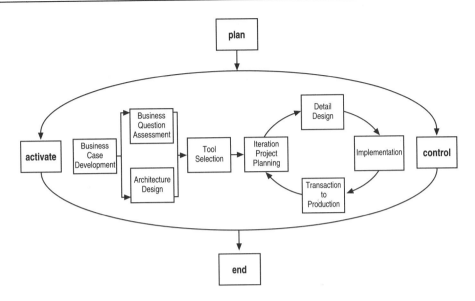

Figure 3.2   PACE and the data warehouse process.

Plan

Establish the project objectives, scope, and standards, list the deliverables, and discover any constraints. In this phase you select the approach, which for a data warehouse project can include consultants. See the Data Warehouse Institute (www.dw-institute.com) article on "10 Mistakes to Avoid When Choosing a Data Warehousing Consultant."

Planning should also assess risks, chief among which is cost. Rule of thumb: figure three to four months per iteration. Using a mix of consultants with your own staff, this can cost about $100,000/ month.

To develop the project plan, you have to create a work breakdown structure, estimate effort, allocate resources, schedule resources, develop a budget, and track it. You need a tool such as Microsoft Project 98 to do this. There are also more advanced ones such as the PLATINUM Process Continuum Suite (www.platinum.com) that use a library of industry best practices derived from consulting experience.

Other resources include trade shows, magazines, and organizations such as the Data Warehouse Institute. These sources can provide proven, formal processes for project development. Don't reinvent the wheel. Available products don't just suggest steps: they define resource requirements, show how to calculate timelines, contain example documents, and explain techniques.

The plan must, of course, be presented, finalized, and approved. All these steps (and the ones that follow) can become quite complex for large projects within large organizations. The Microsoft Solutions Framework (MSF) is an adaptable model for project planning and execution. Look into it for clear explanations and suggestions.

Activate

To activate the project you must:

- Publicize the project
- Equip team members
- Train team members

Data warehouse technology will change an organization's business, procedures, and staffing. Hold a kick-off meeting to educate *all* users on what a data warehouse is and how it can help them. Use meetings and publications to educate personnel and to manage their expectations.

Business users should drive the technology by helping to define the initial requirements and requirements for future iterations. IT staff should know the general needs of the business community, but it takes business analysts to drive the actual information requirements based on the needs of the user community.

The final part of this stage, especially if you are bringing in outside consultants or contractors, is to train the project team on the general tools it will use (such as e-mail, project management software, word processors). DW tools will be obtained later.

Control

Control continues day by day until the end of the project. There are four steps:

- Assign project tasks
- Motivate project participants
- Track the project process
- Revise the project plan

To assign project tasks from the work breakdown structure (WBS, discussed below) you have to match the assigned tasks with the skill sets of the available resources. This is a new type of technology, so the majority of the staff probably will not have worked a data warehouse project or used any of the software tools associated with it. A consultant can be a big help in this phase.

Make staff available for the project. To plan properly from the start of the project, you need to evaluate skills and assign tasks. A data warehouse is an *ongoing* project—not a one-shot deal like installing an office software package, then letting Tech Support handle the calls.

Because this will be a long-range project, managers should work to promote individual development, create incentives for teamwork, monitor progress, and acknowledge achievements. There is a shortage of data warehouse professionals; you'll be lucky if 20 percent of the team has prior experience. If you don't develop, track, and acknowledge team members, they probably will not be around for the next project and you will have to start from scratch again.

The project manager should constantly assess the state of the project and disseminate information regularly to the team, users, and sponsors.

The manager also has to watch out for *scope creep*. The project bases warehouse requirements on business drivers and user input, and you must evaluate user suggestions and requests carefully to weed out the "nice to have" features that can, inch by inch, increase cost drastically. If a feature tests out but cannot be incorporated in the initial design, document it and save it for future inclusion. Every phase of the project gives you an opportunity to track issues for future growth as well as for current tasks: don't waste it.

Rule of thumb: 15 percent of a project time is spent on the Planning, Activating, Controlling, and Ending tasks of project management. Many companies hire a data warehouse consultant as the project manager, instantly acquiring experience that helps control the project, mentor and train staff, and develop an operational method.

End

Well, everything ends sooner or later, for one reason or another, but a project must be brought down to a documented conclusion. When the DW is up and running and people are using it, there is more to do than just go home. You have to capture the lessons learned during design, implementation, and testing (for future iterations), archive the project materials, report on the project's performance, turn over the project results to the operations and support staffs, and release the project resources for use on other projects. There are more details on this phase at the end of the chapter.

Business Case Stage

Before construction begins, the scope and value objectives of the project must be defined in the data warehouse business case stage. Normally given four to six weeks, this process includes:

- Strategic visioning
- Enterprise engineering assessment
- Business process reengineering
- Value stream assessment
- Business case development

Strategic Visioning

This ongoing process, sometimes also called a Strategic Information Plan (SIP), aligns the company's business and technological strategies within the market. It is a prerequisite to enterprise engineering and business process reengineering stages. Some companies have an SIP in place, and it can serve as the seed from which the data warehouse project grows.

Enterprise Engineering Assessment

EEA develops an enterprise-wide view of the organization's need for change and its readiness to accept it. A data warehouse is not a cure-all. If an organization lacks data sources and resources, a warehouse cannot be effective. Before undertaking a data warehouse project, organizations must decide if they want to fix operational data problems by business reengineering, systems development, or information systems planning. This assessment is normally a prerequisite to business process reengineering or a value stream assessment.

Business Process Reengineering

Business process reengineering (BPR) reworks an enterprise's cross-functional processes, jobs, structures, and controls so they can better satisfy customer needs. This is not a firm prerequisite to creating a data warehouse: some companies hold off on this process until they have a data warehouse up and running. They can then use what they learn from the data warehouse to reengineer the business process and use the warehouse to measure any changes made in the organization. For example, specific, focussed sales pattern knowledge derived through DW queries may make it possible to evaluate and tune an advertising campaign.

Value Stream Assessment

The value stream assessment (VSA) solves business problems by studying an enterprise's value stream(s) from a high level over a short time (six to eight weeks), looking for ways to improve managerial, operational, social, and technological performance. The process identifies the company's *predator value stream*—the unique capability that allows it to move faster and produce better than its competition—and its vulnerable market share areas. The knowledge provided by data warehouse technology supports the VSA.

Business Case Development

This identifies the tasks needed to build the *business case* for the data warehouse. At this point, the team that will justify, design, and implement the data warehouse enters the process. They use collateral already developed by consultants or internal personnel (interviews, focus sessions, statistical analyses) to document:

- A high-level work breakdown structure for the entire project
- A cost/benefit analysis, including a return on investment if possible
- The critical success factors
- The critical success inhibitors
- The project assumptions

The business case specifies and supports the justification for a data warehouse, estimates the immediate and extended costs so that the company can budget, and identifies the project's executive sponsor(s) and gets their approval, so that development can begin.

Lower cost, ease of use, reduced staff requirements, and products such as Microsoft SQL Server 7.0 make it easy to design, develop, and implement local, desktop datamarts. But regardless of resources and desire, it is a mistake to pursue a data warehouse project without a thorough business case analysis.

The next sections describe business case assessment deliverables.

High-Level Work Breakdown Structure for the Entire Project

This structure does not need to include the low-level tasks that would be used in the actual project, but should contain the summary-level tasks and stages that reflect the major efforts. Still, you should build in detail: it helps management understand the project better, and it helps the team budget time and money more accurately.

If no one on the team has data warehouse project experience, specifying tasks becomes much more difficult. At this point, you can see the value of an experienced consultant. If you decide to hire one, investigate the company's use of a process or method, its staff's technical ability, and its data warehouse experience (number and type).

Choose a method or tool that allows you to import tasks into the organization's project management tool.

A Cost/Benefit Analysis, Including Return on Investment (ROI), if Possible

Work with business managers and key business users to identify and assign relative weights to the high-level business benefits of implementing a data warehouse to support the value streams or strategic initiatives. Management and key business users can provide the objectives, critical success factors, and future development plans for the enterprise, along with a strategy for achieving them. An effectively designed data warehouse should help an organization make strategic decisions that cannot be made through operational transaction systems.

You can sometimes find potential benefits by looking for existing business problems. Ask:

- Do business analysts, executives, and managers need more timely access to critical business information for decision-making purposes?

- Does business information reside in multiple systems requiring users to compile data from multiple reports to obtain meaningful business information?

- Does the IT organization spend too much time providing the business community with custom reports?

- Do reports return inconsistent information?

Try to get users to identify *hard* ROI figures. Many requests are tagged with "we just have to have it." This may indicate growing acceptance of DW technology, but it is not as useful as hard ROI.

Some examples of organizational benefits:

- Faster market share gains (increased revenue).

- Reduced costs due to faster information access.

- Protection of customer base through better knowledge of internal and external customer requirements and satisfiers.

- Target marketing for the development of new products and services.

- Ability to respond quickly to marketplace shifts.

- Ability to analyze trends rather than merely capture and store data.

- Ability to use information to respond to business questions, even unpredictable ones.

- Ability to adapt to a constantly changing internal business environment (that is, distributed decision making and the need for information that crosses applications).

- Ability to adapt to new business rules governed by external forces (downsizing trends, market fragmentation/segmentation, deregulation laws, regulations, etc.).

- Improved staff utilization: less time spent accessing and gathering data, more time available for analyzing, understanding, and acting on it.

Next you need to estimate at a high level the costs to develop and implement the data warehouse. Include a ballpark estimate of architecture costs; this is not a thorough analysis of technical and applications architecture requirements (done later or in a separate project). Identify costs as short-term or long-term.

Examples of cost categories:

- Current systems analysis

- Design

- Implementation, including costs to extract, transform, cleanse source data

- Personnel

- Software/middleware

- Infrastructure/hardware

- Facilities

- Maintenance/enhancement

The chart below represents a total cost of ownership that could be used in an ROI analysis.

	Total DW Cost of Ownership														
Months	1-4	5-7	8-11	12-15	16-19	20-23	24-27	28-31	32-35	36-39	40-43	44-47	48-51	52-55	56-59
Iteration	DM	EWDW	DM	DM	DM	MAINT	MAINT	MAINT	MAINT	MAINT	MAINT	MAINT	MAINT	MAINT	MAINT
Operational Support Costs															
IT Support	50.0	37.5	50.0	50.0	50.0	150.0	150.0	150.0	150.0	150.0	150.0	150.0	150.0	150.0	150.0
User Training ($200 per user)	2.4	5.0	5.0	5.0	5.0	0.5	0.5	0.5	0.5	0.5	0.5	0.5	0.5	0.5	0.5
User Mentoring (one FTE)	42.0	33.0	42.0	42.0	42.0	42.0	42.0	42.0	42.0	42.0	42.0	42.0	42.0	42.0	42.0
Sub-Total operational Costs	94.4	75.5	97.0	97.0	97.0	192.5	192.5	192.5	192.5	192.5	192.5	192.5	192.5	192.5	192.5
Capital Costs															
Hardware Purchase/Upgrade	40.0	75.0	40.0	40.0	40.0	5.0	5.0	5.0	5.0	3.0	3.0	3.0	3.0	3.0	3.0
Extraction Software	50.0	50.0	0.0	0.0	0.0	0.0	0.0	0.0	0.0	0.0	0.0	0.0	0.0	0.0	0.0
Cleansing Software	0.0	50.0	0.0	0.0	0.0	0.0	0.0	0.0	0.0	0.0	0.0	0.0	0.0	0.0	0.0
DW Manager Software	0.0	25.0	0.0	0.0	0.0	0.0	0.0	0.0	0.0	0.0	0.0	0.0	0.0	0.0	0.0
RDBMS	50.0	300.0	50.0	50.0	50.0	0.0	0.0	0.0	0.0	0.0	0.0	0.0	0.0	0.0	0.0
Metadata	10.0	50.0	10.0	10.0	10.0	0.0	0.0	0.0	0.0	0.0	0.0	0.0	0.0	0.0	0.0
Front End	20.0	20.0	40.0	40.0	40.0	0.0	0.0	0.0	0.0	0.0	0.0	0.0	0.0	0.0	0.0
Software Maintenance (15%)	0.0	0.0	7.0	7.0	7.0	37.0	37.0	37.0	37.0	37.0	37.0	37.0	37.0	37.0	37.0
Design & Implementation	440.0	330.0	440.0	440.0	440.0	78.0	78.0	78.0	78.0	78.0	78.0	78.0	78.0	78.0	78.0
Sub-Total Capital Costs	610.0	900.0	587.0	587.0	587.0	120.0	120.0	120.0	120.0	118.0	118.0	118.0	118.0	118.0	118.0
Total per Iteration	704.4	975.5	684.0	684.0	684.0	312.5	312.5	312.5	312.5	310.5	310.5	310.5	310.5	310.5	310.5
EDW Cumulative Total to Date		1,679.9	2,363.0	3,047.9	3,731.9	4,044.4	4,356.9	4,669.4	4,981.9	5,292.4	5,602.9	5,913.4	6,223.9	6,534.4	6,844.9

Legend: *All costs represented in thousands of dollars

DM = Datamart   EDW = Enterprise Data Warehouse   MAINT = Maintenance Mode

Figure 3.3   Total DW Cost of Ownership.

Assumptions:

- Hardware and software estimates are obtained from representative DW engagements.
- Software maintenance is the industry norm: 15 percent of the purchase price, charged annually after the first 12 months of use.
- Operational costs are based on industry norms.
- Design and implementation costs represent estimated costs for development labor.

If several business cases justify the project, compare their merits and do-ability. Use focus sessions to decide on the business justification and data requirements, and analyze the source data to make sure it can provide the information required. This step makes sure that the data available on the source system really answers the business questions.

Sometimes this information is most easily grasped in a chart. It should show which business case offers the highest possibility of success for the first data warehouse project. In the focus sessions and interviews, make sure users realize that all their requirements are considered important, but to test out the new technology one area has to be selected based on its likelihood of success. If it succeeds it validates the project and benefits the entire company.

In focus sessions and interviews, ask users about their current information capabilities and what requirements they feel would add efficiency and business value. Encourage them to "think out of the box" so they don't limit requirements to fit the existing source systems. A small incentive (say, $500 for the suggestion that brings the highest ROI) can spark a lot of user interest.

In focus sessions:

- Groups of less than a dozen people are easiest to manage.
- Schedule in advance for maximum attendance.
- Allow all users to attend—they all have knowledge of the organization.
- Schedule two half-day sessions. This gives you time between the two days to evaluate what you obtained the first session and decide if you need more detail.
- Consider hiring an experienced facilitator: it can be well worth it.

Critical Success Factors

Focus sessions help identify and document the critical success factors (CSFs) that have to be in place for the project to succeed.

Examples of CSFs:

- Well-defined business case
- Sound architecture design, including potential for scalability
- Realistic project scope
- Manageable amount of data
- Approved and available budget
- Dedicated internal and external staff

Critical Success Inhibitors

Focus sessions also help you identify and document the Critical Success Inhibitors (CSIs) that can impede or derail the project.

Examples of CSIs:

- Lack of commitment and awareness from executive sponsors
- Impact of other strategic information technology projects
- Inability to extract data from source systems without adversely affecting transaction system performance
- Unmanageable degree of organizational change during project
- Lack of access to necessary source data
- Disruption/change in high-level management or sponsor appointments
- Lack of involvement or cooperation by affected business or IT areas
- Unrealistic expectations
- Unrealistic schedule
- Unskilled/untrained resources or lack of resources in general
- Part-time staff assignments
- Failure to use standards and models for data management
- Non-supportive organizational culture

Project Assumptions

Based on thorough analysis and derived from the CSFs and CSIs, project assumptions must be in place for the project to be conducted as planned. Violating them endangers the project. These are gathered during focus sessions and interviews, are based on facts, and are critical reference points for project phases.

Here are some examples of assumptions. They are written in formal contractual language to stress their importance:

- Project will begin no later than [date].
- Scope will be limited to X.
- [Group A] will help evaluate and select tools; [Group B] will select and purchase tools. (This may be one group.)
- Defined resources will be available.
- Business and IT personnel will be available for strategy sessions, interviews, and meetings to identify and prioritize business and system information requirements.
- Required information systems documentation that affects the data warehouse will be made available to the team:
  - Source system data will be available.
  - Quality and cleanliness of source data will be no less than X percent.
  - Organizational change issues will be limited to X.
  - Technology platform will be X.

The Finished Business Case Document

Present the finished business case document to the proper management and budget approval members. It serves as the first formal project document. It makes a handy training document, providing context and history for team members and users who come aboard later. It is also a good model document for the next DW project, by which time you will know where the document did well and where it failed.

The Business Question Assessment

When the project is approved, it's time to move into detailed project planning.

The business question assessment (BQA) establishes the data warehouse subject areas, the scope of individual project iterations, and the short-term implementation strategy by:

- Deciding DW scope and intended use
- Defining and prioritizing business requirements, as set forth in the business case, and other information needs the DW will address
- Identifying business directions and objectives that may influence the required data and application architectures
- Deciding which business subject areas provide the most needed information, and prioritizing and sequencing implementation projects accordingly

- Developing the logical data model that will direct the physical implementation model

- Measuring the quality, availability, and related costs of needed source data at a high level

- Defining the iterative population projects based on business needs and data validation

Analyze the prioritized predator value stream or most important strategic initiative to decide which business questions the implementation has to answer. Business questions pose issues that determine strategic direction. For example, a business question for a retailer could be: "What were the top ten items sold in all stores in Region X for the second quarter of this fiscal year, where *top ten* is defined as the ten highest items in terms of total revenue per item?"

Assess each question to evaluate its overall importance to the organization, then perform a high-level analysis of the data needed to provide the answers. Assess the data's quality, availability, and cost (to bring it into the data warehouse). Use this information to reprioritize the business questions according to importance, cost, and feasibility (of acquiring the required data).

Use this analysis to decide on the scope of the foreseeable DW iterations, in the form of population projects. Estimate, within practical data acquisition limits, how many business questions can be answered in a three- to six-month implementation.

A business question must be answerable by objective analysis of available data. Business questions should:

- Focus on verifiable issues. A DW implementation cannot be created to satisfy a need that can't be stated as a business question. "Easier querying" is of little or no use in designing a technical solution.

- Help define project scope.

- Directly guide logical data model development by identifying the data objects that provide needed information to the warehouse.

- Define the tests for system acceptance. The developed system should answer any in-scope business questions.

Conduct focus sessions and interviews to develop the list of key business questions for which the DW should provide answers. Concentrate on actions that can be accomplished through user queries and on data acquisition. Use this search to:

- Establish the DW scope and intended use.

- Define and prioritize the business requirements and information (data) needs the DW will address.

- Identify business directions and objectives that may influence required data and application architectures.

- Reveal which business subject areas provide the most needed information.

- Flesh out the logical data model that will direct the physical implementation model.

- Measure the quality, availability, and related costs of needed source data at a high level.

- Decide on the iterative projects to populate the DW based on the business needs and data validation.

BQA tasks:

- Implement a change management program.

- Use focus sessions and interviews to find out:

    - Information requirements

    - Data requirements

    - Data availability

- Develop the logical model.

- Perform a source system audit to estimate the feasibility of obtaining the needed data elements.

- Choose and prioritize the population projects.

- Estimate the first iteration project costs.

- Gain approval of the first project.

- Confirm executive sponsors.

Hasn't this last item already been accomplished? The BQA stage may begin long after initial approval: the original sponsor may no longer be with the organization. You may need to find new sponsors, in which case you can dust off the business case and re-present it.

Following are more detailed looks at each BQA task.

Implement a Change Management Program

Install a change management program to monitor and prioritize change requests and prevent unplanned changes to project scope. Whether the process is formal or informal, a system must be in place before any development occurs. If your organization already has a serviceable process, adapt and use it.

Hold Focus Sessions and Interviews

First: identify the stakeholders—the key employees (managers, users, IT) — who have a vested interest in the project. Use focus sessions and interviews to help these people identify the key business questions that the data warehouse must satisfy and their associated data sources. Business management uses this information to conduct the strategic analysis.

Second: prepare an agenda and a schedule. These are important information-gathering activities and should be modeled on facilitated workshops and held over one to two weeks. Have each group meet for at least two half-day sessions so that you can assess what was gathered in the first session, then tune the discussion in the second. You can interview individuals if necessary, but group sessions instigate dialogue and tend to be more productive.

Unlike transactional operational systems, data warehouses retain comprehensive histories of a data element and its progression over time. Any database can provide sales information, but a warehouse can allow a business manager to see how many widgets were sold over a five-year period, then look at the answer from different views, such as region or sales person. Make these benefits clear in the focus sessions, so that the stakeholders can identify and refine the data warehouse requirements in the form of business needs, detailed objectives, type and granularity level of data needed, reporting and query capabilities, and related priorities. Asking "Which data do you want?" invites users to ask for all the data in the operational databases, not all of which can be delivered in the first implementation or is even useful in a warehouse. Instead, ask "Which data do you want first?"

Use the focus sessions to get a general idea of business users' criteria for performance, response, and access (workstation, Web-based, etc.). These requirements are explored and defined more fully in the architecture review and design stage.

In this stage you are trying to develop lists of:

- Information requirements for the project (in business question format)
- Data elements needed to answer the information requirements
- Source systems from which to obtain the data elements
- Possible external sources for data elements
- Data elements that currently are unavailable (to establish system enhancements)
- Data quality issues on the source systems
- Performance requirements
- Data retention requirements (how much history and how long to keep it)

Develop a formal list of the business questions and the needed elements and have the stakeholders approve it. It serves as a scorecard when you develop acceptance criteria later in the project.

Data warehouses cross business functional areas by integrating enterprise-wide information and serving multiple user communities. Individual source data systems serve specific subject areas (retail, financial, marketing, distribution, etc.), and business requirements tend to congregate into subject areas. As a result, a warehouse is typically developed to serve across subject areas but is populated in an iterative fashion, one subject area at a time, depending on the data available and the relative importance of the business requirements.

This leads to the tricky proposition of deciding who goes first. Group the business questions according to the high-level subject areas and the associated source systems that provide the necessary information to answer the questions. (Some business questions will cross subject areas.) This grouping will begin to reveal the subject areas most likely to profit from a data warehouse, which will indicate the most logical business area for the first implementation project.

Determine Data Availability

Data elements answer business questions and guide the development of the logical data model (entity or object types and their relationships). You need to collect pertinent information on them, then add to and refine it as the project proceeds. This activity starts with high-level business information, moves down into detail-level data requirements, and finally deals with candidate subject areas that will become sequenced population projects. As part of this process, you should develop a source data map: for each business question, set up a table containing the rows of data element information and columns in which to record:

- Name
- Description
- Source system(s)
- Primary source (Y or N)
- Format
- Valid values
- Update rate
- Derived (Y or N)
- Derivation algorithm
- Data steward
- Availability factor
- Extraction factor
- Cleanliness factor
- Value to warehouse

Decide which data elements are needed to answer each business question. If one element is normally derived from others, record its derivation formula. For example: Average Monthly Sales = Year Sales/12).

Identify the steward and owner of each data element and record this information in the source data map. A data *steward* is typically a functional area or IT management role responsible for overseeing and tracking changes to specific data elements and their use across systems. A data *owner* has primary responsibility for the data held within a given business subject area. (If your organization already has a data ownership program, you can use it to find this information.) You may not be able to discover ownership for a given element, in which case project management can take ownership. This phase is not merely administrative: failure to reach agreement on data access can stymie a project.

(A program for managing data ownership issues should be developed as part of the data architecture in the architecture review and design stage.)

Once you know what elements you need, and perhaps who controls them, list the systems and other internal and external sources that can contribute the necessary data elements. The majority of the data in the warehouse comes from the organization's operational systems (relational databases, mainframe systems, and flat files), and these most likely are centered on business functional areas (billing, inventory, sales, etc.). Other internal sources may include PC-based systems, files, databases, spreadsheets, etc. External sources such as tapes and files are often used to capture information on the stock market, bond ratings, competitors, partners, etc.

Gather as much information as possible when researching data source systems. Obtain information on system operations, including update rates, type of processing, and whether a data element has originated in that source system or another. Obtain a copy of the system's data dictionary, if it exists, and comments from the data steward or system owner on the data quality. Obtain key contact information for each source system. Record the source system information in the source data map.

Review the formal data dictionary for each source system identified. Record in the source data map the element name, source, size, format, update information, and description of what the element really represents. This information also serves as metadata: it will be captured and catalogued in a special repository during subsequent stages or projects, including the architecture and iterative design/development stages. If no data dictionary is available, try to get information directly from the source system, the data owner, and the data steward.

After identifying the necessary data elements and their source systems, select the most appropriate source for each element and record it as the primary source in the source data map. To do this, ask these questions:

■   Where is the data element created?

■   Is the element "pure" in this source system (not transformed or derived)?

■   If not, what transformation has taken place on the element in this source system? For example, a data element called *Part Number*, originally coded PT_NMR, has had a prefix added to its code by this system. It now carries an identifying code of DE_PT_NMR but represents the same data element as in the original system.

■   How many other elements will be extracted from this system?

Tip   Each data element extraction takes time and resources, so for each population project try to get as many elements as possible from a single source system.

To maximize the data quality and minimize cleansing and transformation, use the system of record as the primary source system whenever possible. The system of record is the source system that contains the data element in the form that is most timely, accurate, appropriate, and structurally suitable to the form to be contained in the DW. For example, the billing system would be the system of record for invoice and payment data elements.

You now have a list of information requirements, needed data elements, and sources for the elements. You can use this information to determine and prioritize population projects in the final steps of the BQA.

Develop the Logical Data Model

You can create the logical data model as an entity relationship diagram (ERD) or an object relationship diagram (ORD). Each is based on the business questions and the data elements needed to answer them. The data elements congregate around central subject areas; they define the necessary entity or object types that are the cornerstones of the detail-level subject-area data models developed during the iterative design/development stages.

Dimensions (broad categories of attributes) are part of the physical rather than logical schema of the data warehouse but you have to start envisioning the physical database schema early in the process. This is because you have to perform a source data audit, and it is affected by how attributes are categorized into dimensions and how the dimensions are arranged hierarchically. By identifying the entity or object types and the central subject areas around which the logical data elements congregate, the audit helps determine the initial implementation and the population projects that follow.

You develop a model that answers the business questions by studying how data elements in the primary source systems relate to the information requirements. Group the data elements into broad dimensions (such as geography, time, product, customer, etc.) and then study the elements for drill paths (the hierarchical progression of dimension detail from high to low). For example, a *time* dimension drill path would be year, quarter, month, day, hour, etc. A *geography* dimension might drill down to country, region, state, city, etc. Use drill paths to identify dimensions.

Next you need to analyze the business questions and data elements by asking, "Report by *what*?" This reveals the high-level entity types: report by *customer*, by *region*, by *product*, etc. Construct a logical data model in the form of an entity relationship diagram or object relationship diagram that represents the high-level entity or object types and their relationships, including the cardinality and optionality status.

At this stage, the logical data model is an overview. Rather than be limited to a single subject area, it should illustrate the integration points between subject areas that will ultimately be incorporated into the warehouse. You need to start considering how many fact tables (that is, subject areas) will be included in the physical warehouse because the preliminary data model will eventually drill down into subject-area data models, which will become physical schemas, each containing a fact table. A fact table contains the data element from the lowest hierarchical detail level for each dimension in a single subject area, and the values for that data element that you want to track.

Some multi-functional data modeling tools that are designed for developing data warehouse applications include PowerDesigner, EasyER, and Erwin ERX.

Perform a Source System Audit

A source system audit collects detailed information on each data element in the primary source systems, evaluates its quality and relative value, and assesses the feasibility and cost of acquiring the data elements needed to populate the warehouse. Combine this information with the priority lists for business questions and data quality, and you can derive the initial DW population project design.

Thoroughly analyze each data element's existing state in the primary source system, asking:

- Is the data element useful to the warehouse (should it be kept)?

  Assess each data element's value to the enterprise; discard useless ones. Of course, this must be done within the context of the operational source system and the target warehouse. Flags such as *Deleted-Flag,* and *Row-Last-Update-Date* are data elements that lack business meaning and should probably be discarded. Retain data elements such as *Company-Name*, *Class-Code*, and *Transaction-Date* that provide significant business information. Assess usefulness carefully and get rid of clunkers. Users and developers tend to include every operational data element in the warehouse without analyzing its usefulness, which severely affects warehouse size, speed, and efficiency.

■ How clean is the data element?

Assess the data element's value and format to see if the element is acceptable or can be made so with justifiable effort.

■ How easy is the data element to extract from the source system?

■ To which dimension does the data element belong?

Some data elements do not align with a dimension (for example, *cost*), but need to be retained for their atomic detail.

Enter the relative values for these items into the source data map, then identify and reconcile redundant data elements.

Evaluate the information collected for each data element (summing weighted values where appropriate) in the source data map. Use each element's availability, quality, and cost to assess the feasibility of extracting and using it. Finally, use the data's status to assess the feasibility of answering each business question, taking into account the relative importance of each question. These steps help you define the population projects.

Determine and Prioritize the Population Projects

Now it's time to develop implementation alternatives and propose them to the stakeholders and executive sponsors for review. Specify a recommendation for a first iteration of the warehouse, or the first population project. Typically, the first iteration constructs the warehouse and populates it with data for a single subject area, thus answering that area's set of business questions. This normally takes longer than subsequent population iterations, which typically last three to six months, with an average of three or four projects in 18 to 24 months.

The first iteration answers the subset of business questions selected as most effective or important. It helps to have a second subset ready, along with the pros and cons for using either as a first cut at the warehouse. If a problem develops with the first set (practical or political), you have an alternative to pitch to the stakeholders and executive sponsors.

This is also a good time, now that the data costs are known, to let users evaluate the importance of the business questions that the warehouse will answer, and agree or disagree with the recommendations. Depending on what you discover during these activities, you may need to meet with the stakeholders to reprioritize the business questions and subsequent population projects.

Ultimately, this phase results in a consensus that the proposed population projects will provide the best return from the DW development.

Estimate the First Iteration Project Costs

Now you can estimate the cost of the re-scoped first population project, and update the long-term project budget. If your estimate was good, so much the better. If the project is falling short, be prepared to explain why.

Staffing needs can increase costs beyond original estimates. Project plans sometimes allot in-house staff for the first iteration, only to find out that people have moved on and contractors or consultants are needed to fill the empty positions.

Gain Approval of the First Project

After racking and stacking the population projects and estimating the costs of the first iteration, you are ready to present the first iteration project to the audience responsible for making the go/no go decision. If you have completed the steps diligently so far, and have kept stakeholders involved and informed, approval should be a formality. Once you have the green light, you and the team are ready to start designing.

Architecture Review and Design

The architecture sets the overall technology and process framework. The architecture review and design stage assesses what pieces of the architecture already exist in the organization (a requirement analysis) and what pieces are missing (a gap analysis).

This phase develops the DW logical architecture—the configuration map of the necessary component data stores, including a central enterprise data store, an optional operational data store, one or more (optional) individual business area datamarts, and one or more metadata stores (containing two different kinds of catalog reference information about the primary data).

Next, the data, application, technical, and support architectures are designed to physically implement the logical architecture. The requirements for these architectures (explained below) are carefully analyzed so that the DW can be optimized for users. A gap analysis finds out which components of each architecture already exist in the organization and can be reused, and which must be developed (or purchased) and configured.

The **data architecture** organizes the sources and stores of business information and defines the quality and management standards for data and metadata. It sets the structure in which users see business meaning for the data in the data stores, and provides a mechanism for cataloging the data transformation processes that are necessary in warehouse development.

The **application architecture** is the software framework that guides the overall implementation of business functionality within the warehouse environment. It controls the movement of data from source to user, including extraction, cleansing, transformation, loading, refreshing, and accessing (reporting, querying).

The **technical architecture** provides the underlying computing infrastructure that enables the data and application architectures. It includes platform/server, network, communications and connectivity hardware/software/middleware, DBMS, client/server two-tier vs.three-tier approach, and end-user workstation hardware/software. Technical architecture design must address the requirements of scalability, capacity and volume handling (including table sizing and partitioning), performance, availability, stability, charge-back, and security.

The **support architecture** includes the functions necessary to manage the technology investment effectively, and the DW software components: tools and structures for backup/recovery, disaster recovery, performance monitoring, reliability/stability compliance reporting, data archiving, and version control/configuration management.

Architecture review and design applies to the long-term strategy for DW development and refinement, and is not conducted merely for a single iteration. It blueprints the data and technical structure, software application configuration, and organizational support structure for the warehouse. It forms a foundation on which iterative detail design activities can take place. Detail design tells you *what* to do: architecture review and design tells you what pieces you need to do it.

You can conduct this stage more or less in parallel with the business question assessment stage. The infrastructure that enables information storage and access is generally independent from the business requirements that drive the DW. But the efforts cannot be completely separate: data architecture definition requires some BQA input (such as data source system identification and data modeling), so the BQA must conclude before the architecture stage.

Microsoft Data Warehousing Framework

The Microsoft Data Warehousing Framework provides an overall structure for many of the processes within the architecture design stage.

The Microsoft SQL Server 7.0 database provides the cornerstone, serving as the enterprise data store, the operational data store, or datamarts within the architecture. Scalable from small to terabyte-level systems, it can fill a variety of database roles, and it provides utilities and services that are used throughout the technical and application architectures.

Microsoft's Data Transformation Services (DTS) provides data extraction and transformation capabilities. Providing simple transformations through a GUI-interface and more complex ones through a variety of scripting languages, it loads the SQL Server 7.0 engine and imports data from legacy sources, flat files, and Oracle databases.

Similarly, the SQL Server 7.0 Online Analytic Processing (OLAP) Services provides a multi-dimensional engine for data storage and analysis. OLAP Services can function as either a multi-dimensional OLAP (MOLAP) server which pre-aggregates data, a relational OLAP (ROLAP) server which allows analysis to the lowest level of detail, or a hybrid OLAP (HOLAP) server which allows for a solution that includes a balance between pre-aggregation and drill-down. Business requirements drive the aggregation and cubing strategies, based on need and the trade-off between high performance (MOLAP) and detailed analysis (ROLAP). (Cubing creates multi-dimensional databases of pre-summarized, localized data from the central warehouse.)

Another resource is the Microsoft data warehousing coalition of vendors who have fit their products within the Microsoft Data Warehousing Framework. It has produced third-party analysis and transformation solutions that augment the framework, comply with the Microsoft data warehousing architecture, and facilitate component design.

During the architecture design, you must evaluate many components for the warehouse architecture. The Microsoft Data Warehousing Framework makes it easier to design processes that provide a scalable and flexible architecture.

Review Business Plans and Existing Architecture Documentation

First, the project team should review the existing enterprise architecture to identify reusable components and tools. (Most organizations, for instance, have tools in place for data access, transformation, and extraction.) Second, if there have been any in-house DW projects, the team should survey them to identify best practices, technologies, and other potential infrastructure components. (For example, if a previous project selected a database platform or tool, using these components could promote sharing of reporting components or metadata.) Third, the team should evaluate how well existing architectural components fulfill any requirements generated so far. The team should see, on the basis of this early examination, which parts of the DW architecture are pre-determined (by existing conditions) and which parts need to be designed.

The enterprise architecture documentation is a primary resource: it shows the current and planned architecture, and it identifies architectural components (data, application, technical, and support) that are already in place. The team should also review the organization's strategic, business, and information systems plans, and the value stream assessment documentation. DW planning must support the enterprise architecture standards to encourage component reusability and information sharing across the enterprise, and to avoid reinventing the wheel.

The project team can use a checklist to track existing components such as:

- Data standards and management processes
- Metadata management processes
- Performance requirements
- Capacity requirements
- Availability requirements
- Stability requirements
- Charge-back requirements
- Security requirements
- Data archive tools/strategies/requirements
- Data extraction/tools/strategies/requirements
- Data transformation tools/strategies/requirements
- Data cleansing tools/strategies/requirements
- Data load tools/strategies/requirements
- Data access tools/strategies/requirements
- Data refresh tools/strategies/requirements

Develop Logical Data Warehouse Architecture

Logical architecture is the conceptual configuration map of the overall structure for presenting information to users. It is the first step in the DW design, identifying the necessary data stores and containing these components:

- **One enterprise data store (EDS).** A central repository that supplies atomic (detail level) integrated information to the whole organization.
- **One operational data store (optional).** A "snapshot" of enterprise-wide data.
- **One or more individual datamarts (optional).** Summarized subsets of enterprise data specific to a functional area or department, geographical region, or time period.
- **One or more metadata stores or repositories.** Catalogs of reference information about the primary data. Metadata is divided into two categories: technical and business.

The EDS is the cornerstone of the data warehouse—the source for informational needs, analytical processing, and drill-down support for the datamarts, which contain only summarized data. The EDS consolidates related data from subject-area systems and external sources; the datamarts distribute it into logical categories such as business functional departments or geographical regions, then supply it to users issuing queries. Because the EDS is a collection of daily "snapshots" of enterprise-wide data, it can supply a history of a data element's changes over time, and this aids effective strategic analysis. By definition, the EDS contains a huge amount of data, so access can be slow when users access it directly. It is more efficient to use datamarts to filter, condense, and summarize data for specific business areas.

The operational data store also supports (near) real-time data access, but, unlike the EDS, does not track data changes over time. Instead, it is updated several times a day (the frequency depends on need) with snapshots of the enterprise data. These can be accessed quicker than the EDS, so an operational data store should be part of a data warehouse design if you regularly need current (not historical) information and want reports to run quickly and immediately. Data extraction to update an operational data store does affect system performance, however.

A datamart is a data repository focused to meet the needs of a specific business function, department, geographical division, time period, or other subset. It is a conduit through which that data is distributed from the EDS to users' workstations, where it is available for quick, easy access through ad hoc or canned queries. Like the EDS, the datamart retains history, so it can be used for strategic analysis queries.

Metadata is data about data—a sort of library card catalog of comprehensive information about the warehouse's data. It helps administrators, developers, technicians, and users to find, use, and understand warehouse data, to trace data from the warehouse to its operational source, and to relate it to data in other subject areas. There are two types—business and technical metadata—each kept in one or more repositories that service the EDS.

Business metadata provides users with information on what reports, queries, and data reside in the warehouse: the location, reliability, context, transformation rules, and source operational systems of data.

Technical metadata provides critical information that helps administrators, developers, and technical users track data movement between operational systems as they maintain the DW, control its growth, and plan for future releases. (Types are listed in the "Metadata Management" section below.) Technical metadata is more explicit and complicated because the technical staff needs to manage the data, populate the warehouse, ensure that users can access data, etc. Administrators, developers, and technical users need to understand how the programs extract, transform, and load the data into the warehouse, which programs, files, and tables are affected by warehouse changes, how and how frequently users access the warehouse. (Types are listed in the "Metadata Management" section below.)

Every warehouse design requires an enterprise data store and one or more metadata stores, but datamarts and an operational data store are judgment calls. The project team should develop a logical architecture by evaluating potential configurations against business requirements.

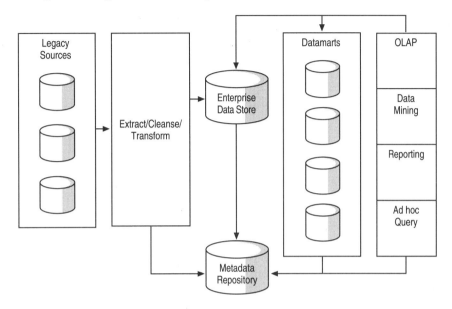

Figure 3.4   Sample logical data warehouse architecture.

Develop Data Architecture

The data architecture defines, monitors, and manages the data standards and procedures for data quality control, data ownership, source data tracking, and metadata handling. It must ensure that data loaded into the warehouse is timely, useful, and accurate. The following sections discuss functions the team should address when developing the data architecture.

Metadata Management

It is paramount to build an effective metadata strategy within the warehouse environment.

Business metadata helps business users navigate to the data they need. (The IT community typically knows its operational source systems intimately enough to navigate them without needing metadata.) Examples include:

■ Subject areas for which data is available

■ Mapping and transformational information on each data element (source field name, destination field code, transformation routines/calculations, etc.)

- Source system of each data element
- Level of summarization and detail kept on each data element
- Data element (attribute) names and business definitions (for example, "ACCT_CD" represents "Account Code for Small Business")
- Table names and business definitions
- Domain values
- Business rules
- Common access routines to warehouse data
- DW refresh schedule (date and time of latest data)
- Access estimates for queries and report executions
- Data owner of each data element

Technical metadata provides administrators, developers, and technical users a means to track the data movement from operational systems to the warehouse, so that they can maintain DW operation, control growth over its life cycle, and efficiently plan for future releases. Examples include:

- Structural information about the data (table names, table structures, format, key, size, index, etc.)
- Source system of each data element
- Source system field codes
- Mapping and transformational information on each data element (source field name, destination field code, transformation routines/calculations, etc.)
- Data model relationships
- Encoding conversions
- User report and query access patterns, frequency, and execution times
- History of data extractions
- Program names and descriptions
- Version maintenance information
- Security access levels
- Growth metrics
- Load frequencies
- Data archiving
- Purge criteria
- Table access patterns

Metadata exists throughout the enterprise in programs, data dictionaries, file layouts, data models, and other components of legacy systems and enterprise architectures. It also is in external data sources, in corporate knowledge, policies, guidelines, and in other information that people "just know." It must be collected, consolidated, and made available to the enterprise data store in a separate repository that is designed in the detail design stage and built in the implementation stage. Some metadata is captured and can be loaded into the repository with tools that extract, transform, and load primary data (some metadata comes bundled with the primary data). There are metadata management tools, but they are costly and there are as yet no leading vendors or industry standards. Unless there is a great deal of metadata, it may be cheaper to manage and publish it using a front-end tool, reporting tool, manual updates, on-line help file, word-processor document, or other means. To ensure user confidence in data, pick a metadata solution that allows users to see how warehouse data elements have been created.

If you build a data warehouse using the Microsoft Framework, you can use the Microsoft Repository, which resides on a Windows NT server, to consolidate information from SQL Server 7.0, DTS, and metadata from Microsoft data warehouse coalition products. The Microsoft Repository provides a foundation for integrating metadata from several sources. For a detailed discussion of this topic, see the "Metadata Management Infrastructure" section in Chapter 11.

Some products can share metadata easily. For example, Informatica, a leading extraction and transformation tool, can share metadata with MicroStrategy, a relational OLAP product. Rather than simply exchange metadata, these products display each other's metadata. With them, users can look up the business meaning of an element within the OLAP environment, then use the technical metadata from the extraction/transformation product to trace the data back to the source. The industry is moving toward metadata standards, and project teams should look for integrated metadata opportunities.

The project team should establish policies and procedures for collecting metadata from enterprise sources, and for managing and making changes to metadata in the data warehouse. The team should find out how metadata is extracted, loaded, updated, and made available, and whether metadata is stored in a separate database or kept on a different technical platform than the other data stores. The team should also review any of the organization's existing metadata management programs and apply them if necessary or practical.

Data Quality

As data is extracted from source systems and loaded into the warehouse, it must be checked for quality: timeliness, usefulness, completeness, and accuracy. Data quality is directly tied to its source. To maximize data quality and minimize the need for cleansing and transformation, always try to draw data primarily from the system of record, where data elements are the most timely, accurate, appropriate, and structurally suitable for use in the warehouse. For example, the billing system should be the system of record for invoice and payment data elements.

The data architecture should establish policies and procedures for managing and monitoring source data quality. The project team should define and document how data quality issues will be resolved and who has the final approval on any issue. Ask users to evaluate the data in the source system(s). They tend to know the data quality issues and can help keep bad data out of the warehouse.

The data quality control program should also ensure that data is as accurate and complete as the source system data, and that warehouse update rates and transformation procedures do not adversely affect it.

Source Data Tracking

The project team should also establish policies and procedures for tracking warehouse source data that crosses organizational systems. The team should maintain a list of all source systems, the contact point for each system, a description of what each system does, and a listing of its constituent data elements that is as complete as is feasible. Assuming the data elements needed to satisfy business requirements exist within the organization's databases, the DW designers need a data tracking system to ascertain where to find them. The information can be kept in a small database or spreadsheet.

Data Population Standards

The team should also establish data standards that define data elements in terms of:

- Acceptable range of values
- Format (numeric, alphabetic, alphanumeric, date, etc.)
- Number of characters permitted
- How they are stored
- How long they are stored
- Rules for transformation (changing a source system data element into a warehouse data element)

The standards should include a strategy for managing data granularity (the level of detail maintained). The strategy should cover:

- Levels of detail for each division
- Levels of detail for each region
- Amount of granularity duplication between the region and division, if any
- Method for drill down from division to region
- Method for maintaining consistency between division and region data

- Method for maintaining consistency between detailed and summarized data
- Historical information needs

Data Ownership Program

A data ownership program ensures that changes to data are published and implemented in all affected operational and informational systems. Ensuring that someone is responsible for data ownership is often a critical success factor: changes to source data elements affect the data warehouse, so they must be published and implemented in all affected systems. As new business questions develop and additional details about existing questions materialize, you must be able to track data elements to their owners. The team should review any existing data management programs, and should adopt applicable ownership standards.

Develop Technical Architecture

To provide infrastructure support for the data warehouse application processes and data architecture, the technical architecture must look at the long-term strategy and build in scalability so that the warehouse can continue to provide value as business needs and technologies change. The team should review the enterprise architecture technology documentation of current and projected technologies, and meet with IT and business representatives to collect the technical requirements for performance, availability, stability, security, capacity, and charge-back. Gaps can be filled by implementing new technical components or using existing hardware, software, and middleware components.

The team should use the enterprise architecture documentation's description of technology to inventory available technical components and products. If the IT organization keeps an up-to-date component inventory, the team can review it; otherwise, the team should compile one. The inventory should:

- **Consider current/planned operational workload.** Who are the main users, to what degree are the facilities used now, and what future use is expected?
- **Identify local environmental and policy factors.** Architecture is constrained by a number of factors imposed by management or corporate headquarters, or by external influences. The team needs to review policy documents or conduct interviews with IT and communications management.
- **Interview management.** IT management can provide important insight into how the current architecture evolved and its strengths and weaknesses. Interview early in the analysis phase and be sure to address:
  - Policies that govern the technical architecture, and their origin and impact on the existing architecture
  - Constraints imposed by internal or external environmental factors
  - Problem areas

- Existing plans and strategies, written or not
- Technical architecture support for the business objectives
- Objectives and critical success factors for the technical architecture

- **Identify technology trends.** Trends can be identified by IT management, by reference to technical publications, by attending vendor briefings, or by external consultants. Categorize trends by the amount of impact they will have on potential DW architecture, then analyze the more significant ones.

- **Assess technical position.** The time and intermediate steps needed to attain the target architecture depend on the current level of sophistication. (Do not mistake complexity for sophistication.)

Technical Requirements

Once the existing technical components have been identified, the next step is to identify the business requirements and key metrics that the warehouse must support. A solid technical architecture foundation collects requirements in the areas discussed below.

Identify Technical Architecture Components

The team should compare the current and proposed technical environments to decide what components are needed to support the requirements. The team should consider:

- **Client-server architecture approach.** DW applications are client-server applications, and can be implemented in either two-tier or three-tier architectures. Three-tier implements a logic component on a server between the DW and the presentation layer. Increased use of the Web and intranets as servers is shifting current DW architectures to a more "server-centric" environment, "thinning" clients (desktops) by distributing much of the logic among multiple communicating servers.

- **End-user workstation hardware/software.** In addition to the data access tools that perform query and report functions (covered in the "Develop Application Architecture" section below), users need other access tools: computer, monitor, network connectivity and communications (TCP/IP, NetWare), drivers for accessing the database, operating systems upgrades, OCX controls, Web browser, etc.

- **Platform/server.** Numerous servers support warehouse development. The Microsoft Data Warehousing Framework is based on Windows NT architecture, which offers enhanced scalability and performance. Whatever platform is used, servers must be sized properly. The DW may contain huge amounts of data to support trend analysis, and its servers must be sized for this and to scale as demands increase.

- **Security enforcement software.** This keeps unauthorized users away from sensitive data, especially outsiders if the DW uses an extranet or is Web-based.

- **DBMS.** The DW consolidates data from internal and external source systems. The database management system (DBMS) needed to support the database must be scalable to maintain performance as capacity increases over about three to five years. SQL Server 7.0 is the key database platform for the Microsoft Data Warehousing Framework. It supports key data warehousing features such as parallel loading, parallel processing, and multi-processor support. To evaluate a DBMS, ask:

  - What is its initial cost?

  - What are its maintenance costs, including upgrades and support?

  - How easy is it to use?

  - What skills are needed to use it and how readily available are those skills?

  - How many processors does it support?

  - Can it load and process queries in parallel?

  - Does the vendor have good industry standing and a substantial customer base?

- **Network.** The network must support data access and file transfers for remote and local users. Important factors include range (international or domestic), Web-based, degree of complexity, and technical requirements. Network management software may be required to manage network traffic and individual network nodes. Include essential middleware components.

This evaluation yields a preliminary short-list of recommended technical components for further investigation, which can, in another phase, be narrowed to a set of tools and vendors.

The configuration of these components is the data warehouse technical architecture, which works in conjunction with the components of the data, application, and support architectures to create the scalable infrastructure that runs and supports the DW system.

Develop Application Architecture

The application architecture is the software framework that enables the overall implementation of business functionality. Its development is based on the business requirements, which are part of the physical implementation of the logical architecture. It includes all elements that affect how data is moved from source to user, including tools and programs that extract, transform, cleanse, load, refresh, and access (report, query) data. And it provides the framework on which tool selection and program design are based.

The team should review (and adopt) any existing organizational standards, policies, programs, and tools applicable to the application architecture for existing or proposed systems.

The Microsoft Data Warehousing Framework provides tools and technologies that support many application architecture processes. The project team needs to design the processes described below.

Data Extraction, Cleansing, Transformation, and Loading

Data is extracted from the source systems, cleansed, transformed, and loaded into the DW. These processes usually are performed together.

Extraction can be performed by software tools or by programs written in a language such as COBOL, C++, or C. Extraction tools often perform data transformation as well. Microsoft supports the data extraction and transformation process through Data Transformation Services (DTS), which can extract data from sources such as Oracle, DB2 on Windows NT, flat files, AS/400, and host-based sources that use Microsoft SNA Server.

Cleansing removes or fixes unwanted or incorrect data. Available cleansing tools automatically correct or reject values such as salutations, abbreviations, and state or postal codes. The project team can create code that corrects or rejects other unwanted values. Generally, you have to buy tools only when dealing with large warehouses that collect data from multiple sources that pose cleanliness problems; smaller efforts can usually get by with a data extraction/transformation tool or scripts.

Next, source data is transformed to a dimensional format, placed into standardized codes, and divided into fact records and dimensional records ready for loading into the warehouse. Some tools perform data transformation in conjunction with extraction. DTS handles simple transformations through its GUI, and complex transformations through JAVA or VB script. Its steps can be executed in parallel on an SMP machine. For complex activities beyond the scope of DTS, Microsoft supports the process through allied vendors such as Prism, Informatica, and Sagent.

The team needs to consider many extraction/transformation options, chief among which is whether to use a tool or custom coding. This depends on the number and types of sources involved. Usually, extraction/transformation tools support only limited types of data. First-generation tools are code generators that can usually handle mainframe-based sources very well since they can generate COBOL. Second-generation tools are function-based and usually handle relational non-MVS databases very well but struggle to extract from MVS sources. Usually, these tools require that an extracted flat-file be produced from legacy sources. All tools require some learning time, but they create reusable modules that pay off in subsequent iterations. Most tools also capture metadata.

Native database utilities can often be used to load transformed data into the DW. If native drivers are available, loading can be part of the extraction/transformation process. Microsoft uses DTS. Usually, stored procedures or database scripts handle DW updates and corrections.

The data extraction/transformation/cleansing/loading architecture identifies only *if* tools will be used to implement the processes. The specific tools are selected in a later stage. Don't be fooled into believing that tools can do it all: factor in some time for custom coding.

Data Refresh Process

A data refresh strategy dictates whether DW data receives full or incremental refreshes.

A full refresh strategy consists of three steps:

1. Delete all existing warehouse data (or simply drop and re-create the tables)
2. Extract all data from the operational systems
3. Load the new data into the warehouse

A full refresh works with relatively small amounts of data, but increasing volume also increases the time required for a refresh. Eventually, this can become too slow.

An incremental refresh extracts and loads only new or changed operational data. It still takes longer as data volume increases, but not so long as a full refresh. Many vendors now recommend using the log tapes as incremental data sources.

The team should pick a method, determine whether it will be handled by a tool or by custom-coded programs, and decide what language (such as COBOL, C++ , or C) custom programs should be developed in. (Candidate tools are evaluated later.) If data extraction and transformation tools are to be used for the refresh process, the team should investigate their ability to handle changed data.

Data Access Process

DW users can be diverse in location, type, platforms, workstation interfaces, and reporting/querying needs. The team should gather information on user locations and types, and should map user types to locations and subject areas. The team also needs to know user hardware and presentation interface requirements: will they access the DW through a GUI built with a front-end development tool such as Visual Basic or C++, or through the Web? Some parts of this investigation use information gathered when deciding on the technology architecture, because the technical infrastructure drives user hardware configurations. This is the time to identify the power users and others that will be involved in tool selection, testing, and the transition into production. Document each power user's name, location, business area, type of computer, memory available, and any other relevant information. Use this when upgrading or purchasing user workstation software.

Data access tools are considered decision support system/executive information system (DSS/EIS) software applications. Users can be classified as novices (limited understanding of databases) and power/expert users (understand database structures). All DSS/EIS tools must link to a data management (metadata) layer that resides between the user and the database and is managed by IT staff (or a power user) so that it is kept in sync with the underlying database tables. There are three types of tools:

- MOLAP or ROLAP
- Production reporting
- Ad hoc query (usually with report writing functionality)

MOLAP (multidimensional on-line analytical processing) and ROLAP (relational on-line analytical processing) tools provide strong reporting and drill-down capabilities for multi-dimensional power analysis. With ROLAP tools users can directly access DW data (single datamart or full enterprise data store) to the lowest level of atomic detail. MOLAP tools are similar in function but permit direct access only to *cubes* (multi-dimensional databases) of pre-summarized, localized data from the central warehouse. Cubes are portable, making them useful for DW demo presentations. Microsoft SQL Server OLAP Services supports these types and HOLAP (hybrid OLAP), which enables pre-aggregated cubes as well as drill-down to a lower level of detail in the enterprise data store. (Microsoft provides the plumbing for OLAP analysis; third-party vendors provide the front-end user interface.)

Production reporting tools are used mostly by developers or power/expert users to create production reports for end-users. Complex analytical reports require IT skills, because they often involve programming and graphics manipulation. These tools can be set up in a two-tier architecture to allow users to access the database directly to produce less-complex reports. Setting them up in a three-tier architecture requires placing an interim report server between the database and the user workstation, but this is recommended if complex reports are needed or heavy report scheduling is expected.

Ad hoc query tools allow novice and power users to access the DW directly to retrieve information to queries such as "what are total sales by region?"

Developers can use tools such as Visual Basic or C++ to create GUI front ends through which users can access the DW. Microsoft has provided the OLE DB for OLAP API that allows custom-built applications to access OLAP Services. The team should outline the data access processes and user requirements to decide which tools or custom-coded applications to use. Specific tools are selected in a later stage.

Develop Support Architecture

Some functions are not directly tied to DW construction but must be in place to ensure that the system operates smoothly over time and serves users effectively: user training, system performance monitoring, backup and recovery, help desk, version control, configuration management, change management, etc. The team must therefore develop a fourth architecture (support) to work in conjunction with the data, application, and technical architectures.

Support architecture provides technical, management, and customer support. The team should investigate and adapt (if practical) any hardware components, software tools, policies, programs, and procedures that already exist within the organization. The team can conduct a gap analysis, then itemize the support architecture component matrix, including recommendations to adopt, adapt, or develop.

Support architecture technical functions include:

- DW transition from development to production environment
- DW maintenance, including management coordination of multiple source systems
- Software upgrades
- Version control
- Configuration management
- Data archiving
- Backup and recovery
- Disaster recovery

The team should outline the requirements for these and itemize potential issues.

Support architecture management functions of the support architecture include performance/usage monitoring and reporting activities such as:

- Query response time/complexity ratio
- Volume of users
- Types of usage
- Volume of data and growth rate

Management can use some of the performance information collected here to evaluate the DW's usage and acceptance level within the organization.

Support architecture customer functions include:

- Developing a user service level agreement detailing DW availability and data currency.

- Training users on front-end tools, including requirements for what levels of users will be trained, and how training will be developed and delivered.

- Help desk operation (technical support to users).

- Management of tool vendor support agreements.

- Organizational/cultural change and rollout procedures to help users adapt to the DW approach.

- Change management procedures for controlling user requests during development. (This can be the change management program developed during the BQA.)

Based on the support requirements, the team should conduct a complete gap analysis on the components of the support architecture, using the itemized requirements for technical, management, and customer support functions as a baseline. The enterprise architecture documents (including component checklists) can serve as a baseline for existing components and programs. The team should also analyze the enterprise's source systems and DW structures to see if any elements of these functions already exist.

The team now uses everything learned so far to identify the best candidate hardware and software components, including tools, to perform these support functions:

- Backup and recovery

- Disaster recovery

- Performance monitoring

- Data archiving

- Version control

- Configuration management

This yields a short-list of recommended support components for further investigation in a later stage.

Getting the MOST out of the Project

The **MOST** concept helps you examine and assess four components of a DW project:

- **Management**

- **Organization**

- **Social**

- **Technology**

Teams often are so concerned about the project's technical aspects that they forget the organizational and social implications. But the technology can bring big changes to an organization's day-to-day operations. Management aspects also are often carefully studied, probably because management starts the project, pays the bills, and must be kept happy.

But the organization and social factors are also important, sometimes more so than the technology. When implementing a new technology, a project team must understand how changes affect staff and the organization as a whole.

The value stream discussed earlier looks at the different operational and functional "stovepipes" of an organization as a process is evaluated, concentrating on the impact of each step—not just in terms of technology and management, but to the entire organization and social culture.

For example, a data warehouse report containing important company information affects management, but in so doing it can also affect the entire organization, because management decisions affect the entire company. If improved information management helps business, all employees may realize larger raises or bonuses. These and other social effects derive from the data warehouse.

Evaluate all changes for their possible impact on all four of the **MOST** components.

Obtain Approval and Sign-off

After the application, technical, data, and support architectures have been defined, the entire data warehouse architecture is usually proposed to the executive sponsors, the business community, and key architects within the organization. The executive sponsors must sign off on the DW architecture, and they must be assured that the DW's proposed direction fits the enterprise's business needs and architectural strategy. The business community needs to believe that the architecture will fit scalability and functionality requirements as the DW is rolled out. The key architects need a more thorough technical briefing, to ensure that the team has not overlooked any key technical issues. Once these parties have approved the architecture, the team can move forward.

Conclusion

The processes outlined in this section are crucial to building a successful warehouse. All architectural processes should be thoroughly documented and reviewed across the enterprise. The architecture is the basis for all future DW iterations: it must be developed and reviewed effectively before any development begins.

The Right Tools for the Right Job

How do you select the right set of tools? It will necessarily be a *set*: no single tool can do the job. Simple answer: decide what the job is, then you can decide what set of tools to buy and use.

You won't do this once. Remember that the data warehouse is a process that changes over time. New tools will hit the market, existing tools will change. You will end up looking at new tools as the warehouse grows, users become more competent, and the tools themselves mature.

Tools Overview

In this stage you identify the candidate tools for developing and implementing the data and application architectures, and for performing technical and support architecture functions where appropriate. Then you select the ones that best meet the business and technical requirements defined by your DW architecture. Then you purchase and install the tools, and train users.

Tool selection depends on existing technical infrastructure. Many organizations try to avoid buying tools by using the ones they already have in place, so the team must thoroughly evaluate existing tools and the feasibility of using them. Some can be form-fitted to the DW, but special circumstances will often require new ones.

If management insists on using particular tools or if tools have already been assessed and selected for this project, you can skip this stage. If the mandated tools are not good choices, you may want skip the project.

You can categorize tools according to data, technical, application, or support functions:

- Source data extraction and transformation
- Data cleansing
- Data load
- Data refresh
- Data access
- Security enforcement
- Version control
- Configuration management
- Backup and recovery
- Disaster recovery
- Performance monitoring

- Database management
- Platform
- Data modeling
- Metadata management

Identify the Players

Compile the technical and business requirements for all the categories of tools to be selected, then develop the key evaluation criteria against which qualified vendors and their product offerings will be assessed. Reduce the list of all vendors to a list of candidates that is large enough to include all needed tools and small enough to work with. Use queries, requests for information (RFIs), and research to build information. Check out some of the DW Web sites for vendor lists and reviews; the Data Warehouse Institute is an excellent place to start.

To identify the key candidates, work through the four stages below.

Develop Tool Requirements

Categorize required tools. The architecture review and design phase developed business requirements for technical, application, and support architectures. Data modeling (related to the data architecture) is another category. If there was no review and design phase, the team will have to define tool requirements and specifications before proceeding.

Identify Candidate Vendors

Identify vendors who sell the tools specified above. Use the list developed in the architecture review and design phase. If that phase was skipped, evaluate vendors now, based on general knowledge of the industry and its players, industry analysts' reports and ratings, the specific business and technical requirements of the tools, and the degree to which a given vendor is likely to meet the requirements criteria.

Choose Evaluation Criteria

Choose criteria that will eliminate some tools (and vendors) from further consideration, and use them to focus the list. Some good ones:

- Market reputation
- Industry analysts' ratings
- Requirements and limitations of technical infrastructure (such as Windows NT compatibility)
- Compatibility with existing tools to be used

- Price
- Vendor responsiveness
- Availability
- Scalability
- Ease of use

Get Down to the Short List

Narrow the vendor list to a short-list of no more than five finalists per category. Contact them for more information. They will need a minimum tool requirement list.

You could instead send them a request for information (RFI) with a deadline. This method provides you with vendors' ideas and alternatives, which you can use to narrow the vendor list further, to specify and envision your proposed solution, and to feel out the marketplace. These are all good things, but an RFI cycle can add a month to the project schedule because vendors need time to gather information and respond. If you want to speed things up, you can gather a lot of this information off the Internet.

Delete vendors from the short-list, prioritize the remaining candidates, and adjust the tool selection criteria matrix.

Develop the Test Plan

Many vendors will tell you that they will supply test data, and while this may be helpful you still have to test tools against your data in your environment. Some vendors will offer to come in and run tests for a charge, thus offsetting *your* costs, but if you decide to do this make sure they fit *your* schedule. See how easy it is to deal with the company: if they are difficult to work with now, what can you expect after you buy?

Develop a matrix that lists the critical evaluation criteria for each tool. List the candidate tools as columns, and the requirements (technical or business) and key performance factors as rows. Allow room in the cells for evaluative comments. As you fill in the matrix, rate each tool on each point and then use the matrix to determine the winners.

Below is an example of itemized matrix evaluations. Customize these criteria to meet your situation.

Company characteristics

- Established customer base
- Size of established client base

- Main customers using their tools
- Company stability
- Financial condition
- Strategic partners
- Market share
- Percentage of revenue spent on R&D

Technical support/vendor service

- Technical support available during normal working hours
- Possibility of special support arrangements
- Speed of technical support responses
- E-mail/bulletin board support
- Internet technical forums and user groups
- Web page
- Quality of maintenance support after installation
- Maintenance cost
- Upgrade costs separate from maintenance

Price

System requirements

- Open architecture
- Does tool run as a service on server/workstation
- Does tool require user to be logged on
- Does tool have to be loaded on the DB server

Memory requirements

- Disk space requirements
- Middleware requirements

Operating system requirements

Training

- User manuals
- Animated icons
- Computer-based training materials
- Quality/usefulness of training materials

Data extraction functionality

- Capability to distinguish data type differences between source and target
- Can users build a query using a GUI
- Can users run a query and filter the result set
- Can results be sorted
- Can results from other fields be calculated
- Can query be saved for reusability
- Can query be previewed before run
- Can results be auto-pasted into another application
- Can null values, zero values, blanks, etc., be extracted
- Can query be displayed before execution
- Can extraction commands be displayed and edited

Data cleansing functionality

- Removal of unwanted duplicates
- Removal of unwanted characters
- Correct field values to match field definitions
- Capability to replace missing data
- Test data integrity rules
- Storage of calculations

Data exporting functionality

- Move data in a single pass
- Extract data in any format and sort order
- Ease of exporting data

Metadata functionality

- Help feature availability
- Repository for queries and reports
- Microsoft Repository
- Integration
- Publish to Web
- Usage statistics/job statistics

Summarization/aggregation functionality

- Loading of summarized tables
- Loading of aggregate tables

Matching functionality

- Match records across multiple sources
- Merge records

Transformation functionality

- Code translation
- Tag translation
- Smart-code translation

Data load functionality

- Quality of loading capabilities
- Loading to various platforms
- Loading many-to-one tables
- Loading one-to-one tables
- Automatic loading
- Parallel loading

Performance

- Simple query run-time
- Complex query run-time
- Ease of installation
- Scalability
- Code generation
- Temporary storage utilization
- Exception reporting/error logs
- Scheduling
- Retry capability
- Backup/restore

Schedule and Test

Arrange for vendors to demonstrate their tools, and test each of the finalists on how efficiently and effectively each tool addresses performance and capability requirements. Test formally: install each tool in a test environment similar to the target environment and run test scenarios to see how well the tool handles the key performance factors. Analyze the results, rating each criterion for each tool. Record this information, along with total scores, in the tool selection criteria matrix.

Create a plan that identifies the tests to be performed, test participants (include a representative group of end-users), test sites, environment(s), and preparation steps. You may need to make different test plans for different tool classes. Define the test cases and test data to be used. These should help the team evaluate how well each tool addresses key performance factors. Obtain the test data required for the test cases.

Create a scripted scenario for each test procedure, including expected results. Consider creating multiple scenarios to evaluate different tool requirements.

Prepare the test environment so that it mirrors the production environment's technical infrastructure (server, DBMS, network configuration, workstations, etc.) as closely as possible. This may entail using vendor laboratories or other offsite facilities.

Schedule tests with each short-list vendor. They should be willing to provide comprehensive information on their tools, to demonstrate features, and to run the prepared tests. Rule of thumb: it normally takes a half-day per vendor to set up and run an evaluation. Be sure to update the tool evaluation test plan within the project schedule.

Research the industry and in-house standards against which vendor performance will be measured, including level of customer service. Analyze each vendor's strategic direction and future plans for its candidate tools, as well as its policies, procedures, and performance record for service. If a vendor has no information on the future of its product line, take this into consideration: your organization probably expects to have a long-term relationship with each vendor.

The last step is to perform the evaluation. Use the same team members and users for each test to make sure you get ratings from the same set of raters.

Consider releasing your results (or a subset of them) to the vendors. They are putting a lot of time and effort into helping you select the correct tool, and they may learn something useful from your reasons for not choosing one of their products.

Estimate the Tool Life-Cycle Costs

Although purchase price is important, you also need to estimate other costs. Estimate the total life cycle costs for each tool by considering:

- Implementation
- Upgrade
- Operation
- Technical support

Estimate the cost of implementing each tool according to the requirements and strategies defined by the data, application, technical, and support architectures. Remember to look at the impact of implementing tools at remote sites. Can it be done remotely, or will IT staff have to visit every machine?

Estimate upgrade and maintenance costs for each tool throughout its estimated life. Consider purchase and installation costs for upgrades, and expected frequency, if possible.

Estimate the cost of operating each tool in the production environment over its expected life: labor, facilities, outsourcing, equipment, and training costs. Don't overlook the cost to upgrade individual PCs to run the product: a $200 piece of update software may require a new machine.

Estimate support costs. Consider the types and levels of support available. If proposed DW requires 24 x 7 availability, tool support should be available on the same schedule. Find out how much support can be provided by your help desk. The more support you can provide in-house, the lower your overall costs.

Select and Purchase

If you have done all this, selection becomes straightforward. If at this point you find that tools from two competitive vendors are roughly equal, consider haggling. A vendor may be willing to discount a tool if you say you are ready to go with a competitor to save money. You may be able to get a better tool cheaper, or perhaps get a deal on training, upgrade, or maintenance costs.

If you are using a consulting or contractor service, they may have relationships with vendors that are good for a discount. Some firms are value added resellers (VARs) for tool vendors and are willing to pass on savings if you sign with them for services. (This is worth considering when you research consulting or contractor services.) Some firms won't tell you this unless you ask.

Add up everything you have learned this far and select the tools you need. Be sure to document the recommendations in each tool category, supported by the results of the analysis. Include short-term and long-term costs for each tool.

If you can't find or afford the tool you need, consider developing a custom-coded application. Consider your organization's ability to develop and maintain custom software, and the estimated life-cycle costs. These usually cost more than off-the-shelf solutions.

If necessary, submit the tool recommendations for approval. Include all relevant supporting documentation, such as the completed tool selection criteria matrix. Be prepared to support your choices in the face of political or management resistance.

When you get the green light, procure the tools. You can put this off until implementation, but don't forget that delivery, installation, testing, and training take time. Some companies take months to purchase a tool. Factor your company's buying process into the schedule.

Finally, Iteration Project Planning

Some organizations move quickly from considering a data warehouse to designing and building it, but most take a long time to work through the budget process, staffing requirements, consultant selection, etc. This section is based on the more realistic assumption that weeks or months have gone by since the project was approved and funded during the BQA.

If architecture design or tool selection took place during or after the BQA, or if much time has elapsed since the BQA, be sure to follow the iteration project planning steps in this section. If you have just finished the BQA, you still need to follow this procedure, but will find that you merely have to add detail to what you have already developed.

The data warehouse is implemented (populated) one subject area at a time, driven by specific business questions to be answered by each implementation cycle as planned during the BQA. Now it is time to plan the subject-area implementation project. The first step is to conduct user interviews and focus sessions to refine the business requirements discovered in the BQA and the technical requirements of the architecture review and design stage. You need to refine them to the subject-area level, then analyze them to yield the detail needed to design and implement a single population project. The project team has to be expanded to include the people who will construct and deploy the warehouse. A detailed design and implementation plan has to be developed for the iteration project. Implementation steps include:

- Construct a detailed project plan for the current iteration project

- Refine the overall information requirements into those pertinent to the current subject area of implementation

- Provide for the identification and acquisition of detail-level population data

- Account for any project scope change that might have resulted from discovery of detail-level information requirements since the completion of the BQA

- Revise estimates for the total development cost for the first iteration project

- Identify the cycle's critical success factors, inhibitors, and project assumptions

- Identify the development facilities needed by the project team

- Identify the full project team and their responsibilities

If you set out to gather more detailed information, be prepared to explain to management and users why you are once again verifying design issues and user requirements. You may be able to avoid focus sessions by just checking with key management and users for possible requirement changes.

A data warehouse project is unlike most projects in that it will change and develop as improved technologies (such as Microsoft SQL Server 7.0) simplify design and implementation. Successful data warehouses grow to satisfy user needs, and these needs develop as users define new business and information requirements. Users should understand that the data warehouse team will come back often for more input. The "Roll Out the Data Warehouse" section later in this chapter details some creative ways to gather information from users after the initial project is up and running.

Information gathering doesn't have to be formal. Team members can often learn useful things simply by chatting with the business managers and staff. This is no substitute for regular meetings, but it can add a lot of value with little effort.

The rest of this section details the tasks you have to accomplish to prepare for the iteration project.

Refine Business and Technical Requirements

Population cycles are defined in the BQA stage. If there was no BQA, the team must now identify and prioritize the DW subject areas to be implemented, based on business requirements and the data to be extracted from the source systems and loaded into the warehouse to support queries within each subject area. The most critical area becomes the first population project.

All the pieces must be in place before you can design and implement the first iteration. This includes the conventional project management and startup activities associated with any project, which are detailed in the plan, activate, and control stages. During the first iteration, the warehouse is built and populated with the first cut of data. Subsequent iterations install successive cuts of data.

To prepare for the detail-level information-gathering sessions, review the key business and architectural information generated in the business case development, business question assessment, and architecture review and design stages. If new team members have come on since these stages, have them review the documents, then hold a team meeting to cover any issues.

It is time to define the business information and technical requirements to a level of detail sufficient for populating the warehouse one subject area at a time and making its contents accessible to users. This may require focus sessions and interviews with users of the subject area to be implemented, to further refine the business and technical requirements and identify what data users need. Use the same stakeholders interviewed during the BQA session. If you are sure nothing has changed, you can forgo these sessions.

You can also use sessions to identify special application and technical requirements that will permit users to access the data they need, when they need it, to produce what they need, so that the iteration development project can be effectively designed to meet user expectations.

Focus sessions should define these requirements for the current iteration:

- What data is needed to answer the business questions
- Level of data granularity/summarization
- Reporting specifications
- Ad hoc query specifications
- Timing and frequency of data refresh
- Historical retention/archiving
- Backup and recovery
- Performance monitoring
- Charge-back requirements permitting IT to charge individuals or departments for connect time, queries, reports, special processing, etc.
- Business and technical metadata
- Security

If you gather more information, be sure to update the business requirements documentation.

Refine Data Model and Source Data Inventory

Using the high-level logical data model created in the BQA stage, drill down and refine it to the subject-area level to isolate and define the entity (or object) types, attributes, and relationships pertinent to the current iteration subject area. You are now ready to model the specific subject area, but keep the higher-level integration points with other subject areas in mind. When modeling, always try to think ahead to where the model may need to go to accommodate future requirements.

Revisit the source data map created in the BQA and refine the inventory of physical data elements needed for this population project. Review the data quality findings for the needed data elements.

This develops the final logical requirements that the database administrator (DBA) uses when developing the physical model. You should also consider having the DBA help to develop the logical model, because by the end of the project the DBA often knows more about the DW than anyone else: business requirements, acquisition, loading, storage process, and tools. In short, the DBA is an excellent backup for other team members—a fact you can exploit when trying to contain costs.

Develop the Iteration Project Plan

If focus sessions changed the original scope projections, revise the project scope and be prepared to present the changes to management, if required. The high-level business case provides the basic work plan for the iteration; with it you can revise the original project plan to include a work plan for this cycle's population tasks. You may have to revise your original development cost estimates, and the critical success factors, inhibitors, and project assumptions. Identify the development team members, and get them to commit and schedule the necessary people and resources. Be sure to identify the development facilities needed by the team.

This is also the time to make sure that management understands that the development team will not manage the DW once it has been fully developed, tested, and placed in production. Depending on internal staffing requirements, some team members may be committed to DW management, but the team members generally move on to other projects. Managers will have to be found and appointed.

Obtain Iteration Project Approval and Funding

Preliminary approval and funding for the first iteration was secured in the BQA. If subsequent studies have caused changes to the first iteration project plan and you need re-approval, present the revised project to the decision makers, including business managers, stakeholders, and executive sponsors. If no significant changes have been made, skip this step.

If this is a follow-on iteration (to add a new subject area to the warehouse), update the decision makers on the project. Give them the detail they need to secure funding to incorporate the new subject area (information to answer a new set of business questions) and increase the user pool.

Once you have approval and funding, it is time to design and build the iteration. It has been a long path, but well-defined business needs, detailed planning, and tool selection based on organizational requirements, all serving a well thought-out architecture, increase the project's chances for success. The process also provides a set of lessons that the company can use on future data warehouse projects.

Detailed Design: The Down and Dirty

The architecture defines the overall strategy and processes by which the warehouse is developed; the detailed design maps out the implementation of those processes for the iteration.

The detailed design stage develops the physical DW model (database schema), defines metadata, and updates, expands, and verifies (with users) the inventory of source data needed for the subject-area implementation. It also designs and documents procedures for:

- Warehouse capacity growth
- Data extraction/transformation/cleansing
- Data loading
- Security
- Data refresh
- Data access
- Backup and recovery
- Disaster recovery
- Data archiving
- Configuration management
- Testing
- Transition to production
- User training
- Help desk
- Change management

When the design activities are completed, conduct a critical design review before beginning implementation.

Create the Physical Model

The database schema is the heart of the data warehouse. A strong data model makes for good performance and allows users to access the data and find what they need. The project team should use the subject-area logical model, the refined data element inventory, and user requirements identified during the BQA to develop the physical data model.

The *logical* data model identifies the entities, attributes, and relationships between different business processes in the iteration implementation; the *physical* model defines the physical layout of the database tables within the warehouse. The physical model is created in two steps. First, the team identifies the facts, fact groups, and dimensions as part of the subject-area implementation. (A **fact** is a measurement; a **dimension** is a collection of descriptive attributes used to analyze facts; a **fact group** is a collection of similar facts that share a grain and a set of dimensions; a **grain** is the lowest level of detail within a fact group. Examples of facts and dimensions are given below.) Second, the team converts this set of fact groups and dimensions into fact tables and dimension tables. The physical schema can take the form of a star schema (denormalized, multi-dimensional model) or a snowflaked schema (a normalized multi-dimensional model). The team also decides the indexing strategies for the physical model, and any aggregate tables that need to be developed.

This is a challenging task, the specifics of which are beyond the scope of this chapter. For detailed information, see Ralph Kimball's *Data Warehousing Toolkit* or *Data Warehousing Lifecycle Toolkit*. The rest of this section provides an overview of the process.

To identify the facts, fact groups, and dimensions from the detailed subject-area logical model, the team must first review the detail-level entity or object types and their attributes. A subject area contains consolidated groupings of attributes called dimensions. The team should sort the needed data elements (attributes) for this subject area into dimensions, building on the dimensions identified in the BQA. Examples include geography, time, product, and customer. Data elements follow natural drill paths—the hierarchical progression of dimension detail from high level to low. For example, a *time* dimension would drill down to year, quarter, month, day, hour, etc., a *geography* dimension to country, region, state, city, etc. Dimension drill paths ultimately reveal attributes at the level on which the business analysis must be performed. (For example: "How many diapers were sold in the Kansas City region in April 1997 to commercial customers?")

Next, the team should identify fact and fact-group attributes for the subject-area implementation. Facts are measurements with which users can analyze warehouse data. Fact groups are collections of similar facts of the same grain. Examples of facts include *total sales*, *total quantity sold*, and *number of customers*. To be useful in analysis, facts need to be identified at the lowest level of granularity, which can be defined as the intersection of dimensions in a fact group. It determines the lowest level of detail to which analysis can be performed. For example, a fact group may contain facts about telephone billing information such as number of minutes and cost of call. The dimensions that determine this group's grain could be geographic location with dialing code (as the lowest hierarchical level), customer, or time. The analyst could then identify the total number of calls generated to a particular region at a particular time. (Dimensional modeling is also beyond the scope of this chapter. For more information, refer to Ralph Kimball's *Data Warehousing Toolkit* or *Data Warehousing Lifecycle Toolkit*.)

Once the facts, fact groups, and dimensions have been identified, the team should create the database model that defines the DW physical table structures as either a star or a snowflake schema.

A star schema represents a single subject area with a minimal number of tables. Each dimension has one table containing all its attributes; different levels of attributes do not have separate dimension tables. There may be several fact tables based on the fact groups that share these denormalized dimensional tables. A star schema structure increases data access performance for reporting and analysis because redundant data exists to provide quick access. An advantage is that there are fewer table joins, so performance tends to be faster; a disadvantage is that the redundancy requires more storage space.

The snowflake schema contains a separate table for each hierarchical level of each dimension, which limits the number of attributes in a single table. The tables in the dimension hierarchy have a 1-to-many (1:M) relationship, from the top level down. In very general terms, a snowflake schema contains many tables linked through defined relationships (key structures or pointers) to define a single subject area in a hierarchy. A snowflake schema increases the efficiency of data entry and update, and reduces occurrences of invalid data by eliminating redundant data. An advantage is that data is efficiently stored and space is not wasted; a disadvantage is that there are more table joins, so performance tends to be slower.

Some access tools work better in one environment than in the other. Usually, fact groups translate directly into fact tables in both schemas; dimensions translate into multiple-dimensional tables in the star schema and single-dimensional tables in the snowflake schema.

Once the team has identified the fact tables and dimensional structure, it must develop the indexes, aggregates, and partitioning to complete the physical model. Indexing and partitioning should match the DBMS requirements to enhance performance. Partitioning is also influenced by DW size and whether the DW is implemented on a special server such as NUMA (non-uniform memory architecture) or MPP (massively parallel processing). Study these factors carefully before developing indexes and partitions. Aggregation strategy also depends on the database platform and (possibly) the data access tool, some of which make strong use of aggregates. The team should work with the data access tool vendor to identify the appropriate aggregation strategy.

Microsoft SQL Server 7.0 has new features to support parallel queries, multi-indexing operations, smart hashing, merge joins, improved scan, fetch, and sort, and other features. If the system uses SQL Server 7.0, the team can take advantage of these features in the physical database design to enhance query performance.

The physical dimensional model is crucial to the data warehouse's usefulness. Designers should study dimensional modeling thoroughly. If you are thinking about bringing in a specialist, this is a good place to do it.

When the dimensional model is complete, the team should review the list of available data sources and refine the list for this iteration, including all known sources of data, internal and external. The team should define the availability, location, format, size, refresh rate, and other details for the data elements, and use that information to narrow the list of source systems. Assess source data quality. This was done initially in the BQA, and it should be done again, now with respect to the more specific subject-area requirements.

Once the dimensional model is complete and the data elements have been identified, the team should conduct a business design walkthrough with users to validate that all DW requirements have been met. The dimensional model and the data elements are directly tied to the business requirements and must be reviewed with users.

Define Metadata

Metadata (information about the primary data elements) is stored in a special repository. It serves business and technical purposes for business and technical users (including warehouse developers and administrators).

The team should design the procedures for gathering the metadata and populating the metadata repository, according to the metadata management program and the metadata requirements. The team should now, if necessary, refine metadata requirements to accommodate any information discovered during definition of the architecture requirements or the iteration's subject-area details.

The team should examine the physical data elements and define the transformational mappings from the source data systems to the DW. This produces **technical** metadata, which defines how a field name in a source system is transformed into a data element that conforms to warehouse conventions. For example, a data element called "Name" from the BILLING source system might be transformed into "CUST_ID, LEFT(5)" for use by the warehouse. (Note that size and format information is recorded as part of the metadata for this element.) The metadata also defines the transformation routines that move data from operational systems to the warehouse, and the business rules for usage and derivation, key, index, and other relevant transformational and structural information about the data elements.

The team should also define **business** metadata such as the business meaning of the data elements, and the codes (which are often cryptic) that represent warehouse data elements. For example, user metadata might define the data element "ACCT_CD" as "Account Code for Small Business," "COST_CTR_CD" as "Code for Cost Centers in East Region," etc.

Design the Iteration Implementation Plans

Using the strategies and programs outlined as part of the data, application, technical, and support architectures, the team should design or refine all required implementation procedures. Some of these plans might be informal, taking the form of a spreadsheet or list rather than a detailed plan. Some plans are created for a specific population cycle, others are created initially and evolve through successive population projects. Each plan should be customized for the current population project, and the information should be consolidated into one comprehensive detailed design plan.

The next sections describe plans that should be drafted as part of the detailed design stage.

Data Extraction, Cleansing, Transformation, and Load Plan

The detailed design phase drafts the design for extracting, cleansing, transforming, and loading data into the warehouse. The architecture identifies the framework, but the implementation plan identifies the *process* for the iteration. Based on the dimensional model, the identified data elements, and the source systems, the team should detail how elements are to be extracted from source systems, which tools will be used, what format the data will be received in, and the staging area for data storage. The team should then specify how data will be validated and cleansed, and the specific cleansing and transformation routines. It should specify and document the logic under which data elements are converted to a dimensional model format, the transformations (so that they can be coded during the implementation), and the data loading process.

Design Security Plan

The team should reassess system security, incorporating any changes required by new information to the model developed in the architecture review and design stage. Authorized users and IT staff need proper levels of access to the warehouse. The plan should specify:

- Which departments have access
- Access procedures
- Required security levels for all categories of users and administrators
- Ongoing monitoring of users and query types
- Measures for revoking authorization when necessary

The team should decide which tools and functions require passwords, and should provide assignment and verification methods. Front-end tool users should use passwords for database access. Source system data access through the extraction tool should also be secure.

Data Refresh Plan

Using the data refresh strategy developed in the architecture review and design stage, the team should decide on the rate, procedures, and schedule, and should estimate the time needed to stage and move data into the warehouse.

Data Access Procedures

Based on the data access strategy developed in the architecture review and design stage and any pertinent focus session results, the team should detail how warehouse data will be accessed by the set of users targeted for this iteration. If data access is to be custom-coded using a front-end tool, the team will have to design routines. If access tools are to be used, the team should define and document their implementation procedures. The team should also determine and document which reports will run batch, and the specific requirements for canned and ad hoc query capability and how these requirements will be met. Finally, it should specify any reporting templates and any drill-down and report navigation strategies.

Backup and Recovery Plan

The plan should specify:

- Where backup media are stored
- Which data will be backed up and when (calendar)
- Which staff members perform backup and restore activities

Disaster Recovery Plan

Disaster recovery plan particulars depend on the business and technical environment—every organization has its own rules and regulations for off-site tape storage, insurance coverage, conducting drills, etc. The team can test the plan by simulating system destruction and recovery. One way is to develop two identical parallel DW systems, shut one down, then test how quickly (and in what state) and to what degree the backup can be put online.

Data Archive Plan

A data archive plan defines how and how long to maintain data that is no longer needed for regular reporting purposes. An archive plan should address:

- Storage media (tape drive, optical disk, etc.) and location
- Access methods
- Archive schedules
- Archive processes
- Restore processes
- Data structure and format

An optimal strategy considers:

- **Amount of history.** How much data should be available for trend analysis and research? The goal is to minimize retrieval of archived data by keeping enough online (in the warehouse or the operational systems) to suit normal purposes.
- **Level of detail.** The less detail maintained in the warehouse for the accepted duration, the more must be maintained in the operational systems.

- **Archived data access needs.** If archived data is to be retrieved using the same reports and tools used for non-archived data, the archived data format must support extraction.

- **Response time expectations.** What is a reasonable amount of time for retrieving archived data? This depends on user expectations, the archived data format, and the storage media.

Historic data requirements should have been developed during the architecture review and design stage. The team now specifies how to implement them.

Charge-back Plan

Charge-back allows IT to charge DW users for connect time, performed queries, generated reports, special processing, etc. The architecture review and design stage should have specified DW charge-back requirements, if any.

Charge-back is not common, because most companies feel users should not be charged for exploring the warehouse for useful information. Attitudes vary, however, and if charge-back is to be used, the team should design its procedures. If there are no charges for warehouse use, skip this task.

Configuration Management Plan

The configuration management plan details procedures for implementing and ensuring system stability through these modifications:

- New or upgraded software installation.

- Efficient configuration of additional warehouse users.

- Deployment and release of new reports to users as new subject areas are added.

- Management of concurrent development of different versions of reports and databases. For example, if two teams concurrently integrate different subject areas into the warehouse, they must share data models and resources without conflict.

If the company already has configuration management policies and procedures in place, the team should adopt and apply them to the DW as appropriate, making sure to provide coverage for warehouse-specific issues.

If any of the tools selected for implementing and operating the warehouse have applicable automated configuration management features or components, use them.

Test Plan

The team should design an implementation component test plan that specifies:

- Unit test procedures for extraction/cleansing/transformation routines
- Unit test procedures for data load routines
- Unit test procedures for data refresh routines
- Test procedures to validate database security
- Test procedures to validate data archiving
- Test procedures to validate backup and recovery
- Test procedures to validate disaster recovery
- Test procedures to validate charge-back
- Scripted system integration test procedures for testing the fully operational production warehouse populated with actual data (including extraction/cleansing/transformation, load and refresh activities)
- Procedures for free-form user acceptance testing (including data access) of the production DW system
- Test personnel, frequency, methods, and pass/fail criteria

User Training Plan

The project team should design a program that trains users to access and analyze data. The plan should identify necessary trainer skills, determine the training rollout strategy, and outline procedures for instruction in:

- How to produce reports, including how to use all categories of reporting tools
- How to query the warehouse, including how to use ad hoc query tools
- How to analyze reports and results of queries
- How to respond to organizational cultural change issues that result from introducing new methods for accessing, storing, and processing data

Transition to Production Plan

The production plan describes the steps to move the DW to fully operational status. It must scope and script out all necessary activities, including:

- Preparation of technical architecture (hardware and software) in the production environment
- Execution of source data extraction, transformation, cleansing routines
- Initial data load and first refresh cycle
- Movement of files, programs, documentation to new server

- Update of production libraries and catalogs
- Establishment of user support infrastructure and services
- Refinement of production system components if necessary

Help Desk Plan

The team needs to plan for instituting and maintaining a help desk that supports DW users. If the company has a help desk in place, a DW section can be integrated. The plan should document procedures for training help desk personnel, provide for compiling and delivering technical support information, and publish the help desk schedule.

Conclusion

The detailed design revisits many of the strategies identified in the architecture design and solidifies them for the iteration. Once the detailed design is complete, the specifications are in place for easy routine coding during implementation.

Implement All the Planning

Everything accomplished up to this point paves the way for an easy implementation. Hardware, software, and middleware have been purchased and installed. The development and test environments have been established, and the configuration management processes have been implemented. Programs for extracting, cleansing, transforming, and loading source data, and for refreshing existing data, have been designed and run against a test database. Load process metrics have been captured. The metadata repository has been loaded with transformational and business user metadata. Canned production reports have been developed, sample ad hoc queries have been run against the test database, and output validity has been measured. User access policies and procedures have been established. System functionality and user acceptance testing has been conducted for the complete, integrated DW system. System support processes for security, backup, recovery, and archiving have been implemented and tested.

The next step is to conduct the production readiness review, evaluating the system before it is put into production.

Purchase and Install Data Warehouse Components

The first step is to purchase and install the hardware, software, and middleware components specified in the data warehouse architecture, according to the configuration management process specified in the detailed design.

When everything is in hand, install and test these components:

- Server hardware and software.

- DBMS software.

- User hardware and software. These components include computer, monitor, network connectivity and communications (TCP/IP, NetWare), drivers for accessing the database, operating system upgrades, ActiveX controls, Web browser, and data access software for querying and reporting.

- Application software. These components include software for metadata management, and for data extraction, transformation, cleansing, loading, and refresh.

- Support components. These include backup and recovery (may be embedded in the DBMS), disaster recovery (may be same as backup/recovery components), archiving (tape drives, optical disks, etc.—may be same as backup/recovery or disaster recovery), performance monitoring, security enforcement, and configuration management (may be an embedded component of other tools).

The team should implement and follow the configuration management plan developed in the detailed design.

Prepare Test Data

Once all components are installed, the team should create a test data set using sample data from the source systems, and using data definition language (DDL) to implement the physical schema. These are used to create the programs and access routines necessary for implementation. Although smaller than the production data files, the samples should be created in accordance with the detailed design to ensure that the transformation programs match the production routines.

Create and Test Extraction, Cleansing, Transformation, and Loading Programs

Now the team can begin to develop the programs and routines to extract, cleanse, and transform operational source system data so it can be loaded into the DW. (Some data will not need to be transformed.) The programs will be used in conjunction with the tools selected for these functions, so make sure to use the tool to modify the generated code. Within a single cycle, data is extracted from the source system, cleansed to fit a range of values, and transformed to comply with warehouse format requirements, registering the conversion formulas in the metadata (derivation formulas, summary computations, etc.). It is not feasible to separate these functions into individual programs or to unit test them as separate activities.

The team should document the data sources, the platforms extracted, and the progression of the data through the extraction application. Use consistent naming conventions for the programs.

Using the sample source data, the team should conduct a unit test of each data extract/cleanse/transform program using a small number of records. Test cleansing functions against transformed and non-transformed data. Use the appropriate tools to debug and modify programs.

Load and Test Data to the DBMS

When the routines have been tested, the team should run them to create a sample set of clean, transformed data, then load the data in the test database tables, using the load scripts in conjunction with any tools designated for this purpose. Time and benchmark the processes for small, medium, and large data files.

When the data is in the warehouse, run queries to ensure validity, and run reports to ensure correctness. Meet with the users to discuss any issues.

Create and Test the Refresh Programs

The team should now use the refresh plan (from the detailed design) and the data refresh tool to develop programs to load updated replacement data, then use the sample, extracted data to unit test each data refresh program against a small number of records. Debug and modify the programs as needed.

Set Up the User Access Modules, Then Grant Access to Users

First, the team should set up the administration or management modules on the server with the query and reporting tools. These must be set up first because varying configurations on user workstations may require customizing user modules on the server, developer workstations, and/or user workstations. Next, the team should populate the user profiles and security access levels for the data access tool and establish user access to data through the access tool. Implement and test charge-back mechanisms, if any are required.

Turn On and Test Metadata

The data access tool must be able to access the metadata to make reports, so the team must load the technical and business metadata into the test database before testing any canned or ad hoc queries. Load technical metadata (IT staff needs it to develop and maintain the warehouse), then business metadata (users need it to find the data elements they need).

Create and Test Canned Queries and Reports

Now the team can begin to create sample queries and reports to test the business questions defined in the BQA, way back when. First the team should create the MOLAP/ROLAP queries and production reports (power analysis canned queries) in accordance with the data access procedures specified in the detail design. These queries test the MOLAP/ROLAP and production reporting data access tools and coded routines to make sure the correct results are returned and to measure data validity.

Establish benchmarks to measure the query complexity against system impact and response time. Fine tune the canned queries if performance problems are uncovered. The team should also issue a variety of ad hoc queries to ensure that the data content is accurate, the calculations produce correct results, and response time meets the architecture requirements.

Perform System Testing

Test:

- At the developer level for integrated component functionality
- At the user level to assure that the system produces the results users want and has a satisfactory interface

Load the test version of the warehouse with the full contingent of source data for system testing. Load technical metadata first, then business metadata, then the entire operational data set. The warehouse must contain all representative source data before you can test integration and user acceptance at the system level.

Use the system integration test scripts (from the test plan) and the fully loaded test database to make sure all components and routines function correctly with one another. Test all data extraction, cleansing, transformation, load, and refresh routines. Run all programs against high data volumes.

Obtain the Acceptance Sign-Off from Users

Prepare a user acceptance agreement that *specifies* performance factors, distribute it to users, and have them sign it. If you can't get sufficient acceptance, evaluate the problems, and make modifications if they are feasible and within scope.

Implement and Test the Support Processes

Before moving the system into production, implement and test backup, recovery, disaster recovery, data archiving, and security. When this is complete, the team should conduct a review with the executive sponsors, IT and business managers, and stakeholders to validate that the warehouse is ready for production use.

Implement and test these support functions:

- **Database security.** Make sure the database is protected against unauthorized use. If you find problems, modify the security plan and take corrective steps.
- **Backup and recovery.** Implement the procedures, then test them against the fully loaded test database. Tune, if necessary.
- **Disaster recovery.** Implement the disaster protection procedures and test them. Conduct a "fire drill" to ensure that the system can continue to operate in the event of catastrophic failure. If the plan calls for two systems in parallel, throw the switch to the alternate system.
- **Archiving.** Implement and test the data archiving procedures outlined in the data archive strategy section of the detailed design.

When testing is done, the team should conduct a comprehensive review of the pre-production system with the executive sponsors, IT and business managers, and stakeholders to secure agreement that the warehouse is ready to be put into production.

The warehouse is now ready to be moved into production.

Move into Production and Start Again

If you have carefully planned and executed all the steps outlined and documented the results, transition should be quick and smooth. If you failed to plan adequately, the team may have to perform both development and production tasks during the next iteration. Here are the steps for a smooth transfer of technology and responsibilities.

This stage moves the data warehouse development project into the production environment. The development team works with the operations staff to load data into the warehouse and execute the first refresh cycle. Then the operations staff is trained, the DW programs and processes are moved into the production libraries and catalogs, and the system documentation is created. Create and present rollout and tool demonstrations to the user community, schedule and conduct user training, put the help desk online.

Finally, the team creates a change management board and implements change control procedures for future development cycles. It seems like a lot of steps, but before the team can move on to the next population project it must transfer what it has created.

The primary objectives of this stage are to:

- Move all system components from the development environment to the production environment
- Train the operations staff and end users

- Document the operational system
- Position the new system for ongoing maintenance
- Provide a warehouse that is fully operational and available to users

Install the Production System

Installing the production system transfers all installed technical and application architecture components, programs, files, and documentation to the production environment, and updates production libraries and catalogs. The development database administrator (DBA) should coordinate with the production DBA to procure a new empty database to be populated as the full-production DW, then the production DBA should create the database physical schema and define the space necessary to accommodate the indexes. The production DBA should then generate the data definition language (DDL) statements to develop the database table definitions, using the tools provided with the DBMS, if feasible. Data modeling tools also provide DDL creation modules that support most DBMSs.

Show the production staff how the extraction/cleansing/transformation programs perform on the source data in the operational systems. Usually this can be done in the development/test system, but if this is not possible you'll have to install the programs on the operational system. If you use the test environment, run the refresh programs to sync the DW with the operational world when the load is complete, then implement the specified refresh schedule to keep the DW current.

Training sessions for the operations staff vary, but one effective method is to have the development staff work hand-in-hand with them for several weeks, then be on call for problem-solving and consultation.

If it has not yet been done, the development team should now formally document all user, managerial, and operational procedures. After later iterations, production staff should update the documentation.

Make complete documentation a sign-off requirement for the development staff. Do not settle for a promise of later delivery: it will never get done.

Roll Out the Data Warehouse

Plan a big kick-off presentation and demonstration for management and users. Be creative.

Make a brief presentation to users on the new tool to jump-start their use of the new technology. Have the warehouse staff on hand to answer questions. Have several stations set up to demo the warehouse and front-end tools. Don't let development team members stand up there and show things: let users test drive it.

If you offered incentives for user suggestions (best query, best money or time saving idea), have the project manager and senior organizational staff present the prizes.

If you have a large company or a huge user base, you may have to take the show on the road for presentations at different company sites.

User training is key. Now is the time to put into operation the program you developed to teach business management and users how to access warehouse data and analyze the results. A half-day or one-day (maximum) training session with a small group is recommended. The effort should continue until everyone is trained; this arrangement lets trainers incorporate student input as they go. Don't just cover the tools—explain the business issues that drive queries and analysis. For this purpose, trainers might invite representative users to explain how the DW can be used in their area, following up with sample queries that address business questions. Inviting users to participate can forge stronger relations between the IT and user communities, and this can help IT learn more about DW design and implementation. You can sometimes get business units to fund this effort.

Sessions should provide instruction and guidance on:

- Concepts and use of all data access tools
- How to produce reports, including how to use all categories of reporting tools
- How to query the warehouse, including how to use ad hoc query tools
- How to analyze reports and query results
- Organizational cultural changes that will result from the introduction of new methods for accessing, storing, and processing data

Implement the User Technical Support

Data warehouse access tools are new types of tools to most users, so your support effort can expect questions. Users need answers, and they often need (or want) them fast. Poor support may cause users to throw up their hands and simply avoid using the warehouse.

If your company has a help desk in place, you may be able to assign DW support responsibilities to them—after you train and equip them. Make sure they work through the user training materials. Invite them to the rollout meetings and ask them to talk about *how* they are set up to assist users.

The necessary help desk procedures were worked out in the detail design. If you change or adapt procedures to accommodate issues you discover while setting things up, make sure to amend the detailed design for future data warehouse projects.

Establish the Service Level Agreement

Now is the time to put into place the service level agreement worked out during support architecture development. It should cover the current iteration and should be reevaluated for each future iteration.

The agreement should:

- Establish the acceptable uptime for the warehouse. Constant availability is probably not achievable: how much is sufficient?
- Establish problem reporting methods.
- Establish a formal modification request method.
- Establish a user training agreement.
- Establish acceptable performance criteria.

Make it specific and thorough and write it out. Present it to the user community and secure their acceptance. This is a key performance measurement tool for the warehouse and its support effort. Make sure everything is in place to fulfill it.

Establish the Maintenance Program

Finally for this stage, you have to establish the warehouse maintenance program. This requires identifying and appointing a change management board. One was established during the BQA to control scope changes during development; now you have to establish a long-term maintenance process that the board can oversee to monitor and manage change to the technical, data, application, and support environments over multiple development cycles.

This is necessary because a data warehouse grows and changes over time. There may be new hardware, new software, additional source systems, additional application processes, changes to the refresh cycle, changes to version control activities and responsibilities, modified help desk procedures, changes to user training, and new requirements for performance monitoring. If not properly managed, this growth can quickly get out of control.

To identify process improvements that can be incorporated into the DW, you should consider implementing Kaizen techniques, wherein *everyone* takes responsibility for the ongoing improvement of the system.

As change requests are submitted, the change management board should assess and prioritize them, document and archive them, and accept or reject them. If major changes are deemed necessary, they may require a new development iteration. Naturally, the board should evaluate and prioritize them with respect to the predator value streams and planned iterations.

If this is not the first iteration, these programs may already be in place. All you have to do is modify them to reflect any changes created by this release.

Finish with a PACE Check

All that remains is to **END** the project in an orderly manner.

Do this by capturing all the lessons learned during design, implementation, and testing. Iterations give you a chance to learn from your mistakes. Each future attempt can go smoother and faster if you end the project correctly: archive the project materials, report on the project's performance, turn over the project results to the operations and support staffs, and release the project resources for use on other projects.

You need to produce a deliverable in this stage, too. It should indicate that:

- The technical tasks have been completed and the products and results are in place
- The project has been canceled or postponed indefinitely, with or without completing anticipated products or results
- The project plan is not approved
- The project resources have been consumed

Notice that not all of these events indicate success. For instance, the project plan may not have been approved, leaving things in the planning stage. Even so, a thorough, archived project history will help the current team determine why the plan was not adopted, and may help the next team prepare more effectively.

Prepare and Deliver a Project Completion Report

Document the project history for the benefit of teams that come along later. A final report should start with a project overview, describe what happened, explain what was learned, and provide measurements of the process and the final DW. It should also describe the technical architecture, the technology in use, metrics, reusable objects, etc.

A handy way to gather material for the report is to ask each team member to provide input. (It helps to ask them at the beginning to keep track of their experiences and ideas throughout the project.) Besides helping you complete the report, team input provides you with a list of each member's accomplishments. You can use this to write reviews, award bonuses, give awards, or promote workers.

The report should document the project history with a management-level overview of what occurred, the scope, objectives, and pertinent metrics for time, resources, or money. Define what products were produced, describe the technology and tools used, discuss their impact on productivity, standards, etc. Recap the project performance, recommendations for subsequent actions, major decisions and the reasons behind them. Describe accomplishments and lessons learned—good and bad, things worth doing again and things worth avoiding.

This information can help future teams understand how projects really work and provide input for risk management. Make it available to project managers, process designers, etc. for project planning, processes, tasks, techniques, and approach.

Try to break down costs, timeframe, and resources for individual project tasks. Quantify when possible or meaningful: number of interviews, number of walkthroughs, number of entity types, etc.

Some numbers to derive and include:

- Project team members
- Other people involved
- Business/organizational units
- Interviews/focus groups/workshops
- Locations
- Subject areas
- Business areas
- First-level business functions
- Lowest-level business functions
- Entity types
- Proposed business systems
- Proposed data stores
- Number of elementary processes
- Design areas
- Entity lifecycles
- Current systems
- Final data stores
- Elementary processes
- Owned entity types
- Procedures and procedure steps
- Record types
- Users to be trained

Turn Over the Results

Everything produced in the course of a project has the potential for reuse, so you should review products with this in mind. Rule of thumb: if a product was important enough to create, it probably is important enough to save. Identify the ones that can be used by other projects, and the ones that can be modified to create a generic model or template. Catalog potential reusable objects and store them in an accessible format and medium.

Identify how and where to archive project output and products; document everything, including the media on which they should be kept and how long they should be maintained. Make sure that the correct versions of shared objects are passed to other teams, as appropriate, and that the recipients know how to access and update these objects.

Some objects to consider for reuse:

- Documents
- Task plans
- Quality assurance plans
- Business models
- Industry-specific value streams
- Technical architectures
- Development environments
- Project standards
- Code
- Project control mechanisms
- Project organization and role descriptions

If for some reason project results are rejected, get the reasons in writing, identify what must done to gain acceptance, then follow up.

It is a good idea to make hard copies of the major deliverables produced during the project and present them to team members and, if you think it worthwhile, users. The team created the documentation, and while soft copies are fine for project archives and sharing with other organizations, team members should each have a hard copy. As project manager you may want to include a page in the front of each binder that contains a personal note from you or a member of upper management thanking the member for helping with the project. It takes very little effort to do this, and it can generate a lot of good will.

Release Project Resources

Assess the quality of the contribution made by each project participant. If you used contractors or consultants, write a letter to their company commenting on their contribution, and on the areas in which they excelled or in which they needed or made improvement. Management can always use input on how their staff members performed on a project.

Document internal staff members' performance and contribution for their record. Recognize and reward individual contributions. Throw a project completion party.

People are the most important DW asset: take care of them. This project has trained them, and if they enjoyed this challenge they will look forward to the next iteration. Don't lose their expertise.

Finally, complete the project accounting, including resource utilization and budget. Reconcile actual and planned utilization of project resources, and actual and planned costs. Terminate all arrangements for the use of project resources, including leases and contractual agreements, then release them.

Lessons Learned

This chapter is based on field experience in data warehouse engagements performed by jm+co. It would be nice to close with a top ten list of things to remember, but there are far more than that. Data warehousing is a young and rapidly changing technical field, and there are always lessons to learn.

To find out what these lessons are, attend the conferences, read the magazines, check out the Internet sites, and read some of the books. Avail yourself of the experience of people who have done this before. Everyone makes mistakes; the smart ones learn from them.

The list below summarizes some lessons alluded to in this chapter. You may want to copy them and refer to them during your project. By the time you're done, you'll have some of your own.

1. Make sure your team has at least one experienced data warehouse team member. Either hire one for your staff, or bring in a contractor or an experienced consulting firm.

2. If you do hire a consulting staff, hire a good one. Check out the Data Warehouse Institute (www.dw-institute.com) article, "10 Mistakes to Avoid When Choosing a Data Warehousing Consultant."

3. Don't re-invent the wheel. Use a proven data warehouse method.

4. Remember that the project *must* be driven by business needs to succeed. This is not just another IT project.

5. Educate as many people as possible in the organization. Invite everyone from senior management to users to the kick off meeting that explains the project and the technology.

6. Make sure contractors or consultants agree to transfer knowledge to the team, then make sure that you make it happen.

7. Make sure that you have staff available to work on the project. Plan on having a production staff in place when you are ready to transfer the project to the operations staff.

8. Watch out for scope creep. Make sure no one on the team promises users capabilities that have not gone through the change management process.

9. Make sure you have a change management process in place.

10. As the project starts, check to see if the company has already done a strategic information plan (SIP). If there is one, use it.

11. Explore data quality issues early. Don't let a data quality problem become an issue after the data warehouse is up and running. Identify problems early, and fix them.

12. Don't build a data warehouse just to play with the technology. Even if it is going to be a small implementation, go though the entire process.

13. During the BQA, get users to provide hard return on investment assessments. They know best where money can be saved.

14. Use incentives to get users to develop queries that add business value. They know the business and where the savings are.

15. Keep new arrivals informed on the project's goals and history.

16. Develop a data steward and data ownership program early. As more datamarts begin to surface, the ownership of data becomes more important.

17. See if you can use any existing tools for data extraction, transformation, etc., to reduce cost.

18. Create a plan for capturing business and technical metadata.

19. Plan on security early. It is easier to build it in than to add it on.

20. You probably will need more than one tool. Different tools for different users.

21. Consider ROLAP or HOLAP tools for detailed drill-down.

22. Create datamarts and warehouses by following a higher-level blueprint that stresses iteration.

23. Be sure to have, and use, a strong backup and recovery plan. Test it.

24. Buy hardware and software early to avoid development and production delays.

25. Use tools like Excel 2000. Most users know Excel and can easily pick up on the use of PivotTable service, keeping down training and application software costs.

26. Know your project's internal politics and company culture. Be realistic—they can affect the project.

27. Conduct quickie meetings to inform business managers and end users on the project and gain their input.

28. If new team members comes on board during the project, have them review the materials and meet with them to review and discuss the project's goals and history.

29. Include the database administrator (DBA) in the project as early as possible. DBAs should be key players and they make good backups for other team members.

30. Plan ahead on how the project will be transferred to the operational staff. Remember that the development staff may be busy working on the next iteration and won't be able to provide full-time support to the new system.

31. Be sure to have a rollout meeting. Cake, balloons, prizes. Get the word out with a bang.

32. Keep the warehouse staff active in training users. Use business members, too.

33. At the end, debrief team members on what they did for the project.

34. Provide copies of key deliverables to your staff, management, and the company project management office.

35. One more thing: *have fun*! This is a lot of hard work, but it should also be exciting and fun.

[Start adding your ideas here.]

Conclusion

It's tempting to think that all you need to do to build a data warehouse is get some tools, come up with a general idea of what you need to build, then spend a few weeks throwing something together. Build it and they will come. After all, you might end up with a great application, the right data, the right queries, and the right database design. On the other hand, you might spend a lot of time and money only to end up with an application that your end users try, dislike, and never want to take the time to try again.

You can dramatically increase your chances for success by following a few simple rules:

- Have a proven recipe for success. Use a data warehouse plan that has been used to design and implement a successful project.

- Use the right stuff: industry-proven tools and experienced team members.

- Start small. Build the warehouse on a small, solid success story. Remember, it is an iterative process.

- Use proven project skills to manage time, budget, and resources. Time spent planning pays off.
- And *always* know what users need. Keep the project focused on the business.

That process should:

- Use the **PACE** management concept
- Be based on a business case
- Work through a BQA early to define requirements
- Use an architecture review and design to provide a plan that will last
- Create a detailed design
- Select the right tools
- Plan for first and later iterations
- Implement all planning
- Transfer the project to the operations staff gracefully
- Provide thorough closure
- Get the staff ready to do it all again

In the end, all that matters is how happy your users are. Do they use what you have designed and given them? The answer to that question is the measure of your success.

About the Authors

Howard Burkett is a Senior Consultant with the Western Region of jm+co, based in Costa Mesa, CA. He was a member of the initial team that developed the current data warehouse method. He has worked on numerous data warehouse projects since 1982. He can be reached at hburkett@jamesmartin.com.

Vijay Sankaran is a practice catalyst in jm+co's North America data warehousing solution center. He has several years of experience designing and building data warehouses in various industries. He can be reached at vsankaran@jamesmartin.com.

This article also contains input from projects and jm+co staff members worldwide. Their contributions continually improve the company's methods and deliverable formats on all data warehouse engagements.

For information on the data warehouse process library please contact Howard Burkett.

PART 2

Very Large Database Solutions

Time, as they say, flies. Sometimes we have to fly with it or be left behind. Yesterday you were strolling along configuring Microsoft SNA Server to mine that old mainframe databank, and today you're racing to complete the migration of the human resources database to SQL Server. Maybe your head is spinning after ramming into one imponderable after another, maybe your legs are tiring and your lungs are burning, or maybe you've slumped over your keyboard, brought down by the weight of one very large database project.

To help you recover, this section walks you through the key issues in designing, building, tuning, and managing very large database (VLDB) systems. It arranges them topically, addresses them thoroughly, and offers lots of examples drawn from real-world cases. Because of its complexity, a VLDB project needs complete and accurate documentation to mitigate risk, and Chapter 4 describes how to organize and record each design and implementation step to ensure security, reliability, and expandability. Like a good pair of running shoes and a regular stretching regimen, Chapter 5 limbers you up on the basic hardware choices and SQL Server configuration issues. Chapter 6 surveys best practices for mapping your logical design in to a physical data model, and Chapter 7 sketches the course for optimal query and transaction coding. Chapter 8 describes how to plan and perform backups, reorganize indexes, and use the database consistency checker (DBCC) statements.

CHAPTER 4

VLDB Issues at Broadband Cable Communications

By Frank Rabeler, g&h Database Technologies GmbH

A VLDB system is complex and is designed to address specific business problems. Because of this, every essential fact about its design, development, testing, and evolution must be documented for the system to be usable. Without complete and accurate documentation, development can become inefficient and more costly, testing can fail to verify functionality and resolve problems, usability can be compromised, and maintenance can become difficult and labor-intensive. Most important, the resulting system can fail to satisfy the business requirements for which it was proposed.

The Solution in Focus

This chapter reviews how a VLDB was designed at Broadband Cable Communications, using this process to explain and demonstrate the documentation needed to describe, record, and track each design and implementation step. It examines the major project stages, stressing how documentation can ensure security, reliability, and expandability.

All the information in this chapter (and the others in this section) is drawn from the experiences of companies that have implemented VLDBs using SQL Server 7.0 as recorded by Microsoft Consulting Services. It has been combined into case studies under the fictional names of Broadband Cable Communications, Bound Galley Book Cellars, and others. Taken together, these chapters discuss the challenges of VLDB solutions from preliminary design to fine-tuning the system in the production environment, providing examples, explanation, and field-tested recommendations.

What You'll Find in This Chapter

- An overview of VLDB design and implementation.

- Stage-by-stage guidelines for database project documentation—how it should be organized and what it should contain.

- How to create tables for detailed information in a VLDB.

- The importance of using naming and drawing conventions in the design.

- The benefits of using separate environments in development.

Case Overview

A very large database (VLDB) design project is similar to any large project, having the same phases and considering the same issues. Still, there are some differences that dictate or influence decisions and can affect scheduling and budget. Documentation is a similarity, but it is also one of the differences, in that a VLDB project creates special documentation needs and requires a thoroughness not necessary in many other projects. The first part of this chapter reviews the VLDB design process; the remaining sections discuss the documentation that should be created to specify, record, and track each step.

The first step in developing a VLDB system is to assess business and user requirements so that you can design the technology to meet specific needs. Right from the beginning (and throughout the project) you must distinguish between *needs* and *wants*. Some features are necessary (these are needs) and some represent things people would like to have (these are wants). There is nothing wrong with including things that people want, but deal with needs first and remember that indulging wants can explode the scope of a project, incurring costs and complication out of proportion to value derived.

An organization decides that it needs a software system to support certain processes, meet goals, or solve problems. In sum, what is needed is the solution to a business problem. Fair enough, but to develop an effective and usable software solution, designers need to create a comprehensive problem definition, and to do this they must collect and analyze information about the business process to be supported and the problems (there may be several, related or not) to be solved. Before a solution can be developed, the business problem must be defined.

A good problem definition *does not* describe the proposed software system; it concentrates on the problem so that users and developers can agree on what problem to solve. The proposed system will be designed in an effort to improve things, but it is not simply a better mousetrap. There may not be a system already in place, in which case *improvement* becomes more difficult to quantify. And in any case there are probably many diverse users and each may have different wants, some of which conflict, some of which are too vague to be useful, some of which are impractical or impossible.

VLDB development projects follow the standard path:

- Prototyping
- Design
- Implementation

- Testing
- Production
- Maintenance

Along the way you have to consider security, quality assurance, configuration and change management, and, lest we forget, documentation.

Prototyping

A prototype refines and clarifies design and local architecture by:

- Demonstrating feasibility
- Determining the cost effectiveness of various design alternatives
- Discovering or confirming requirements
- Proving the technology or the implementation approach
- Soliciting users for information that will help create a working system
- Detecting possible performance problems

Allow users to interact with the prototype so that they can suggest changes and additions. Users will, after all, be the ones using the system, and they are the people who understand the business at the ground level. While gathering user input in focus sessions, interviews, and prototype test runs, remember to separate needs from "nice to have" features. The team can assess, prioritize, and include changes, then retest with users within the limits of budget, time, and common sense.

Design

Database design is perhaps *the* critical element of a SQL Server solution, especially with respect to performance. The structure of the database is decided first, then applications are built around it rather than vice versa. Design requires detailed technical knowledge of the implementation environment.

Data Models

The design process develops three models, in this order:

- **Conceptual data model.** This describes database contents, not storage structures or management.
- **Logical data model.** This is built off the conceptual data model, and describes the database structure (the *relational* model is the most widely used). This must be refined as far as is practical before defining the physical model.

■ **Physical data model.** This describes the database implementation—primarily the storage structures and access methods—so it is tailored to a specific DBMS (such as SQL Server 7.0).

To get from the conceptual data model to a robust and efficient physical data model, system designers and technical specialists collaborate to achieve a compromise between business needs and technical constraints.

Software Architecture

This defines how components interact. The first question is where to locate the running code. Should most of the work be done on the client, in the central database, or on a separate application server?

Client/server software architecture divides an application into three logical components:

■ **Data services,** which join records and maintain database integrity by defining valid values for attributes and enforcing foreign key relationships.

■ **Business services,** which apply business rules and logic such as defining how customer orders are added or how customer credit is checked.

■ **Presentation services,** which establish the user interface and handle user input.

These logical layers can be implemented on physical machines in several ways: two-tier with FAT clients or with FAT servers, three-tier, or using the Internet. For most large-scale implementations, three-tier provides the best distribution of functionality and expansion potential.

For example, for its online order shipment system, Bound Galley Book Cellars uses a three-tier architecture consisting of the application itself, Microsoft Transaction Server (MTS), and the database under SQL Server 7.0. Most of the business logic is housed in the MTS packages. Stored procedures are used for all data manipulation, but they are simplified so that they minimize the use of logic in the structured query language (SQL) statement. This creates a scalable environment by concentrating most work on the MTS servers, where it can be increased as needed. Currently the database comprises about 4,600,000 book titles from 60,000 publishers. Expected volume is about 12,000,000 order details per year (33,000 order details per day).

Planning Operations

Plan for:

- **Backup and recovery.** Get a solid plan in place before moving any application from development into production. Procedures are driven mostly by data availability requirements.

- **Reorganization.** Reorganize data on the data and index pages by rebuilding indexes with a new FILLFACTOR to ensure that database pages facilitate growth by containing an equally distributed amount of data and free space.

- **Updating index statistics.** This ensures that the query engine has up-to-date information on the spread of data in the tables, so that it can access data more efficiently. SQL Server automatically updates index statistics periodically; you can arrange for immediate updates.

- **Performance tuning.** You may need to create new indexes to boost performance, and the production system will require maintenance—consider these issues during design to minimize the effect on users, time taken to perform the task, and effort involved.

- **Consistency checks.** These find damaged data so that it can be corrected. Use database consistency checker (DBCC) statements.

- **Database Maintenance Plan Wizard.** It helps you set up and automate the core maintenance tasks necessary to ensure that the database performs acceptably, is regularly backed up, and is checked for inconsistencies.

Chapter 8, "Field Observations on Managing Operations," has a detailed discussion on this topic.

Implementation

Application requirements determine which physical implementation of the three-tier model is best. Consider:

- **Performance and scalability.** For high throughput and good price/performance, pick an implementation that uses business logic in stored procedures. For resource-intensive distributed applications, pick a physical three-tier implementation.

- **Client platform and access.** If a variety of client platforms must have access to your application, pick an Internet implementation.

- **Developer skills.** If team members are skilled in a particular language or the current system has a lot of existing code in that language, pick an implementation supported by it.

- **Administration.** Different implementations require different administrative overhead.

There is no one correct answer—the best course of action is to thoroughly understand the alternatives and the trade-offs before choosing an implementation.

Hardware Environment

SQL Server hardware planning is primarily concerned with system processors, memory, disk subsystems, and the network.

- **CPU.** Estimate the level of **CPU-bound** work that will occur on the hardware platform. (This is the amount of work that is computation-bound—the CPU overloads with calculations.) With SQL Server, CPU-bound work can occur when a large cache is heavily or completely used.

- **Memory.** Memory configuration is crucial for performance. SQL Server uses memory for its procedure cache, data and index page caching, static server overhead, and configurable overhead.

- **Disk Subsystem.** Optimizing disk I/O is the most important aspect in SQL Server solution design. Select a subsystem that complements SQL Server performance characteristics. To determine numbers of disk controllers and drives, and their size and configuration, consider user and application performance requirements. You have to understand the logical database design and the nature of associated data, and the interplay between system memory and disk I/O with respect to Windows NT and SQL Server.

See Chapter 5, "Hardware Selection and Configuration," for more information.

Configuration

After completing the database development process and appropriate tuning, the next step is to focus on SQL Server configuration settings. Start with the default values, establish a performance baseline, then tune parameter values as you monitor performance. Chapter 5 includes a more detailed discussion.

Tools

You need tools that support:

- Modeling (data and procedures)
- Application development
- Testing
- Documentation
- Configuration and change management
- Quality assurance
- Project management

Try to get the best tools of each category but be sure to create an integrated tool set so that output from one tool can always be processed by the next one in the chain.

Testing

Testing the system verifies it (shows that it meets its specifications) and validates it (shows that it does what users want it to do). It is an expensive process, normally consuming a significant amount of development time to complete testing on the module, subsystem, integration, and acceptance levels. For VLDB projects it should include stress and performance testing and this may require developing special applications to simulate high concurrent-user traffic.

Test planning is essential and you should include it in the process from the beginning. It should set out standards rather than describe specific tests, and should ensure that all requirements are individually tested. Record all tests and test results so that the process can be audited. Specify all system parts and use this specification to derive a complete set of test cases for each component.

Other Development Aspects

Security

You must secure data from internal and external attacks to control who has access to which data and how. SQL Server can help you manage user access. Remember that too-stringent security can get in the way of productivity: you need to balance restriction with access.

Configuration Management

Once a system is in production, you must control and manage changes. Configuration management (CM) is an essential part of software development—it brings stability to design, to implementation, and to evolution (large software systems have long lifetimes and can change often). Ill-conceived or poorly documented changes can disrupt performance, undermine system maintenance, and stifle growth.

CM systems provide version control and configuration identification by controlling the release of a product and changes to it throughout its lifecycle, ensuring consistent software by establishing baselines and by recording and reporting the status of components. It serves as the development team's central repository, organizing and synchronizing all their work, documents, and deliverables.

Quality Assurance

Quality assurance (QA) consists of procedures, techniques, and tools that help ensure that the product meets or exceeds requirements.

In the early phase of development, quality assurance certifies that product development is progressing according to the requirement specification. After the project reaches testable milestones, quality assurance performs independent application testing and reports bugs and other problems to the developers.

Introduce a formal review process (walkthroughs or inspections) to monitor quality throughout development, test thoroughly, document system metrics, and perform post-implementation reviews. A good QA plan explicitly identifies all significant system attributes and shows how they should be measured and judged.

Production

Transition from the Former System

When moving to a new database system you have to transform data from previous systems and other data sources. These can be older versions of SQL Server, Microsoft Access, Microsoft Excel, or Oracle spreadsheets, or text files. Transformation often includes formatting.

Microsoft Data Transformation Services (DTS) is a new SQL Server 7.0 feature that supports many types of transformations, such as simple column mappings, calculation of new values from one or more source fields, decomposition of a single field into multiple destination columns, and so on. Complex transformation and data validation logic can be implemented with ActiveX scripts, which can invoke methods from any object linking and embedding (OLE) object to modify or validate column values.

Data Loading

Before they are used for the first time, most SQL Server applications need an initial load of historical reporting data, current operational data (from a legacy system), static reference data required by the application, or new data required by the application to describe the initial state of the operation. Before spending the time and resources to fully load a database, test the entire application on a subset of the data to identify data loading errors or inconsistencies.

To extract existing data and transfer it into the new application's SQL Server database requires:

- Using DTS to import, export, and transform data between SQL Server and any OLE DB, ODBC, or text file format.

- Using the SQL Server bulk copy program (**bcp** utility) to import data into the database tables. The most flexible and common option, the **bcp** utility can be configured to read different file formats and efficiently import large amounts of data into SQL Server.

- Using the SQL Server BULK INSERT command (new in SQL Server 7.0) to quickly copy a data file into a database table or view it in a user-specified format. BULK INSERT offers superior load performance while DTS provides data transformation for imports from or exports to heterogeneous data sources.

Starting Operations

When the database is populated, run a test production environment for a long enough time (some weeks) under real load to make sure it is operating correctly. Carefully monitor and document all database activities, check all database issues, test the backup strategy, and verify that the restore process works.

Maintain contact with key users to make sure their needs are being met. An effective way to accomplish this is to perform user satisfaction surveys to gather information on:

- Latent problems
- Perceptions of problem areas that have not surfaced through other means
- Requirements for future versions
- Shifts in usage patterns that can affect the network

Use what you learn to develop support and maintenance programs that address user satisfaction.

When you are comfortable with database operation and production environment stability, it is time to go into real production.

Maintenance

SQL Server requires preventive maintenance and periodic tune-ups. Develop a maintenance plan to minimize system downtime.

Keeping the System in the Best Shape

Daily SQL Server operation requires some time to manage the database engine to its fullest potential. You'll need to back up the database regularly, and you may need to re-create some indexes to improve performance. Taking these issues into consideration during database design minimizes later impact on users, time required, and effort involved. Plan for maintenance in three areas: SQL Server, database, and table/object. Perform regular maintenance and be sure to:

- Document any configuration change
- Monitor error logs
- Back up your databases and transaction logs
- Check database consistency
- Monitor performance
- Monitor user activity
- Update statistics and maintain good indexes
- Check fragmentation

Application, system, and user needs determine the frequency of regular maintenance tasks, which can be scheduled and automated with the SQL Server 7.0 Database Maintenance Plan Wizard. The Index Tuning Wizard is also useful.

Change Request Management

Change control procedures help you predict the effects of system changes before they are made. Change requests must be managed during development and after the system is moved into production. Use a change control board to decide whether to approve the request and how to solve the problem. Use a change request tracking tool.

Integrate this with the configuration management system and follow a consistent change process.

Documentation Guidelines from Broadband Cable Communications

Full documentation that captures and develops all important information from the initial requirement specification to the final acceptance test plan is essential if the system is to be understood and maintained. As the system is modified, all associated documentation must be studied and corrected; if it is not, the record of the system will diverge from the reality it is supposed to describe, complicating maintenance, development, evaluation, testing, and so on.

This section proposes guidelines for database project documentation, stressing the kinds of documentation needed during the development and maintenance process, and explaining why each is necessary. There are sample templates for each type, and examples derived from a SQL Server project done at Broadband Cable Communications (BCC)—a project that was successful, in large part, because of how documentation was planned and created.

Everyone realizes that documentation provides a record of a completed project; not everyone realizes that *during* the project it supports communication between:

- End users
- Analysts
- Database administrators (DBAs)
- Developers
- Management

Communication is always important, and it is crucial in large projects involving numerous teams in complex overlapping phases of planning, development, implementation, maintenance, and support.

Of course, it is not enough simply to create a pile of documentation: to be useful it must be *good*, meaning that it must be:

- Reliable (up to date)
- Complete (include all aspects of development and maintenance)
- Correct (doubt free)
- Accessible to every project member

The sections that follow look at the working phases in a database development project, and show what kinds of documentation should be created at each step.

Working Phases and Their Documentation

Figure 4.1 shows the working phases in the database development process.

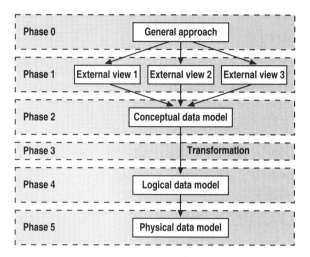

Figure 4.1   Phases in the database development process.

Phase 0

In this phase, the general scope of the database project is defined. When this has been staked out, it is possible to define **subject areas** (also called **external views**) that identify the different points of view users have on the data. BCC uses the expression *subject area* instead of *external view*.

Main focus: group the whole work into logical units.

Phase 1

A preliminary conceptual model is created for each external view.

Phase 2

All external views are consolidated into one conceptual data model, which should become the most stable part in the project, presenting a normalized view of the daily-business data structures. (See "Data Modeling" for more on normalization.)

Phase 3

Entities are transformed into tables. This should be accomplished as a distinct phase because it is not a simple one-to-one process: several entities may result in one table, and attributes/columns holding derived values can be added to tables for performance purposes.

Phase 4

All tables, views, triggers, and synonyms are defined.

Phase 5

All details for implementation (indexes, locations, users, groups, grants, etc.) are defined, and all database system specifics (syntax, features) are added. The database is now ready for installation.

Figure 4.2 shows the phases and the kind of documentation each requires. (It also provides a handy overview of this chapter.)

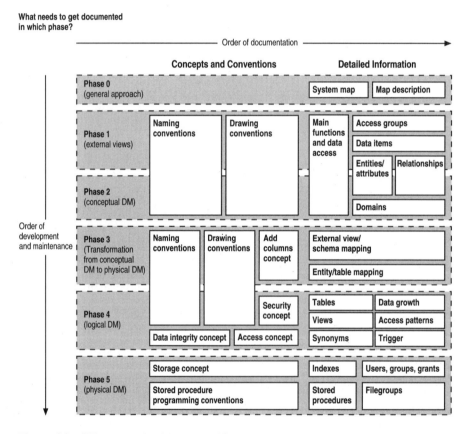

Figure 4.2 What must be documented?

Design information is of two basic types and this distinction is maintained in the organization of the sections that follow: *Concepts and Conventions* and *Detailed Information*.

Concepts and Conventions are general and help to produce consistent detailed information. They are the entry point for every new project member and a reference for the whole project. Later sections in this chapter explain the advantages of concepts and give hints and examples. Define concepts at the beginning of the project and include them in the database documentation.

Detailed Information results from analysis, including specifics on all database objects.

Each shaded box in the figure represents a type of documentation and is explained in the following sections.

Phase 0 (General Approach)

You have to identify and document the project's general approach, describing project scope in terms of:

- Existing systems and applications involved
- Future (planned) systems and applications
- Project database location within existing/future systems and applications
- Information flow between applications and databases

This overview provides the basis for splitting the project into different external views (subject areas or modules), which are useful groupings of entities (real-world objects).

Concepts and Conventions

At this point, besides using commonly known symbols and descriptive text (see Figure 4.3 below) in the system map, no conventions or concepts are needed to arrive at the detailed information.

Detailed Information

System Map

Figure 4.3 is taken from the BCC database project. It provides an excellent example of a system map, and shows all the information mentioned above.

From this map you can derive all the information mentioned above.

BCC identified these subject areas.

- Parties (People and Organizations)
- Addresses (People and Organizations)
- Products (Products)

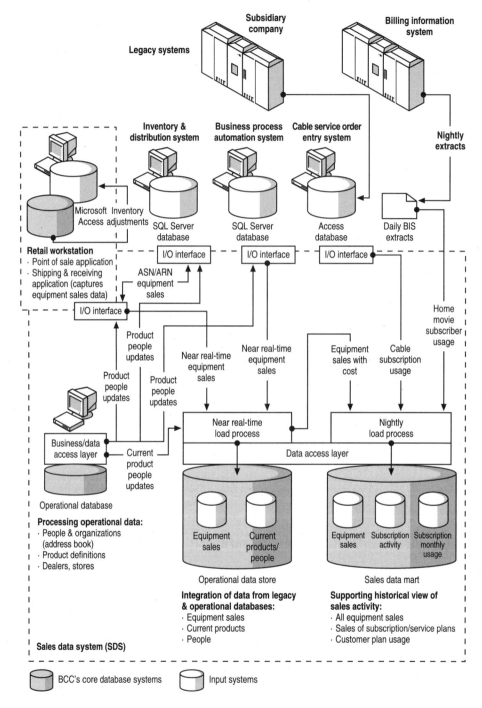

Figure 4.3   Broadband Cable Communications database project system map.

- Positions (People and Organizations)
- Contact Mechanism (People and Organizations)
- Equipment Sales (Equipment Sales)
- Phone in the Box Transaction statuses (Equipment Sales)
- Sales Datamart

Map Descriptions

The most important areas are then described literally but briefly. Two examples from the BCC map show how this works: *People and Organizations* and *Products*.

- **People and Organizations.** Examples include BCC employees, as well as external people and organizations that BCC interacts with such as MarconiVille. Telephone numbers and e-mail addresses are associated with people and organizations. Also included are positions that an organization creates and positions that it fills.

- **Products.** Examples include all physical items that BCC sells, such as phones, batteries, and pagers. Prices, substitutes, aliases, and classifications are associated with products.

All inputs and outputs are also briefly described.

This documentation required only three and a half pages, but it provided BCC with an excellent overview that everybody involved in the project could use to get up to speed.

Because there are no specific conventions for database project documentation, the next sections provide general concepts and suggested conventions.

Phases 1 and 2 (External Views, Conceptual Data Modeling)

These phases achieve a **conceptual data model** (CDM). This represents the overall logical structure of a database, which is independent of any software or data storage structure and often contains data objects not yet implemented in the physical databases. To represent the data needed to run an enterprise or a business activity, it:

- Represents data organization graphically
- Verifies the validity of data design
- Provides a solid and stable basis for generating the **logical data model** (LDM) which specifies the database's implementation of tables and columns

External views help to:

- Identify the scope of knowledge needed for analysis and concepts in a certain area
- Define the right working teams
- Identify main user groups and the ways they access data
- Work in parallel teams

Although phase 2 consolidates all external views into one conceptual model, the project can keep the main structure derived from the external views. As a result the team may find shortcuts for each external view as part of the database table's naming conventions (see Phase 4).

Definitions

Definitions for the expressions used in these phases.

Object	Description
Domain	Set of values for which a data item is valid
Data item	Elementary piece of information
Entity	Person, place, thing, or concept that has characteristics of interest to the enterprise and for which information should be stored
Entity attribute	Elementary piece of information (a characteristic) attached to an entity
Relationship	Named connection or association between entities
Inheritance link	Special relationship that defines an entity as a special case of a more general entity (also known as super/subtyping)

Concepts and Conventions

Naming and drawing conventions used in Phases 1 and 2 should make things clear to users.

Naming Conventions

Here are recommended naming conventions for all documented database objects (entities, attributes, etc.):

- Use *talking* names for every object—names that mean something when you see them.

- Name should not be longer than 30 characters (SQL Server limits size). Object names are part of the data model and when they get too long the resulting diagram becomes too difficult to read. And object names in later phases are usually derived from object names defined now, so leave some room.

- Don't use abbreviations not commonly known by users.

- Use a label (80 characters max) for every object.

- Create a description field of variable length for every object. Document ranges or lists of valid values as well as business rules. CASE tools usually have extra entry fields for these purposes; the recommendations here describe the minimum requirement.

- Use users' native language if the project language is different.

- Whenever possible, provide place holders for each object name to support the mapping between names used in the conceptual data model and names used in the database later on (see the examples in the following sections).

Drawing Conventions

The conventions discussed here are options, derived from commonly used conventions. The intent is to show what information is essential in an entity relationship diagram (ER diagram). This diagram is an essential part of the planning process: it specifies and graphically represents the type of relationships between all system entities. As such, it is a roadmap to the logical and physical architectures and it should be carefully, thoroughly, and accurately thought out and designed. ER diagrams are by far more compact and easier to understand than a textual description. They are used to discuss design decisions or design options with users (who define the requirements) and programmers (who implement the application). After a while, all participants in the design process will start to "think in diagrams" rather than words, so it is essential to organize and lay out a diagram that is clear and understandable.

Entities

Each entity is represented by a box. Descriptions should include:

- Entity name
- Attributes that form the primary key
- All remaining attributes
- Entity type:
    - **Kernel.** These provide a source of data to the model. These are the model's "master" entities and are essential for the model's proper operation. They are denoted with a shadow.

- **Characteristic.** These provide a mechanism to add a type to an element in another entity, and are referenced by other entities. They are denoted with a normal box.

- **Associative.** These relate two other entities in a many-to-many relationship. They are denoted with a dotted-line box.

- Inheritance (see example below)

- Relationships between entities (cardinality, optionality, and label if necessary)

  - **Cardinality** defines the type of the relation, usually one-to-one, one-to-many, many-to-one, or many-to-many. In some cases you know how many entities belong to a relation and can specify the term: for example, the relation from weeks to days is one-to-many but it can be expressed as one-to-seven.

  - **Optionality** specifies whether at least one entity must take part in the relation (see the examples below).

Master entities should always be on top or to the left from their detail entities (see one-to-many relationships below). This reflects normal reading order: left to right, top to bottom.

The next section explains in detail the chosen notation for document relationships. (Primary key attributes are always underlined.)

Notations for one-to-many relationships.

One-to-many Relationships	Description
Division — Division number, Division name, Division address ○⟨ **Employee** — Employee number, First name, Last name, Employee Function	**Cardinality** and **Optionality:** Each division may have zero or more employees; each employee may belong to zero or one divisions **Keys:** *Division number* becomes foreign key in *Employee*
Division — Division number, Division name, Division address ○—⟨ **Employee** — Employee number, First name, Last name, Employee Function	**Cardinality** and **Optionality:** Each division must have one or more employees; each employee may belong to zero or one divisions **Keys:** *Division number* becomes foreign key in *Employee*
Division — Division number, Division name, Division address ⊢⟨ **Employee** — Employee number, First name, Last name, Employee Function	**Cardinality** and **Optionality:** Each division may have zero or more employees; each employee must belong to one and only one division **Keys:** *Division number* becomes foreign key in *Employee*

One-to-many Relationships	Description
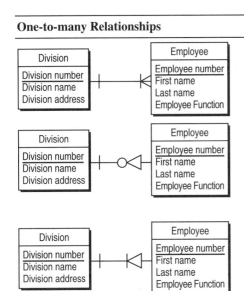	**Cardinality** and **Optionality:** Each division must have one or more employees; each employee must belong to one and only one division **Keys:** *Division number* becomes foreign key in *Employee*
	Cardinality and **Optionality:** Each division may have zero or more employees; each employee must belong to one and only one division **Keys:** *Division number* becomes part of the primary key in *Employee,* so an employee is uniquely identified by *employee number* <u>plus</u> *division number*
	Cardinality and **Optionality:** Each division must have zero or more employees; each employee must belong to one and only one division **Keys:** *Division number* becomes part of the primary key in *Employee,* so an employee is uniquely identified by *employee number* <u>plus</u> *division number*

Notations for one-to-one relationships.

One-to-one Relationships	Description
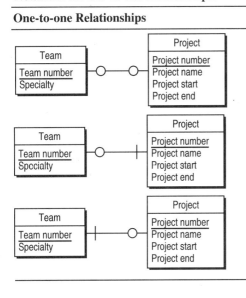	**Cardinality** and **Optionality:** Each team works on zero or one projects; each project is managed by zero or one team. **Keys:** *Team number* becomes foreign key in *Project*; *Project number* becomes foreign key in *Team.*
	Cardinality and **Optionality:** Each team has to work on one project; each project is managed by zero or one team. **Keys:** *Team number* becomes foreign key in *Project*; *Project number* becomes foreign key in *Team.*
	Cardinality and **Optionality:** Each team works on zero or one projects; each project has to be managed by one team. **Keys:** *Team number* becomes foreign key in *Project*; *Project number* becomes foreign key in *Team.*

Notations for many-to-many relationships.

Many-to-many Relationships	Description	Associative entity

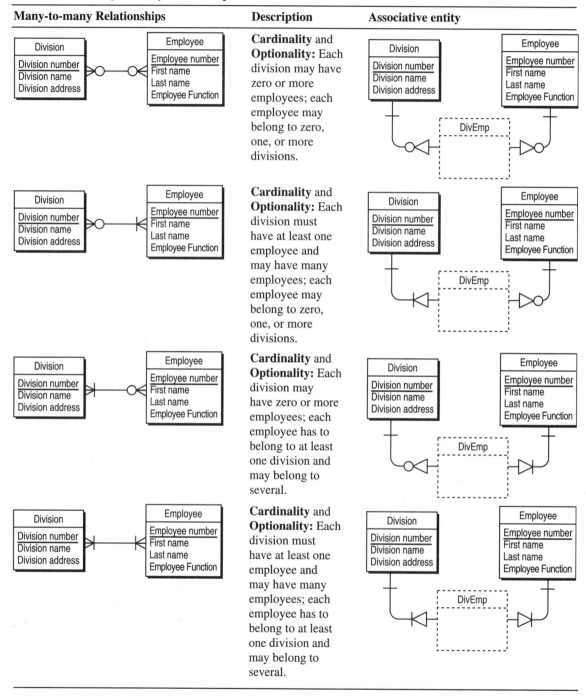

Inheritance

Inheritance allows you to define an entity as a special case of a more general entity. The entities involved in an inheritance are different, even though they may have many similar characteristics. The general entity is known as a **supertype** (or parent) entity and contains all of the common characteristics. The special case entity is known as a **subtype** (or child) entity and contains all of the particular characteristics.

You can also define an **inheritance link** between entities that causes one or more subtype (or child) entities to inherit, at the physical level, all or part of the attributes carried by one supertype (or parent) entity.

The example below shows a supertype *Employee*. The subtypes *Freelancer* and *Company employee* hold attributes specific for each type. So freelancers have special contract numbers and a defined number of working hours. Company employees have a company car.

The X inside the inheritance symbols says: "An employee is either of type freelancer or of type company employee."

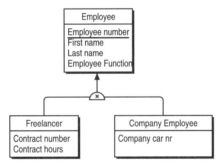

Figure 4.4   An inheritance link.

Omitting the X inside the inheritance symbol says: "An employee is freelancer and/or company employee" (which doesn't make sense in this example).

Supertype and subtype entities can have any kind of relationship with other entities. If just company employees belong to divisions the example could look like this:

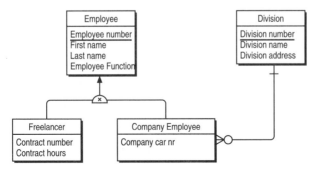

Figure 4.5   Breakdown possible if only company employees belong to divisions.

Figure 4.6 shows a subset of a data model that represents the drawing conventions described above:

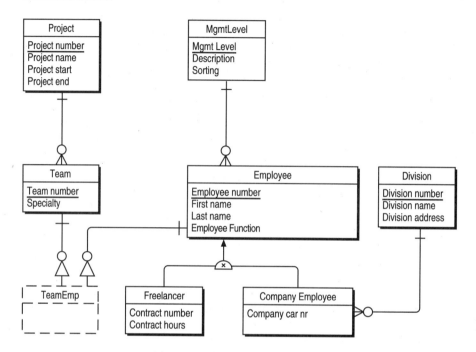

Figure 4.6   Data model subset representing drawing conventions.

The entity relationship diagram (ER diagram) is the most important output of Phases 1 and 2.

Detailed Information

Access Groups

This documentation indicates who is accessing the data, and how, and causing how much load.

For each external view, the documentation should describe the main groups of users (or batch jobs) accessing data. A user group is something like *controllers*, *order entry clerks*, or *customers*. It should also describe the type of data access (read, write) and should estimate the number of transactions caused by each group in each area.

Here is an example:

Example table for external views.

Group name	Group description	Read	Write	No. of Transactions

External view descriptions.

External view name:	Clear name for the external view (to improve readability of the model).
Label:	Descriptive label for the external view
Group name:	Name of the user group accessing data
Group description:	Description of the group itself and its usual method of access
Read:	X if the transactions are *read*s
Write:	X if the transactions are *write*s
No. of transactions:	Transaction/time. For example: 500/day, 2/second, etc.

Groups that perform read *and* write transactions have two entries.

Data Items

Data items are elementary pieces of information. A first step of data analysis usually is to identify all data items relevant for each external view. Later these items are assigned to entities and become entity attributes. Here is an example:

Example table for detail Information.

Name	Label	Data Type	Domain

Example table for long description.

Name	Long description (unlimited)

Detail information must be entered for each data item. If an item needs more description or annotations, use the long description table.

Data item descriptions.

Name:	Clear name for the data item (to improve readability of the model).
Label:	Descriptive label for the entity
Data Type:	Initial indicating the data format (numeric, alphanumeric, Boolean, etc.) followed by the number of characters
Domain:	Later, when domains are defined, they can be referenced in this column
Long description:	If needed

Domains

Domains help you to identify types of project information. They define the set of values for which a data item is valid. Properties include data types, lengths, lists of values, and so on. Applying domains to data items makes it easier to standardize data characteristics for attributes in different entities.

Example table for domains.

Name	Code	Data type	Length	Precision	Minimum	Maximum	Value-label

Domain descriptions.

Name:	Clear name for the domain (to improve readability of the model).
Code:	**Reference Name** for a domain. For example: short cuts used as part of naming conventions in the logical model (see naming conventions in logical data model).
Data Type:	Form of the data corresponding to the domain (numeric, alphanumeric, Boolean, etc.)
Length:	Maximum number of characters
Precision:	Number of places after the decimal point (if appropriate)
Minimum:	If a range is defined for the domain, this column holds the min-value
Maximum:	If a range is defined for a domain, this column holds the max-value
Value-label:	Values for labels such as 1-Mr., 2-Mrs, etc.

Create characteristic entities for value labels; use a defined set of columns such as:

■ <value_name>

■ description

■ sorting

MgmtLevel
Mgmt Level
Description
Sorting

Most *value labels* require a maintenance environment because in general they are not static (even if users say they are). If characteristic tables (with the same structure) are identified in the logical model, it is easy to use the model to generate a maintenance environment for them automatically. A standard structure also makes it possible to generate standard list boxes for value labels in business applications' user dialogs.

Entities and Their Attributes

Example table for documenting entities and their attributes.

Entity name:	Entity label:
Entity long description:	

Example table for detail Information.

Attribute name	Label	Domain	Data type	PK	M

Example table for long description.

Attribute name	Long description (unlimited)

Entity descriptions.

Entity Name:	Clear name for the entity (to improve readability of the model)
Entity Label:	Descriptive label for the entity
Entity long description:	Long description if needed
Attribute name:	Clear name for the attribute (to improve readability of the model).
Attribute label:	Descriptive label for the attribute
Data Type:	Initial indicating the data format, such as numeric, alphanumeric, Boolean, etc., followed by the number of characters
Domain:	Name of the domain used for an attribute
PK:	Primary key flag: X if an attribute is part of the primary key
M:	Mandatory flag; X if an attribute is mandatory
Attribute long description:	If needed

Relationships

Relationships document cardinality and optionality between entities (see "Drawing Conventions" on page 143). Document every relationship—its meaning is not always obvious in the ER diagram.

Example table for relationships.

Name	Label	Entity1	Entity2	Integrity	Description

Relationship descriptions.

Name:	Clear name for the relationship (to improve readability of the model)
Label:	Descriptive label for the relationship
Entity1:	First entity of the relationship (usually the master entity)
Entity2:	Second entity of the relationship (usually the detail entity)
Integrity:	Delete integrity rule. When a transaction tries to delete a master who still has detail rows, the result can be:
	Reject the transaction
	Cascade delete of detail rows
	Nullify detail rows (set key information to a dummy key that collects all orphan rows)
Description:	Long description of the relationship and any special integrity checks required

Phase 3 (From Conceptual Data Model to Logical Data Model)

Concepts and Conventions

This documentation is mainly for database administrators (DBAs) and developers, and should reflect their needs.

Drawing Conventions

These are the same as the ER diagram drawing conventions. Use boxes to represent tables. Include:

- Table name

- Column names (foreign key columns are displayed here because they became part of a table when the logical data model was derived from the conceptual data model)
- Underlining for primary key columns (pk)
- Foreign key information (fk)
- Data type and length
- Nullability information

The logical data model represents every ER diagram relationship by an arrow pointing from detail to master, and representing the join conditions between two tables. Figure 4.7 is an example derived from the ER diagram.

The supertype/subtypes for entity *Employee* are resolved by putting all subtype attributes to the supertype. This is just one possible solution, and it requires installing special check constraints for the supertype columns.

Naming Conventions

Include the database object type in the object name.

Database object types.

Object type	Description
CO	Constraint
FU	Function
IN	Index
SU	Stored procedure updating and inserting to the database
SR	Stored procedure reading from the database
SD	Stored procedures deleting from the database
SE	Sequence
TA	Table
TR	Trigger
VI	View

Synonyms don't have a special type because they can refer to any type.

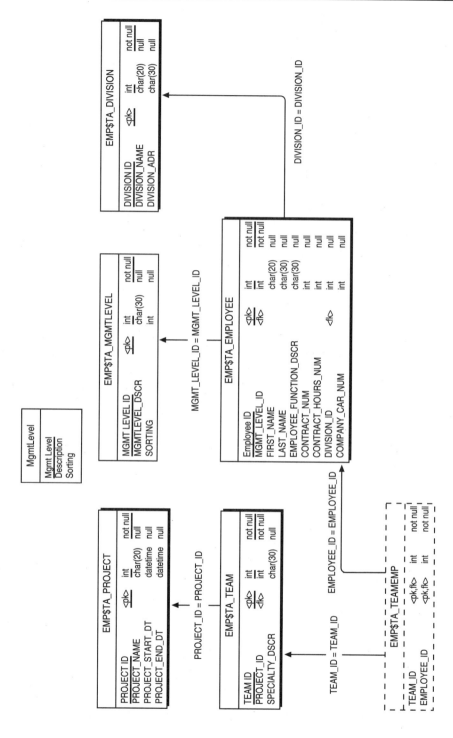

Figure 4.7   **Resolution of super/sub types for entity** *employee.*

Including the object type within the object name makes it much easier to read and debug scripts and source code. If every external view results in an extra database schema, you can put a schema shortcut in front of every database object. The example in Figure 4.8 illustrates this:

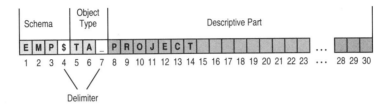

Figure 4.8   Including the object type labels within the object name

For column names, use clear naming conventions for the primary key column. BCC, for instance, added the extension *Inst* to every primary key column. Some designers add *ID*. It is strictly a matter of taste.

You can also add a shortcut of the domain referenced by a column to improve readability of code and scripts (see examples below). Some possibilities:

- ADR for address
- NAME for names
- NUM for numeric values
- DSCR for description

See Figure 4.7 for examples.

The Concept for Standard Columns to Add

When transforming entities into tables, it is highly recommended that you have a rule or concept for identifying the columns you add to tables. Rules standardize the database for purposes of:

1. Primary key definition
2. Optimistic locking strategy
3. Data historization
4. Auditing
5. Data archiving techniques

Primary Key Definition

Even though there are always primary key columns defined at entity level, you may want to enforce a system-defined primary key. BCC added a special key column to every table, so there are no composed primary keys. This greatly simplifies coding joins between tables. The performance planning process (not covered in this chapter) will show you if this standard is useful for your project.

Optimistic Locking Strategy

BCC also added a **timestamp** (TS) column to every table that increments whenever a record is updated—a feature that can be advantageous. Consider this example:

1. Read a row from the database

2. Show it to the user and allow it to be changed

3. Write it back to the database, if any changes were made

Obviously, some mechanism must be in place to deal with concurrent use. The database has many users and they occasionally will attempt to access the same record simultaneously. There are several ways to lock records to prevent lost or overlapping changes.

Pessimistic locking locks the row while the data is being read, releasing it only when the update is done. This blocks other users from accessing the row. While safe, this is inconvenient because the lock lasts as long as it takes the user to make the change—and there is no way to tell how long this will be.

Optimistic locking can alleviate some of this problem by using a timestamp. For every write operation, this sets a timestamp that is read along with the row. When the user enters the update, the timestamp is checked: if is not the same as when the row was read somebody changed the row in the meantime. In this case, the change record will not be written to the database. Instead, the user should re-read the record in its new shape and decide whether to insist on the change. The code sample below shows how this is done.

```
Step1:
SELECT value_col into prog_var1 ,
              ts into prog_ts
FROM    table1
WHERE   id = '4711';
/* no locks are held due to autocommit */

Step3:
Modify prog_var1

Step 2:
BEGIN TRANSACTION;
UPDATE table1
```

```
SET         value_col = :prog_var1
WHERE    id = ´4711´
AND         ts = :prog_ts;

Check rowcount; if rowcount is 0 then somebody else has been modified
that record.
COMMIT;
```

This obviates the need for locking the record while an update is in progress. If the record is changed by one user while another is working with it, the rowcount will show it. The UPDATE statement will not find any matching rows and thus not change the database contents. The application should ask the user how to proceed. The user can either overwrite the last change or re-read the record to see the change.

Data Historization (Chronology)

Not all tables need chronology, so you have to figure out which do. Chronology has two cases:

- **Physical chronology.** Certain tables do not allow data to be changed or deleted. (For example, the case of *rule given by law* means that the state of the database at any given point in the past must be reconstructable. This means that old data must be there for the reconstruction.) For every data manipulation, a record is replaced by a new record and the old one is marked *out of date*. In this case two columns should be added:

  - CreateDate
  - CloseDate (Not all records have a *CloseDate*)

- **Logical chronology.** This stores data with *valid from* and *valid to* characteristics. For example: credit card data shows an identification number and an expiration date, after which the number will change. To store this kind of information (two versions of the same record, one for today one for the future) add these columns to a table:

  - ValidFrom
  - ValidTo
  - Version (Note that *Version* will become part of the primary key)

Chronology is a complex topic because integrity is protected by special user-defined integrity checks. If your business data has chronology characteristics, you have to define a standard that handles it in one of the ways described above.

Auditing

This allows DBAs to see who created or modified a record, and when. Add these columns:

- CreateDate
- CreateUser
- ModifyDate
- ModifyUser

Data Archiving

Add this column:

- ArchiveDate

The date can be set when archiving has taken place successfully.

Detailed Information

External View/Schema Mapping

A **schema** is a collection of logical data structures in a physical database. External views can require that you develop one or more schemas. This section discusses schema mapping.

Example table for documenting schemas.

External view name	Schema name	Schema shortcut1	Schema owner	Description

Schema descriptions.

Schema	Description
External view name	Clear name for the external view (to improve readability of the model)
Schema name	Clear name for the schema (to improve readability of the model)
Schema shortcut	Shortcut for a schema (use just three digits so that you can use the schema as part of a naming convention later on)
Schema owner	Owner of a schema in the database
Description	Long description of the schema

Entity/Table Mapping

The entity table cross-references entities (from the conceptual model) and tables (from the logical model).

Example entity table (based on the table above).

Entity	Table	Description
Project	EMP$TA_Project	
Team	EMP$TA_Team	
Employee	EMP$TA_Employee	
Freelancer	EMP$TA_employee	Parent *Employee* inherited all *Freelancer* attributes
Company Employee	EMP$TA_ Employee	Parent *Employee* inherited all *Company Employee* attributes
MgmtLevel	EMP$TA_MgmtLevel	
Division	EMP$TA_Division	
TeamEmp	EMP$TA_TeamEmp	

Phase 4 (Logical Data Model)

Concepts and Conventions

Data Integrity Concept

The integrity concept is specific to every project. It is necessary because it shows the DBA and the developers which integrity relationships exist and how to manage them.

Here are the data integrity guidelines from the BCC project documentation:

Data integrity involves preserving data consistency and correctness. The project will use the following features of SQL Server to preserve and maintain data integrity:

- **Domain integrity.** This refers to the range (domain) of valid entries for a column. The project uses CHECK and FOREIGN KEY to ensure integrity.

- **Referential integrity.** This preserves the defined relationships between tables when records are entered or deleted. When creating tables the project uses PRIMARY KEY and FOREIGN KEY constraints to ensure domain integrity (DRI=declarative referential integrity). Because DRI is used, the project uses stored procedures to provide cascading deletes.

- **User defined integrity.** The project uses stored procedures and triggers to enforce other data integrity considerations. Because several tables contain historical data, several issues should be considered to maintain the historical integrity for tables. (These considerations are discussed in another section of the BCC documentation.)

Security Concept

SQL Server has three security modes:

- **Integrated.** This allows SQL Server to use the Windows NT authentication mechanism to validate SQL Server logons for all connections. Only trusted (multi-protocol or named-pipe) connections are allowed.
- **Standard.** This uses SQL Server's logon validation process for all connections.
- **Mixed.** This allows SQL Server logon requests to be validated by using either integrated or standard security methods. It supports trusted connections (as used by integrated security) and non-trusted connections (as used by standard security).

The documentation should clearly point out which mode will be used for the project.

Access Concept

Do not allow applications to access data directly. For flexibility and optimized maintenance, there should be a logical layer around the data. This layer can be implemented in several ways:

- Views for read access plus stored procedures for write access (BCC solution)
- Only stored procedures for read and write access

The documentation should clearly point out that no other data access methods are allowed.

Detailed Information

Access Patterns

Identifying and defining the best logical data structure is an iterative process: it takes successive efforts to optimize performance and satisfy business requirements. To find the right structure, it is important to document the database access patterns resulting from transactions that are critical for a project's success. Document headers whether they hold global information or detail information, because an access may have several steps that touch different tables.

Example table for accesses and details (steps).

Access name:

Access type:

Access long description:

Average number of users:

Maximum number of users:

Active time from: to:

Average frequency:

Maximum frequency:

Expected response time:

Access detail information.

Step	Tables joined	Projection	Restriction	Access type	Rowcnt max	Rowcnt avg	Comment

Access header descriptions.

Header	Description
Access name	Access's descriptive name
Access type	Access type can be *user dialog* or *batch process* or *procedure*
Access long description	Long description
Average number of users	Average number of users (or processes) using this access
Maximum number of users	Maximum number of users (or processes) using this access
Active time from: to:	Span during which the access takes (for example, from 8 a.m. to 5 p.m. workdays)
Average frequency	How often an access is processed on average (for example: 10/minute, 20/day, etc.)
Maximum frequency	How often an access is processed at maximum (for example: 30/minute, 500/day, etc.)
Expected response time	Response time needed for daily business

Access detail descriptions.

Detail	Description
Step	Step number in the detailed access documentation (tells the order in which the different steps of an access are processed)
Tables joined	List of tables that are joined in a certain step
Projection	List of columns retrieved
Restriction	Join conditions and further restrictions
Access type	Access type is either *read*, *delete*, *insert* or *update*
RowCnt max	Maximum number of rows possibly accessed
RowCnt avg	Average number of rows possibly accessed
Comment	A step's comment (description)

This documentation is used in performance planning (tests that will tell which physical structures to choose).

Tables

The next section has an example explaining the structure of this part of documentation:

Table name:	EMP$TA_EMPLOYEE
Label:	
Description:	
File Group:	

Column List.

Column name	Column code	Domain	Type	K	M	N	Default value
Employee number	EMPLOYEE_ID	ID	int	PK	Yes	No	None
Company car #	COMPANY_ CAR_NUM	NUM	int		No	Yes	None
Contract hours	CONTRACT_ HOURS_NUM	NUM	int		No	Yes	None
Contract number	CONTRACT_NUM	NUM	int		No	Yes	None
Division number	DIVISION_ID	ID	int	FK	Yes	No	No
Employee function	EMPLOYEE_ FUNCTION_DSCR	DSCR	char(30)		No	No	No description given

Column name	Column code	Domain	Type	K	M	N	Default value
First name	FIRST_NAME	NAME)	char(20)		No	No	BLANK
Last name	LAST_NAME	NAME	char(30)		Yes	No	No
Mgmt Level	MGMT_LEVEL_ID	ID	int	FK	Yes	Yes	Yes

Table descriptions.

Item	Description
Table name	Table name
Label	Table short description
Description	Table long description
File Group	SQL Server file group a table is assigned to (see Phase 5: "Physical Data Model")
Column name	Step number in the detailed access documentation; tells the order in which the different steps of an access are processed
Column code	List of tables that are joined in a certain step
Domain	Shortcut of the domain this column is based on
Type	Data type and length
K	Type of key which can either be blank: *PK* (for primary key) or *FK* (for foreign key)
M	Mandatory or not
N	Null values allowed or not
Default value	Default value (if nulls not allowed)

Data Growth

You need to know the size and growth dynamics for tables for the last phase ("Physical Database Implementation").

Example table for data growth.

Table name	Growing type	Initial size	Factor

Data growth descriptions.

Item	Description
Table name	Table name the documentation refers to
Growing type	Possibilities:
	Static (no changes in table size, just initial insert, no deletes)
	Transient (no changes in table size but heavy delete and insert)
	Growing (table is growing over the time)
Initial size	Table size at the end of initial data loading
Factor	For transient tables this tells the number of rows deleted and inserted over time (for example: 200 deletes and inserts/hour)
	For growing tables this is the growing factor (for example: 1000 rows/day)

Triggers

Triggers cause Transact-SQL statements (typically a single statement or a stored procedure) to be executed automatically on insertions, updates, or deletions on a given table.

Triggers are essential to data integrity because they perform additional actions to keep the database consistent.

Example table for triggers.

Trigger name	Table name	Time	Scope	Statement	Condition	Type	Comment

Trigger descriptions.

Item	Description
Trigger name	Name of the trigger in the database
Table name	Table name the trigger refers to
Time	When the trigger will be fired with respect to a time:
	Before
	After
Scope	Possibilities:
	Statement
	Row

Item	Description
Statement	Statement that fires the trigger:
	Insert
	Update
	Delete
Condition	Data condition that causes the trigger (where-clause)
Type	Possibilities:
	Referencing foreign key
	Self referencing
	Business logic
Comment	Additional trigger descriptions

Views

Views build a collection of data derived from one or more tables. They are defined by an appropriate SELECT statement collecting the information.

Example table for views.

View name	Table names	Projection	Restriction	Comment

View descriptions.

Item	Description
View name	Name of the view in the database
Table names	Table name(s) the view refers to
Projection	List of columns in the view
Restriction	Join conditions and further restrictions
Comment	Additional view descriptions

Synonyms

The documentation should map database object names to their synonyms.

Example table for synonyms.

Synonym name	Object name	Object type	Comment

Synonym descriptions.

Item	Description
Synonym name	Name of the synonym in the database
Object name	Database object name the synonym refers to
Object type	Type of database object (for example: table, view, etc.—needed only if object type is not part of the naming conventions)
Comment	Synonym purpose

Phase 5 (Physical Data Model)

Concepts and Conventions

Storage Concept

This provides guidelines about where to store data physically. The design can physically separate:

- Tables and indexes
- Static tables and those with heavy write activities
- Logical data groups
- Business tables and indexes from archive tables and indexes

Or any combination of these options.

The documentation should define clear guidelines because storage can influence database performance and scalability.

Stored Procedures Programming Conventions

At the very least, document the basic programming conventions for:

- Error handling
- Transaction handling
- Logging
- Tracing

Detailed Information

Filegroups

Filegroups are essential building blocks: data files are logically grouped into them, tables and indexes are assigned to them, and logging files are organized in them.

Example table for filegroups.

Filegroup name	Database	Drive	Chunk size	%age	No. of files	Description

Filegroup descriptions.

Item	Description
Filegroup name	Name of the filegroup
Database	Database name that a filegroup refers to
Drive	Drive the filegroup refers to
Chunk size	Chunk size if growth is defined by chunks
%age	Percentage if growth is defined a percentage
Number of files	Number of files belonging to a group
Description	Filegroup description

Indexes

Indexes are access paths to the table. Frequent access patterns should be supported by indexes to ensure acceptable response times.

Example table for indexes.

Index name	Filegroup	Table name	Columns	Type	Uniqueness	Description

Index descriptions.

Item	Description
Index name	Name of the index
File group	Name of the file group an index belongs to
Table name	Table name the index refers to

(continued)

Item	Description
Columns	List of columns that are part of the index
Type	Possibilities:
	Non-clustered
	Clustered
	Covered
Uniqueness	Tells if an index is unique or not
Description	Common index description

Users, Groups, Access Rights

You need to map:

- Which users belong to which groups
- Which access rights (privileges, grants) are given to which group

Example table for group name.

List of users

Group name descriptions.

Item	Description
Group name	Name of the user group the listing is for
List of users	List of users belonging to the group

Document the access rights given to each group.

Example table for access rights.

Database object name **Access rights**

Access rights descriptions.

Item	Description
Group name	Name of the user group the listing is for
Database object name	Name of the database object an access right is given for
Access rights	List of access rights (select, update, delete etc.)

Stored Procedures

Stored procedures are collections of Transact-SQL statements being executed within the database server and returning a result to the calling application.

Minimum documentation for each stored procedure.

Stored procedure name:

Description

Example table for parameters.

Parameter name	Type	Parameter Description

Stored procedure descriptions.

Item	Description
Stored procedure name	Name of the stored procedure
Description	Long description for the stored procedure
Parameter name	Parameter name
Type	Parameter data type
Parameter Description	Parameter description (purpose, meaning)

Defining Separate Environments

When planning the development of a new application, you should consider defining separate environments for development, roll-out, maintenance, and so on. These environments can resemble the production system to varying degrees.

Bound Galley Book Cellars set up a very good set of environments that enabled rapid high-quality development. For details, see the last section of this chapter and Chapter 5, "Hardware Selection and Configuration."

Advantages of Separate Environments

Installing a set of separate environments during the development process has two main purposes:

1. Speed up development
2. Ensure the quality of the application being developed

Speed Up Development

Separate environments help accelerate the development process, primarily by allowing you to perform different tasks in parallel and to prevent one task from interfering with another. You can run these sorts of tasks in parallel:

- Ongoing software module development
- Demonstration of intermediate results to users, checking their acceptance and integrating additional requirements into the development process
- Production environment setup

Ensure the Quality of the Application Being Developed

High quality depends on controlled delivery of components from the development environment to an integration environment and, finally, to the production environment. A well defined procedure for delivering components ensures stability by proving that the running application does not depend on specific settings in the development environment.

Quality must also be assured for system throughput and query response times. Complex queries should be analyzed and optimized. This can be done in parallel with ongoing development, but it cannot be allowed to interfere with the development or production environments.

Separate environments also expand training possibilities. Software systems achieve high availability through failover systems, replication, or other kinds of redundancy, all of which have to be tested thoroughly to ensure that they behave as expected. Database administrators have to be trained to handle problems, especially if the in-place mechanisms are not fully automated. System failures create high stress, and the ability to react quickly and correctly is developed through training.

Tasks Requiring or Accelerated by Separate Environments

The tasks described in this section must not interfere with each other. To ensure this you can either run them sequentially in the same environment or in parallel in separate environments. The latter, of course, allows for faster development.

Module Development

In a large project, several developers work on different modules and they need to test queries and transactions on a database with a few records. For some types of applications they might need to create data constellations against which to test the module behavior. If they use a development tool that stores results in a SQL Server database, a separate database will be necessary—one that will never be migrated to the production environment.

Separate development environments can be a drawback if developers over-customize them for specific needs. This speeds up development and eliminates some recurrent actions, but it can create a situation in which modules depend on customized settings to function correctly. These problems will show up during integration because that environment will import the modules but not the specialized development settings. Still, it is better to avoid such problems completely.

Performance Planning

Complex queries have to be run against reasonable data volumes so that their response times can be accurately estimated for tuning purposes. Tuning usually entails creating additional indexes and replacing parts of the query statements with semantic equivalents. For SQL statements, tuning requires reproducible measurements, and these cannot be guaranteed in a development environment; in fact, they cannot even be guaranteed in the production environment if it is running an earlier version of the application. You need a development environment that closely resembles the production environment. For examples of the tuning process, see Chapter 7, "Field Observations on Coding Queries and Transactions."

Integration and System Tests

At specific points in the development process (milestones) modules are integrated with preliminary versions of the application and tested. If you maintain separate environments, module development can continue during integration testing if no activities interfere with each other. Some modules may be rejected as a result of the integration tests, in which case they are returned to development. The accepted modules remain in the integration stage and should not be changed by developers, which is usually accomplished by restricting access to the integration environment more tightly than access to the development environment.

Quality Assurance

After acceptance, modules must pass quality assurance evaluation, which checks them against criteria such as accordance to previously defined guidelines, coding styles, etc. Regression tests check to make sure that new versions produce the same results on given input data as previous versions. Automation of these tests (using other tools) allows the use of larger test suites and leads to more thorough testing and higher-quality software. Regression tests can also be performed during integration and system testing.

Developing and Testing Administration Jobs

Complex software systems and VLDBs place some administrative burden on the production system in the form of backup and recovery, reorganization (defragmentation), archiving of old database contents, and other ways of "polishing" the data. These tasks (and some availability concepts) have to be tested before they can be installed on the production system. Testing should not interfere with other development steps.

Simulating Failures

High availability requires additional hardware and software components and these must also be tested. Every kind of failure addressed by these components must be simulated, usually by shutting off hardware components or intentionally writing invalid data to disks to make sure the system recovers automatically. If these tests indicate that other administrative tasks are necessary to enable the automatic recovery, the tasks will have to be defined and tested in an appropriate environment.

Checking User Acceptance

After these tests have been completed the system is presented to users, who will agree with the implementation or suggest further refinements. This adds overhead but is necessary for a smooth roll-out.

Environment Size and Configuration Requirements

Regardless of how many separate environments you use to accomplish these tasks, the better they are separated the easier it will be to complete tasks in parallel. Effective environment separation leads to earlier completion and higher quality.

Separation

While it is obvious that some environments must be separated, it is not so obvious in other instances. But *all effective* separation increases development speed and system quality.

Everybody agrees that the development environment must be separate from the production system. Otherwise, all intermediate states of the modules would be visible to the production system and would reduce its stability.

Separating the development environment from a dedicated integration and system test environment helps detect module dependencies on special development settings. It also allows you to continue development while modules are integrated and the whole system is tested. The integration and system test environment must not interfere with the production system, to keep the latter clear from any defects in the modules being tested.

The next stage of separation is using a dedicated performance planning environment to develop and tune complex database queries and transactions. In most cases, the response times of queries and the throughput of the transactions are regarded critical and must meet defined requirements. Some queries and transactions should be prototyped to ensure that they meet requirements with the designed data model. This environment can also be used for post-production analysis and tuning of queries and transactions.

Queries are tuned by checking for appropriate indexes and, if necessary, replacing parts of the query with semantically equivalent Transact-SQL phrases. Transactions are tuned by improving index design and checking for potential lock conflicts. Both types of tuning require measuring resource consumption in different formulations and comparing results, so this environment must not have any background load. (Details on tuning are in Chapter 7, "Field Observations on Coding Queries and Transactions.")

Quality assurance should be an ongoing activity performed in parallel to other activities but separated so as not to interfere with them. If you perform it after system integration, it can use the integration environment.

Fault tolerance and recovery tests require an environment in which you can simulate all kinds of failures. Obviously, it must be completely separate from all other environments.

Finally, when presenting prototypes and intermediate milestones to users, performance should not be affected by other development activities such as stress or recovery tests. This can be guaranteed only in a separate environment.

Sizes and Configuration

The environments just discussed have different size and configuration requirements.

The development environment must have enough CPU power and disk capacity to satisfy developer needs. The kind of application being developed determines how many databases must reside in this environment so developers can work on modules in parallel. This environment does not need production-size databases or high availability components such as Windows NT clusters or database replication.

The performance planning environment must first of all allow you to run a database as large as the production database is estimated to be. Query execution plans (evaluated by the query engine), response times, and system throughput all depend on the table size. Query plans depend on the statistics and thus on the actual data distribution. To measure, compare, and evaluate alternatives for queries and transactions, the database must also contain reasonable table and attribute values. This environment should also run production components such as replication, because they consume a certain amount of resources and affect achievable throughput and response times.

The integration and system test environment must be as similar to the production system as possible. It should have a database as large as the production database is expected to be, not only for performance testing but to detect problems that might appear only on databases of a certain size. This environment should have all production system components—middleware, other software, fault tolerance components, etc.—because any of these can interfere with the modules being tested.

The test environment for administrative jobs and recovery has the same requirements for the same reasons. Only a production-size environment will show how long certain tasks will run and how long recovery takes.

The requirements for an environment in which to demonstrate the prototype to users depends on what features you want to present to them. You can present the UI and basic functionality on a small set of data and without high availability components. If you want to demonstrate throughput and response times fairly, you will need appropriately sized databases with reasonable contents. Demonstrating fault tolerance or recovery times requires all production components.

Multiple Environments on the Same Machine

Although dedicated machines simplify things, they are expensive and you can often get by running some environments on the same computer, although this usually requires loosening requirements to some extent. If you reduce the number of tasks performed in parallel, you can get by with three machines containing:

- The development environment with small development databases
- One machine similar to the production system in database size and availability features
- The production system.

Use the second computer for integration and system testing, performance planning, developing and testing administrative jobs, simulating failures, and demonstrating the prototype to users. These things cannot be done in parallel, and you may have to prepare the computer for the next job by saving the database and configuration to a backup medium and restoring the original database and settings for the next activity.

A Good Set of Environments at Bound Galley Book Cellars

Bound Galley Book Cellars had little time in which to develop their POD Receiving and Integrated Shipping Management System (PRISM). In only four months they completed the first release of the system, tested it, rolled it out and started the production system. This was feasible only because they defined dedicated, separated environments for performing as many activities as possible in parallel without reducing quality.

They defined separate environments for:

- Development
- Integration and system test
- Quality assurance
- User acceptance
- Production
- "Burn box"

The "burn box" was used to test new software releases such as Windows NT option packs, SQL Server beta releases, and other components. They were released to the other environments only if they passed testing.

All environments were located on separate machines and shared no resources (except the network) to prevent interference. Developers configured most of the machines as clusters and with the same memory size and disk capacity as the production environment, to avoid any unpleasant surprises when moving components between environments. The only exception to this was the user acceptance environment, which was smaller.

CHAPTER 5

Hardware Selection and Configuration

By Christopher Etz, g&h Database Technologies GmbH

Very large database (VLDB) system hardware must support specialized data storage and access requirements while assuring acceptable throughput in a high-transaction environment characterized by heavy concurrent use. This chapter begins by addressing general requirements and making some recommendations, then moves on to discuss hardware-related configuration issues.

The Solution in Focus

Obviously hardware configuration is a central concern in any system design and deployment. But, as in just about every other aspect, VLDB systems pose special requirements and not a few challenges. For starters, you need to decide on and set up basic hardware *in the early stages of the design process*, so that you can test design factors against basic performance requirements. For another, once you have basic components figured out, you have to decide how they will interact: by definition you are creating a high-transaction-rate system that needs access to huge amounts of data. Performance is critical and even small design decisions can have large effects. How processing is handled, how much auto-tuning the system does, how processing flow uses hardware—all of these things determine how effectively the production system will let users do their jobs.

All the information in this chapter (and the others in this section) is drawn from the experiences of companies that have implemented VLDBs using SQL Server 7.0 as recorded by Microsoft Consulting Services. It has been combined into case studies under the fictional names of Broadband Cable Communications, Bound Galley Book Cellars, and others. Taken together, these chapters discuss the challenges of VLDB solutions from preliminary design to fine-tuning the system in the production environment, providing examples, explanation, and field-tested recommendations.

What You'll Find in This Chapter

- Basic hardware types needed for VLDB design, how they interact, how to configure them for performance, how specific companies configured their systems.

- How SQL Server 7.0 auto-tunes the configuration and how to choose when to intercede to customize effectively.

- How fiber channel processing works, and how you can use it to reduce CPU overhead and improve performance.

- Specific recommendations for configuring SAP on SQL Server 7.0, using case study examples for individual issues and a large SAP system at Microsoft for an overview of how it improved overall system performance.

Warning   This chapter makes recommendations for tuning the Microsoft Windows NT registry. Using the Registry Editor incorrectly can cause serious, system-wide problems that require you to reinstall Windows NT. Microsoft cannot guarantee that any problems resulting from the use of Registry Editor can be solved. Use this tool at your own risk.

Hardware Selection

You should select hardware early in a database application development project because, from the outset, you need hardware for:

- The database server
- The application server (if you plan to develop a 3-tier application)
- Testing some of the client systems in the planned configuration

Configuring basic hardware greatly increases tuning potential during the design stage; it is easier and cheaper to change the design at this point in the project than it will be later. During the early planning phases you make design and architecture decisions that can lead to bottlenecks or other problems in production. You can eliminate these early, through performance and stress tests, if the database server has access to disk storage capacity similar to that calculated for the production system. (For information on performance planning, see Chapter 7, "Field Observations on Coding Queries and Transactions.")

To discuss hardware selection, this section uses three fictionalized deployments as primary examples: a book shipment system designed for Bound Galley Book Cellars, the subscriber activation system at the mobile telephone provider A&G Phone, and a "customer behavior and profitability" application at MultiForm Industries. The other companies referred to in this section of the book are used occasionally.

Computers

The database server computer determines achievable throughput. If it is at all possible, you should dedicate separate computer systems to the different environments needed during development (see the section "Defining Separate Environments," in Chapter 4).

Processor Architectures

SQL Server 7.0 runs on the Intel and DEC Alpha processor architectures supported by Windows NT. Of the cases used in this chapter, A&G Phone used 600-MHz DEC Alpha processors, which they decided offered better throughput than Intel-based computers. The other clients chose Intel-based architectures ranging from PentiumPro, Pentium II, to Xeon processors at different clock rates. Most systems belong to the family of Compaq ProLiant family 5500, 6000, and 7000 lines.

Intel and DEC Alpha turned out to be well suited for running big database systems. Both platforms support data warehouse and online transaction processing (OLTP)-type applications. Intel processors have achieved greater power in recent years and now offer systems that can cope with VLDBs. DEC Alpha processors are well supported by Microsoft products and make stable VLDB servers. Intel Xeon and DEC Alpha processors work well in systems with high CPU power requirements.

SMP Issues

VLDBs require a lot of CPU power, especially for OLTP applications, which typically form hot spots by performing many operations on a small set of data. A small data set almost always remains in the database cache, reducing physical disk I/Os, and well tuned database systems can reach cache hit ratios of 99% or higher. CPU power is also needed to drive compact transactions that are often contained in stored procedures running within the database server, especially if the transactions are designed to allow high concurrency. If well tuned applications experience a bottleneck, it commonly is due to insufficient CPU power. When the CPU becomes the limiting resource, you must add more CPUs, increase the clock rate, or distribute tasks and implement replication.

Symmetric multiprocessor (SMP) machines can boost database server CPU power. The cases referenced in this chapter all run SMP machines, some with four processors per machine, some with two.

One potential problem on SMP machines arises from how runnable threads are assigned to processors. In one of the systems mentioned above, the fourth processor became saturated because it was assigned to handle all network interrupts in addition to its share of the database server threads. This was easily solved by restricting database activity to the first three processors, saving the fourth for operating system services. In the Windows NT registry (as shown below) the ProcessorAffinityMask for the first three processors was set to 0x7:

```
HKEY_LOCAL_MACHINE\System\CurrentControlSet\Services\NDIS\Parameters
\ProcessorAffinityMask
```

Memory

SQL Server 7.0 makes the best use of available memory by allocating for itself as much as it can get, using most of it for the database cache to reduce physical disk I/Os. If other processes require more memory, SQL Server releases some, always leaving about 5 MB of memory free. Increasing physical memory usually improves performance, reduces application response times, and increases system throughput.

SQL Server installations run on Windows NT 4.0, and its memory model limits the address area of each process to 4 GB: Windows NT Enterprise Edition reserves 1 GB for the kernel and leaves up to 3 GB for user data, all other editions reserve 2 GB for the kernel and leave 2 GB for user data. Because the database cache uses the greatest amount of available memory, the database server can use the 2 or 3 GB allocated for user data (depending on the edition), but cannot use more, even if it is available.

The companies referred to in this chapter installed large amounts of database server memory to run SQL Server 7.0 applications on VLDBs—between 1.5 and 3 GB of physical memory. This put them at (or close to) the maximum. These figures represent practical maximums, because in a 32-bit architecture there is no way to make more main memory accessible to SQL Server.

Disk Controllers

The three companies put their databases on external disk storage systems connected to the computer via SCSI or fiber channel. The machines have multiple disk controllers, so parallel I/O requests can be sent over different controllers. Qlogic, Adaptec, and Adaptec clones are the most commonly used brands.

One company used an Adaptec clone but ran into throughput problems with high I/O rates. Analysis showed that the system could not handle outstanding I/O requests on more than three of the controllers, and a problem developed whenever the fourth controller received an I/O request. To maximize throughput, the database files were organized so that no more than three controllers are involved at one time.

If your system plan has extremely high I/O requirements, consider GTL bus systems (instead of the more widely used PCI bus systems) and fiber channel controllers (instead of SCSI controllers). Plan for enough disk controllers to enable high-volume parallel I/O requests.

Bus Systems

Bound Galley Book Cellars found that their e-commerce system throughput was limited, not by the disk storage system or the controllers themselves, but by the internal PCI bus, which could not cope with the frequency of interrupts generated by four or more disk controllers accessing the database disks in parallel. They solved this by installing GTL bus-based systems of fiber channel disk controllers.

Disk Systems

VLDBs do not fit on internal disks; they require external disk systems.

Besides storage and access characteristics, you have to consider disk system mean time between failure (MTBF) stats. Every disk model has its own. In most cases, this figure is large enough that data can be protected with conventional backup systems. As more disks are installed, however, MTBF figures accumulate and the threat of a failure increases. To avoid data loss due to hardware failure, run all environments on RAID (redundant arrays of inexpensive disks) systems.

RAID Levels

The commonly used RAID levels are 0, 1, and 5.

RAID levels.

RAID level	Function	Advantage
0	Striping without redundancy	Very high performance
1	Transparent mirroring, storing all data twice	Easy recovery
5	Striping with parity	Enough redundancy to recover from a single disk failure

RAID level 0 offers good performance, but does not protect data from hardware failures. This RAID level is always used in combination with RAID level 1, never on its own.

RAID level 1 stores every data block on two disk drives. Should one disk fail, data access shifts to the second drive. In combination with RAID level 0, this provides very high performance on writing I/O requests. This combination is also known as RAID level 10 or 1/0.

RAID level 5 protects against data loss due to single disk drive failure. It requires less system capacity to store the redundant information (parity). Its complexity, however, reduces I/O write request performance below that of RAID level 10.

All the companies referred to in this chapter applied the same two rules to determine RAID level:

- Store the data files of the application databases on RAID level 5.

- Store the temporary database (**tempdb**) and the log files of all databases (these files have the highest write I/O rates) on the combination of RAID levels 0 and 1.

Software vs. Hardware RAID

RAID levels are provided by software that can be located either in the disk storage system (hardware RAID) or within the computer itself (software RAID). In hardware RAID, the disk storage system performs the operations on behalf of the I/O requests. RAID operations are transparent to the computer, so SQL Server can use all the CPU power. In software RAID, Windows NT uses some of the computer system CPU power to perform RAID operations.

MultiForm Industries used software RAID to create a demonstration system, one purpose of which was to test using SQL Server 7.0 to handle 2 terabytes of data. This resulted in CPU bottlenecks. For their deliverable system they plan to establish hardware RAID, which is generally preferable in VLDB applications.

Backup Systems

SQL Server 7.0 throughput is limited only by the backup hardware, and can be maximized by storing the backup on disks first, then copying it to backup media such as individual DLT tapes, DLT libraries, or jukeboxes of writeable CD-ROMs. With this method, Bound Galley Book Cellars and MultiForm Industries achieved a maximum throughput of 60 GB/hour on their DLT libraries. Designing, implementing, and testing the backup and recovery strategy is described in Chapter 8, "Field Observations on Managing Operations."

Network

Network requirements are largely determined by application architecture. High transaction rates require more network bandwidth. A 3-tier architecture, in which business logic is performed by an application server, causes a lot of SQL statements and results, all of which use bandwidth when they are exchanged between the application server and the database server. Encapsulating the business logic in stored procedures reduces bandwidth requirements.

None of the companies referred to in this chapter found a conventional Ethernet with a bandwidth of 10 Mbit/second to be sufficient. They installed either a higher capacity Ethernet (100-Mbit) or an ATM network. All of them use TCP/IP network protocol because others (such as SPX/IPX) put too much traffic on the network.

Clustering

You can increase system availability by running SQL Server on a Windows NT cluster (a set of two or more machines accessing the same disk storage system). Each has its own hostname and Internet address, as well as a second hostname and Internet address identifying the cluster as a unit. One cluster member serves requests to the cluster hostname or the cluster IP address. If it fails, the other member takes over.

Clustering tends to work well, although the process of installing SQL Server on a Windows NT cluster requires that you meet some prerequisites and perform the installation steps in the right order.

Prerequisites

- Hardware must be compatible with a Windows NT cluster.
- The cluster operating system must be Windows NT Server, Enterprise Edition.
- The cluster must have a static IP address and subnet mask, on which it will answer the requests as a unit.

- Cluster members should be connected to at least two different networks (to eliminate the network as a single point of failure).
- Drive letters must be assigned to the drives *before* they are connected to the shared SCSI bus.

Installation

1. Install the Microsoft Cluster Server on the first machine.
2. Install the Microsoft Cluster Server on the second machine and make sure that it joins the (already existing) cluster.
3. Verify the cluster installation by finding both machines in the Cluster Administrator.
4. Install Windows NT Option Pack 4 on both machines. Do not boot either machine until both have Option Pack 4 installed.
5. Install SQL Server 7.0 on both members. Include named pipes as one of the network protocols.
6. Check both installations.
7. Set up a virtual server using the SQL Failover Cluster Wizard and configure it to handle the cluster's IP address and subnet mask.

When the installation is done, you can move the virtual SQL Server between cluster members.

For more information, see the Microsoft Cluster Server and the SQL Server Books Online.

Hardware at Bound Galley Book Cellars E-Commerce Site

Bound Galley Book Cellars operates an Internet book ordering system. Orders are processed by the POD Receiving and Integrated Shipping Manager (PRISM) application running on SQL Server 7.0. PRISM is Web-based, using the intranet to implement smart, rapid, and real-time sourcing and shipping methods.

The production system, including backup systems, has this configuration:

- IIS 1 and IIS 2 are the Web servers, providing HTML, active server pages (ASPs) and FTP access.
- MSMQ 1 is the primary site controller (PSC) for the Microsoft Message Queuing System, MSMQ 2 is the backup site controller (BSC).
- MTS 1 and MTS 2 form a cluster and provide Microsoft Transaction Services. MTS 1 is active and MTS 2 is backup. MTS 3 is a further backup system that is activated if the cluster fails. For systems that cannot tolerate unavailability (most sales systems) it is advisable to provide a backup for worst-cases of even the most remote possibility.

- SQL 1 and SQL 2 form the production cluster in an active/active configuration. SQL 3 and SQL 4 form a backup cluster. Transactions are replicated from the production cluster to the backup cluster by copying and applying the log files. SQL 5 and SQL 6 are a third cluster of database machines dedicated to reports, which can degrade performance when run on the production cluster. Replication from the production system to the reporting system is performed by dumping the database daily and restoring on the reporting system, so that reports never conflict with concurrent transactions.

Configuration: Auto-Tuning

If you do not specify optional values, SQL Server 7.0 auto-tunes many of them: amount of memory used for the database cache, number of open connections, open database objects, locks, etc. It also monitors system use to determine the amount of memory available in the hardware.

Auto-tuning allows you to use all or part of the default configuration supplied by SQL Server 7.0. The companies referred to in these chapters used auto-configured parameters except in a few cases: Bound Galley Book Cellars set the amount of memory to use for the database cache, MultiForm Industries and BCC limited file size growth to absolute values instead of percentages, and Black Dinosaur Oil Co. and A&G Phone configured their SAP environment. These changes are described later in this chapter.

A&G Phone noticed a slow start and CPU utilization near 100% when the first transactions and queries were executed against its newly populated database. At first it seemed that the design had seriously underestimated the amount of CPU power required, but after a few hours CPU utilization dropped and throughput increased as the database system self-calibrated. When you set up an implementation project schedule, include some hours (after the database is populated but before it is available for general use) for executing some typical transactions and queries so that SQL Server can find its optimal configuration. If you cannot initiate transactions without changing database contents, run some typical queries such as online data retrieval or reports instead.

How to Set Configuration Options Explicitly

The configuration options are generally accessed through Transact-SQL. You can set the most common configuration options with SQL Server Enterprise Manager. It calls two stored SQL Server procedures (**sp_configure** and **sp_dboption**) to read the settings and display them to you. If you make any changes, Enterprise Manager calls the procedures again and updates the SQL Server settings.

Access SQL Server Enterprise Manager from the **Start** menu, then select **Programs** and **Microsoft SQL Server 7.0**, where you find the item **Enterprise Manager**. Here is the start screen:

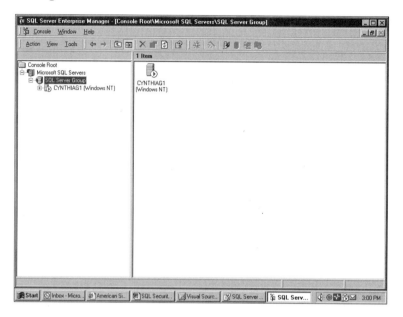

Figure 5.1   SQL Server Enterprise Manager start screen.

On the right side, place the cursor over the SQL Server installation in which you want to change configuration options, right-click, then select **Properties**. This window is displayed:

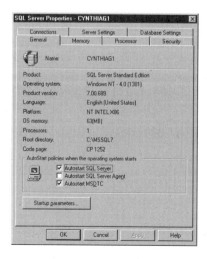

Figure 5.2   Properties window in SQL Server Enterprise Manager.

The register cards show the configuration options you can set.

You can also set any configuration option directly through Transact-SQL. You can call the stored procedures with any front-end tool that allows you to enter arbitrary Transact-SQL statements, such as the Query Analyzer or the command-line oriented front-end tools ISQL and OSQL.

Access Query Analyzer from the **Start** menu, then select **Programs** and **Microsoft SQL Server 7.0**. This shows the item **Query Analyzer**. It offers two windows, one for entering the Transact-SQL statements, and the other showing the output.

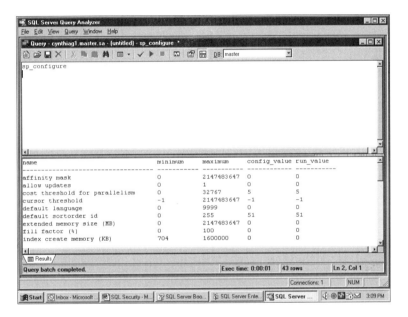

Figure 5.3   Input and output windows for Query Analyzer.

The command-line tools ISQL and OSQL have the same user interface although they communicate with SQL Server differently (ISQL uses the DB-library, OSQL uses ODBC). You can use these tools to redirect input and output. For instance, you can prepare configuration settings in a script file and store the output in another file. This allows you to keep your last settings in a file as a record—highly recommended because you can use this file to configure another installation with the same values.

The input script for showing all configuration options can look like this:

```
sp_configure 'show advanced options', 1
goreconfiguregosp_configurego
```

The command to execute is:

```
isql -E < input_file > output_file
```

Setting the Memory for SQL Server

Unlike SQL Server 6.5, SQL Server version 7.0 manages memory by grabbing all but about 5 MB of the available memory and dedicating most of it to the database cache. If memory requirements for other applications running on the same computer reduce free memory below 5 MB, SQL Server releases some; if free memory on the system increases, SQL Server grabs all but the last 5 MB. This works well except in some cases when the same computer is also running other applications such as:

- Full-text search support (MSSearch)
- Web servers such as Microsoft Internet Information Server
- Application servers such as an SAP installation's update processes

 If you run these sorts applications on the SQL Server computer, you may want to limit the amount of memory that the SQL Server is allowed to grab. In practice, most real VLDB environments dedicate a computer for the SQL Server installation—all of the companies referred to in this chapter did—and this is not a factor.

Memory configuration options.

Configuration option	Allowable range	Unit	Description
Min server memory	0 ... 2,147,483,647	MB	Guarantees a minimum amount of memory to SQL server.
Max server memory	0 ... 2,147,483,647	MB	Prevents SQL Server from using more than the specified amount of memory.
Set working set size	0 or 1		Allows you to lock SQL Server memory into the physical memory of the computer and thereby eliminate SQL Server paging activity.

If you set **min server memory** and **max server memory** to the same value, that value is the fixed amount of memory to allocate to SQL Server.

To set **max server memory**, evaluate the answers to these questions:

- Can other applications be transferred to another computer? (If possible, you should dedicate a computer to SQL Server, in which case you don't need to set these options.)
- How many other applications are there? The more things you run on the computer, the less memory is available for SQL Server.
- Don't make virtual memory any larger than 1.5 times physical memory. This ratio causes a certain amount of paging but does not severely affect system throughput.
- Which application serves the most users? Obviously, if the database is used most often it should get most of the memory.

Rule of thumb: if one other application runs concurrently on the same computer, grant about 70% of the physical memory to SQL Server; if more than one runs concurrently, grant 40% to 50%.

You can set maximum memory with the stored procedure **sp_configure**. Enable the advanced options, set each value, then issue the RECONFIGURE command for the changes to take effect.

You can also set it with SQL Server Enterprise Manager, or with Transact-SQL in ISQL, OSQL, or the Query Analyzer. These procedures are described above.

Number of Asynchronous I/O Requests

SQL Server sends I/O requests asynchronously to the disks. The default setting allows a maximum of 32 outstanding I/O requests per file, which normally is adequate for servers with non-specialized disk subsystems such as SCSI disks. But if the database resides on a high speed RAID system connected through several SCSI-channels or even faster bus systems, SQL Server can send more I/O requests to the disk system before the first one has to be answered. This is because "intelligent storage systems" can take advantage of more I/O requests by reordering them to minimize disk head movements and by processing requests out of order if the corresponding block happens to pass by the disk head. This can improve overall throughput.

Use the **max async IO** option to control the maximum number of outstanding I/O requests per file. Increasing it may improve performance during disk-intensive operations, but there will be an upper limit after which performance will decline. Use Windows NT Performance Monitor as you adjust it to find this limit.

You can set **max async IO** only with Transact-SQL using ISQL, OSQL or the Query Analyzer.

Here is an example. A&G Phone improved I/O system throughput by setting **max async IO** to 100. Their environment included a DEC alpha server 7300 5/600 with three Qlogic controllers connected to a Storage Work system RA 10000 including three HSZ70 controllers. They used these Transact-SQL statements:

```
sp_configure 'max async IO', 100
go
reconfigure
go
```

Configuration: Fiber Mode

OLTP-type applications are often used by high numbers of users concurrently, resulting in a high volume of compact transactions being sent to the database. For every database connection, SQL Server has to keep its own context, which must be switched each time another user executes a new transaction or query. Context switching causes CPU overhead, but you can reduce this by using fibers. (The concept of fibers is described in the SQL Server Books Online. See "Thread and Task Architecture" in the "Server Architecture" section of "SQL Server Architecture.")

Default Behavior

The standard SQL Server configuration keeps the context of the database connections by using threads—an operating system feature that allows concurrent execution paths within a single process. Here, SQL Server forms the process and every user has an execution path within the server to perform a transaction or query.

Different threads can run on the same CPU. The CPU switches from one thread to another at, for instance, the end of a given time slice (a configurable option) or when an action such as a disk operation cannot be completed immediately. For SMP systems with up to four CPUs (the most common configuration), threads of one process can run truly parallel on CPUs.

SQL Server maintains a pool of worker threads for user connections, and their quantity is defined by the **max worker threads** configuration option. Its default is the maximum (255).

A SQL Server batch is a set of one or more Transact-SQL statements sent from a client to SQL Server for execution as a unit. When SQL Server receives a batch, it assigns a free worker thread to the user connection. If no free worker threads are available but the limit has not been reached, it allocates a new one. If the limit has been reached, the batch waits until a worker thread is freed.

If a lot of SQL Server batches arrive while others are still executing, SQL Server has to switch from one thread to another. Switching is performed by Windows NT, which has to change from user to kernel mode to perform the switch, then back to user mode in the context of the other thread. Frequent context switches cause a great deal of CPU overhead.

Fiber Mode

Fibers are independent execution paths within a thread. They are performed in parallel, but they reduce CPU overhead by using library calls (on top of native Windows NT threading) to perform context switching in user mode rather than in kernel mode (used for threads).

To configure SQL Server to use fibers, use the **lightweight pooling** option. The default value is 0, which uses native Windows NT threads for the worker threads. Change this to 1 to use fibers.

Fibers cannot run on their own, but must be contained in threads. For this reason, SQL Server starts a few threads within which the fibers are executed. Windows NT can use only one processor to handle the thread as a whole, regardless of its number of fibers. SQL Server starts one thread (containing fibers) per processor.

When Transact-SQL batches execute, only the fibers are relevant, so the term *worker thread* now applies to a fiber instead of a thread. The number of worker threads, however, is still limited by the **max worker threads** option.

Whether worker threads are executed as native Windows NT threads or as fibers affects how context switches are done, how the Transact-SQL batches are assigned to the different processors in an SMP system, and how the operating system schedules thread execution.

Context Switches

Context switching should have an impact on system throughput only when CPU power is the limiting resource. Some application activities (concurrent SQL batch execution, for instance) initiate more context switching than others, and this determines how much improvement you can expect when tuning. OLTP-type systems with a high number of concurrently executed, small transactions will benefit from using fibers; data warehouse-type applications, with fewer but more complex queries, will derive no measurable benefit. If you change to fiber mode and still experience a CPU bottleneck, your may have to add CPUs, remove other applications from the SQL Server computer, or divide the database into smaller units and spread them over different machines (if feasible).

SMP Effects

In a multiple-processor computer, a context switch can move a thread to a processor other than the one on which it began. This deprives the thread of any cached information it was using on the first processor, so it starts executing on the new processor slowly, speeding up as it completes memory accesses to create a new cache. Fiber mode runs only one thread (composed of concurrently executing fibers) on the same processor, so it makes better use of the processor cache by reducing context switches for threads. Fibers can be shut down and later restarted, but fiber mode increases the chances they will resume on the same processor and have access to the existing processor cache.

Scheduling

The operating system prioritizes and schedules threads. Fiber mode has fewer threads, although each of them can contain numerous fibers and thus serve several clients, and SQL Server assigns all of them the same priority. This can slow down database throughput if there is any other activity on the system, so you can use fiber mode only if the machine is dedicated to SQL Server.

You should not try to circumvent this problem by boosting the priority of the SQL Server threads: it can cause problems by preventing network requests from being served fast enough.

Recommendations

To evaluate the usefulness of fiber mode in your system:

- Make sure the computer is dedicated to SQL Server.

  If it is not, use native Windows NT threads to ensure acceptable scheduling between system tasks.

- See if CPU power is the limiting resource.

  You can expect fiber mode to help only if CPU utilization is at or near to 100%. Use Windows NT Performance Monitor to check overall CPU utilization. If it stays below 80%, continue running worker threads as native Windows NT threads.

- See if you have a high number of context switches.

  Use the Windows NT Performance Monitor to check totals. If the number is not extremely high, continue running worker threads as native Windows NT threads.

If these do not alleviate the problem, run fiber mode.

Configuring Fiber Mode

Enable fiber mode with the **lightweight pooling** option. It is an advanced option (not available in SQL Server Enterprise Manager) and you must use Transact-SQL ISQL, OSQL, or Query Analyzer to set it. First, enable the advanced options:

```
sp_configure 'show advanced options', 1
go
reconfigure
go
```

Then enable the fiber mode:

```
sp_configure 'lightweight pooling', 1
go
reconfigure
go
```

You have to restart SQL Server for the setting to take effect. Start the SQL Server Service Manager and click the **Stop** button. When the **Start/Continue** button becomes available, click it to restart the server.

Figure 5.4   Service Manager screen for stopping/restarting SQL Server.

You can also use SQL Server Enterprise Manager to stop the server: right-click on the **SQL Server** icon, select **Stop**, then right-click again and select **Start**.

Subscriber Activation System at A&G Phone

A&G Phone runs its subscriber activation system as an SQL Server 7.0 application. This forms a big OLTP system with a 3-tier architecture to boost availability, scalability, and transaction throughput. The system supports 1600 users, with 350 working on the database at any one time, and can process as many as 6,000,000 transactions per day.

A&G Phone database environment systems.

System	SQL Server	Hardware
Reporting and customer services	SQL Server 6.5	Windows NT 4.0 cluster of 2 DEC Alpha 4100 5/466s
Subscriber activation system (OLTP)	SQL Server 7.0	Windows NT 4.0 cluster of 2 DEC Alpha 7300 5/600s
Sales support and system management	SQL Server 6.5	Windows NT 4.0 cluster of 2 DEC Alpha 7300 5/533s
Fuzzy retrieval	SQL Server 6.5	Windows NT 4.0 cluster of 2 DEC Alpha 7300 5/400s

The OLTP servers have 4 processors at 600 MHz and 2 GB of main memory, each. They include 3 Qlogic disk controllers and 2 DE 500 NIC network adapters.

The disk system is an RA 10000 Storage Works system with 3 HSZ 70 controller in dual redundancy mode, and 45 4-GB disks. All database-related disks run in RAID level 10.

The subscriber activation system takes its input from clients connected via ISDN or modems. Some orders arrive as faxes and are passed through an online character recognition system run by an external provider. After orders are entered into the system, credit checks are performed by connecting to the appropriate providers on the WAN. If credit is OKed, the information is passed to the billing system, replicated to the customer service system, and archived on CD-ROM.

Testing Fiber Mode Impact

After enabling the fiber mode, A&G Phone noticed 30% increase in system throughput. Figure 5.5 shows a comparable case on a test system, where the effects of implementing fiber mode are smaller but still considerable.

The diagram shows normal mode first (the left side of the graph), then shutting down SQL Server (the drop in the middle), then restarting in fiber mode (the right side). The percentage of total processor time (the line on the bottom) is at 80% or slightly above in both phases. During normal mode, the top two lines are close together, showing that system calls roughly equal context switches—that is, almost every system call results in a context switch. In fiber mode, the top two lines are farther apart, showing that there is a greater difference between system calls and context switches—that is, fewer system calls cause context switches, and the thread runs longer because threads now have fibers, which can continue operating.

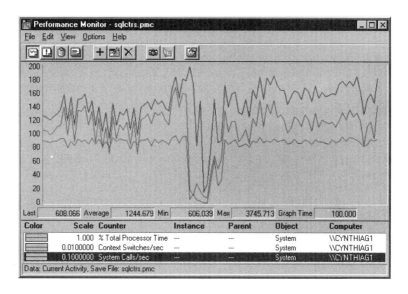

Figure 5.5   Effects of implementing fiber mode on a test SQL Server system.

Configuration: Considerations for SAP

SAP R/3 is an integrated set of business applications covering accounting and controlling, production and material management, quality management, plant maintenance, sales and distributions, human resources management, and project management. It runs on a variety of database systems, including SQL Server 7.0.

SAP uses thin-client architecture: clients connect to application servers that contain the business logic and send transactions asynchronously to so-called update processes. In SAP R/3, you can configure where processes run, a capability you must consider when setting up a database system. Black Dinosaur Oil Co. and MS Sales run SQL Server 7.0 as the database management system for SAP R/3. This section describes their experiences and configuration issues.

Black Dinosaur Oil Co.

Black Dinosaur Oil is a large energy company with three primary business operations—oil and gas exploration and production, manufacturing and marketing of motor oil and other petrochemical and automotive products, and franchising and operating fast oil-change centers. It currently has a global network of approximately 4,000 PCs and 200 servers. As a result of a recent merger, it gained 600 retail outlets (for a total of 1,800) and expects to process more than twice as many daily business transactions (approximately 1.2 million dialog steps per day).

To cope with the estimated transaction volume, they installed SQL Server 7.0 beta 3 on a Windows NT cluster consisting of a primary Compaq ProLiant 7000 with 4 Xeon processors at 400 MHz and a secondary ProLiant 6000 with 4 PentiumPro processors at 200 MHz, each with 2 GB of main memory. The database is located on an EMC^2 Symmetrix 3700-18 Enterprise Storage System with 2.3 terabytes of disk space, connected to the cluster via four controllers.

The SAP R/3 application servers run on 6 Compaq ProLiant 6500 server computers, each with 4 200-MHz PentiumPro processors, 1.5 GB of memory, and 24 GB of disk space. Two run the R/3 sales and distribution online functions, two run all other SAP online functions, one runs batch processes, and one runs the SAP central instance and update processes.

Automatically Updated Statistics

By default, SQL Server automatically updates statistics on table indexes, enabling the query engine to select better query plans by looking at actual data distribution.

Statistics are created automatically when an index is created. You can suppress this by adding the clause *with statistics_norecompute* to the CREATE INDEX statement. If you later decide to create statistical information on a column, you can do so by adding the statement CREATE STATISTICS. You can create statistics on indexed and non-indexed columns. Use this command to see statistics:

```
dbcc show_statistics ('table', 'column')
```

A typical output looks like this:

```
Updated                 Rows    Rows Sampled Steps   Density        Average key length
--------------------    -------  ------------ -------  -------------  ------------------
Feb 28 1999  7:19PM  10000        10000       100    4.3901554E-3       8.0004282

(1 row(s) affected)

All density             Columns
----------------------  -------------------------
5.0251256E-3                 j

(1 row(s) affected)
```

The first block shows the date and time of the most recent update, the number of rows in the table, the number of rows in the sample used to calculate the statistics, the number of histogram cells and the average space used to store the values. The interval from the smallest to the largest value is divided into histogram cells, each cell containing the number of rows where the actual value fits into the range covered by the histogram cell.

The second block shows the column(s) belonging to the index, and their selectivity (All density).

A third block (too large to display above) shows the statistics' individual cells.

You can set a trigger that automatically updates statistics after a specific number of row modifications. The update is performed in the context of the actual transaction and thus increases the response time of the triggering statement. The distribution of the table contents is calculated based on a sample of rows. It does not lock the affected table, so other queries can continue to access it.

Statistic maintenance causes overhead, mostly in the form of additional I/O requests to collect the sample data, but this cost is usually outweighed by the improved query plans and response times that accurate data distribution statistics make possible. Automatically updated statistics are recommended unless a system is already experiencing a severe I/O bottleneck.

You can switch automatic update of statistics on or off with the Transact-SQL statement:

```
sp_dboption 'database', 'auto update statistics', 'value'
go
```

where *database* is the actual name of the database and *value* is **true**, **false**, **on**, or **off**.

You can switch statistics collection on or off at the table level with the command:

```
sp_autostats 'table_name', 'value', 'index_name'
go
```

where *table_name* is the name of the table, *value* is **on** or **off**, and *index_name* is the name of the index or column on which to collect the statistics.

Even with a huge database, Black Dinosaur Oil Co. updated statistics automatically under SQL Server 7.0 and never experienced bottlenecks or unacceptable delays.

File Setup

SAP R/3 consists of many tables (the number depends on the SAP modules installed) so to insure optimal SAP throughput you must size and place the database files correctly. This process is explained in Chapter 6, "Building the Physical Data Model."

Data Files

Although SQL Server 7.0 now supports filegroups, SAP does not: a SAP installation uses only one group containing all files.

Rule of thumb: spread the I/O requests by using at least three different data files per production database. Place the files on different partitions so that file names contain different drive letters. If SQL Server has to access all partitions for a query or transaction, it generates I/O requests for these files in parallel.

SQL Server uses a proportional fill strategy across all the files within each filegroup, writing an amount of data proportional to the free space in the file and allowing the new file starts to be used immediately. This tends to fill all files at about the same time. And concurrent I/O requests are handled optimally if the partitions on which the files are located are accessed by different disk controllers.

SAP R/3 releases 4.0B and 4.5A automatically install three files in the default filegroup.

Autogrowth and Proportional Fill

SQL Server 7.0 now supports autogrowth and autoshrinking of data files and transaction log files. A default SAP installation exploits the default behavior of automatically growing files.

However, proportional fill of data files stops working once a data file fills up and must be extended (see Chapter 6, "Building the Physical Data Model"). When a disk is used for other purposes, autogrowth can lead to fragmentation if the next few disk blocks are already in use and the extension must be placed elsewhere.

For these reasons, you should start with a reasonable size for data files so that autogrowth does not occur from the beginning. Observe the fill rate and the amount of fragmentation before deciding on a strategy. Use Windows Explorer to check the fill rate of the disk or partition. Select a drive letter, right-click on it, and select **Properties**. The resulting diagram shows the used and the free space on the disk or partition.

To check the fill rate within a database, execute the stored procedure **sp_spaceused** from Query Analyzer, ISQL, or OSQL. The output looks like this:

```
database            database size        unallocated space
----------------    ------------------   ------------------
cedb                5.06 MB              3.03 MB

(1 row(s) affected)

reserved            data                 index size           unused
----------------    ------------------   ------------------   ---------------
2080 KB             1088 KB              864 KB               128 KB

(1 row(s) affected)
```

The first block shows the name of the database, its actual size, and its amount of unused space. The second block displays the used space as *reserved* and divides it up into the amounts used for tables (*data*) and indexes. The last number contains the unused space within the reserved area.

You can also check fragmentation with the Transact-SQL statement DBCC SHOWCONTIG, which produces this kind of output:

```
DBCC SHOWCONTIG scanning 'test' table...
[SHOW_CONTIG - SCAN ANALYSIS
----------------------------------------------------------------------
Table: 'test' (117575457)  Indid: 1  dbid:7
TABLE level scan performed.
- Pages Scanned................................: 78
- Extents Scanned.............................: 11
- Extent Switches.............................: 10
- Avg. Pages per Extent.......................: 7.1
- Scan Density [Best Count:Actual Count].......: 90.91% [10:11]
- Logical Scan Fragmentation ..................: 0.00%
- Extent Scan Fragmentation ...................: 18.18%
- Avg. Bytes free per page....................: 45.4
- Avg. Page density (full)....................: 99.44%

(11 row(s) affected)

DBCC execution completed. If DBCC printed error messages, contact your
system administrator.
```

The first value to assess is the scan density. It is 100 (percent) if everything is contiguous, less if there is fragmentation. To increase scan density, rebuild the index with the statement

```
CREATE [UNIQUE] [CLUSTERED | NONCLUSTERED]
INDEX index_name ON table (column [,...n])
[WITH
[PAD_INDEX]
[[,] FILLFACTOR = fillfactor]
[[,] IGNORE_DUP_KEY]
[[,] DROP_EXISTING]
[[,] STATISTICS_NORECOMPUTE]
]
[ON filegroup]
```

Database Size

SAP database space requirements are smaller under SQL Server 7.0 than they were for SQL Server 6.5. There are three reasons: SQL Server 7.0 can store more than just one **image**, **text**, or **ntext** field per data page, it allows **varchar** to be up to 8000 characters long (so SAP has been able to change the data type of some columns from **text** to **varchar**), and its 8-KB page size reduces space requirements for some indexes.

SQL Server 7.0 accesses **tempdb** more often than SQL Server 6.5 did. This improves response times because the query processor can now evaluate joins with hash strategies, but it requires extra disk space because the generated hash table is stored in **tempdb**. Because **tempdb** is accessed more frequently, you should place **tempdb** files (data file and its transaction log file) on separate disks with a separate controller to keep performance levels high.

Transaction Log Files

Transaction log files are associated with the individual databases. Configure them to grow automatically so they can store the information of ongoing transactions, but make sure to allot them sufficient disk space to grow with long batch jobs or client copies.

During transactions, database data files are read from and written to, and the transaction logs are written in parallel to the transaction log files. If there is a media failure, you must have either the data files or the log files to recover the database, so you should store them on different disks.

Organize disks to reflect the fact that transaction log files normally are only *read* for backups or to perform transaction ROLLBACKs, but they are frequently *written* to. If you use RAID systems to store the transaction log files, do not use RAID level 5, which supports automatic recovery on failures of a single disk at the cost of a reduced throughput for I/O writes. Use RAID level 1, which writes all data onto two independent disks. It has higher space requirements than RAID level 5, but offers a better throughput on writing I/Os. You can also use RAID level 0, which stripes data over several disks.

Back up transaction log files regularly to prevent them from growing indefinitely. Backup interval depends on transaction frequency and is generally in the range of 10 minutes to 4 hours. Black Dinosaur Oil Co. and MS Sales set an interval of 15 minutes.

In some systems you can truncate log files on every checkpoint to free up space, but you cannot do this in a production database because committed transactions are saved with the transaction log backup and you need all of them to restore a database from a backup. The default configuration disables truncation.

Buffer Pool Size

By default, SQL Server grabs all available main memory except for 5 MB. This is optimal for computers running only the database server, but it does not leave enough memory to run other applications on the same computer.

To allocate memory for SQL Server, you have to decide where to locate the main SAP components. You can distribute:

- The database server itself
- The SAP update instances (middle-tier application servers performing the transactions asynchronously to SAP clients)
- The SAP application servers executing the queries and the application logic for the SAP clients

Depending on the SAP R/3 installation type, the database server computer may or may not run some of these components.

To break down the available memory for each components, consider these scenarios (examined in detail in the following section):

- The computer is dedicated to the database server
- The computer runs the database server and the SAP update processes
- The computer serves as the only central system for the SAP installation

Scenarios

Scenario 1: Dedicated Database Server

Large SAP installations dedicate a computer to SQL Server, running update instances and application servers on different computers. This offers the best performance and obviates the need to configure memory usage—SQL Server by default optimizes use of the available memory.

Scenario 2: Database Server with Update Instance

Smaller SAP installations run the database server and the update instances on the same computer.

You must configure available memory to support these components or SQL Server will grab it all, limiting the memory available to the update instances (which have high paging activity) and decreasing throughput. SQL Server frees some memory if availability becomes low, but when SQL Server memory shrinks and grows the cache cannot achieve an optimal hit ratio. All of which means you must limit the maximum memory available to SQL Server. The recommendation based on SAP's experience is to limit it to 65% of the physical memory.

On the other hand, the memory for SQL Server should always be large enough to provide a suitable cache. If it is reduced too far, the cache hit ratio decreases, forcing SQL Server to perform more disk I/Os which in turn increases application response times and the transaction queue on the update instances. All of which means you must define a minimum memory allotment for SQL Server. A good value is 40%.

Settings for a computer with 2 GB of physical memory.

Configuration option	Percentage	Value	Transact-SQL statement
Maximum memory for SQL Server	65%	1300	sp_configure 'max server memory', 1300
Minimum memory for SQL Server	40%	800	sp_configure 'min server memory', 800

Scenario 3: Central System

Very small SAP installations use only one computer as a server. It has to run the database system, the update processes, and the application servers. A single computer can handle these functions if it serves a small number of clients.

This requires configuring maximum and minimum SQL Server memory allotments. The maximum prevents SQL Server from grabbing all available memory, which would force components into high paging rates. The minimum guarantees that SQL Server will have enough memory—most of which it will use as the database cache, thereby reducing the I/O volume.

Settings for a computer with 2 GB of physical memory.

Configuration option	Percentage	Value	Trans-SQL statement
Maximum memory for SQL server	45%	900	sp_configure 'max server memory', 900
Minimum memory for SQL server	45%	900	sp_configure 'min server memory', 900

Number of SAP Update Processes

A SAP installation has dedicated update processes that perform data manipulation. Applications send transaction requests to these processes asynchronously, where they are collected, queued, and executed against the database. If a transaction fails for any reason, the application is informed and the user can try it again. Obviously, transaction queue length depends on transaction complexity and server performance. It also depends on the number of update processes serving the transaction queue.

SQL Server 6.5 could lock only individual pages. Since a page consists of several records, SQL Server 6.5 sometimes locked records unnecessarily, and running more than one update process could result in a deadlock if the records being manipulated resided on the same page. SQL Server 7.0 can lock individual records, which significantly reduces deadlocks. Normally, records are worked on by only one user, and that can now be done without causing concurrency problems with other users.

If you migrate from SQL Server 6.5 to SQL Server 7.0, you should increase the number of update processes. MS Sales increased them to 6 and did not experience unacceptable deadlock rates. For testing purposes they increased the number as high as 10 without having any deadlocks in various batch scenarios running against these update processes.

You can specify the number of locks SQL Server can allocate by setting the **locks** option, although it is recommended that you leave it set to 0 so that SQL Server decides how many locks to use. It is an advanced option (not available in SQL Server Enterprise Manager) and to set it you must use ISQL, OSQL, or Query Analyzer to execute this sequence of Transact-SQL statements:

```
sp_configure 'show advanced options', 1
go
reconfigure
go
sp_configure 'locks', 0
go
reconfigure with override
go
```

Complete list of configuration recommendations and SAP recommendations for SQL Server setup.

Parameter	Default value	Recommended value	Comment
Allow updates	0	1	
Index create memory	12000	1216	
Locks	0	5000	
Max sync I/O	32	up to 255	For very efficient hard disks
Max server memory	0	see above	
Min server memory	0	see above	
Network packet size	4096	8192	
Open objects	500	0	Lets SQL Server handle any amount of open objects
Set working set size	0	1	Locks virtual memory into physical memory

Database options.

Parameter	Default value	Recommended value	Comment
Auto create statistics	ON	ON	Unless you experience severe I/O bottlenecks
Auto update statistics	ON	ON	Unless you experience severe I/O bottlenecks
ANSI Nulls	OFF	ON	*Column* = NULL always returns NULL; required for some WHERE conditions to return correct results
Select into/bulkcopy	OFF	OFF	To log all data manipulation operations

Configuration: Example Large SAP Installation on SQL Server 7.0

For an example, what more natural place to turn than Microsoft, which runs a large SAP installation on SQL Server 7.0. This section outlines the implementation of SAP R/3 on SQL Server 7.0 and compares it to a previous implementation on SQL Server 6.5.

SAP Modules

SAP divides its whole system into components (called **modules**) that you can purchase and install separately. The sales division of Microsoft currently uses:

Module	Description
SD	Sales and distribution
MM	Material management
FI	Financial accounting
CO	Controlling
AM	Assets management
HR	Human resources

Hardware Environment

The SAP environment consists of a single database server on a Compaq ProLiant 7000 with 4 PentiumPros at 200 MHz and 3 GB of main memory. The database requires about 100 GB of disk space. An identical computer serves as warm backup.

The application servers run on 16 computers, each with 4 processors at 133 – 200 MHz and 512 MB – 1 GB main memory.

Backup Strategy

The first level of backup is to keep the warm backup database server in sync by shipping the transaction log files to it and applying them on the backup database every 10 minutes. The second level consists of a nightly database backup to a DLT tape array. The tapes are stored off site.

Maintenance Tasks

Scheduled maintenance tasks.

Maintenance task	Frequency	Remarks
DBCC Checkdb	Twice/week	No corruption detected since migration to SQL Server 7.0
Update statistics	Once/week	Not done automatically; based on sample or whole table contents depending on the table size
Table growth and fragmentation monitoring	Once/week	
Checking free disk space	Once/week	
Monitoring deadlocks	Once/week	
Monitoring number of outstanding updates	Once/week	

System Load and Response Times

The SAP installation currently has about 2000 users, about 600 concurrent users around noon every day. The average response times for interactive dialogs used to be about 1.5 seconds. Because there was only one update process in the SQL Server 6.5 implementation, its response time increased from below 2 seconds in September 1997 to over 7 seconds in July 1998. Now, SQL Server 7.0 runs six update processes in parallel, reducing response times significantly.

Results of migrating to SQL Server 7.0.

Topic	SQL Server 6.5	SQL Server 7.0	Comment
Database size	130 GB	85 GB	Mostly because several image or text fields are stored on the same page
Average response time of interactive queries	1.25 seconds	.92 seconds	
Average response times of transactions	4.7 seconds	1.3 seconds	Because 6 update processes run in parallel
Backup duration	3.5 hours	45 minutes	
DBCC duration	over 100 hours	8.5 hours	No longer necessary

CHAPTER 6

Building the Physical Data Model

By Christopher Etz, g&h Database Technologies GmbH

The more thorough the planning, the better the system works. That is almost always true, but it becomes more meaningful as systems become more complex. Very large database (VLDB) solutions are created to enable high-performance querying and reporting that effectively use huge amounts of data, and their planning requirements are correspondingly large. This chapter looks at basic planning for the physical data model, beginning with the general process and moving quickly into specific considerations, calculations, and examples. Of particular interest is the extended discussion of table and index planning. These elements form the core of a VLDB solution, the overall effectiveness of which is determined by how thoroughly and intelligently you plan before you build.

The Solution in Focus

This chapter discusses basic planning considerations for VLDB physical data design. After some introductory remarks on fundamental modeling concepts, it dives into the specifics of physical design, concentrating on designing the basic components: databases, files/filegroups, tables, and indexes. Along the way, it discusses functionality, shows how to estimate or calculate space requirements, uses examples drawn from actual cases, and provides recommendations for informed decision making.

All the information in this chapter (and the others in this section) is drawn from the experiences of companies that have implemented VLDBs using SQL Server 7.0 as recorded by Microsoft Consulting Services. It has been combined into case studies under the fictional names of Broadband Cable Communications, Bound Galley Book Cellars, and others. Taken together, these chapters discuss the challenges of VLDB solutions from preliminary design to fine-tuning the system in the production environment, providing examples, explanation, and field-tested recommendations.

What You'll Find in This Chapter

- Explanation of the three phases of data modeling: conceptual, logical, and physical.

- How to translate the logical model to the physical.

- Explanations of how to define files and filegroups, how to organize and place them.

- How to plan tables: calculating space requirements, partitioning schemes, selectivity.

- How to plan indexes: calculating space and performance, clustered vs. nonclustered.

- Performance considerations and recommendations based on field observation.

Data Modeling

Data modeling is the design process phase that creates an efficient, final database schema that satisfies user requirements. Obviously, this process can be long and involved, so it is normally divided into three stages:

- Conceptual data model
- Logical data model
- Physical data model

The next three sections describe how to achieve the schema. For detailed information on how to document a VLDB design, see Chapter 4 "VLDB Issues at Broadband Cable Communications."

Conceptual Data Model

The conceptual data model deals with entities and relations.

Entities represent the pieces of information to store in the database; they correspond to the real-world objects to be modeled. Entity **attributes** are atomic pieces of information, even if they are subdivided on other design levels. For example, the entity *customer* may have attributes such as *name*, *address*, on so forth, and even if the address attribute is subdivided into *street*, *town*, *zip code*, etc., it still is considered atomic.

Relations represent object correspondence or interdependence. There are four basic types.

Relation types.

Relation type	Description	Notation
One-to-one	Every entity of the entity class A corresponds to one entity of the class B and vice versa.	
One-to-many	Every entity of the entity class A may correspond to several entities of the class B, but every entity of B can correspond to only one entity of A.	

Relation type	Description	Notation
Many-to-many	Every entity of the entity class A may correspond to several entities of the class B and vice versa.	
Superclass-subclass	Every entity of the superclass A corresponds to exactly one entity of one of the subclasses B, C or D. The relations are mutually exclusive.	

On each side, relations can be **mandatory** (there must be a corresponding entity) or **optional** (there does not need to be a corresponding entity). Mandatory relations are represented by a small bar, optional relations by a small circle.

For example, a customer may or may not have one or more addresses, but any address in a given data model must belong to a customer: So the customer-address relation is one-to-many and optional, and the address-customer relation is many-to-one, mandatory. The notation is:

Figure 6.1   Mandatory and optional relations.

Entities and relations are the common terms when designing a relational database. Entities can also be called **object classes**.

The conceptual data model specifies all entities to be represented in the database, their most important attributes, and the relations (including type, and whether they are optional or mandatory).

Logical Data Model

The logical data model deals with the possibilities of a relational database. It converts the conceptual data model's entities into tables and its attributes into columns. It specifies the tables to be created in the database, all their columns, and all columns' data types. Relations are converted depending on their type. Many-to-many relations and relations that are optional on both sides are converted into (mapping) tables. All other relations become foreign keys in one of the tables.

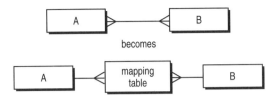

Figure 6.2   Mapping relations.

Physical Data Model

The physical data model deals with database system (Microsoft SQL Server version 7.0) features. It takes the tables and columns from the logical data model and adds storage-specific information and other performance features. It specifies the tables and their assignment to filegroups (placement), the columns and their data types and constraints, the indexes and their type (clustered or nonclustered) including fillfactors etc., and other database objects such as views, stored procedures, and triggers.

The logical model describes the tables in general; the physical data model takes into account the requirements for throughput and response times of queries and transactions. It adapts the logical data model to meet the performance requirements.

The result of a physical data model can be a Transact-SQL script containing all the statements to create the whole database with its objects—tables, columns, constraints, indexes, stored procedures, triggers, and so on.

From Logical to Physical Data Model

The logical data model results in tables and relationships between them. Once the logical design is complete, the next step is to plan the physical layout of the database or databases (the physical data model).

The physical data model describes the layout and placement of objects:

- **Databases.** The number of databases to use for the data, their names and placement
- **Files and filegroups.** The database's data files and transaction log files. Data files can be arranged in filegroups, which offers a way to control table and index placement.
- **Tables.** The structure of the tables, including their columns and data types.
- **Indexes.** The physical accesses to the data defining the achievable response times within the database.

The next section describes the physical data model design considerations and experiences of the companies referred to in these chapters.

Planning Databases

The first step in planning the physical data model is to consider the three types of databases involved in the application:

- The **master** database
- One or more application databases
- Temporary database (**tempdb**)

Other databases may be needed for replication, etc., but these three types are always present.

The master Database

Every installation of SQL Server has a **master** database in which is stored the system catalogs describing all databases, users, configuration settings, system stored procedures, etc. The master database is used by SQL Server internally—even by sessions that are connected to other databases—and it must always be accessible. Because of these demands, it is highly recommended that the master database never be used for any application database objects.

Application Database

Data belonging to the application is stored in one or more databases. Though tables of all databases can be used in queries, there is generally no need to separate the data into different databases. In rare instances when database tables have totally different access patterns, it may be beneficial to put them in separate databases, but as a rule it is preferable to use files and filegroups to define table placement.

To find out if tables have disparate access patterns, ask these questions:

- Is there a subset of tables serving a different purpose than the others? For example, are users and access administered by an application instead of through SQL Server?
- Are there tables with static contents that you want to put in a read-only database? For example, tables of messages in different languages to be read by the application.
- Are there user groups that do not need to share any data?

■ Do you plan to separate the online transactional processing (OLTP) part of the database from the reporting part? Tables used by reports typically are filled or updated regularly by a batch job (nightly, weekly, etc.). If the reports use only certain tables, you can separate them into different databases. If you are running SQL Server on a cluster, you can run the reports on a different machine than the OLTP database to spread CPU use over both machines. If there is a failure, both databases would then be served by the same computer running SQL Server.

Bound Galley Book Cellars uses a similar approach, but goes even further, running a complete, separate cluster for reporting purposes. The batch job for updating the report database uses a network connection to transfer the data.

In OLTP environments, applications are often contained in a single production database. Of the companies referred to in these chapters, Bound Galley Book Cellars and Black Dinosaur Oil Co. run typical OLTP applications, storing all OLTP tables in a single database. A&G Phone puts data for determining access rights into a separate database, to meet high, specific security requirements. SQL Server allows you to grant privileges on stored procedures, tables, views and their columns, but A&G Phone needed to specify access rights on application dialogs and on specific records. To accomplish this level of control, they set up their own privilege system within the application server, and stored the data describing access rights in a separate database.

In data warehouse environments, it is common to separate data into different databases because different user groups typically run their own sets of reports and use different drilling methods. To support different access patterns, data is often stored redundantly in separate databases, often with different data models. In general, report requirements lead to pre-aggregated facts, which can be used as a common basis for several reports. These aggregated facts and the participating dimensions form the datamarts.

Separated datamarts are used at James Wilkie Publishing, Broadband Cable Communications, and MSSales. See Chapter 10 "MS Sales Data Warehouse" for a description of this solution.

Temporary Database

Temporary database objects are created explicitly by CREATE statements or implicitly by execution of a query. They are stored in the temporary database (**tempdb**). All complex queries require a certain amount of space in the temporary database because they build intermediate result sets that are used in later stages of the query. Typical cases are sorts and hash joins. SQL Server 7.0 has several algorithms to perform a join of two or more tables. The hash join, for instance, is efficient when several records match the search condition, and it stores the hash table in **tempdb**.

To achieve optimal response times on complex queries you have to take special care when creating **tempdb** so that it can handle its high volume of reads and writes. To optimize I/O throughput:

- Place **tempdb** on its own disk to eliminate competition with I/O requests to other database objects.

- Use a fast disk (short latency, high bandwidth connection). If you use RAID, avoid RAID level 5 for **tempdb**—it reduces throughput on write requests. Instead, use RAID level 0 (striping), optionally in combination with RAID level 1 (mirroring).

- Consider dedicating a disk controller to the **tempdb** disk.

The space requirements for **tempdb** depend on the number of concurrently executed queries and the amount of data they have to work on; **tempdb** use can vary, and you can provide for this by allowing **tempdb** to expand automatically as needed. If a query generates larger than expected intermediate result sets, automatic expansion prevents the query from terminating unsuccessfully. Frequent expansion can affect system performance, so the first tactic should be to create a **tempdb** sized to handle normal operations.

To find a reasonable **tempdb** size:

- Multiply the largest amount of temporary disk space used by any query by the number of concurrently running database connections.

- Monitor **tempdb** size in the first production phase and adjust it until you avoid expansion. (There might be some minor expansion while it is not being monitored; use this method to prevent significant expansion.)

To monitor the size of the temporary database, use this sequence of Transact-SQL statements in the Query Analyzer (or any other tool that allows you to execute arbitrary SQL statements):

```
use tempdb
go
sp_space_used
go
```

The output looks like this:

database_name	database_size	unallocated space
tempdb	8.50 MB	7.98 MB

(1 row(s) affected)

reserved	data	index_size	unused
536 KB	240 KB	384 KB	-88 KB

(1 row(s) affected)

The first block shows the database name (**tempdb**), the actual size of the database (8.50 MB), and the amount of currently unallocated space (7.98 MB).

Both approaches have advantages and disadvantages. Estimating an upper limit for **tempdb** avoids any expansion, but the space you reserve might never be used. This can happen if the query you measure to find the highest space consumption is a report that runs only rarely (such as nightly) and never in parallel. If you monitor **tempdb** size, you see its actual size, but only at one moment in time—this is only a snapshot.

The best practice is to combine approaches: estimate the space requirements for a large complex query, multiply by an estimated number of concurrent executions, size the initial disk space for the temporary database, then monitor real use and adjust the size. Sizing during initial production will require a lot of monitoring to compare estimates with real use.

Replication

You have to run replication, so you also have to estimate space for replica databases. Many backup plans simplify this by replicating the production database to a second machine. In the event of a failure, you can switch instantly to the replica and continue operations instead of taking time to recover the production database from a tape or disk backup. There are two basic ways to replicate the production database:

- Conventional replication between SQL Server databases, as described in Chapter 13. You can select tables or parts of tables in this method.
- Replication by backing up the transaction log file, moving it to the second machine, and applying it on the replica ("log shipping"). This requires that the production and replica databases be structured identically.

Most of the companies referred to in these chapters use log shipping as one level in their backup and recovery method. This entails minimum overhead and the log files have to be backed up regularly anyway. It does impose some activity on the production database (copying the archived log files to the replication machine) and does not capture transactions that occurred during the last backup interval.

Planning Files and Filegroups

After considering which and how many databases to use, the next step is to plan their data and log files. Data files can be organized into filegroups so that you can more specifically control the placement of database objects (tables and indexes).

Raw Devices

For creating database files, SQL Server supports the use of **raw partitions**—disk partitions that are formatted only on the low level, but do not have a Windows NT file system, such as FAT and NTFS. When creating a database file on a raw partition, you specify only the drive letter assigned to it; you do not specify a file name because there is no file system.

Raw partitions impose several limitations:

- You can create only one database file on each raw partition. The logical partition must be configured as a single database file because there is no file system on the raw partition.

- You cannot perform normal file system operations such as copy, move, and delete.

- You cannot back up database files located on raw partitions with the Windows NT Backup utility, although you can still create SQL Server database or transaction log backups.

- You cannot configure automatic expansion for database files. Create the files at their full size.

- You have to use lettered partitions (such as E:) not numbered devices.

- You cannot take advantage of file system services such as bad block replacement.

Raw partitions can yield a slight performance gain over NTFS or FAT, because they eliminate file system overhead, but you can usually tune performance as well and more easily by reviewing indexes or data placement, so for most installations the preferred method is to use files created on NTFS or FAT partitions. Raw devices would help avoid any file system failures (bugs) or limitations, but currently there aren't any that are severe enough to compel you to use raw devices.

None of the companies referred to in these chapters use raw devices, even though they are running extremely large databases with high I/O volumes.

Data Files

Every database contains at least one data file, and often many. Assigning them to filegroups helps you specify table placement, but consider the individual data files before you consider filegroups.

Names and Location

While there are no restrictions on data file location in the directory trees, nor on names or extensions, you should follow some guidelines:

- Place data files on a uniform level within the directory tree. For example:

  drive:\Mssql7\Data

- Construct the file name from the database name, an identification of the filegroup, and a sequential number. For example:

  dbname_filegroup_n, where *n* = 1, ...

- Use consistent extensions:

Extension	File type
.MDF	Data files of the primary filegroup
.NDF	Data files of the secondary filegroup
.LDF	Transaction log files

A database can have only one primary filegroup; this is where the database system tables are stored. All other filegroups are secondary. You can put user tables in any filegroup.

Don't create too many data files. Normally, you should have one data file per disk or partition (drive letter). It should be as large as you need or as large as the disk space allows.

Growth and Shrinkage

You can configure the data and log files of a SQL Server installation to grow or shrink automatically as their contents require more or less disk space. You can specify growth to occur in chunks of a specific size or as percentages (the default).

Growth can lead to disk fragmentation: if the file shares a disk or partition with other growing files, chunks of files probably will become intermixed. This raises the risk of fragmentation if they grow in different chunk sizes, and raises it more if files are also allowed to shrink.

Some recommendations:

- If you use automatic file growth, impose a uniform chunk size for all files on the same disk or partition. Don't use percentage growth factors.

- Avoid automatic shrinkage: it is more useful in desktop environments than in VLDB environments.

■ With or without file growth, the database administrator must monitor the remaining free disk space, either within the fixed-size data files or on the file system.

The companies referred to in these chapters differed in their approach to automatic file growth. A&G Phone and Broadband Cable use autogrowth, but use absolute increments to avoid file system fragmentation. Others use fixed-size files and monitor space, increasing files manually, if necessary. Some monitor used space with the stored procedure **sp_spaceused** (see example above) and set a growth increment by examining database size and the insertion rate of new records. If they expect the database to shrink again, they use a fixed size for all increments on the same file system to reduce the probability of fragmentation.

Parallel I/O Requests

You can set up the number and location of the data files to enable parallel execution of I/O requests. SQL Server uses drive letters to select I/O requests that can be executed in parallel, so the presence of different drive letters clears I/O requests for simultaneous execution. A&G Phone, for instance, uses separate filegroups for tables and indexes that are frequently used together in joins, so that SQL Server can read all data sources for a query in parallel.

Log Files

Every database has at least one transaction log file, which stores information on ongoing transactions. This file is not read during normal ongoing operations, but it is needed for:

■ Transaction rollback, both explicit (using the ROLLBACK statement) or implicit (due to errors, constraint violations, deadlocks, etc., that can happen during execution of SQL statements).

■ Recovery after a database backup has been read from the backup medium. The file re-executes all transactions that have been committed since the time of the database backup.

The transaction log file experiences a lot of I/Os while recording transactions and it is crucial to recovery. To satisfy its security and performance requirements, you must consider its placement carefully.

Placement: Security Restrictions

A transaction log file must never share any disks with the database it belongs to: if that disk fails, both the database and the transaction log file are lost. Even if you could recover the database from a backup, you would have no way to apply all committed transaction if the transaction log file (or parts of it) are lost. The database and its transaction log file(s) must never have any disks in common.

The transaction log files always belong to one database, so you *can* place the transaction log file for one database on the same disks as the data files for another database. This is even good practice for spreading I/O load over all disks if you have multiple databases with similar loads. You can place database X data files on disk set A and the log file on disk set B; for database Y, put the data files on disk set B and the log file on disk set A.

A&G Phone separated tables into two databases, because they use a security database to administer users and privileges and the production database for all other tables. Security database data files reside on the same disks as the transaction log files of the production database; the security database transaction log file resides on the least active disk of the production database.

Placement: Performance Restrictions

The transaction log file usually is written serially as transactions proceed, so it is best if the disk head stays in place for the next write operation. For this reason, separating transaction log and data files has performance as well as security implications. To minimize impact from other activities, use a separate, dedicated disk for the transaction log file.

Growth and Shrinkage

Like the data files, the transaction log file can grow and shrink during normal operations. This might lead to fragmentation on the disk or partition, but it can help performance by allowing the transaction log file to expand so that transactions can continue if the original allotment fills up.

Performance considerations for the size and growth of the transaction log:

- Create a transaction log file of "reasonable" size to prevent automatic expansion. You can monitor performance and use your knowledge of system activity to estimate a size. Frequent expansion affects performance because no writes are made to the transaction log while the expansion creates a virtual log file.

- Set a reasonable growth increment to make sure the file grows enough. If it grows too little to accommodate the number of log records being written to it, it will expand frequently, affecting performance.

- Set a uniform chunk size for file growth to reduce disk fragmentation; avoid setting a growth percentage.

- If you find that the log is too big, reduce it manually rather than letting SQL Server size it automatically, which can hurt a busy system's performance with page moves and locking.

For peak performance, dedicate a disk and configure the log file to take all of it. This eliminates the need to create a strategy for automatic growth configuration. The companies referred to in these chapters all keep their production database transaction log files on dedicated disk sets of their RAID systems. They use the whole file system for their transaction log files and never shrink them. Shrinking files to save disk space can be worthwhile with desktop systems but usually is not worth it in large OLTP databases.

Filegroups

Filegroups are collections of data files that specify table and index location. Every database has one primary filegroup (the system catalogs are stored in it). If no other filegroup is specified, the primary filegroup becomes the default filegroup (where tables and indexes are located).

You can create secondary filegroups (MultiForm Industries found an undocumented, hard-wired limit of 256) and create tables and indexes in them. You can denote one of the secondaries as the default filegroup for the database (in which case the previous default loses its status as *primary*).

Some general recommendations for files and filegroups:

- If you use multiple files, create one or more secondary filegroups for the additional files and make that filegroup the default. Use the primary file to contain only system tables and objects.

- To maximize performance, create files or filegroups on as many different physical disks as possible, and place objects that compete heavily for space in different filegroups.

- Use filegroups to place objects on specific physical disks.

- Place different tables used in the same join queries in different filegroups. This improves performance by allowing parallel disk I/O searches for joined data.

- Place heavily accessed tables and their nonclustered indexes on different filegroups. This improves performance by allowing parallel I/O if the files are on different physical disks.

Here is a process for following these recommendations:

1. Write the most important tables and indexes on separate cards.
2. Group the cards that contain tables and indexes most frequently used in joins.
3. Put big tables in separate groups from small tables and nonclustered indexes.
4. Try to have as few groups as possible.
5. Count the number of disks to be used for data files. This is the maximum number of filegroups.
6. If you have more groups than disks, start again and put more tables in the groups.

7. If you have fewer groups than disks, you can define filegroups with more than one data file, thereby spreading tables over more than one disk:

   a) Assign a disk to every group.

   b) Go through the groups with the big tables and assign the remaining disks to these filegroups. This spreads I/O requests and offers the best performance.

Proportional Fill

When tables or indexes grow, new space must be allocated. Space allocation does not happen page by page with 8-KB pages, but by **extents** (8 coherent pages). Tables smaller than 8 pages (64 KB) are placed in mixed extents (with other small tables). Tables 8 pages or larger have uniform extents (the entire extent belongs to only one table).

Filegroups determine which data file to allocate extents from. This enables proportional filling: as data is written to a filegroup, SQL Server writes an amount proportional to the free space in the file to each file within the filegroup, rather than filling the first file then writing to the next. If the filegroup consists of several data files of the same size, every table in the filegroup is uniformly spread across all files. This optimizes performance on heavily used tables by spreading I/O requests over all participating disks.

Filegroups can contain different numbers of files. You can spread any large and central tables over several disks, and keep the contents of small tables together by putting them in a filegroup containing only one file.

Impacts If Several Data Files Are in One Filegroup

A&G Phone found that the autogrowth feature does not work on filegroups with more than one data file.

As long as all data files belonging to a filegroup have free space, the proportional fill works perfectly, spreading tables uniformly over the files. But when one file fills up, it is the only one extended. All further inserted data goes only into the most recently enlarged file until it fills up again, then the next data file is enlarged and all insertions go into it. This concentrates insertions into one file. One central table in the A&G Phone database stores incoming activation orders, and A&G Phone found that the response time of the order entry transactions increased considerably after the first data file filled up. This caused severe problems that harried them until they located the cause. To correct this situation, they defined all data files to be as large as possible, and disabled autogrowth.

So you should not allow autogrowth for the files of any filegroups that consist of more than one data file. If they tend to become full, extend them manually. More precisely, if you have filegroups with more than one data file, make the files large enough to prevent them from growing automatically. The Transact-SQL statement to prevent automatic growth of data files is:

```
ALTER DATABASE dbname MODIFY FILE (NAME = name, FILEGROWTH = 0)
Go
```

You can execute the statement with the Query Analyzer or any other tool that executes arbitrary SQL statements (OSQL, etc.).

Then, monitor the free space of each file of the filegroup by the Transact-SQL statement

```
DBCC SHRINKFILE ('name', size, NOTRUNCATE)
```

Use the actual size in MB to avoid any real shrinkage. The output of the command contains columns titled **CurrentSize** and **MinimumSize**. These tell you, respectively, how big the file is and how much space is used. If the minimum size approaches the current size, use this command to increase the files:

```
ALTER DATABASE dbname MODIFY FILE (NAME = name, SIZE = new_size)
```

goAdding Files

You can add individual files and filegroups to a database with the Transact-SQL statement ALTER DATABASE.

MultiForm Industries experienced a problem when adding files to a database currently in use. Adding a large data file to an existing database requires a considerable amount of time. During this time, the file is formatted (filled with internally needed information). Newly added files are registered in the database's system tables, during which the system table is locked and concurrently running transactions and queries cannot complete.

They found a workaround: add new files to the database at minimum size. The operation still issues the lock, but small files are added so quickly that concurrent transactions are not appreciably delayed. When the new file has been added, it is then enlarged to the required size. The enlargement takes as long as adding a large file, but it does not hold locks that delay transactions and queries.

The two steps in this workaround are:

1. Initially add a file of 1 MB:

   ```
   ALTER DATABASE dbname ADD FILE (NAME = logical_filename,
       FILENAME = 'physical_filename', SIZE = 1)
   Go
   ```

2. Expand to the desired size:

   ```
   ALTER DATABASE dbname MODIFY FILE (NAME = logical_filename,
       SIZE = required_size)
   ```

goAdministration

Besides specifying table and index placement, filegroups also help administration, so you should take your maintenance plan into account when you design the physical data model.

You can back up individual files, filegroups, or the whole database. It is best to back up a whole filegroup if it contains more than one file, because the tables will probably have parts in every data file belonging to the filegroup. But you don't always have to back up the whole database.

It can take hours to back up large databases to individual tapes or tape libraries. Even if you back up online, so that the database remains accessible to all applications, the process causes so much I/O that it might be acceptable only during a short backup window.

If the backup window is tight, you can reduce the backup to one filegroup per day, as shown below.

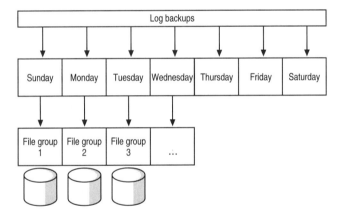

Figure 6.3   Backup window.

The diagram shows that each day the backup captures the transaction log files and one filegroup selected round-robin (filegroup 1 on Sunday, filegroup 2 on Monday, etc.). When the last filegroup has been backed up, the first filegroup is backed up on the next day.

Planning Tables

The most important point when planning the physical data model is the layout of the individual tables. Layouts are derived from the logical data model, but some further considerations are described in this section.

Nullability Considerations

Nullability is the ability of a column to store NULL values. Columns can be defined to contain NULL (WITH NULL) values or not (NOT NULL). The ANSI standard of SQL defines WITH NULL as the default. This has some impact on system design:

1. Each nullable column in a row requires an additional bit to store the information for a NULL value.

2. All predicates on these columns use a three-way logic (TRUE, FALSE, or NULL) which is more difficult to handle than two-way.

3. Empty strings and NULL values are evaluated differently and must be searched for separately.

Use nullable columns only if you need them (that is, the database system uses NULL to represent a special piece of information such as *not appropriate* or *unknown*). If your system has no such requirements, define columns NOT NULL.

When you convert the logical data model into a physical data model, reconsider which columns really need to store NULL values. Here are two examples:

- **Addresses.** A missing address can be represented by an empty string as easily as by NULL. Define the column NOT NULL.

- **Measurements.** In this column, any value can appear and represent a valid measurement, so NULL is the best way to represent a missing measurement, especially if information about missing measurements is to be stored. Define the column WITH NULL.

Calculating Space Requirements

When deciding which data types to use, you usually have to estimate the size of the resulting tables. The first step is to know the space requirements of the data types.

Space requirements by data type.

Data type	Bytes	Range	Remark
int	4	-2,147,483,648 to 2,147,483,647	
smallint	2	-32,768 to 32,767	
tinyint	1	0 to 255	
bit	1	0 or 1	

Data type	Bytes	Range	Remark
decimal[(p[,s)]] or numeric[(p[,s)]]	5, if $1 \leq p \leq 9$ 9, if $10 \leq p \leq 19$ 13, if $20 \leq p \leq 28$ 17, if $29 \leq p \leq 38$	$-(10^p-1)$ to 10^p-1	p specifies the precision and s the scale. The default precision is 28, unless SQL server is started with the flag /p, in which case it is 38. The default scale is 0.
money	8	approx. –922 billion to +922 billion with 4 decimal digits	
smallmoney	4	approx. –214,748 to 214,748 with 4 decimal digits	
float[(n)]	4, if $1 \leq n \leq 24$ 8, if $25 \leq n \leq 53$	approx. -10^{308} to 10^{308}	n is the number of bits used to store the mantissa. The default is 53.
double precision	8	approx. -10^{308} to 10^{308}	a synonym for float(53)
real	4	approx. -10^{38} to 10^{38}	a synonym for float(24)
datetime	8	January 1, 1753 to December 31, 9999 with a precision of milliseconds	
smalldatetime	4	January 1, 1900 to June 6, 2079 with a precision of minutes	
char(n)	n	$n \leq 8000$	1-byte characters
varchar(n)	$n + 2$	$n \leq 8000$	1-byte characters
text		up to 2,147,483,647 characters	1-byte characters
nchar(n)	$2n$	$n \leq 4000$	Unicode strings
nvarchar(n)	$2n + 2$	$n \leq 4000$	Unicode strings
ntext		up to 1,073,741,823 characters	Unicode strings
binary(n)	n	$n \leq 8000$	arbitrary binary contents
varbinary(n)	$n + 2$	$n \leq 8000$	arbitrary binary contents
image		up to 2,147,483,647 characters	arbitrary binary contents

The variable length data types **varchar**, **nvarchar**, and **varbinary** require two additional bytes to store the actual length of the value, but they require only enough space to store the actual value. If you know the average size of a data type, use it for n instead of the maximum size. For tables with variable-length columns you have to add two bytes to the record length.

The nullability information is stored in a bitmap and requires

$$2 + \left\lfloor \frac{n+7}{8} \right\rfloor$$

bytes, where n is the number of nullable columns. ($\lfloor ... \rfloor$ denotes the integer portion of the fraction, discarding any remainder.)

To calculate the space required by one row:

1. Calculate the space requirements for all columns depending on their data type as shown in the table above.
2. Add all column sizes.
3. Add two bytes if there are any variable-size data types in the table.
4. Add the number of bytes for the nullability information as described above.

The result is the number of bytes required for every row.

SQL Server 7.0 has 8-KB data pages; rows can use up to 8096 bytes. Each row requires two more bytes to store the offset where the row actually begins on the page. Thus, the number of rows per page is

$$\left\lfloor \frac{8096}{\text{row\_size} + 2} \right\rfloor$$

Finally, the number of pages is

$$\left\lceil \frac{\text{number\_of\_rows}}{\text{rows\_per\_pages}} \right\rceil$$

and the table size in bytes is 8192 × number_of_pages. ($\lceil \text{expression} \rceil$ denotes the smallest integer greater than or equal to the expression.)

Example: The Broadband Cable database stores addresses in a table.

Broadband Cable address-table columns.

Column	Type	Nullability	Description
AddressInst	**int**	IDENTITY	Primary key
CreateDate	**datetime**	NOT NULL	Date record was created
CreateUser	**varchar(30)**	NOT NULL	SQL server login that created record

Column	Type	Nullability	Description
ModifyDate	**datetime**	NOT NULL	Date record was updated
ModifyUser	**varchar(30)**	NOT NULL	SQL server login that updated record
CityPostalCodeInst	**int**	NOT NULL	FK: CityPostalCode
Address1	**varchar(40)**	NOT NULL	The first line of the address
Address2	**varchar(40)**	NULL	The second line of the address
Directions	**varchar(255)**	NULL	Step by step instructions on how to arrive at this address

The logins used in the columns *CreateUser* and *ModifyUser* average 10 bytes. The column *Address1* averages 20 bytes, *Address2* (which is not always filled) averages 10 bytes, and *Directions* (rarely filled) averages 20 bytes.

Size calculations.

Item	Used size	Variable size offset	Total size
Column AddressInst	4 bytes		4 bytes
Column CreateDate	8 bytes		8 bytes
Column CreateUser	10 bytes	2 bytes	12 bytes
Column ModifyDate	8 bytes		8 bytes
Column ModifyUser	10 bytes	2 bytes	12 bytes
Column CityPostalCodeInst	4 bytes		4 bytes
Column Address1	20 bytes	2 bytes	22 bytes
Column Address2	10 bytes	2 bytes	12 bytes
Column Directions	20 bytes	2 bytes	22 bytes
Sum of columns			104 bytes
Addition for variable size columns			2 bytes
Addition for nullable columns			3 bytes
Total sum per row			109 bytes

Rows require 109 bytes each. The number of rows fitting on one page is:

$$\left\lfloor \frac{8096}{row\_size + 2} \right\rfloor = \left\lfloor \frac{8096}{109 + 2} \right\rfloor = \left\lfloor \frac{8096}{111} \right\rfloor = \lfloor 72.9... \rfloor = 72$$

(An average of 72 rows fit on every page.)

Impact of Declarative Referential Integrity

The declarative referential integrity (DRI) is defined in the SQL-92 standard and is supported by SQL Server. When you are creating tables, it allows you to specify which columns of which tables are referenced by foreign keys. Referential integrity guarantees that the foreign keys reference existing rows.

The advantage of DRI is that you have to define these integrity constraints only once, typically when creating the tables. From then on, SQL Server ensures that the constraints are always met. Whenever an INSERT or UPDATE is performed against a table with such constraints, SQL Server checks for the referenced row. On DELETEs against the referenced table, it makes sure that the row is not referenced by any other table. The system performs these checks automatically, so you don't have to implement the process in application code.

For example, the table above has a column labeled *CityPostalCodeInst*, which is a foreign key to the table *CityPostalCode*. You can enforce DRI with the statement

```
ALTER TABLE Address ALTER COLUMN CityPostalCodeInst
CONSTRAINT fkCityPostalCode REFERENCES
CityPostalCode(CityPostalCodeInst)
```

Now every insertion into the table Address and every update on the column *CityPostalCodeInst* checks that the value of the column *CityPostalCodeInst* exists in the table *CityPostalCode*, and every deletion from the table *CityPostalCode* first checks to make sure the value is not referenced by the table *Address*.

Declarative referential integrity creates CPU overhead and I/Os for these checks, and this sometimes reduces throughput slightly (causing longer response times).

Some environments can avoid this overhead by ensuring data integrity through other means:

- Read-only databases where the check is part of the data load. From then on, no further data manipulation takes place and no constraints are needed.
- Applications with a defined data-manipulation layer, such as stored procedures or 3-tier architectures, where the checks are part of the data-manipulation layer. These applications do not execute any SQL statements directly on the database, so they do not need to be evaluated a second time.

The companies referred to in these chapters opted to avoid overhead by not using DRI. They had either read-only environments of data warehouses or datamarts, or a defined data-manipulation layer, where necessary checks were performed. In fact, most OLTP applications have such a layer, so declarative referential integrity checks are redundant.

Considering the Selectivity of Column Values

Once you know which columns belong to a table, you can still choose which values will be used to represent the information.

For example, at A&G Phone, orders for the activation of mobile telephone cards pass several status values. The order is entered (status: *entered*) then an employee starts to work on the order (status changes to: *working*). One step is to check the customer's credit using an external system (status changes to: *credit check*). Then the status is changed accordingly to *accepted* or *rejected*. Accepted orders are transferred to the rating system. While the transfer is pending, the status is set to *to be transferred*. Finally, the status is set to *completed*, until a batch job deletes the order from the system.

The order table has integer columns for the primary key, the status, and several other items. The first approach was to represent the most frequent status value by NULL so the column was created WITH NULL. The most frequent query on this table looks for a given status value other than NULL. In order to support this query, an index was defined on the status.

Status values index.

Status value	Description
NULL	Entered
1	Working
2	Credit check
3	Accepted
4	Rejected
5	To be transferred
6	Completed

The Transact-SQL statement to look for all orders waiting for the credit check is:

```
SELECT * FROM Orders WHERE Status = 2;
```

As the system was originally set up, the query engine did not to use the index, because the table statistics indicated that too many rows contained NULL values, even though the query was looking for a non-NULL value. So the query engine ignored the index and performed a full-table scan instead, which led to poor response times.

The problem was to find a way to fill the column to achieve better value selectivity. All meaningful status values are positive numbers, so a negative value could effectively represent any non-status value. The designers replaced the NULL value with negative values. The primary key contained only positive values, too, so they replaced the NULL values with the negated value of the primary key. This increased the selectivity of the column drastically.

You can see the differences in the table contents by comparing both approaches.

Boosting selectivity.

First approach				Second approach			
OrderID	Customer ID	Status	Further columns	OrderID	Customer ID	Status	Further columns
1	6511	NULL	...	1	6511	-1	...
2	73	NULL	...	2	73	-2	...
3	923	NULL	...	3	923	-3	...
4	838	2	...	4	838	2	...
5	9189	NULL	...	5	9189	-5	...
6	2945	NULL	...	6	2945	-6	...
7	73	6	...	7	73	6	...

The column *Status* has a secondary index in both cases.

In this new approach, the statistics contained the information that the column is highly selective because all rows that formerly contained a status value of NULL now contain unique values derived from the primary key. The statistics indicate to the query engine that the index is highly valuable, so it always uses it. Query response times decreased dramatically. There was no need to change the Transact-SQL statement.

Rule of thumb: look for a highly selective value (for example, one derived from the primary key) instead of the most frequent value (NULL in this example) if these arbitrarily inserted values can be distinguished from any other meaningful entry.

Temporary Tables

Sometimes applications have to create temporary tables. You can use normal tables for these instances, but then the application has to ensure that they are dropped at some point.

To fill this need, SQL Server creates temporary tables in the temporary database (**tempdb**) and gives them names prefixed by one or two hash signs (#) that determine how long they reside in **tempdb**.

SQL Server 7.0 temporary table characteristics.

Prefix	Description
#	A temporary table with this prefix exists only for the duration of a user session or the procedure that created it. It is automatically dropped when the user logs off or the procedure that created the table completes. No other users can share or access this table. Permissions cannot be granted or revoked on this table.
##	A temporary table with this prefix is a global temporary table. It also typically exists for the duration of a user session or procedure that created it, but it can be shared by multiple users. It is automatically dropped when the last user session referencing it disconnects. All other database users can access this table. Permissions cannot be granted or revoked on this table.

These prefixes simplify the handling of temporary tables by telling SQL Server that a table is temporary so it can drop them automatically. This simplifies application design and avoids situations in which an application loses its database connection because of network problems and cannot drop its temporary table.

Partitioning

When planning the physical data model, you also have to consider table partitioning. Tables can be partitioned vertically or horizontally.

Vertical partitioning separates columns logically belonging to one table into different physical tables, usually based on use: the most frequently used and small (narrow) columns go into one table, and the larger columns (such as remarks or other kinds of strings) go into another. The advantage is more compact storage of frequently used columns, which reduces I/Os on full-table scans and increases cache hit ratios. The disadvantage is overhead: when columns from both tables have to be read, a join is created between them. Only rarely is vertical partitioning worth its overhead. None of the companies referred to in these chapters partitioned any tables vertically.

Horizontal partitioning separates rows into different tables, usually based on one column's value: each partition holds the rows for a given range of values. For example, you can horizontally partition on product groups, geographical areas, etc.

The advantage is that you create smaller partitions compared to the whole table, which can accelerate all operations on the table if only one partition has to be accessed. INSERTs into indexed tables have to maintain the indexes, and as more rows appear in the table the index can fill. Then, index pages have to be split and the different branches of the index's B-tree may get different numbers of levels. The storage engine then re-balances the B-Tree, rearranging the index pages to equalize the numbers of levels on all branches. On smaller tables, a smaller B-tree has to be re-balanced, which is faster and causes less locking. If UPDATEs, DELETEs, or SELECTs have to be done by a full-table scan, fewer pages are read and examined. If they are supported by appropriate indexes, fewer index levels have to be passed. (For a deeper discussion of indexes see the "Planning Indexes" section, below. For more information on the internals of B-trees, refer to *indexes* in *Microsoft SQL Server Books Online*.)

However, if a query needs to search a row but does not know on which partition it is stored, it has to examine all tables. This leads to more SQL statements or (by the use of the UNION operator) to a more complex query. This disadvantage is acceptable if such statements are rare (if the partition to be searched is known in most cases).

For example, consider this section of a very large customer table:

Customer table section.

Region	CustomerID	Name	Further columns
North	3874	Smith	...
North	912733	Constanza	...
North	28461	Jones	...
North	9181	Rumplestiltzken	...
West	238947	deNiro	...
West	872	Vandelay	...

You can partition this table vertically into tables holding customers for only one region. If there are four regions (north, west, south, and east) there will be four tables, each with the same columns, and named *NorthernCustomers*, *WesternCustomers*, *SouthernCustomers*, and *EasternCustomers*.

To make sure insertions go into the appropriate region table, you can include constraints such as:

```
ALTER TABLE NorthernCustomers
     ADD NorthernCheck CONSTRAINT CHECK (region = 'north');
ALTER TABLE WesternCustomers
     ADD WesternCheck CONSTRAINT CHECK (region = 'west');
ALTER TABLE SouthernCustomers
     ADD SouthernCheck CONSTRAINT CHECK (region = 'south');
ALTER TABLE EasternCustomers
     ADD EasternCheck CONSTRAINT CHECK (region = 'east');
```

If you need to retrieve a value without knowing the region, you can use the UNION operator to create a view that combines all partitioned tables:

```
CREATE VIEW AllCustomers AS
    SELECT * FROM NorthernCustomers
    UNION ALL
SELECT * FROM NorthernCustomers
    UNION ALL
SELECT * FROM WesternCustomers
    UNION ALL
SELECT * FROM SouthernCustomers
    UNION ALL
SELECT * FROM EasternCustomers;
```

This view contains the same information as the whole table without partitioning. You can use the view, even if you know the region, as in a Transact-SQL statement such as:

```
SELECT * FROM AllCustomers WHERE region = 'north' AND further search
conditions
```

In general, this leads to reading the four partitioned tables, although only *NorthernCustomers* can contain matches for the query.

These constraints tell the query engine where to search for matches, so it accesses only the table *NorthernCustomers* even in this case. When building an execution plan for the SELECT statement, the query engine uses constraints to access only tables that, according to the partitioning criteria, potentially contain matching columns.

MultiForm Industries and Broadband Cable used partitioned tables with constraints on the partitions and a UNION view for SELECTs. The query engine could restrict the partitions to those potentially containing matching rows, when executing SELECTs against the view. But if the view was used in a more complex query (such as a join with other tables) the query engine could not find an optimal execution plan. Instead, it materialized the whole view in the temporary database and then performed the query against this intermediate result set, which yielded poor response times. The workaround is to code the query using the partitions instead of the UNION view.

Using the example above, a query such as:

```
SELECT *
    FROM  AllCustomers, Orders
    WHERE region = :program_variable
    AND   AllCustomers.CustomerID = Orders.CustomerID
    AND   further conditions
```

might suffer from bad response times. The workaround is to separate the different cases within the program this way:

```
if (program_variable = 'north')
    SELECT *
        FROM  NorthernCustomers, Orders
        AND   NorthernCustomers.CustomerID = Orders.CustomerID
        AND   further conditions
else if (program_variable = 'west')
    SELECT *
        FROM  WesternCustomers, Orders
        AND   WesternCustomers.CustomerID = Orders.CustomerID
        AND   further conditions
else ...
```

Rule of thumb: before implementing partitioning, evaluate its impact carefully. Examine and tune the queries using the partitioned view, and evaluate performance. See Chapter 7 for more information on execution plans, and coding queries and transactions.

Planning Indexes

Without indexes, finding matching rows would require scanning the whole table and evaluating the search condition on every row. Indexes speed up this process by storing the values of the indexed columns and a reference to the row in the table.

SQL Server does not automatically use any defined index. Rather it constructs execution plans with and without the index, compares estimated response times, and chooses the faster plan. If indexes are insufficiently selective, it does not use them because a full-table scan returns the result faster. If there are too many indexes, the optimizer spends too much time creating and evaluating potential execution plans.

So you have to plan the indexes carefully, trying for a minimal set of good ones. The next few sections describe the index types supported by SQL Server; later sections offer indexing guidelines.

Index Types

SQL Server's indexes always store the values of the indexed columns in a B-tree—a hierarchical data structure where all branches have the same number of levels. When data is added to or deleted from the table, the index is reorganized to maintain the same number of levels on all branches. The lowest level of the B-tree (leaf nodes) can contain a complete table row (called a clustered index) or just a reference to it (called a nonclustered index).

Nonclustered Indexes

Ordinary indexes are nonclustered. The index is stored separately from the contents of the table, and forms a B-tree with the values of the indexed columns. References to the corresponding row in the base table are stored at the leaf node level.

Nonclustered indexes are created with the Transact-SQL statement

```
CREATE [UNIQUE] INDEX index_name
ON table_name (column_name, ...)
[WITH FILLFACTOR = value]
[ON file_group]
```

The **fillfactor** value specifies how much leaf page space is used; the remainder is kept free so that further insertions can be made without splitting the pages and rebalancing the B-tree. The default value of 0 behaves like a fillfactor of 100: it stores as many values in the leaf pages as possible. If the table will grow in the future, use a fillfactor between 0 and 100, but only if the newly inserted rows have arbitrary values. If the values are increasing (typical for primary keys), stay with the default. Otherwise, all newly inserted values will go into the leaf page with the highest values and the reserved space within the other leaf pages will use up disk space without ever being used.

You can put the index on a different filegroup than the base table. This is beneficial for queries that return large result sets because the index and the base table can be read in parallel from different disks without the disk head movements required to read them both on the same filegroup.

Clustered Indexes

A clustered index combines an index with the table contents: its leaf pages contain the table rows rather than references to them. This means there can be only one clustered index per table.

Clustered indexes are created with the Transact-SQL statement:

```
CREATE [UNIQUE] CLUSTERED INDEX index_name
ON table_name (column_name, ...)
[WITH FILLFACTOR = value]
[ON file_group]
```

The same nonclustered indexes fillfactor considerations apply.

Because the clustered index is intermixed with the rows of the table, it cannot be separated onto different filegroups, nor is there any need to do so.

Comparison

Generally, base table rows are not stored next to the values of an indexed column (only a small part of the index has to be read when selecting a range of values from it). Corresponding rows of the base table tend to be spread all over the table. This results in only a few I/Os in the index but one per row when accessing the base table. Other rows read on a page probably will not belong to the result set, so the number of I/Os is approximately equal to the number of rows fetched.

A clustered index sorts rows on the indexed columns. In this case, selecting a range of values results in reading a few inner index pages and the corresponding leaf pages, and the leaf page rows match the search condition and belong to the result set. So the number of I/Os is approximately equal to the number of pages necessary to store the matching rows.

This means range searches supported by a clustered index require considerably less I/O than range searches on a nonclustered index.

For example, the table *Customers* has a column *CustomerID* serving as the primary key. The data has been inserted in an arbitrary sequence (not sequentially according to the primary key values).

In a table without clustered indexes, the rows are placed on the data pages in the sequence in which they have been entered. If you create a nonclustered index on this table, all values of the primary key appear on the index leaf level and the next higher level contains the ranges of the values in the lower-level pages and pointers to them. The number of levels depends on how many are needed until a single page (called the root page) can reference all pages of the previous level. The values of all entries in the index are sorted (necessary for B-trees).

A clustered index stores the rows of the table on the leaf level. The data pages are now part of the index and are sorted on the values of the indexed column. The higher levels are created just as they are in a nonclustered index.

Figure 6.4 shows both types of indexes based on two assumptions:

- 3 rows of the table fit on every data page
- Every inner index page references 10 pages on the next level

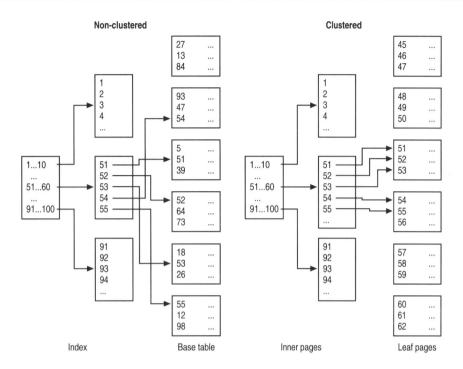

Figure 6.4   Nonclustered vs. clustered index.

On the left side, notice that the rows have been inserted in this *CustomerID* sequence: 27,13, 84, 93, 47, 54, 5,…. On the right side, the clustered index will always look as it does now; it does not reflect the sequence in which the rows are inserted.

Impact of Clustered Indexes on Other Secondary Indexes

Nonclustered indexes contain references (called row locators) to the corresponding row in the base table. Row locator structure depends on whether the data pages are clustered. In nonclustered cases, the row locator is a pointer to the row, for a table with a clustered index the row locator is the clustered index key (it contains the columns of the clustered index).

So the existence of a clustered index affects the contents of all other indexes on the same table. Unless the columns of the clustered index are extremely slim (8 bytes or less) all secondary indexes become larger when there is a clustered index.

Impact of Clustered Indexes on I/Os

When a table has a clustered index, it accelerates SELECTs with search conditions on the indexed columns, because the actual contents of the rows are already found on the index leaf level, eliminating the need to read a separate base table. This advantage is enhanced if the SELECT returns several rows, because they are clustered by the index and fewer I/Os are required to build the result set.

However, all accesses supported by other indexes experience an overhead. If there is no clustered index, a nonclustered index would point directly to the row within the base table; if there is one, a nonclustered index uses the clustered index values as pointers to rows. Any read operation going through a nonclustered index first has to descend the B-tree of this index. It finds the values of the clustered index on the leaf level, then descends the B-tree of the clustered index until it finds the matching rows on its leaf level. This means operations supported by a nonclustered index on a table with a clustered index create more I/Os than they do on tables without clustered indexes. The impact increases along with indexed column sizes on both indexes: larger (broader) columns mean there are fewer index rows on every page, and this means more index levels have to be traversed.

If UPDATE operations change the contents of columns belonging to a clustered index, the index has to be maintained and so do all other indexes because they contain pointers to UPDATEd clustered index values (not to base table rows). The maintenance causes a high volume of I/O writes, slows down the transaction, and may (by imposing locks) delay or deadlock other running transactions.

Recommendations

Clustered indexes accelerate operations going through the index, but slow down operations on any other indexes. This decrease is acceptable only if the clustered index offers stronger advantages.

Recommendations:

- Don't use a clustered index for the primary key without carefully assessing the structure and performance issues.
- Don't use clustered indexes on columns that are frequently UPDATEd.
- Use a clustered index for the most frequent query that returns more than one row (a set-oriented query).
- If the columns of the clustered index differ from the primary key, support the primary key with a unique, nonclustered index.
- Keep the clustered index as slim as possible.

The companies referred to in these chapters differed significantly in their use of clustered indexes. MS Sales, James Wilkie, Broadband Cable, and Black Dinosaur (as defined by SAP) used clustered indexes for their primary key. Bound Galley Book Cellars used clustered indexes only in the few cases where set-oriented queries got the maximum benefit, and avoided them on tables with heavy write operations. MultiForm Industries used clustered indexes to support the most frequent joins.

These actions seem contradictory, but each company based its decision on which types of queries and transactions are most frequent:

- If there are heavy write operations, use clustered indexes only with caution.

- If an application mostly reads and manipulates one row of a table at a time, use a clustered index for the primary key.

- If there are lots of joins with result sets of many rows, use clustered indexes on the joined columns.

This is only a starting point. You have to initiate a plan then check the most important queries on different physical data models to achieve best response times. (For more details and some examples, see Chapter 7, "Field Observations on Coding Queries and Transactions.")

Index Disk Space Calculation

Index disk space is calculated somewhat differently than table disk space.

Index pages contain the values of the indexes columns plus references to the next index level or to the base table, so the calculation of space requirement for the values of indexed columns is based on the data types as described in the section "Calculating Space Requirements" on page 224. Remember to add for nullable columns and variable-length data types.

There are four formulas for calculating index row size, depending on page and index type.

- For inner (non-leaf) index pages:

  Add 8 bytes for the reference to the next index level and 1 byte for the index row header. The result is the size of 1 index row.

  The number of index rows per inner index page is then calculated as

  $$\left\lfloor \frac{8096}{\text{index\_row\_size} + 2} \right\rfloor$$

■ For leaf pages of clustered indexes:

This is calculated just as it is for ordinary tables. If you use an explicit fillfactor, multiply the number of leaf pages by (100/fillfactor).

■ For leaf pages of nonclustered indexes on tables without a clustered index:

The leaf pages contain values of the indexed columns and the row locator referencing the base table. Add 8 bytes for the row locator and 1 byte for the index row header. The number of index rows per leaf page again is

$$\left\lfloor \frac{8096}{index\_row\_size + 2} \right\rfloor$$

and the number of leaf pages is

$$\left\lceil \frac{base\_table\_rows}{number\_of\_leaf\_pages} \right\rceil$$

Multiply the result by (100/fillfactor) if you are using an explicit fillfactor.

■ For leaf pages of nonclustered indexes on tables with a clustered index:

The leaf pages contain the values of the indexed columns and the values of the clustered index columns. The space requirement for the columns of the clustered index is calculated as before, based on column data types. Remember to add for nullable and variable-length columns. The index row length on the leaf pages is the sum of the indexed column sizes and clustered index column sizes.

The number of index rows/leaf page is again

$$\left\lfloor \frac{8096}{index\_row\_size + 2} \right\rfloor$$

and the number of leaf pages is

$$\left\lceil \frac{base\_table\_rows}{number\_of\_leaf\_pages} \right\rceil$$

Multiply the result by (100/fillfactor) if you are using an explicit fillfactor.

This gives the number of leaf pages for any case. The number of non-leaf pages on the first level is

$$\left\lceil \frac{number\_of\_leaf\_pages}{index\_rows\_per\_page} \right\rceil$$

The next level has

$$\left\lceil \frac{number\_pages\_on\_previous\_level}{index\_rows\_per\_pages} \right\rceil$$

pages. Repeat this calculation for the inner levels, until the result is 1. This is the root page of the index. Add the number of pages of all levels. This is the total number of pages required for the index.

Covered Indexes

SQL Server 7.0 can use indexes even if not all index columns are used in the search condition (SQL Server 6.5 sometimes had problems doing this). To make optimum use of an index, however, the values for the left-most index columns are given. The remaining columns of the index can be used to build the result set of the query. If all needed columns are found in the index, SQL Server does not look up the base table (the table being indexed). Indexes that support the whole query without needing to read the base table are called covered indexes.

For example:

Customers table columns.

Column	Data type	Description
CustomerID	**int**	Primary key
Name	**varchar(30)**	Customer's name
Town	**varchar(30)**	Customer's town
Profession	**varchar(30)**	Customer's profession
further columns		

The query in question is: find all *CustomerID*s of customers in a specific town with a given pattern for the name. The Transact-SQL statement for a specific search is

```
SELECT    CustomerID
   FROM   Customers
   WHERE  Town =     'Seattle'
   AND    Name LIKE 'S%';
```

The first idea will be to create an index on the columns *Town* and *Name*. The query will find the matches in the index, and use the reference to the base table, where it will find the selected *CustomerID*s.

With SQL Server 7.0, if the index contains any further columns (such as *Profession*) it will still be used **if** the columns used in the search condition (*Town* and *Name* in the example) appear first in the index. An index on *Profession*,

Town, and *Name*, for example, would be of no use: a covered index would include the columns *Town*, *Name*, and *CustomerID*, and the query engine would use it because the search condition names the left-most columns. Unlike the first index (*Town* and *Name*) the values for the *CustomerID*s are now found within the index. There is no need to access the base table, and the query engine will eliminate this step, answering the query by accessing the index only.

This shows the advantage of covered indexes: they reduce I/Os by eliminating the base table search, which constructs a result set faster, decreasing query response times. The disadvantage is that additional space is required to store the additional columns, which leads to larger index rows and (possibly) more index levels.

The advantages often outweigh the disadvantages. In environments with many concurrently running transactions, the absence of covered indexes can lead to deadlocks. A&G Phone experienced this. One operation started with the base table and had to maintain the index, so it locked the appropriate rows in the base table then tried to lock the corresponding part of the index. A concurrent operation started with the index, locking the appropriate section, and then tried to lock the rows in the base table. Result: deadlock. Designers created some covered indexes, which eliminated the need to access the base table, skipped the corresponding lock requests, and cleared things up. (This is relevant only for nonclustered indexes: clustered indexes have the actual rows on the leaf level.)

Rule of thumb: you can consider adding columns to a nonclustered index to create covered indexes, but there is no rule of thumb for how many columns you can add and still derive benefit. You have to measure the effect of covered indexes in *your* environment. For more detail, go to the next chapter, "Field Observations on Coding Queries and Transactions."

Field Observations on Coding Queries and Transactions

By Christopher Etz, g&h Database Technologies GmbH

Queries access the database to retrieve data; transactions access it to manipulate data. These two actions have, by far, the highest impact on database performance, stability, and error rates, so it is crucial that you develop them carefully. Applications are also important, of course, but their performance implications differ. Queries and transactions are executed on the same database server for all participating applications; application logic is performed within the application on the client or on an application server. Problems with an application's logic will bother *its* users, but problems with queries and transactions will bother *all* users.

The Solution in Focus

Having taken care of all the ground work, you now have a system either in production or very near to being so. Time has come to start seriously tuning queries and transactions. The VLDB system was designed and built to enable users to execute queries and transaction: they are the system's *raisons d'être*, they place the greatest demand on its processing infrastructure, and they ultimately determine whether it succeeds or fails in its purpose.

All the information in this chapter (and the others in this section) is drawn from the experiences of companies that have implemented VLDBs using SQL Server 7.0 as recorded by Microsoft Consulting Services. It has been combined into case studies under the fictional names of Broadband Cable Communications, Bound Galley Book Cellars, and others. Taken together, these chapters discuss the challenges of VLDB solutions from preliminary design to fine-tuning the system in the production environment, providing examples, explanation, and field-tested recommendations.

What You'll Find in This Chapter

- How to assess performance requirements, then tune queries to meet them.

- The general procedure for optimizing query performance; this section uses a detailed example to demonstrate how to analyze the execution plan developed by the SQL Server 7.0 query engine and tune the query to hit performance goals.

- How to tune transactions, particularly how to identify and avoid blocks, locks, and deadlocks.

- General tuning tips developed at the case study companies used in this section.

Case Overview

There are only a few general guidelines for developing high-performance queries. Once you have considered them you have to develop and test most queries—especially complex ones—one by one. The next section describes how to develop, test, and tune queries for high performance, and provides an example case to illustrate the procedure.

Performance Requirements

Performance requirements for queries and transactions are described by throughput or response time. **Throughput** is the number of operations (statements or transactions) performed per unit of time. **Response time** is the interval between sending an instruction to the database server and receiving the result. **Query results** are rows matching the search condition. **Data manipulation** or **transaction results** are status codes (describing the success of the operation) or error codes (indicating a deadlock, duplicate key, etc.). Transaction performance is normally assessed by throughput, query performance by response time.

Single-User and Multi-User Tests

You have to test queries and transactions to see if they are meeting performance requirements. Tests are generally done on two levels:

- **Single-user tests.** First, test the query or transaction in single-user mode to measure the response time. If necessary, tune the query until the response time is acceptable.
- **Multi-user tests.** Then test the query or transaction in multi-user mode to assess its behavior when it is executed several times in parallel. This also helps you assess its scalability. Multi-user tests are necessary for data manipulations, to make sure there are no locking problems (deadlocks or blocking locks).

Procedure for Developing High-Performance Queries

The general procedure is straightforward and always the same:

1. Measure the response time and/or throughput

   If you meet the performance requirements, you are done.

2. Measure the resource consumption

   The critical resources are processor (CPU) time and I/O requests. Depending on the type of application, you may want to measure other resources such as network bandwidth. This step should give you an idea of where to start tuning. If the query is I/O bound, it probably is missing an index or not using an existing index. If the query is CPU bound, the problem could be that it is performing sorts inefficiently during execution, or some other inefficiency in the execution plan.

3. Consider the execution plan

   The SQL Server 7.0 query engine develops a plan for executing the query based on data distribution statistics. You can't assume which of its many different strategies it is using: you have to study the plan to assess it, especially its estimates of rows matching the search condition and response time.

4. Construct alternatives and test them in the same way

   The execution plan shows you which operations use the most resources or time. Find preferable alternatives by changing Transact-SQL statement syntax, adding or modifying indexes, adding hints, etc.

5. Run the best-performing alternative through a multi-user test

   Measure and compare the alternatives' resource consumption and execution plans, then multi-user test the winner and assess its performance. If it meets the requirements, you are done. If not, try another alternative.

Measuring Resource Consumption

When you develop a query, you have to see if its resource consumption is in line with its complexity.

Resources to measure for query evaluation.

Resource name	Description
Response time (elapsed time)	Time from sending the query to the SQL Server to the receipt of the result
Processor time (CPU time)	Amount of processor activity on the database server needed to execute the query
Number of I/O requests	Number of disk reads and writes on the database server needed to execute the query

To see the amount of resources consumed, execute these statements:

- SET STATISTICS TIME ON (to see response and processor times)
- SET STATISTICS IO ON (to see numbers of I/Os)

Wherever arbitrary Transact-SQL statements are allowed you can execute these with Query Analyzer, or from the command line using ISQL (database connection via the DB-library) and OSQL (database connection via ODBC).

Note   The QueryAnalyzer is easy to use and interactive. ISQL and OSQL allow you to redirect input and output and store results in files with commands such as:

```
isql -E < SQL-script > output_file
```

If the query you are tuning takes too long to complete you can't measure its actual resource consumption so you have to use the query engine's estimates. To see them, execute the statement:

```
SET SHOWPLAN_ALL ON.
```

Displaying the Execution Plan

When the SQL Server 7.0 query engine receives a query, it assesses the possible methods of execution, taking into account factors such as indexes, numbers of matching rows required to satisfy the conditions, and so on, then selects the plan that offers the best estimated performance. To understand resource consumption for the query, you have to display and study the execution plan. How you display it depends on the tool you are using.

In Query Analyzer, click on the **Query** menu and select **Display SQL execution plan**. In ISQL or OSQL, execute SET SHOWPLAN_TEXT ON or SET SHOWPLAN_ALL ON (for more detailed information).

For instructions on reading and interpreting execution plans, see "Graphically Displaying the Execution Plan Using SQL Server Query Analyzer" in SQL Server Books Online.

Example: There are two tables, *Parent* and *Detail*, with the following columns:

Table *Parent*.

Column	Data type	Description
ParentID	**int**	Identifies every record
ParentShortText	**varchar(30)**	A short string column, always filled
ParentLongText	**varchar(200)**	A longer string, sometimes filled

This has 20,000 records and occupies 3 MB in the database.

Table *Detail*.

Column	Data type	Description
DetailID	**int**	Identifies every record
ParentID	**int**	Foreign key
DetailShortText	**varchar(30)**	A short string column, always filled
DetailLongText	**varchar(200)**	A longer string, sometimes filled

This has 1,000,000 records and occupies 42 MB in the database.

The query to be tuned (to complete in less than one second) selects a few records of the *Parent* and their *Details*:

```
SELECT Parent.ParentId, ParentShortText, DetailID, DetailShortText
FROM Parent JOIN Detail ON Parent.ParentID = Detail.ParentID
WHERE Parent.ParentID IN (0, 1, 2)
ORDER BY Parent.ParentId, DetailID
```

To tune the query, you need to know the physical primary keys and any other indexes. To measure the initial resource consumption, execute these statements in the Query Analyzer:

```
SET STATISTICS TIME ON
go
SET STATISTICS IO ON
go
SELECT Parent.ParentId, ParentShortText, DetailID, DetailShortText
FROM Parent JOIN Detail ON Parent.ParentID = Detail.ParentID
WHERE Parent.ParentID IN (0, 1, 2)
ORDER BY Parent.ParentId, DetailID
```

The output window shows the query result and resource consumption:

```
Table 'Detail'. Scan count 2, logical reads 85910, physical reads 511,
read-ahead reads 5152.
Table 'Parent'. Scan count 1, logical reads 29977, physical reads 56,
read-ahead reads 336.

SQL Server Execution Times:
   CPU time = 136313 ms,  elapsed time = 165287 ms.
```

The first part of the output shows the I/O statistics: scan count (number of scans over the tables) and logical reads (number of pages accessed). For tuning, these are less important than the next numbers: physical reads (reads of single pages) and read-ahead reads (reads of several pages by a single operation). The totals here are $511 + 5152 + 56 + 336 = 6055$.

The second part of the output shows processor time (about 136 seconds) and response time (165 seconds). At almost 3 minutes this is far from meeting the performance requirement of less than 1 second.

If it had not been necessary to wait for the output, the query would have proceeded in line with the query engine estimates displayed by the statements:

```
SET SHOWPLAN_ALL ON
go
SELECT Parent.ParentId, ParentShortText, DetailID, DetailShortText
FROM Parent JOIN Detail ON Parent.ParentID = Detail.ParentID
WHERE Parent.ParentID IN (0, 1, 2)
ORDER BY Parent.ParentId, DetailID
```

The output here shows a huge amount of information, of which the query needs only the sums of the columns *EstimateIO* and *EstimateCPU* (54 + 30137). This means the query engine expects to do 54 I/O operations, requiring about 30 seconds of processor time. Although the resource consumption is obviously underestimated, the processor time estimate is correct.

So the next step is to look at the execution plan. The graphical display in the Query Analyzer is easier to read than the textual representation from ISQL or OSQL. In the Query Analyzer **Query** menu click on **Display SQL execution plan**. It shows this:

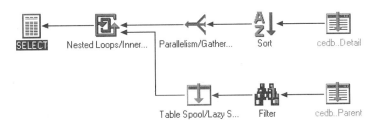

Figure 7.1   Query execution plan.

The output shows that the query engine decided to:

1. Scan the Detail table, sort it, and pipe it into a nested loops join.
2. Scan the Parent table, filter the records by applying the restriction `Parent.ParentID IN (0, 1, 2)`, and use the results as the second stream for the join operation.

The most expensive operation in this execution plan is obviously sorting the whole *Detail* table, which has 1,000,000 rows.

The first tuning idea is to change the SQL statement so that it filters (applies the restriction to) the *Detail* table, too. Now, the statement looks like:

```
SELECT Parent.ParentId, ParentShortText, DetailID, DetailShortText
FROM Parent JOIN Detail ON Parent.ParentID = Detail.ParentID
WHERE Parent.ParentID IN (0, 1, 2)
AND Detail.ParentID IN (0, 1, 2)
ORDER BY Parent.ParentId, DetailID
```

The resulting execution plan shows the filter operations on both branches of the join:

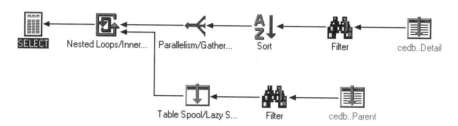

Figure 7.2   Query execution plan—filter operations on both branches of the join.

Resource consumption is reduced significantly.

Query resource with filters on both branches of the join.

Alternative	Response time	Processor time	I/Os
Original version	165287 ms	136313 ms	6055
Restrictions on both tables	26796 ms	6032 ms	5761

Processor time is reduced by a factor of more than 20, but response time is reduced only by a factor of 6 because the number of I/Os did not decrease significantly. An improvement, but still far from meeting the performance requirement.

The next step is to define appropriate indexes on the tables. The restrictions are on the column *ParentID* on both tables. The easiest way to create the indexes is to right-click on the tables within the execution plan. A small menu pops up. Select **Manage Indexes**. In the window, select the column to be indexed and give the index a name.

Creating nonclustered indexes on both tables changes the execution plan:

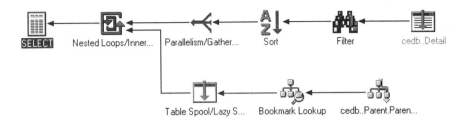

Figure 7.3   Query execution plan with nonclustered indexes on both tables.

It shows that the index on the *Detail* table is ignored (it does not appear), and the index on the *Parent* table is used as expected.

Query resource consumption with nonclustered indexes.

Alternative	Response time	Processor time	I/Os
Nonclustered indexes on both tables	19871 ms	5281 ms	5358

The query accelerated again, but only marginally, and the required response time is not yet reached because the *Detail* table is still being scanned.

There now are two alternatives: use clustered indexes on the *ParentID* columns or make the nonclustered indexes covered. Covered indexes contain all columns mentioned in the query—in this case both result columns *and* columns used in restrictions. This allows the query to find data by accessing the indexes, instead of the base table.

The execution plans of both alternatives look similar.

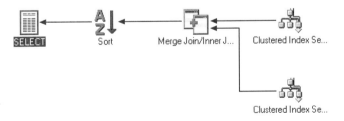

Figure 7.4   Query execution plan with clustered indexes on both tables.

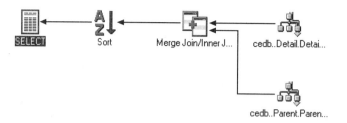

Figure 7.5   Query execution plan with covered indexes on both tables.

Adding the resource consumption of the last two alternatives creates a complete table of results.

Query execution plan summary.

Alternative	Response time	Processor time	I/Os
Original version	165287 ms	136313 ms	6055
Restrictions on both tables	26796 ms	6032 ms	5761
Nonclustered indexes on both tables	19871 ms	5281 ms	5358
Clustered indexes on both tables	135 ms	16 ms	5
Covered indexes on both tables	109 ms	15 ms	5

The final version shrinks the resource consumption of the original by a factor of 1000. The last two alternatives meet the performance requirements and can be regarded as equally suitable. To decide which to use, consider other queries of the application. If another query runs faster with clustered indexes, use covered indexes for this case, and vice versa.

This example was simplified so that the discussion could focus on the procedure instead of the technical issues. The procedure for analyzing and tuning queries is always the same: measure resource consumption, then read the execution plan to understand the measurements and find alternatives. Repeat these steps until you meet the performance requirements.

Field Experiences Coding Queries

Here are some experiences specific to the companies referred to in these chapters.

Retrieving the First Matches

A&G Phone has a lot of queries that should return only the first few matching rows, not all of them. This is a reasonable approach when users are allowed to enter search conditions. If a condition is too weak, a huge number of rows would match and be transferred to the application. This would cause high activity on the database server and the network, hindering concurrent queries and transactions. By returning only the first few matches (say, 100), the query uses less resources and sends fewer rows over the network.

There are two ways to restrict returns to the first few matches:

- Using the SET ROWCOUNT command to limit the number of rows
- Using the TOP operator within a Transact-SQL statement

The query engine does not recognize SET ROWCOUNT, so the execution plan assumes all matching rows are requested. The query is executed, but only the given number of rows are transferred to the application.

The TOP operator is preferable in most instances because the query engine recognizes it and may select a different execution plan, optimized to return the given number of rows. And because the TOP operator is part of the Transact-SQL syntax, you can change the statement to allow the restriction on the first few rows to be evaluated earlier during the execution of the query.

Here is an example using the *Parent* and *Detail* tables from the previous example. Suppose the application retrieves the rows from the join of both tables with an arbitrary search condition, entered by the user. (If no search condition is entered, all rows are returned.) To restrict the size of the result set, the rows are sorted on the column *DetailShortText* and only the first 20 rows are displayed within the application. There are three ways to code the query:

1. With the command SET ROWCOUNT:

```
SET ROWCOUNT 20
go
SELECT DetailID, DetailShortText, Parent.ParentID, ParentShortText
FROM Parent JOIN Detail ON Parent.ParentID = Detail.ParentID
ORDER BY DetailShortText
```

2. With the TOP operator applied to the whole result set:

```
SELECT TOP 20 DetailID, DetailShortText, Parent.ParentID,
ParentShortText
FROM Parent JOIN Detail ON Parent.ParentID = Detail.ParentID
ORDER BY DetailShortText
```

3. With the TOP operator applied to the *Detail* table:

```
SELECT DetailID, DetailShortText, Parent.ParentID, ParentShortText
FROM Parent JOIN (SELECT TOP 20 * FROM Detail ORDER BY
DetailShortText) Detail ON Parent.ParentID = Detail.ParentID
```

This formulation is semantically equivalent to the others but it forces the query engine to read the *Detail* table first, to sort it on the *DetailShortText* column, and to pass only the first 20 rows to the rest of the query, where the data of the table *Parent* are added.

Query resource consumption for code alternatives.

Alternative	Response time	Processor time	I/Os
With the command SET ROWCOUNT	149950 ms	182652 ms	5871
With the TOP operator applied to the whole result set	153563 ms	183297 ms	5892
With the TOP operator applied to the *Detail* table	54299 ms	38280 ms	–

The first two alternatives show no significant differences. The processor time is greater than the response time in both cases, because the alternatives have been measured on a 2-processor machine and the query engine parallelized the query.

The third alternative requires only a third of the response time compared to the other alternatives, reducing processor time by a factor of 5. (The statement SET STATISTICS IO ON returned 0 for the last alternative—obviously an invalid response for a heavily accessed disk.)

This shows that response time is best when the restriction on the first few matching rows is evaluated as early as possible. Thus the third alternative is fastest, although its formulation is more complex.

Checking for NULL Values

The ANSI standard for SQL defines three Boolean values for comparisons: TRUE, FALSE, and UNKNOWN. The last is used whenever at least one expression of a binary comparison operator such as <, <=, =, >, >= or <> evaluates to the NULL value. The expression can be the content of a column, a constant, or any other more complex expression. If you want a result of TRUE or FALSE, when one expression is NULL, you have to use the IS operator.

Results with NULL values.

Expression	Result	Remark
1 = 1	TRUE	Obviously
1 = 0	FALSE	Obviously
0 = NULL	UNKNOWN	Neither TRUE nor FALSE
0 <> NULL	UNKNOWN	Neither TRUE nor FALSE
NOT (0 = NULL)	UNKNOWN	Even the negation makes it neither TRUE nor FALSE
NULL = NULL	UNKNOWN	No chance again
NULL IS NULL	TRUE	The IS operator always returns TRUE or FALSE
0 IS NULL	FALSE	This is FALSE, not UNKNOWN (as you might think)
NOT (0 IS NULL)	TRUE	Same as: 0 IS NOT NULL

The behavior of SQL Server 6.5 differed from the ANSI standard by always returning TRUE or FALSE. (You can force this behavior with the Transact-SQL statement SET ANSI_NULL OFF; you can force ANSI-compliant behavior with SET ANSI_NULL ON.) A&G Phone experienced some problems with this behavioral change when they converted their application from SQL Server version 6.5 to SQL Server version 7.0.

When they converted the database, they used the SQL Server Upgrade Wizard, which switched off the ANSI mode, simplifying conversion. Later in the process, they had to use the SQL Server Enterprise Manager, which switched the ANSI mode back on. Stored procedures entered by the Enterprise Manager behaved differently than those converted by the Upgrade Wizard. The syntax was correct (because a statement such as 0 <> NULL is still correct) but the semantics changed, and that changed the result. As you can imagine, the reason for suddenly differing query results was hard to find.

Experience shows that it is better to stay with ANSI mode. Replace comparisons such as "*expression* = NULL" with "*expression* IS NULL," and "*expression* <> NULL" with " *expression* IS NOT NULL." Double-check all statements to make sure query semantics are as you expect them to be.

Field Experiences Coding Transactions

This section concentrates on locking issues. When coding transactions, you have to minimize locking—both the amount of data being locked and the amount of time locks are held. Even small transactions can cause deadlocks or block other queries and transactions.

A transaction's response time depends primarily on the response times of its Transact-SQL statements. Analyze these statements and tune them as you would a query. Use the same steps described in the "Procedure for Developing High-Performance Queries" section on page 245.

In general, a few deadlocks per day are acceptable if the application handles them automatically and restarts the transaction. The problem worsens if the restarted transaction runs into another deadlock, so you should limit restarts to prevent too-frequent deadlock. Most application developers allow about three tries to complete the transaction, after which the user gets an error message. The user can restart the transaction, call the database administrator, or just plain give up.

You can reduce the likelihood of a transaction repeatedly running into a deadlock by waiting a short time before restarting. Base the wait duration on a random number (between 50 and 200 milliseconds) so that contending transactions don't wait the same amount of time and retry simultaneously.

Analyzing Deadlocks

If there are too many deadlocks you have to find their cause. You know which transaction was rolled back because it gets an error message, but it is harder to locate other participating transactions.

When the deadlock problem intensified at A&G Phone, they shut down the SQL Server, opened a command window, and got details about the deadlocks by executing the command

```
sqlservr -t1204
```

This restarts SQL Server and sends any trace messages to the command window.

Here is an example. You can easily generate a deadlock using two one-column, one-row tables. Initially they look like this:

Table One	Table Two
Col	Col
One ·	Two

One of the transactions performs these Transact-SQL statements:

```
BEGIN TRANSACTION;
UPDATE One SET Col = 'eins';
UPDATE Two SET Col = 'zwei';
COMMIT TRANSACTION;
```

The other performs:

```
BEGIN TRANSACTION;
UPDATE Two SET Col = 'dos';
UPDATE One SET Col = 'uno';
COMMIT TRANSACTION;
```

Because the transactions begin with different tables there is a high probability that they will run into a deadlock. To force it, use two concurrent sessions (open Query Analyzer twice) and execute the first statement of the first transaction in the first window, the first statement of the second transaction in the second window, then the second statements, and so on.

Soon, one of the transactions will deadlock, but the error message does not tell which other transaction participated.

Switch to the command window. There is a trace message:

```
*** Deadlock Detected ***
==> Process 7 chosen as deadlock victim
== Deadlock Detected at: 99/03/18 11:01:16.46
== Session participant information:
SPID: 7 ECID: 0 Statement Type: UPDATE
Input Buf: u p d a t e   t w o   s e t   c o l   =   ' t w o '
SPID: 8 ECID: 0 Statement Type: UPDATE
Input Buf: u p d a t e   o n e   s e t   c o l   =   ' o n e '

== Deadlock Lock participant information:
== Lock: RID: 7:3:16:0
Database: cedb
Table: one
 - Held by: SPID 7 ECID 0 Mode "X"
 - Requested by: SPID 8 ECID 0 Mode "U"
== Lock: RID: 7:3:18:0
Database: cedb
Table: two
 - Held by: SPID 8 ECID 0 Mode "X"
 - Requested by: SPID 7 ECID 0 Mode "U"
```

The upper part of the output shows the two participating database connections with system process IDs (SPIDs—7 and 8), execution context IDs (ECIDs—0 in both cases), and their current Transact-SQL statements.

The lower part shows the locks involved in the deadlock. The RID is the row identifier, consisting of the database ID, the file ID, the page number and the row number. RID 7:3:16:0 specifies the database with ID 7, the 3rd file, the 16th page of the file and row number 0 on that page. The row belongs to table *One* in the database ***cedb***. The first transaction (SPID 7) holds the lock on this resource in exclusive mode (X), and the second transaction (SPID 8) has requested the lock in update mode (U). Meanwhile, on table *Two* in the same database, the second transaction (SPID 8) holds the lock in exclusive mode (X), and the first transaction has requested the lock in update mode (U).

Exclusive locks are not compatible with update locks, so the second transaction waits for the first transaction to release the lock, and the first transaction waits for the second transaction to release the other lock. This is a deadlock, which SQL Server resolves by rolling back one of the transactions, releasing its locks, and sending it an error message. The other transaction can now continue and eventually complete the transaction, performing a COMMIT TRANSACTION and releasing its locks. If the first transaction is restarted, it will either find the second transaction already completed, or block on a lock of the second transaction, if it is still running. At this point it waits for the first transaction's COMMIT to release the lock, then continues running. The likelihood of a second deadlock is very low.

Avoiding Deadlocks

The companies referred to in these chapters used some general procedures to avoid deadlock.

A&G Phone analyzed which transactions took part in the deadlock and found a stored procedure with this structure:

```
CREATE PROC procedure_name AS
BEGIN
    BEGIN TRANSACTION
    SET ROWCOUNT 1
    SELECT columns
        FROM orders
        WHERE search_condition
    /* do some work with the order */
    UPDATE orders
        SET status = new_value
        WHERE orderID = @orderID;
    COMMIT TRANSACTION
END
```

This stored procedure ran frequently in parallel. When two or more procedures selected an order, only one of them could update its status. The other(s) ran into deadlocks.

This was due to default lock behavior: the SELECT statements request shared locks, which are granted to all transactions and are compatible among different transactions. Later on, one of the transactions tried to update the order and requested that the lock be converted to exclusive. Other transactions held the lock in shared mode, so this transaction had to wait for all shared locks to be released. When the next transaction tried to convert the lock to exclusive, it had to wait for the first transaction, which was already waiting for the latter to complete. The deadlock chain was closed, and the SQL Server rolled back one of the transactions and sent it an error message.

The solution is quite simple, once the constellation has been analyzed. Make sure that the SELECT statements request the lock in update mode. You can do this with the UPDLOCK hint. The new procedure in SQL Server 7.0 is:

```
CREATE PROC procedure_name AS
BEGIN
    BEGIN TRANSACTION
    SET ROWCOUNT 1
    SELECT columns
        FROM orders (UPDLOCK)
        WHERE search_condition
    /* do some work with the order */
    UPDATE orders
        SET status = new_value
        WHERE orderID = @orderID;
    COMMIT TRANSACTION
END
```

After that change, the stored procedure no longer caused deadlocks.

Avoiding Blocking Locks

Blocking locks arise when concurrently running transactions access the same data. These locks do not cause deadlocks but they increase transaction response time for the duration of the transaction that holds the lock. To reduce the impact on transactions, tune transactions to run as fast as possible.

MS Sales (see the "Set Processing" section in Chapter 10: MS Sales Data Warehouse) created some guidelines to optimize throughput:

- All transactions are encapsulated in stored procedures. In other words, every stored procedure that manipulates database contents contains the statements BEGIN TRANSACTION and COMMIT TRANSACTION. This has two advantages:

  - The application and SQL Server communicate at the start of the stored procedure and at its end, when the result is returned. These messages are outside of the transaction, so if communication is slowed by the network the lock durations are not extended.

  - A user can't leave an open transaction (with the locks being held) because the stored procedure completes any transaction that it starts.

- All transactions are designed to contain a minimum amount of work. Any calculation that does not need to be contained in the transaction is performed before the transaction is started.

  - Some transactions are broken down into smaller ones. For example, a batch process has to insert a lot of records, and before doing so it has to check if corresponding entries exist in other tables. This can be broken down into two transactions: one that performs the checks and marks the records where the check succeeded, one that inserts the marked records to their final table. The final table is heavily used and any locks placed on it must be of short duration. Splitting the transaction minimizes the lock duration because the second transaction does not have to keep the table locked while the checks are performed—they were completed by the first transaction.

General Guidelines for Coding Queries and Transactions

The companies referred to in these chapters arrived at some guidelines based on what they learned coding queries and transactions.

- MS Sales uses set-oriented processing (rather than record-oriented) wherever possible: Transact-SQL statements are coded so that the maximum number of records are processed by one statement. This approach generally offers higher throughput than looping over all matching records and processing these records one by one within the loop. There are two reasons:

  - Communication between the application and the database is reduced.

  - The query engine is allowed to find execution plans that operate optimally on the complete set of records.

- A&G Phone converted their application from SQL Server 6.5 to SQL Server 7.0 and found that some hints necessary under SQL Server 6.5 caused problems under version 7.0 by forcing the query engine to use a specific execution plan, rather than letting it use the best one. They eliminated all hints within queries and minimized the number of new hints added.

- Bound Galley Book Cellars tuned a lot of complex queries, some of which contained negated predicates in the WHERE clauses. They developed a guideline to avoid the word NOT wherever possible.

    - If you want to delete orphaned detail records (those without a corresponding master record), the statement that first comes to mind is:

    ```
    DELETE FROM Detail
        WHERE ParentID NOT IN (SELECT ParentID FROM Parent)
    ```

    This is equivalent and yields to the same execution plan as:

    ```
    DELETE FROM Detail
        WHERE NOT EXISTS (
            SELECT * FROM Master WHERE Master.MasterID =
    Detail.MasterID)
    ```

    Depending on the sizes of the participating tables and the number of matching rows, it may be faster to code it as:

    ```
    CREATE TABLE #temp (MasterID INT NOT NULL);
    INSERT INTO #temp SELECT DISTINCT MasterID FROM Detail;
    DELETE FROM #temp WHERE MasterID IN (SELECT MasterID FROM Master);
    DELETE FROM Detail WHERE MasterID IN (SELECT MasterID FROM #temp);
    ```

- Bound Galley Book Cellars also developed a guideline for reducing the likelihood of deadlocks: the tables used in a transaction are always mentioned in the same sequence.

    - In most cases, the sequence of the statements within a transaction is not important. It can be relevant, however, if there is some kind of a driving table that provides results necessary to subsequent statements. Bound Galley improved performance by ordering all database tables so that the driving tables come before the others, and requiring that all transactions mention the tables in that sequence.

C H A P T E R   8

Field Observations on Managing Operations

By Christopher Etz, g&h Database Technologies GmbH

Maintenance plans ensure database availability and performance, and good plans are especially important for very large databases. Maintenance for VLDBs is further complicated by the need to plan tasks so that they do not interrupt database use.

The Solution in Focus

This chapter describes how to plan and perform backups, reorganize indexes, and use the database consistency checker (DBCC). These are broad topics, and the information presented here is not exhaustive. Instead, the discussion uses the example companies referred to in these chapters to demonstrate some concepts and methods tested and verified in the field and proven useful for managing VLDB systems.

All the information in this chapter (and the others in this section) is drawn from the experiences of companies that have implemented VLDBs using SQL Server 7.0 as recorded by Microsoft Consulting Services. It has been combined into case studies under the fictional names of Broadband Cable Communications, Bound Galley Book Cellars, and others. Taken together, these chapters discuss the challenges of VLDB solutions from preliminary design to fine-tuning the system in the production environment, providing examples, explanation, and field-tested recommendations.

What You'll Find in This Chapter

- Physical and logical backups—how to pick the one best suited to your needs and how to deal with hardware, software, and configuration issues.

- Procedures for reorganizing tables and indexes—necessary maintenance for finding and clearing up fragmentation that affects system performance. The discussion centers on single command script (developed by MS Sales) that calls a stored procedure and command line tools to find tables with scan densities below 90%. The database objects and code are provided.

- How selected companies use the database consistency checker (DBCC). Although SQL Server 7.0 reduces the need for this somewhat, its performance is improved and it still can prove useful.

Database Backup

This section discusses backup basics, dealing primarily with types and concepts, and using some case study examples to clarify methods. For a thorough discussion of these important topics, see the "Backup and Recovery" section in Chapter 11, "Data Warehouse Management Infrastructure: MetaEdge."

There are different backup methods suited to different purposes.

Database backups are necessary to restore the database in case of a failure. There are two basic types of failure, each addressed by a different method:

- **Corruption due to hardware or software failures.** Database contents can be corrupted by failures such as disk head crashes (hardware failure) or writing a database to a wrong spot on the disk (software failure of the operating system, a driver, or the database server). This requires that the database be restored.

- **User errors.** Users and database administrators can unintentionally destroy (delete or wrongly update) database contents. This requires that the affected part be restored.

To restore the database in case of such errors, there are two types of database backups: physical and logical.

Physical Backups

Physical backups copy database contents to a backup device (a disk location or a tape drive). The contents are not interpreted; they are simply written as a byte stream to the backup device.

These have the advantage of speed (because data is not interpreted, merely transferred). This is also a drawback, because the un-interpreted contents cannot be used to restore a specific database object (such as a table). You can restore only the entire database or specific data files. Another advantage is that you can use this copy in combination with transaction log file backups to restore the database up to the last committed transaction (the time just before the failure and usually long after the last backup was done).

Logical Backups

Logical backups can be used to restore down to the individual table level. They are performed by

- Exporting the data (for example with the DTS Export Wizard)
- Replicating the data to a second database
- Recording the changes in specific tables, commonly called history tables

How to Perform Physical Backups

There are different ways to restore the database after a hardware or software failure that might have corrupted the contents. The hardware methods described in the next section provide a certain amount of protection, but remember that they *augment* a backup strategy—they do not replace it.

Hardware Level

RAID Systems

All of the companies referred to in these chapters placed their databases on RAID systems. RAID levels 1 and greater allow you to use hardware means to recover contents stored on the disks. Only RAID level 0 (striping) does not store any redundant information, so if a disk fails the contents of all logical volumes using that disk are affected.

The commonly used RAID levels 1 (mirroring) and 5 store some redundant information. RAID level 1 writes all data onto two different disks; RAID level 5 stores only parity information. But both allow you to restore the contents after a single-disk crash.

RAID levels reduce mean times between failures (MTBF) but as more disks are added to a RAID system, the cumulative MTBF decreases. Extremely large database installations experience a failure of a single disk about once a week. Although the contents of the database are restored by the RAID system, this indicates a certain probability for a second disk to fail before the first one is restored. And this situation can be handled only by other backup means.

Symmetric's Business Continuous Volumes

Black Dinosaur Oil Co. uses the Symmetric RAID system from EMC, which supports business continuous volumes (BCVs). A BCV is a logical volume (a set of disks) that can be joined into another logical volume, where it serves as a mirror. It can also be removed from that logical volume (called *breaking the mirror*).

Black Dinosaur uses these features to get a database snapshot, which is transferred to the replica: Normally, the BCV is part of the logical volume on which the production database resides, so it contains an up-to-date copy of the database. To refresh their replica, they remove the BCV from the logical volume. The database can continue to work, but subsequent changes are not reflected on the BCV. Next they transfer the BCV contents into the replication database and direct the system to synchronize the appropriate logical volumes from the BCV. Then they remove the BCV from the replication database and re-insert it into the production database, where it receives all production database changes made during its absence.

Black Dinosaur uses this method to create the smallest possible overhead in the production system when extracting the changes for a replica.

Software Level

Although the RAID systems permit restoration of disk contents after hardware failures, normal backups are also strongly recommended.

Backup to Disk

Backups should be performed regularly, in general daily. You can easily define a database maintenance plan with the SQL Server Enterprise Manager. Right-click on **Database Maintenance Plan** on the left side of the window. A pop-up menu appears. Click on **New ...** to open the Database Maintenance Plan Wizard, which guides you through some dialogs. For a backup to disk, you have complete two dialogs: **Database backup plan** and **Backup Disk Directory**. For a direct backup to tape, only the first window appears.

Here is the first dialog:

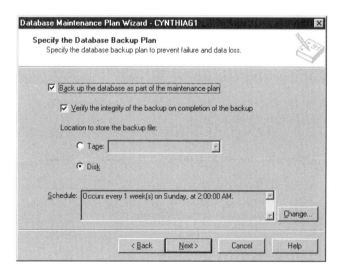

Figure 8.1   Database Backup Plan dialog in the Database Maintenance Plan Wizard.

Click on the check-box **Backup the database as part of the maintenance plan**. Examine the schedule that appears and change it to suit your needs by clicking the **Change...** button. You can schedule one or more backups daily, weekly, or monthly.

Use the second dialog to specify where the backup is stored:

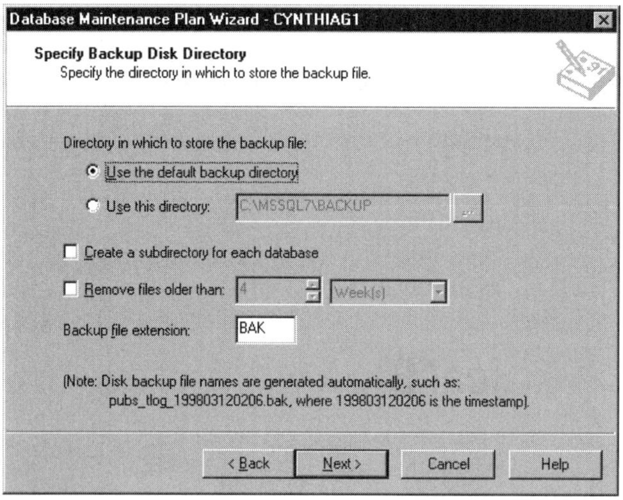

Figure 8.2   Using Database Maintenance Plan Wizard to specify where backups are stored.

MS Sales, James Wilkie Publishers, Bound Galley Book Cellars, Black Dinosaur Oil Co., and A&G Phone write backups to disk first to reduce the time required and the I/O load on the database computer. VLDB administrators should try to complete the backup as fast as possible to minimize system impact.

The duration of a full backup of the database depends on database size and on hardware (disk type, controller, etc.) Some representative statistics:

- Bound Galley Book Cellars needs 35 minutes to back up their 16-GB production database
- A&G Phone needs 8 minutes to back up their 20-GB database
- MultiForm Industries achieved a throughput of 60GB/hour

Transaction log files must also be backed up before their virtual log files can be reused. You can make this part of the same maintenance plan. The Database Maintenance Plan Wizard offers dialogs (similar to the ones shown above) for specifying transaction log files. Generally, you should back these up more frequently than the database.

Some representative tactics:

- MS-Sales backs up the transaction log files every 15 minutes.
- Bound Galley Book Cellars, running a heavily loaded online transactional processing (OLTP) application, backs up the transaction log file every 3 minutes.
- A&G Phone backs up the transaction log files every 30 minutes.

Backup to Tape

The next step is to copy the database and the transaction log files from disk to tape. All the companies referred to in these chapters copy their backups to tape daily, usually in an automated process that runs at night. They do not delete their last backup on the disk, but keep it there to use if they have to restore the database. If the backup disk fails, they can fix the hardware problem then read the backup from the tape.

The companies use different tape systems: DAT tapes, DLT tapes, or even DLT libraries, which resemble RAID systems in that the backup contents are written onto several tapes in parallel.

How to Perform Logical Backups

Logical backups extract the contents of the database so that they can be brought back into the database in small portions—an individual table or row. This becomes necessary when a small section of the database is corrupted (by user error) and it is more sensible to restore the affected portion than the entire database.

You can create logical backups either by exporting the database or by keeping history tables which describe the operations that have been performed on it.

Exporting the Database Contents

You can export the database with the DTS (Data Transformation Services) Wizard or the bulk copy program utility (**bcp**), which uses a command-line interface.

The DTS Wizard guides you through several windows where you specify the table to export and the destination (typically a plain file to store the contents of a table). At the end of the wizard process, you can decide if you want to export the table immediately or create a DTS package to be executed later or on a regular schedule. You have to define the export table by table.

You should export the database whenever you upgrade the operating system, the database system, or the application. Generally, you should export the database before the upgrade, and back up the database after the upgrade. This provides you with a backup you can use if you have to fix minor problems after the upgrade. For bigger problems, you can use the database export that was created before the upgrade. Unlike the backup, the export contains the contents' external representation (not the internal representation), so even if the internal representation of the data changes you can still import the data.

Planning and Maintaining History Tables

Bound Galley Book Cellars included history tables in their data model to audit all operations on the production database. Triggers on the production database tables fire appropriate INSERTs into the history tables, so that they contain a complete description of production database operations. If there is an unintentional operation (a DELETE or UPDATE), the history table can show who performed the operation and when, and the contents of production table can be restored.

Of course, triggers place an additional load on the database, so Bound Galley defined the triggers on a replica of the production database, instead of the database itself. Because every operation is replicated, the history tables are maintained just as they would be if they were triggered from the production database directly.

Every table of the production database has its own history table within the subscribed database. The history table contains the same columns as its base table. Some others can be included.

Optional history table columns.

Column name	Data type	Description
Operation	**char(6)**	contains INSERT, UPDOLD, UPDNEW, or DELETE
Username	**varchar(30)**	User performing the operation
Time	**datetime**	Time stamp of the operation

The remaining columns contain the values of the base table. An INSERT operation inserts the new values in the history table. An UPDATE operation inserts two entries: the old contents with UPDOLD in the column **Operation**, and the new contents with UPDNEW. A DELETE stores the affected record's contents.

The trigger definitions look like this:

```
CREATE TRIGGER BasetableInsert ON Basetable FOR INSERT AS
    INSERT INTO History_table
        SELECT 'INSERT', SESSION_USER, GETDATE(), Basetable_columns
        FROM inserted;

CREATE TRIGGER BasetableUpdate ON Basetable FOR UPDATE AS
BEGIN
    INSERT INTO History_table
        SELECT 'UPDOLD', SESSION_USER, GETDATE(), Basetable_columns
        FROM deleted;
    INSERT INTO History_table
        SELECT 'UPDNEW', SESSION_USER, GETDATE(), Basetable_columns
        FROM inserted;
END;
```

```
CREATE TRIGGER BasetableDelete ON Basetable FOR DELETE AS
    INSERT INTO History_table
        SELECT 'DELETE', SESSION_USER, GETDATE(), Basetable_columns
        FROM deleted;
```

Such triggers allow you to audit every operation on a given base table. The history tables contain the database contents at any given time. If a specific table or a specific row within a table has to be reverted to its contents at a given time, you can find the appropriate values in the history table. If you set up auditing on the replica, there is no impact on the production database.

Guidelines for Establishing Maintenance Jobs

Obviously, it is hard to repair databases that have been corrupted in whole or in part. A complete restore resets the database to its state before the erroneous operation; life goes on, but if the error went undetected for very long, a lot of work probably was done on the database, and it will be lost. History tables (logical backup) can help, but depending on the nature of the erroneous operation it might be hard to extract the correct data from the history tables and to modify operational tables to restore them to the correct state.

Proper maintenance can help recover from such problems, but you must make sure that the maintenance procedure itself does not introduce any errors. Black Dinosaur Oil Co. developed some guidelines to reduce the likelihood of this:

- Every maintenance job is developed in a dedicated development environment. Quality assurance checks are performed by a second person (not the developer) on a second test environment and checked for correctness. Only after this procedure is satisfactorily completed is a new maintenance job established in the production environment.

- No single individual is allowed to perform ad hoc maintenance tasks on the production database: two independent observers must check the necessary statement(s) before they can be run against the production database.

Reorganization

Reorganization is the maintenance process by which fragmentation is removed from indexes and tables. Fragmentation is most often introduced by growing tables. New extents (chunks of memory) cannot always be allocated at the table's current end because those extents might already be allocated for other (also growing) tables.

On tables with clustered indexes, the index determines row placement. After the index is created, all rows are sorted. From then on they lose their order as they are INSERTed, UPDATEd, and DELETEd. Reorganization (index re-creation) re-sorts the rows to re-optimize their placement.

The MS Sales database has many tables with clustered indexes. Because individual reorganization would be too time consuming, they developed a single command script that calls a stored procedure and command line tools to find tables with scan densities below 90%. This section presents the database objects (tables and stored procedures) and the scripts.

Command Script Functionality

The command script completes these steps:

1. Run a Transact-SQL script to create the necessary database objects.
2. Call a stored procedure, which executes DBCC SHOWCONTIG on all tables with clustered indexes.
3. Pass this output through filters to create a Transact-SQL script with appropriate INSERT command into the tables.
4. Re-call the stored procedure, which SELECTs the contents of the tables and executes the DBCC DBREINDEX commands.

The task for the stored procedure used for the steps 2 and 4 is determined by a parameter: if 0, it generates the output from DBCC SHOWCONTIG commands, if greater than 0 it is interpreted as the threshold percentage to run DBCC DBREINDEX.

Tables

The stored procedure needs two tables—**ShowContigName** and **ShowContigValue**—containing these columns:

Table *ShowContigName*.

Column name	Data type	Description
ShowContigId	Identity (1,1)	Primary key
ShowcontigName	sysname	Table name

Table *ShowContigValue*.

Column name	Data type	Description
ShowContigId	Identity (1,1)	Primary key
ShowcontigValue	sysname	Table name

Stored Procedure

The degree of fragmentation is determined by the stored procedure **UtilDBCCDBReIndex**. It is shown below. The error handling has been removed to clarify the procedure's structure.

```
CREATE Proc UtilDBCCDBReIndex
          @DBReIndPct Numeric(6,2) = 90
With Recompile
AS
Begin
    DECLARE @Table_Id          INT,
            @Table_Name        SYSNAME,
            @DBCC_TEXT         char(255),
            @Err               INT,
            @Separator         varchar(255),
            @msg               varchar(255),
            @Sp                SYSNAME,
            @MaxShowContigId   INT,
            @MinShowContigId   INT,
            @ShowContigChar    Char(10),
            @ShowContigValue   Numeric(6,2)

--  Declare a Cursor for Id & Name of the Tables with CLUSTERED Index

    If @DBReIndPct = 0
       Begin
           DECLARE ShowContig_Cur INSENSITIVE CURSOR
           FOR
              Select Id, Name  From SYSOBJECTS
              Where  NAME in ( select object_name(id) from sysindexes
                                  where indid = 1
                                  and   id    > 100
                                  ) -- Only tables with Clustered
           AND    TYPE = "U"
           Order  BY Name
       End
    Else
       Begin

           Select @MaxShowContigId = MAX(ShowContigId) From ShowContigName
           Select @MinShowContigId = MIN(ShowContigId) From ShowContigName

           -- Decision Making Table
           Create Table #t
           (   ShowContigId       Int,
               ShowContigValue    Numeric(6,2)   --  Most Imp DataType
           )
```

(continued)

```
        While  @MinShowContigId  <= @MaxShowContigId
          Begin

             Select  @ShowContigChar  = ltrim(rtrim( ShowContigValue ))
             from     ShowContigValue
             where    ShowContigId = @MinShowContigId

             Select  @ShowContigValue = convert(Numeric(6,2),convert(char(10),
                 substring( @ShowContigChar , 1,
                 charindex('%', @ShowContigChar)-1)))

             Insert into #t
             Select @MinShowContigId , @ShowContigValue

             Select @MinShowContigId = @MinShowContigId + 1
          End

      DECLARE ShowContig_Cur INSENSITIVE CURSOR
      FOR
          Select Object_Id(so.name), so.Name
          From    SYSOBJECTS          so,
                  ShowContigName      n,
                  #t                  t
          Where   n.ShowContigId      = t.ShowContigId
          And     n.ShowContigName    = so.id
          And     so.type             = 'U'
          And     t.ShowContigValue   <= @DBReIndPct
          Order   BY so.Name
    End

-- Open the CURSOR
Open ShowContig_Cur

--   Fetch Records from the CURSOR
FETCH NEXT FROM ShowContig_Cur INTO @Table_ID, @Table_Name

-- Keep looping the CURSOR
WHILE (@@FETCH_STATUS <> -1)
   BEGIN
      IF (@@FETCH_STATUS <> -2)
         BEGIN
            -- Running only ShowContig the First Time
            -- ( When the FE passes the parameter as 0 )
            If @DBReIndPct = 0
              Begin
                 select    @DBCC_TEXT = "dbcc showcontig (" +
                     convert(char(10),@table_id) +")"
                 EXEC    ( @DBCC_TEXT )
                 -- Running the DBCC SHOWCONTIG ( <table_id> )
              End
            Else
```

```
        -- Running only DBCC ReIndex for Selected Tables
        -- ( When the FE passes the parameter > 0 )
            Begin
              select     @DBCC_TEXT = "dbcc dbreindex ('" + @table_name +"',''',90)"
              EXEC     ( @DBCC_TEXT )
              -- Running the DBCC DBREINDEX ( <table_name>, '', 90 )
            End

    END

   FETCH NEXT FROM ShowContig_Cur INTO @Table_ID, @Table_Name
 END

 DEALLOCATE ShowContig_Cur

 Select    @msg = 'Ending the Stored Procedure ' +  @Sp +  ' ' +
    convert(varchar, getdate(), 109)
 Raiserror (@msg, 0,1) with nowait

End
```

Command Script Code

The command script first executes the Transact-SQL script
UtilDBCCDBReIndex.sql, which drops the **ShowContigName** and
ShowContigValue tables and the stored procedure **UtilDBCCDBReIndex** (if
they exist) then re-creates them.

The next step is to call the stored procedure **UtilDBCCDBReIndex** with 0 as the
argument. The output is redirected to a file.

Then, a Transact-SQL script is generated that inserts the table names and the
actual scan densities into the **ShowContigName** and **ShowContigValue** tables.
The first insertion is a small file containing the TRUNCATE TABLE statements.
The next lines are extracted from the output of the previous step by the **grep** and
awk commands (commonly used UNIX filters). Equivalents for Window NT can
be obtained from http://www.cygnus.com. At the end of the generated Transact-
SQL script, **go** is appended from another (very small) file to make the script
complete. The resulting Transact-SQL script looks like this:

```
set nocount on
go
Truncate Table ShowContigName
go
Truncate Table ShowContigValue
go
Insert into ShowContigName Select (object_id1);
```

(continued)

```
Insert into ShowContigName Select (object_id2);
...
Insert into ShowContigValue Select 'percentage1%'
Insert into ShowContigValue Select 'percentage2%'
...
go
```

After the generated Transact-SQL script is executed, the tables contain the names and actual scan densities of all tables with clustered indexes.

Finally, the command script calls the stored procedure again with the actual value of 90%. The stored procedure selects the names of all tables with scan densities below this threshold. For each of these, the statement DBCC DBREINDEX (*table_name*, '', 90) performs the reorganization. All indexes of the given table are re-created with a fillfactor of 90%.

The command script:

```
ECHO   JOB:        Rebuild Indexes
ECHO   FILENAME:   ReIndex.CMD
ECHO
ECHO   DESC:       Step    Description
ECHO           1)  Create the stored procedure
ECHO           2)  Run the procedure with a parameter of 0 so it only
ECHO                   executes a DBCC SHOWCONTIG for all tables with a clustered
ECHO                   index.
ECHO                   The output is written to the log file (defined by %log%)
ECHO           3)  This creates the dbccshowcontigout.txt script with truncate
ECHO               statements.
ECHO           4)  Take the output lines which start with "Table:" and write to the
ECHO               script.
ECHO           5)  Take the Lines which start with "- Scan Density" and write to the
ECHO               script.
ECHO           6)  Execute the dbccshowcontigout.txt script to populate the tables
ECHO           7)  do dbcc reindex on all tables where the Scan Density
ECHO               is under 90%.
ECHO
ECHO   Command Line:   Reindex MyServer MyUserName MyPassword MyDatabase MyLogFile.log
ECHO
ECHO
ECHO   AUTH:       Prasanna Prabhu
ECHO   DATE:       10/21/98
ECHO   FREQUENCY:      On Demand
```

```
echo  **********************************************************************
echo  --- Initializations
echo  **********************************************************************

set svr=%1
set usr=%2
set pwd=%3
set db=%4
set log=%5
set ErrFlag=0

rem This is the initial value so that only dbcc showcontig is executed
set DBReIndPct1=0
rem For the second run of the procedure, this is the lower threshold for Scan Density
set DBReIndPct2=90

echo  *******************************************************************************>>%log%
echo  --- Step 1.  Run the script to create 2 tables and the stored procedure     >>%log%
echo  *******************************************************************************>>%log%
osql /S%Svr% /U%usr% /P%pwd% /d%db% /i UtilDBCCDBReIndex.sql /n /b              >>%log%
if errorlevel 1 set errmsg=***ReIndex.cmd failed & goto problem


echo  *******************************************************************************>>%log%
echo  --- Step 2. do dbcc reindex on all tables                                   >>%log%
echo  *******************************************************************************>>%log%
set qry=osql /S%Svr% /U%usr% /P%pwd% /d%db% /Q "exec UtilDBCCDBReIndex
    %DBReIndPct1% " /n /b
%qry% >>%Log%
if errorlevel 1 set errmsg=***ReIndex.cmd failed on execution of
    SP UtilDBCCDBReIndex & goto problem


echo  *******************************************************************************>>%log%
echo  Steps 3-4 look at the output of dbcc showcontig and append sql statements
echo       to a script    >>%log%
echo  --- Step 3. Truncating tables before populating                             >>%log%
echo  *******************************************************************************>>%log%
cat TruncateShowContig.txt   >  dbccshowcontigout.txt
if errorlevel 1 set errmsg=***ReIndex.cmd failed & goto problem
```

(continued)

```
echo *************************************************************************>>%log%
echo --- Step 4.   Select the Lines which start with "Table:"              >>%log%
echo *************************************************************************>>%log%
grep  "Table: '"              %log%  |  awk   "{print \"Insert into ShowContigName
    Select \" $3 }" >> dbccshowcontigout.txt
if errorlevel 1 set errmsg=***ReIndex.cmd failed & goto problem


echo *************************************************************************>>%log%
echo --- Step 5. Select the Lines which start with "- Scan Density"        >>%log%
echo *************************************************************************>>%log%
grep  "Scan Density "    %log%  |  awk   "{print \"Insert into ShowContigValue
    Select '\" $7 \"'\"}" >> dbccshowcontigout.txt
if errorlevel 1 set errmsg=***ReIndex.cmd failed & goto problem

cat AppendGo.txt       >>dbccshowcontigout.txt
if errorlevel 1 set errmsg=***ReIndex.cmd failed & goto problem


echo *************************************************************************>>%log%
echo --- Step 6. Execute the dbccshowcontigout.txt script to populate the tables   >>%log%
echo *************************************************************************>>%log%
osql /S%Svr% /U%usr% /P%pwd% /d%db% /i dbccshowcontigout.txt /n /b           >>%log%
if errorlevel 1 set errmsg=***ReIndex.cmd failed & goto problem


echo *************************************************************************>>%log%
echo --- Step 7. Perform DBCC DBReindex on tables that need it
echo             (found in previous steps)                                  >>%log%
echo *************************************************************************>>%log%
osql /S%Svr% /U%usr% /P%pwd% /d%db% /Q "exec UtilDBCCDBReIndex
    %DBReIndPct2% " /n /b                                                    >>%log%
if errorlevel 1 set errmsg=***ReIndex.cmd failed & goto problem


:finished
goto done

:problem


:done
echo.
if %ErrFlag%==-1 echo *** ERROR running ReIndex.cmd !!!                      >>%log%
if %ErrFlag%==-1 echo *** ERROR running ReIndex.cmd !!!
if %ErrFlag%==0 echo *** ReIndex completed successfully ***                  >>%log%
if %ErrFlag%==0 echo *** ReIndex completed successfully ***
```

Increasing the Availability

The companies referred to in these chapters have high availability requirements for their production databases. The strongest requirement is 99.99%, which means a maximum downtime of less than one hour per year. No newly installed database with its applications will reach this figure at the beginning. During the first production phase you have to devise maintenance tasks to fix potential problems.

Black Dinosaur Oil Co. provides a good example of how to reach a high level of availability. In the first production phase, they kept the database available during normal working hours. Then, as they grew more comfortable with database operations, they increased availability by defining a maintenance window from 10 p.m. to 1 a.m. every night. The database was available at all other times, including weekends. After the system stabilized further, the administrators noticed that they needed only a small part of the maintenance window so they decided to use it only on Sunday, reducing downtime to only 3 hours per week. The final step is to drop even this maintenance window and to keep the database system available all the time.

One advantage of this procedure is that no regularly running jobs are scheduled between 10 p.m. and 1 a.m. Should they ever need to perform more maintenance, they can do so easily by using the former maintenance window.

Using DBCC Under SQL Server 7.0

With SQL Server 6.5, the database consistency checker (DBCC) was an important tool to check and repair database consistency, especially with the **CHECKDB** option.

With SQL Server 7.0 a new storage engine uses some error detection logic when it accesses the database, so the need for the DBCC is decreased somewhat. But it is still a useful tool and SQL Server 7.0 optimizes its internal algorithms so that it runs significantly faster.

This sections describes the DBCC experiences of the companies referred to in these chapters.

Performance

DBCC performance has been improved significantly, particularly when run on a large database.

At Black Dinosaur Oil Co., DBCC NEWALLOC used to require 24 hours under SQL Server 6.5; under SQL Server 7.0 it takes 6 hours. DBCC CHECKDB took 3 days under SQL Server 6.5. Another company reported a speed increase of 8 – 10 times running DBCC on a 42-GB database.

Necessity

The companies referred to in these chapters, all of which run VLDBs under SQL Server 7.0, were asked about the number of inconsistencies detected and repaired by DBCC.

Only MultiForm Industries reported finding an inconsistency. Their database resides on external disks, mounted on an open system rack (OSR). One of these disks overheated drastically, so the rack was shut down immediately and the bad disk replaced. (From then on, the rumor at MultiForm was that OSR stands for "only smokes randomly.") DBCC CHECKDB detected and repaired two inconsistencies—no doubt caused by the disk's inability to write a block or the hasty shut-down.

Respondents differ on the necessity of running DBCC: Bound Galley Book Cellars no longer runs the DBCC regularly, only in the event of a problem such as a hardware failure. Broadband Cable and Black Dinosaur still run DBCC CHECKDB regularly. They have detected no problems under SQL Server 7.0, but they run it for consistency insurance.

Frequency

The companies still running DBCC schedule it to run once a week as part of a maintenance job. Some plan to enlarge the interval if no inconsistencies appear, but because they need to ensure early detection of production database problems they do not plan to drop DBCC completely from their maintenance jobs.

Data Warehouse Scenarios

The time: 2:11 p.m.

The place: Corporate IT offices for Solutions 'R' Us

The problem: You are just finishing your afternoon carbo-loading—a can of cream soda and a package of Twinkies—when the MIS manager's head flashes past your cubicle wall as he sprints down the aisle doing his best race track announcer imitation (which still is not very good): *"This is it! This is it! The competition rounds the corner; their latest print ad in hand: first quarter sales are up. But coming around the bend, hard on their heels, closing the gap…it's…Solutions 'RRRRRR' U-usssss. We're building a data warehouse for the sales force!"* The singsong 'R' Us 'R' Us 'R' Us is still reverberating when the manager skids to a stop and whistles a panting rendition of the theme from *Star Wars*. You roll the cold cream soda can over your forehead.

The solution: Data warehouse projects require more than enthusiasm and team spirit, and often entail joining forces with a partner company to gather requirements, architect a solution, and manage the rollout. Chapter 3 in Part 1 of this book describes a datamart and data warehouse development and deployment strategy. The chapters in Part 3 highlight several data warehouse (DW) case studies. Chapter 9 explores how Microsoft's human resources DW creates a single secure system for daily reporting. Chapter 10, on MS Sales, describes how the development team created a system to make timely, consistent, and accurate data available for users with divergent needs, *and* boost system performance. Chapter 11 looks at how MetaEdge uses metadata and components built on the Microsoft Repository to manage a data warehouse. And Chapter 12 showcases a simple but highly effective OLAP Services implementation used with a management reporting system.

C H A P T E R   9

HR Data Warehouse
for Microsoft Human Resources

By Erin Blake, John Boen, Spencer Butt, Susan Cushen, Tom Jamieson, Ann Jewett, Keith Klosterman, Allen McDowell, Betsy Norton-Middaugh, David Morts, Tom Niccoli, Lincoln Popp, Chris Stine, and Kathy Watanabe, Microsoft Information Technology Group

Microsoft Human Resources (HR) originally used two data systems for resource planning: one in the U.S. (based on SQL Server) and one for 17 international sites (based on Access 1.1). A complex process collected transactions into a database twice a week. Data volumes and reporting needs gradually necessitated improvement, so in 1997 the SHARP project began work on a new SAP R/3 system and a new HR Data Warehouse (HRDW) to provide a single system capable of daily reporting.

The Solution in Focus

This chapter shows how the SHARP project began by analyzing the unique characteristics of HR data so that business needs and security could be addressed in the earliest phases of HRDW design.

To collect this type of data into a central repository for HR querying and reporting, the design team created the Feedstore—a repository for information destined for outbound interfaces. This is a Microsoft-internal system that acts as a distribution point for common data feeds to synchronize data between numerous applications. Data is also derived from two other logical sections: the Information Desktop, which uses SQL Server 7.0 and OLAP Services to deliver standard, customizable HR functional reports, and HR Online, which can query against multiple databases and is fed through a DCL process that moves the HRDataMart database to a number of publication servers.

Another critical business need was to supply updated HR data current as of the close of the previous business day. To accomplish this, HRDW data is rebuilt nightly—a process so complex that it required creating a metadata SQL solution called the Data Genie. This consists of a Windows NT batch command file wrapper around a set of SQL Server stored procedures and tables that generate batch code dynamically. It allows flexibility in enhancing and maintaining the build process, and some concurrency control.

Specific advice on data warehouse design and implementation—what to do and what not to do—is based on the design team's experience.

What You'll Find in This Chapter

- A detailed explanation of how functional components were designed, built, and integrated.

- How tools and technical environments were used in development.

- How business rules were defined, made consistent, and integrated with a security model.

- Discussion of integration and migration issues.

- Discussions of which decisions worked and which could have worked better.

- How to organize and manage people in this type of project.

Case Overview

Microsoft Human Resources (HR) must be able to collect, manage, and report on data worldwide. Until 1997, HR transactions resided in 18 separate sites and used two Enterprise Resource Planning (ERP) systems: one running on top of Microsoft SQL Server in the United States and 17 running on Access version 1.1 at international subsidiaries. A complex extract and build process was used to combine transactions into a single People Reporting Database (PRDB).

In 1997 a new centralized global HR SAP R/3 system was implemented to contain all HR transactions. At the same time, a new HR Data Warehouse (HRDW) was designed to:

- Provide a central repository for HR querying and reporting
- Supply information destined for outbound interfaces to the Feedstore (a Microsoft-internal system that acts as a distribution point for common data feeds to synchronize data between numerous applications)

This chapter describes how the HRDW was designed, built, and implemented. It discusses how the system is maintained and what sort of work is currently being done to enhance and extend it. The discussion goes into detail on the lessons learned by Microsoft's HR IT group as they designed the HRDW: some things worked well, some not so well, some not at all. These sorts of discoveries are central to the large design effort necessary to create a solid and usable data warehouse.

The discussion begins by looking at challenges that seem peculiar to this project, but which actually arise from the basic concepts of data warehouse design. The nature of the data is crucial: its breadth, depth, frequency of change, interconnections, and uses all dictate the logic that must be built into the data warehouse. HR data of course has some unique characteristics, but all large data collections have their own.

After laying out the challenges, the discussion considers what the project team learned and how it functioned, then moves into testing as a part of design and maintenance. From this point, the chapter presents successive layers of system detail, explains how problems were solved, then examines basic project design and management. A brief glossary concludes the chapter.

By discussing the HRDW project from several points of view and levels of detail, the chapter lets you follow the Microsoft HR IT team as it creates a data warehouse—a task more complex and far reaching than simply designing an extremely large database. During a process of this size and complexity, a development team gets the chance to learn lots of lessons about how to do things—sometimes by finding out how *not* to do them. This chapter is designed to help you see and understand one instance of this process as it unfolded.

Challenges

Nature of HR Data

Experience shows that HR data is much more complex than the data found in a typical financial or sales data warehouse. This complexity arises from:

- **Many more unique attributes.** Typical financial applications manage about 100 attributes: HR manages over 600. Greater complexity (even with smaller volume) creates a need for accurate documentation and effective business rules.

- **Many more entities and relationships.** Data deals with numerous people, positions, and relationships, so the logical model is quite complicated. Entities are often extensively sub-typed. The physical model can be simplified, but doing so requires tradeoffs and these must be understood by users.

- **History is not static.** Errors found in personnel data must be corrected whether they refer to data from last month or years ago.

- **Detail is often required.** Managers tend to study trends and use aggregates, but most daily-use queries seek detailed information (display a person's job history, etc.).

- **Most data has meaning only in relationship to other data.** For example, does a person with the title of manager manage one person, a function, or an organization of 1000 people? You have to take surrounding data into account to answer this question.

- **The time factor.** The business rules associated with legacy data differ from those associated with current data. It becomes a major challenge to make legacy data work with queries designed with the new system's data structures in mind.

Issues Arising from Data Characteristics

- **Design tradeoffs.** As reporting interfaces are made easier to use, more restrictions are placed on the types or complexity of queries that users can write. To keep the system useful but usable by a wide variety of people, HRDW designers had to support different types of queries:

  - Ad hoc queries directly against the database created by business professionals trained in both the business and SQL using a tool such as Microsoft Access or ISQL.

  - Ad hoc queries using a customizable reporting interface (MS Reports).

  - Structured, filtered queries based on standard reports (Information Desktop).

  - Standard reports prewritten by professionals and published periodically.

- **Business rules tend to be subtler** (due to the number of attributes), geographically diverse, and not fully understood by users and IT professionals. Accurate, complete documentation is essential.

- **System maintenance cost is high.** Because individual data elements are highly interrelated, each proposed change must be analyzed to make sure that it will produce only desired effects.

- **Training lag.** It takes longer for new team members (developers, testers, analysts, etc.) to get up to speed on the system.

- **Incremental data refreshes are difficult**, so much so that the data warehouse and datamart are completely rebuilt daily.

SAP R/3

Business requirements forced a ten-month implementation schedule, which constrained the scope of the effort and required design and scope tradeoffs:

- It was decided to minimize data validation in the SAP R/3 UI implementation because:

  Customizing SAP R/3 code might make it too expensive to migrate to subsequent SAP R/3 versions.

  The tight schedule did not allow determination of all relevant business rules for HR data.

  Many business rules needed to be flexible enough to manage different categories of the same data (full-time employees vs. contingent staff, employees of one country vs. employees of another, etc.).

- The code written to extract data from SAP R/3 simply dumped a subset of the columns from each SAP R/3 table to a flat file. This isolated the downstream systems from column additions in SAP R/3 tables, but did not enforce business rules.

  Because of the division of responsibilities between the operations group supporting SAP R/3 and the various business units (such as HR) using SAP R/3, the central operations group used this simpler approach when it saw that enforcing business rules in the extract code would require too much maintenance over time. SAP R/3 warranty restrictions and concern about OLTP performance militated against using remote stored procedures on the SAP R/3 SQL Server box.

- Extracted data, once reloaded into SQL Server, required further transformation before it could be integrated with legacy and other data.

  A number of business rules and audits were enforced at this point in the process to ensure internal consistency of SAP R/3 data. For instance, some data needed to be restated and the 5-character abbreviated German field names were converted to names that were more meaningful in context. Finally, SAP

R/3 stores data in ways suited to *its* functions, not necessarily to those of an HR data warehouse. SAP R/3 data structures and fields were used in ways not originally intended by the SAP R/3 designers, so data warehouse routines had to reinterpret the data as part of the transformation process.

SHARP Project Characteristics

The SHARP project (S A P for H R) implemented SAP R/3 HR modules and superseded a number of other enterprise resource planning (ERP) and client/server systems in use in various parts of Microsoft prior to April 1997.

Some of the challenges were simply due to this being the first phase of a project; others had more to do with project structure and scheduling.

Time Pressure Short Circuited Planning

Project teams are always constrained by time, resources, and scope. For this project, time and resources were tight: few people could be spared from their existing roles, contractors with the required skillset were hard to come by, and it was difficult to use new people quickly and effectively. Thus s*cope* became the factor that varied the most. For instance, the project focused immediately on UI and database issues related to publishing data to existing systems that depend on HR data. This was a good decision. But addressing reporting later, when hard deadlines severely limited the amount of planning, architecture work, and actual deliverables, was not so good, and effects of this decision are still being felt two years later. Over-focusing on feed requirements led to inconsistently normalized tables in the data warehouse design. Reusing these tables for reporting purposes has caused query performance problems.

Rule of thumb: version 1.0 rarely gets it right. Why? Because an implementation team seldom fully understands every concept in a new system and the implications of many decisions become clear only after some time passes.

Bullpen Environment and Its Impact on Documentation

Putting most of the project team in one big room helped meet the hard schedule by optimizing communication and allowing people to meet at a moment's notice. Unfortunately, because everyone tended to understand the project and the system, they tended to under-document business rules for the SAP and legacy systems as well as for the data transformations that were integrated in the nightly build process. Much of the staff has since moved on to other projects at Microsoft, and a great deal of system knowledge has gone with them. Complete documentation is essential.

Legacy Data

Because SHARP replaced two different HR ERP applications used throughout Microsoft, the implementation team had to address more than 1000 shared attributes spread across multiple systems. To get a unified picture of historical data, the team had to sort through over 15,000 variations of attributes across the different HR systems to choose more than 1000 attributes that the HRDW needs to track.

A period of double-keying data into SAP R/3 and the legacy systems during the changeover also created some problems. SAP R/3 was initially implemented only in the US and Latin America. Employees who were put in SAP R/3 had to stay in it, so if they transferred to another subsidiary on a different system, they were maintained in SAP R/3 as well as on the local legacy system. In addition to creating more work at the time, reconciling this data since full implementation has proven difficult and error-prone.

Inconsistent Application of Business Rules in Each System

Different business rules were implemented in each of the legacy HR systems because the existing systems had different structures and features. A further problem was that Microsoft's decentralized management structure allowed subsidiaries to use their systems in ways suited to their individual needs. This made things easier for subsidiary managers, but it also meant that subsidiaries collected different data and applied different rules to it—even if they used the same system. Another "problem" is that business rules change over time but sometimes historical data is not restated to meet new rules. If you want to interpret data correctly, you must understand and program for "magic" dates on which the rules changed. The most important of these magic dates was the date when the SAP 3.0 system went live and many of the business rules and domain values changed.

Weak Documentation Leads to a Dependence on "Tribal Knowledge"

Documentation on the various systems and implementations was spotty, so the conversion team often had to rely on the knowledge of key individuals, especially when dealing with custom modifications that implemented "special case" processing.

Data Ownership Issues Between Systems Were Unclear

In the legacy systems, it was sometimes quite difficult to know where to source the data for a transferred individual, especially when both systems still considered that person as active.

Lack of Built-In Referential Integrity in the Legacy HR Systems

A lack of referential integrity and other business rule enforcement in the legacy HR systems led to data quality problems. Users had to be trained in and responsible for data quality: for input and for fixing data problems highlighted on audit reports.

At the time of the conversion there were significant data quality problems—fixing them is the primary reason that users continue to modify history—and these problems made it difficult to make an accurate conversion.

Project Impacts

Many systems and projects affect the HRDW. To show other teams and management how many issues existed and how they affected productivity, the team created and circulated a diagram nicknamed the wheel of fortune.

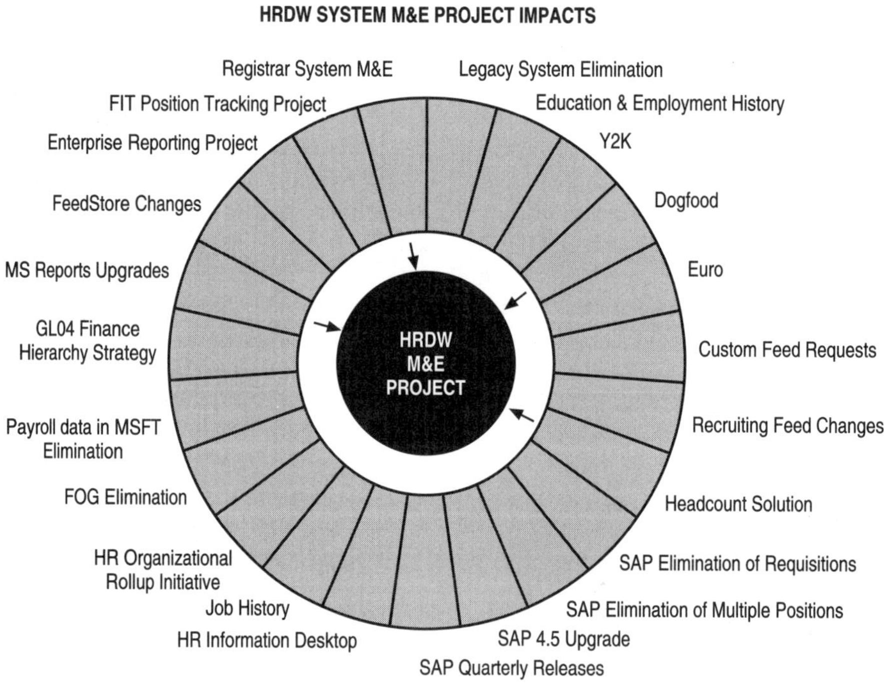

HRDW SYSTEM M&E PROJECT IMPACTS

Figure 9.1   "Wheel of fortune" graphic showing issues in relation to productivity.

Project management separated the HRDW team into sub teams. The M&E (Maintenance and Enhancement) team was assigned bug fixes, responding to SAP R/3 Quarterly releases, helping with any production problems, and making changes as prioritized by business partners. Temporary teams were formed for projects such as adding history, dealing with Y2K issues, and technical upgrades.

MS Reports

To meet the goal of serving as a central repository for HR querying and reporting, the team delivered ad hoc query capability to the business community. Providing users self-service access to data has had mixed results, mostly because users range from novice to expert. The same tool is used by *power* users and *casual* users. The team focused on the power user and (consistent with IT strategy) turned to an in-house application, MS Reports, which was developed by the central IT group for use as a data warehouse query application.

MS Reports uses a Microsoft Visual Basic 6.0 ActiveX add-in to Excel to help users create ad hoc queries that return results in Excel pivot tables, Excel worksheets, or Access databases. A middle tier allows for load balancing and frees up the client while the query is processing.

Security Model

Management strategy required a highly complex security model.

Human Resources data is sensitive. Besides legal and privacy issues, there are morale concerns—users should not have access to sensitive information about their peers. For instance, recruiters need information about jobs and salaries throughout the company to do their jobs, but they do not need salary information about their co-workers.

Two approaches were evaluated to address this issue. One required the reporting application to provide information on a need-to-know basis, so the team would have to analyze the information requirements for each user type (called roles). The other proposed to control data access at a high level (access to the application), and monitor for abuses. This would have been easier and cheaper to implement and maintain, but it would have burdened managers with enforcing access rules and policies, possibly placing them in the position of having to discipline an employee because of a policy violation.

In the end, the team implemented full security in the on-line application, despite increased cost and complexity. The implementation made it possible to restrict user access by column (for example, only selected users could view compensation information) and row (for example, users cannot see certain information about some peers).

Column-Level Security (Data Subject Areas)

To implement the security model, the team categorized the datamart columns into data subject areas (DSAs). For example, social security number and home address information were grouped into the Personal DSA, because the security requirements for those columns are similar. The DSA categorizations helped the team formulate a consistent approach to column-level data permissions.

Row-Level Security (Country and Departmental Restrictions)

Users can be granted access to certain types of data but can be denied access to data subsets depending on role. The two main row-level restriction requirements are *Approved Company Only* and *Peer Exclusion*. Approved Company Only restricts users to information in one or more subsidiary sites. For example, a user in Germany can be limited to seeing confidential data only for employees of Microsoft Germany. Peer Exclusion, on the other hand, prohibits certain employees from seeing sensitive data about their peers.

Production Support Issues

Nightly Processing Window

In order to provide a consistent set of data, the SAP R/3 production support team enforces a keying cut-off. Initially, there was a twelve-hour nightly processing window between the SAP R/3 keying cut-off and the data publication deadline. The keying cut-off was pushed back an hour (to 5:00 p.m.) to provide an extra hour for data processing so that intermediate deadlines for providing data to external systems through data extracts could be met.

The HRDW system was designed to meet a critical business need by supplying updated HR data current as of the close of the previous business day. The publication deadline for this data is 6:00 a.m. PST. Various other external systems need to be refreshed as well, which requires that HR data be made available to them well before the beginning of the business day. The primary interface for delivery of HR data to external systems is the IT Feedstore process.

Dependencies and deadlines for the HRDW build process:

- The extract from SAP R/3 to flat files (6:00 p.m. to 6:50 p.m.). This process must complete before processing can start for current-day HR data.

- The HR01 Feedstore extract from the HR Data Warehouse. This feed depends on successful current point-in-time (CPIT) completion. The deadline for refresh is midnight.

- The HRLoad process refreshes the Registrar system with current-day information; it depends on successful CPIT completion.

- The HRFM01 Feedstore extract from the HR Data Warehouse. This feed depends on successful monthly point-in-time (MPIT) completion. It is used by finance. The deadline for refresh is 2:30 a.m.

- The headcount activity feed. This feed depends on successful MPIT completion and is also used by finance. The deadline for refresh is 2:30 a.m.

- The refresh of the database used by the user query interface, HR Online for MS Reports. This database also supports some ad hoc queries run by the HR department. This refresh depends on successful completion of both PITs and history processing. The deadline for refresh is 6:00 a.m.

- Audit reporting. These reports are used by staff to correct data in the SAP R/3 HR system. They run unattended on the "build" server throughout the day and must be completed before the next day's data warehouse build process starts.

Even though 13 hours seems like a lot of time to process this data, the intermediate deadlines create a very tight schedule. The first deliverable is due about seven hours after processing can start. The next, and most critical finance deliverables are due 2.5 hours later. The most time intensive but least critical deliverable is history processing, which is due 3.5 hours later.

Nightly Batch Problems

The HRDW support analysts must be prepared to deal with a wide variety of problems. Errors during the "build" process may be caused by factors ranging from unexpected data, to SQL Server errors, to network or hardware problems, to file or resource contention issues. Troubleshooting is complicated because it must be timely, but the build process is run overnight when there is no on-site coverage. Most troubleshooting takes place over low-bandwidth Remote Access Services (RAS) telephone connections established from a tech's home.

The HRDW has a set of referential integrity rules enforced by SQL. Because of the implementation approach used by the team, SAP R/3 is not used to enforce many of these rules. Instead referential integrity is handled largely as a set of business rules enforced through data-entry practices. When bad data slips through, the first indication is a primary key violation failure of the data warehouse build process. A support analyst has to correct the problem and restart the build. These types of errors are called build breakers.

The simplest errors are those caused by a temporary network outage or file contention problems. These can usually be fixed by re-submitting the process immediately or after a few minutes.

The two toughest issues are primary key violations caused by unexpected data anomalies and native SQL Server errors. To correct the first type, the analyst uses a RAS connection to study stored procedures and their dependent procedures to identify which data to remove or correct. A typical troubleshooting procedure would include reading the text of the stored procedure(s) involved and then writing an SQL script to cull the problem data. When the bad data is found, it is usually simple to remove it so that the build can continue.

Native SQL Server errors are of several types. Those indicating a shortage of SQL Server storage space can be dealt with by allocating more, or (if the problem is related to temporary storage in **tempdb** or transaction log space) by controlling process concurrency better. Other errors usually can be fixed by stopping and starting the SQL Server services, rebuilding an index, etc.

Even simple problems can affect things when you have to interrupt the nightly build then redo parts of the process. For a process that runs in minutes, fixing a problem and getting back on track can take an hour. For a process that takes hours, deadlines can be missed.

As the HRDW matured, the team reduced or eliminated the most costly errors. The first real attempt at dealing with the primary key violations was to create a procedure that would be called if there was a failure, would check to see if the error was of a known type, and then would use programmatic steps to correct known types without triggering a build failure. In actual practice this solution was only marginally effective because there were many limitations to what the error recovery system could deal with.

The next attempt involved rebuilding indices with the **ignore_dup_row** option. This allows processing to continue after a primary key violation, but does not duplicate data because SQL Server ignores data with duplicate key information. A warning message is generated and placed in the build log file each time a duplicate row is ignored. At the end of the build a separate audit reporting process checks the build log files and reports, so that the underlying data issues can be corrected. Note that this did not remove the underlying error condition: it simply reduced the failure count. These types of "solutions" may hide problems, and it is crucial to follow through, find, and correct them or they will grow until they become unmanageable.

Complexity of Nightly Process

Because of the complexity of the build process, a metadata SQL solution, Data Genie, was designed to rebuild data nightly. It consists of a Windows NT batch command file wrapper around a set of SQL Server stored procedures and tables that generate batch code dynamically. This allows flexibility in enhancing and maintaining the build process, and some concurrency control.

The HRDW nightly build process is run in the Microsoft IT standard batch processing environment. Typically, jobs that are run in this environment consist of a collection of batch files that execute native operating system commands, SQL Scripts, Transact-SQL stored procedures and utilities, and programs or executables. The batch files are normally parameterized using local and global environment variables for such values as server names, share paths, and login and password data. Adding the metadata-driven Data Genie to this system resulted in an elegant and highly configurable system that allows more flexibility than the standard hard-coded batch files. It also added complexity, and the resulting system is a challenge for the support analysts to learn.

The data is also quite complex. It is sourced from current SAP R/3 data extracts as well as from legacy databases, so that history can be pulled forward and data corrections made on old records are reflected. The format of the source data required some pretty complex data transformations in the process.

Testing

The focus and methods of testing must evolve along with the warehouse. Change is driven by changes in business needs and technology, and by lessons learned. Testing must look forward: to make sure proposed changes are efficient and relevant, the team must test them thoroughly before they are delivered. The test team must develop solid and effective communication with the project's business partners, analysts, development, and production support; they must be involved in the project from requirements gathering all the way through to assisting production support.

Challenges

Ensuring that users have access to accurate and complete data is the HRDW test team's biggest challenge. This requires:

- Clear and unambiguous requirements and business rules. The tight project schedule resulted in incomplete documentation of the requirements and business rules. The need for usable documentation was understood, but there was not enough time and resources to get it done. Without a complete and accurate record, it was hard for the team to confirm that data was complete and accurate. Work continues on the documentation, and the team incorporates the information in test procedures whenever possible.

- Holding reviews of functional requirements, physical design, test scenarios, and test cases. These reviews have not always been thorough, resulting in lost time and jeopardized release dates as documentation is corrected or clarified. More personal accountability was assigned to appropriate personnel to clear this up.

- Tracking all test cases against enumerated requirements. The team needs to know what has been tested, what the status of testing is, and when testing should be completed. Tight schedule and staffing problems can relax enforcement of these criteria, but things tend to work well if the team is diligent with the requirements and testing process.

- Significant ramp-up time for new test personnel. Functional requirements and business rules are numerous and complex and often interconnected. People need time to gain a good working knowledge and apply it in their testing. Three to six months of ramp-up time is not unusual.

- That testing is completed using data copied from the production environment. This lengthens the test cycle and can make the discovery of some data issues more difficult, but it shows how most data combinations behave before they are put in production.

- A standard data subset is *not* used for development and testing. Teams sometimes try this as a way of shortening the processing (build) time, but it has not been effective for HR data. For starters, data complexity makes it impossible to create a data set from scratch. Creating a set from production data requires extensive analysis and coding to extract data, then thorough testing to ensure that it is a valid data set. Then the set must be updated as the code base matures or input interfaces change. After making a very serious attempt, the HRDW test team determined that it is prohibitively expensive to create and maintain a representative and valid data subset for the HR data.

Testing in a Production-Like Environment

Initial testing of the HRDW was completed in an environment that simulated but did not exactly replicate the production environment. While this was sufficient at the start of the project, it grew less so as the HRDW expanded and became more complex. Soon it was taking a week or more to successfully install and run in production, making it clear that the test environment had to match the production environment and that a dedicated build environment was necessary.

The Test and Development teams requested hardware that closely matched production hardware. It took significant effort to overcome the objections of key project personnel who were skeptical that the benefits would justify the upgrade costs.

Once the hardware was procured, continuing configuration management effort was required for setup and maintenance. The hardware was configured as closely as possible to the production environment, then all software and applications involved in HRDW processing were matched by version and configured as in production. Standard batch processing environment files (.CMD, etc.) were evaluated and configured to match. Production Support, Test, and Development personnel stayed involved to assure that production, development, and test environment configurations remained consistent.

Even after a year of careful configuration management, differences were being uncovered that affected HRDW processing. The Test and Development teams sometimes have problems with the HRDW build process while builds in other groups work as expected. While these problems can often be traced to an out-of-sync parameter or file, it sometimes cannot be determined if the cause is bad code, incorrect or incomplete installation instructions, or a deviation from the installation instructions.

The HRDW nightly build process has several time-driven intermediate milestones, and it has become harder to meet them as the data warehouse has expanded and become more complex. The project team has to ensure that all milestones are met with each new release, and this requires testing in a production-like environment to derive accurate timing for each step of the process and to see if the milestones can be met. Pre-production testing has helped the team improve the build process and manage users' expectations for data availability.

A fringe benefit of standardizing configuration is that hardware can be moved or loaned around in the project team to meet planned or unplanned needs, with little or no reconfiguration.

Testing in a dedicated, production-like environment has made it possible to get new releases up and running in production within a day. Most team members feel that the improved performance and reduced frustration have more than compensated for the costs.

Personnel

During the project, personnel requirements evolved as management realized the complexity of the testing effort and as deliverable functionality changed.

- The trend in staffing was towards more highly qualified people: strong SQL Server skills are required to test the HRDW.

- HRDW testers needed the same skills as project developers because of the complexity of the business rules, the functional requirements, the physical design, and the schedule.

- Core skills and aptitudes for HRDW testers:

  - Highly intelligent and motivated

  - Advanced SQL Server skills (coding primarily, administration secondarily)

  - Ability to think outside of the box and innovate

  - Ability to analyze and think logically

- The HRDW project testing team used contingent personnel, and it takes time and effort to find, orient, and retain qualified staff. To overcome the difficulty of finding qualified SQL Server testers the team developed strong relationships with recruiters. The team created a list of well-defined required skills, acted quickly and decisively when a qualified candidate was identified, and boosted pay levels for testers.

- Testing requirements and costs for testing grew as the project matured, although efficiency and skills have also increased: it is costing more, but more is being done.

A Brief History of Solutions

PRDB (Pre-SAP R/3 Data)

Before converting to SAP R/3, Microsoft used one ERP system to track US employee data, and another ERP system to track international employee and contingent staff workforce data. These systems were located in 18 sites around the world and stored in separate databases.

Extract files were taken from the international ERP databases twice weekly, consolidated with the US ERP data, into a reporting database called the People Reporting Database (PRDB). HR Online was built as a reporting tool for the consolidated information and attached to the PRDB. PAT (a people tracking tool) and WinOrg were used to track individuals at Microsoft and provide organizational charts of the Microsoft workforce.

The SHARP project was designed to create a single repository for all company HR information, using SAP R/3 as the company-wide solution.

MS Reports

MS Reports is a front-end application designed by Microsoft's central IT Group to provide a user interface to a datamart stored on a SQL Server.

Microsoft Excel is the entry point for MS Reports. An Excel add-in places a **Start MS-Reports** item at the bottom of the **Tools** menu. Selecting it opens another Excel add-in, which adds a single menu and a toolbar to the user's Excel environment. The toolbar and menu item provide access to a Visual Basic 6.0 application. The Visual Basic 6.0 code base handles all of the significant user interface functions including data access. Windows 9*x*, Windows NT 4.0, Windows 2000, Excel 97, and Excel 2000 are supported.

User Interface

MS Reports includes an ad hoc query component and an interface for accessing standard reports.

Query Interface

The ad hoc query interface provides an abstract view of the datamart. Users do not have to know about tables and joins; the only fields displayed are those users may want to include in a report.

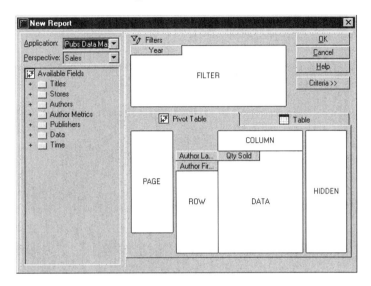

Figure 9.2   MS Reports PivotTable dialog.

To compose queries, users drag fields over to the PivotTable or Table tabs.

The **PivotTable** tab, above, looks very similar to Excel's PivotTable Wizard. When a query is executed from the **PivotTable** tab, query output goes directly to an Excel PivotTable, an Excel spreadsheet, or an Access table. From there the user can refresh the report to retrieve the most current data from the server, edit the report to change criteria or field selections, or drill down on a particular item in the report by bringing back more detailed data.

The **Table** tab provides a place to design queries that will have tabular output. The user can choose between tabular output to an Excel worksheet or to an Access table in a new or existing Access database.

MS Reports provides a single interface to multiple back-end data marts, or *applications*. Currently over 15 applications use MS Reports as their reporting interface or are in the process of implementing it.

Standard Reports Interface

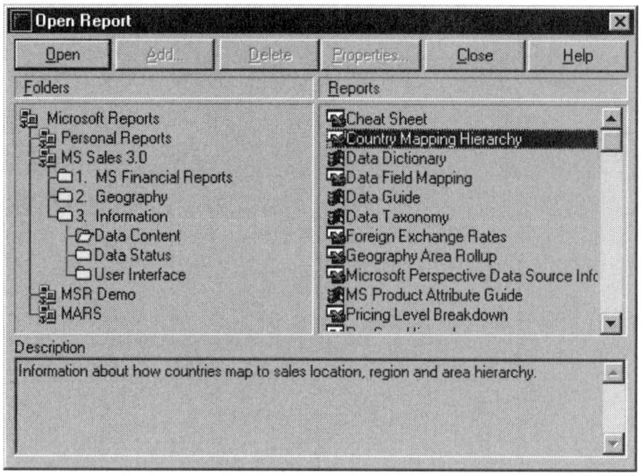

Figure 9.3   The Open Report component—one report interface for multiple applications.

The Open Report component provides the user with a single interface for accessing standard reports for each application. Reports can be Excel spreadsheets, Word documents, links to Web pages, etc., and can be distributed across multiple servers.

Online Help

An extensive Web-based help system guides users through MS Reports and provides context-sensitive help.

Query Engine

Behind the ad hoc query interface is an advanced SQL query engine. MS Reports composes SQL Server code based on the fields the user drags into the query design area.

MS Reports Architecture

The MS Reports Visual Basic code does not change from application to application; MS Reports examines the metadata layer to calculate how to look at a particular datamart. The metadata layer is a group of tables that contain data about a particular datamart, and stored procedures that access those tables. The administrator of the datamart that uses the MS Reports metadata creates the metadata layer.

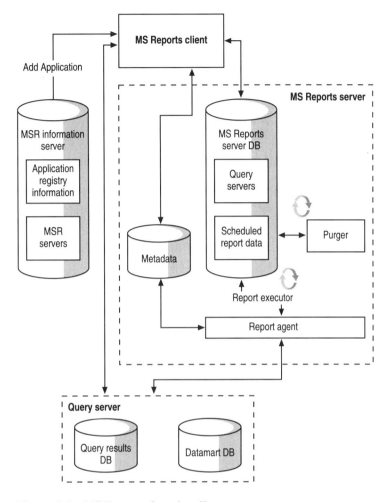

Figure 9.4   MS Reports functionality.

HRDW History

The SHARP project datamart initially contained point-in-time data, but no historic information. The inclusion of history was scheduled for a few months after the initial release of the HRDM PIT (Point In Time) data, but this schedule could not be kept because the job turned out to be much bigger than anticipated. At the same time, the project team found that Management Reporting (the group responsible for ad hoc business reports) had developed some history reports from HRDW source data that the business was using.

In a compromise move to make historical data more widely available rapidly, the team decided to create denormalized tables from the report queries, integrate them into the nightly build process, run them in production for a while, then make any changes needed. This required minimal development work, primarily converting from reports written in a specialized report-writing language to SQL scripts, and adding MS Reports metadata to the reporting tool, HR Online. Testing was limited to comparing the results tables generated by the revised scripts to the tables generated by the original scripts, then thoroughly testing security for the new fields. No attempt was made to document these inherited history scripts, because it was assumed that the history reports had been circulated through the business for some time and were accepted as valid data. The team relied on the business review of the data for any bug reporting, because it had no spec or other documentation for reference.

Because the scripts were written as ad hoc reports, they ran too slowly to be included in nightly processing, so the team originally scheduled them to run on weekends (when a larger build window was available) then optimized them in a later release so they could be run nightly. Few other changes were required.

This 3-month History project exposed a large amount of important historical information to the business. The result was a data structure that is very different from that of PIT. The history tables are completely denormalized. In addition, the code to create the history tables was very monolithic; for example, the Hires, Terms, and Transfers tables are created by completely separate scripts. Operations using shared data (such as salary calculations) are done separately in each script rather than in shared tables so the data is fragmented between tables. A traditional star-schema approach with shared dimensions would have yielded a higher-quality result, but it also would have taken longer to develop. Another outcome was that important mapping information was to be documented after the project was completed. In some cases, it was, in others it was not.

Year 2000 (Y2K) Project

In August of 1998, the team began testing the HRDW for Y2K compliance. Because the HRDW was constructed during a time when people were aware of Y2K issues, the team anticipated few problems. The plan was to demonstrate that HRDW systems were Y2K compliant; few code fixes were predicted.

The team's project vision was:

- Identify and execute code fixes and testing necessary for authenticating that the HRDW systems are Y2K compliant.
- Test and fix only systems that are scheduled to persist beyond 6/30/1999.
- Take advantage of opportunities to structure work efficiently and add long-term value to the HRDW.

The first task was to identify project scope. In scope were core databases used in the nightly build process, source tables, destination databases used for storing feed data, databases used in conjunction with the reporting UI, and all code involved in the nightly build process, including code to generate feeds. Feedstore feeds were considered out of scope because they were owned by another group. When other groups owned sources, the team either verified that the owning group was performing Y2K compliance or did the work itself.

The next step was to select criteria for determining Y2K compliance. These criteria already existed, having been developed by Microsoft's internal Y2K task force.

Next, the team selected a combination of testing methods: code inspection, database checking, and automated black box testing.

For code inspection, the team developer used the **Find in Files** tool in Visual SourceSafe to search for key words in the entire HRDW code base. The number and variety of hits showed which areas to look into further.

These Transact-SQL keywords were searched for:

- CONVERT
- DATETIME
- GETDATE()
- DATEPART
- DATENAME
- DATEDIFF
- DATEADD
- WAITFOR
- ISDATE
- DATEFORMAT
- DATEFIRST
- STOPAT
- EXPIREDATE
- RETAINDAYS

Information from this search was used to determine which HRDW source code should be inspected manually and which could be subjected to automated black box testing. Code inspection was chosen for all code that generates history tables or feeds, Data Genie code, and approximately twenty additional stored procedures that use dates extensively. The only potential Y2K issues found were several hard-coded dates, a couple of which had two-digit years.

Next the team ran SQL scripts against all in-scope databases to look for possible dates or parts of dates in non-date fields, which were then tested. Out of 13 databases, only one potential problem was found: the fiscal year is stored in non-date fields. This would not be a problem in cases where the fiscal year is calculated or copied. Validation would be needed only when users enter the fiscal year into the table.

Automated black box testing was set up to perform date-simulation testing for four key dates: 12/31/1999, 1/1/2000, 2/29/2000, and 12/31/2035. A sample data set was created and tested, then the data was aged and tested to make sure the aging was correct. Data simulation testing then used the Data Genie build process; input was the aged SAP R/3 extract files (sample data set) and output was the aged HRDataMart objects. These steps were used:

- A normal build was run using the sample data set. The resulting objects in the HRDataMart database (called UnAgedHRDataMart) were stored for future comparisons. This served as the groundwork for comparing builds using aged data.

- The sample data set then was aged DDD days using a third-party tool called FileAid. DDD changes with the scenario being tested.

- Using the aged SAP R/3 data set and changing the system date in the build server, another PCB-Dash build was done (called AgedHRDataMart).

- The dates in UnAgedHRDataMart were aged by DDD days (called thisHRDMbase).

- The objects in HRDMbase were compared to the objects in AgedHRDataMart. Corresponding tables should have identical data structures and records.

Once this work was completed, the team had to determine what work should be done to ensure the compliance of new releases. A spreadsheet was designed on which developers could track any code changes involving dates. The developer making the change notes the stored procedure, table, or batch job with the date change, and another developer (or tester) inspects the code that has been added or modified and tracks the results.

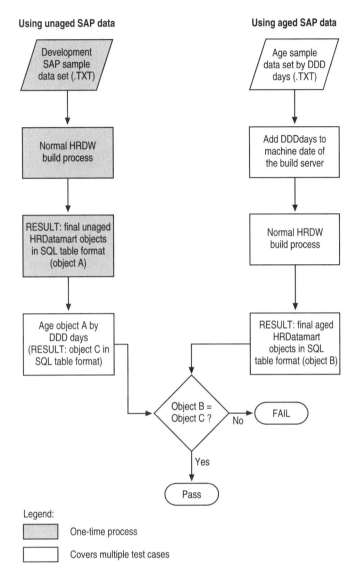

Figure 9.5   Y2K data simulation testing.

Database Upgrade to Microsoft SQL Server 7.0

The database upgrade had two components: the data and the SQL Server code. Because most HRDW databases are recreated each night, most data does not need to be converted with the SQL Server Upgrade Wizard. The remaining portion is from either legacy databases or other supporting databases.

SQL Server source code can be upgraded to SQL Server 7.0 compliance in several ways: SQL Server 7.0 allows for a SQL Server version 6.5 compatibility mode, and, in SQL Server 7.0 mode, options for reducing SQL-92 compliance, such as NULL handling. The team chose to fully upgrade the code for SQL Server 7.0 compliance, hoping to gain any built-in performance boosts and to increase code shelf life.

Code Conversion as Needed

There are additional commands and options available and of course some commands or methods are no longer accessible. In general SQL Server 7.0 is stricter and insures code integrity through more vigorous checking and better-defined operations. Code behavior can sometimes change if the code depends on a peculiarity in previous versions of SQL Server.

The team ran the installation scripts to see what failed. Immediately identified were dependencies on the system tables that had been put in place for conditional processing. This code needed to be altered to reference the new information schema views. The rest of the SQL code installed fine except for a few syntax errors that had been overlooked by SQL Server 6.5, which supports a looser syntax than SQL Server 7.0. For example, it accepts invalid table aliases in the SET clause of an UPDATE statement.

Code Conversion Lessons Learned

Every developer knows that even though code compiles it still may not run correctly. For example, the new SQL Server 7.0 feature called *deferred name resolution* basically means that SQL Server will not try to find a named object until execution time. Even syntactically correct code will not execute at runtime because of missing required objects.

Data warehouses validate or convert data from many different sources, so there can be a lot of string manipulation, NULL checks, or data type conversions. The team encountered runtime problems as it found that some data conversion had to be more explicit or that functions behaved differently than expected. For example, previously the team had checked for both nulls and empty strings in SQL Server 6.5 with the following code:

```
IF RTRIM( @variable ) IS NULL …
```

SQL Server 7.0 requires two steps because empty string or blanks no longer resolve to NULL, now they appropriately resolve to an empty string. The example below works in both SQL Server 6.5 and SQL Server 7.0:

```
IF ( RTRIM( @variable ) IS NULL OR RTRIM( @variable ) =  "" ) …
```

Once the team became aware of common changes, it was possible to search the source code in Visual Source Safe for the suspect keywords and make the changes.

Relative Timings: Minimally Altered Code vs. Appropriately Altered Code

Initial benchmark testing showed that some processes were slower and some faster. Overall there was a 22% decrease in processing time for the build of the PIT and History tables. This time included the use of **bcp** to load text data files into the databases, converting and cleansing, normalizing or de-normalizing, and creating published tables and data feeds.

The conversion to SQL Server 7.0 was an opportunity to clean up code and optimize according to the strengths and weaknesses of SQL Server 7.0. Only timings on the minimally altered code were available for this document.

Testing Through Use of Table Compares: SQL Server 6.5 Results vs. SQL Server 7.0 Results

Because the upgrade to SQL Server 7.0 did not include any feature changes, the team chose to use black box testing, which can ensure that table and feed results appear exactly the same regardless of which version of the source code (SQL Server 6.5 or SQL Server 7.0) produces them. This kept costs down while adequately identifying all of the functionality changes in SQL Server.

Information Desktop

The Business Problem

It is easier to understand the challenge facing HR Management Reporting by considering content and delivery separately. First, content needed to be formalized. Until SHARP made it possible to standardize the HR metrics used to evaluate HR functional programs and organizational health, each HR group researched and created its own system of metrics. This resulted in inconsistent analysis efforts and the development of several manually maintained reporting systems.

The delivery challenge was laid down by HR Management Reporting in a call for standard HR reports based on Excel PivotTables. From the management perspective, the original standard reports:

- Took too long to open.
- Required opening the entire report regardless of intended task.
- Required that users customize each report they viewed to reflect their organizational roll-up structure.
- Were difficult to use.

For these and other reasons, the standard reports were not being fully utilized; several business partners claimed that the reports were of no use at all, even though they contained most of the detailed information that the HR business partners needed. Because HR Management Reporting could not control how the data was rolled up and summarized after reports were published, it felt that the delivery method introduced frequent errors.

The Solution

The Information Desktop tool was created to provide a single systematic view into Microsoft's HR functional business—one that made it possible to measure HR effectiveness and that minimized errors by reducing the need to set reporting structures manually. The current version uses Web technology to deliver standard HR monthly functional reports to HR directors and managers, who can customize roll-up structures to match their business structures and retrieve only the information they need.

During design, the development team considered implementing an SQL Server solution using batch jobs and stored procedures for returning report result sets. The business requirement was to display in less than 30 seconds to users. To speed retrieval of report data, the team proposed a database design in which batch jobs could create tables of pre-set groups. The bad news was that the batch jobs were estimated to take more than eight hours to process one month of data. The good news was that MS OLAP Services already provided this functionality and could process the aggregations in less than one hour for *all* of the report data sets.

The Information Desktop's Web UI allows users to select and personalize reports as needed. The back end uses SQL Server 7.0 (initially SQL Server 6.5) and OLAP Services, into which HRDW data is fed to generate aggregate data. A separate database, specific to the Information Desktop, stores metadata and user-specific report customizations used by the Web UI in displaying the reports.

Legacy Elimination Project

Because of time constraints and inconsistency in historical data, only current information was loaded into SAP R/3, meaning that pre-conversion data remained in several legacy source systems and their downstream databases.

These legacy systems are unsupported by the vendor/developer, use older technologies such as Microsoft Access 1.1, and continue to be a support burden (they require resources to keep them running in production). For these reasons (and to avoid issues with Y2K-compliance and technology upgrades) the Legacy Elimination Project (codename: *Tombstone*) was set up in late 1998 and charged with consolidating legacy data and retiring the legacy OLTP systems. This project is still running as of this writing.

Tombstone has opted for a phased delivery in order to avoid the risks and delayed benefits inherent in a big-bang approach. The phases consist of *consolidation*, *transformation*, and *integration*.

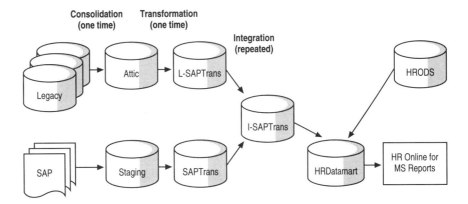

Figure 9.6   Schematic for legacy elimination project.

Consolidation

The consolidation of legacy databases eliminates redundant, unused, and obsolete tables and gathers the remaining ones into a single physical location. After a thorough inventory of the legacy systems documented the disposition of each table in each database on each server, business and IT experts reviewed the results, decided which tables to save, then explained their decision. The *keep*s have been moved to a central database, named *Attic*; the rest were dropped, and many applications have been shut down. Each table moved to the Attic was renamed to avoid namespace clashes. Columns and rows were preserved for each *keep* table, a table cross-referencing old to new table names was added, and the build scripts for the HRDW were modified to pull data from the Attic instead of the legacy databases.

The number of users was scaled back significantly and a user's guide to the Attic was written. The data in the Attic was largely accepted as is. Since no UI was provided and integrity rules for the Attic data were not enforceable, any subsequent corrections to Attic data will require executive business approval, and are expected to be rare and exceptional.

Implementing the Attic immediately (and dramatically) reduced support costs, database objects, and Y2K and other technology upgrade issues.

Consolidation Statistics.

	Legacy	Attic
Servers	5	1
Databases	32	1
Tables	7426	87
Columns	71907	1359
Size	17 G	1 G

Transformation

The next Tombstone phase is transforming the Attic data onto SAP R/3 domains and into tables (called L-SAPTrans) that are similar or identical to the tables used to house the SAP R/3 data (called SAPTrans). For example, an L-SAPTrans table called LTWorkSchedule has been created using the SAPTrans table definition for STWorkSchedule as a model. A simple Microsoft Access database and form are being used to document the mapping and transformation rules from the Attic source columns to the L-SAPTrans target columns. Attic columns used only to locate the source rows are not mapped. The selection criteria are specified at the target *table* level, and the transformation rules at the target *column* level.

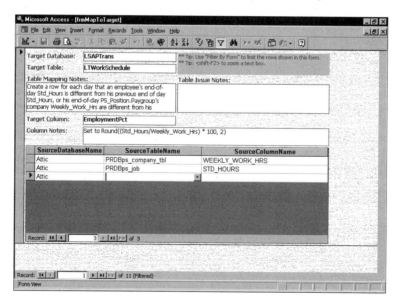

Figure 9.7   Screen for transforming Attic data onto SAP R/3 domains and into tables.

The transformation phase of the Tombstone project is by far the most time-consuming, due to the complexity of the transformation logic and the amount of analysis work required to research and verify business rules.

Integration

After consolidation and transformation, there will be two primary sources of core HR data: SAPTrans (SAP R/3 data) and L-SAPTrans (legacy data in SAP R/3 format). The next phase will integrate them into a single I-SAPTrans source for the HRDW that looks and feels as though it was sourced entirely from SAP R/3. The chief challenge is that L-SAPTrans contains information that occasionally contradicts SAPTrans. This occurs whenever SAP R/3 and the legacy systems hold different facts over the same time period. I-SAPTrans is designed to resolve these contradictions by "stitching" the data from each SAPTrans table and its L-SAPTrans counterpart into a single I-SAPTrans table.

A fundamental business rule the Tombstone team has adopted is that L-SAPTrans serves as the system of record for all transactions before SAP R/3 conversion, and SAPTrans serves as the system of record for all transactions after. The integration step consists of sourcing records from each data set, and adjusting the validity dates (*From* and *To* dates) where overlaps exist, to create a single seamless data set.

Figure 9.8 depicts the integration logic. Each line segment represents a validity period. The blocks represent the From and To dates for that period. In this example the validity period of the second L-SAPTrans record is shortened so that the To date is one day before the From Date of the first SAPTrans record.

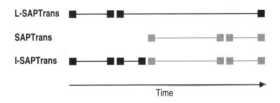

Figure 9.8   Schematic of legacy HR data integration.

An example of this integration is shown in the following SQL script:

```
/* -------------------------------------------------------------------
** Title:   ITWorkSchedule.SQL
** Author:
** Date:    01/18/1999
** Descr:   Creates and populates the table ITWorkSchedule.
**
** Assumptions:
**     each LTWorkSchedule has 12/31/9999 record
```

(continued)

```
**      SequenceNbr is always 0
**      no gaps, no overlaps in LTWorkSchedule, STWorkSchedule
**      FromDate always <= ToDate
**
** MODIFICATIONS:
** Date     Who      Modification
** -------- -------- ----------------------------------------------------
** 01/18/99 tomn     initial version
** --------------------------------------------------------------------
*/


-- Create final destination table
-- Drop existing version of table, if it already exists
IF EXISTS (SELECT * FROM sysobjects WHERE name ='ITWorkSchedule')
   DROP TABLE dbo.ITWorkSchedule
GO


-- create table to be the same as the ST* table wrt:
--     column names, base datatypes, nullability
CREATE TABLE dbo.ITWorkSchedule (
   PersonnelNbr         DECIMAL(8)     NOT NULL
,  ToDate               DATETIME       NOT NULL
,  FromDate             DATETIME       NOT NULL
,  SequenceNbr          DECIMAL(3)     NOT NULL
,  WorkScheduleRuleName CHAR(8)        NULL
,  EmploymentPct        DECIMAL(5,2)   NULL
,  WeeklyHourQty        DECIMAL(5,2)   NULL
,  MonthlyHourQty       DECIMAL(5,2)   NULL
,  PartTimeInd          CHAR(1)        NULL
,  LastModifiedDate     DATETIME       NULL
,  LastModifiedByName   CHAR(12)       NULL
,  DataOrigin           VARCHAR(30)    NULL
)
GO


-- populate table with union query
INSERT dbo.ITWorkSchedule (
   PersonnelNbr
,  FromDate
,  ToDate
,  SequenceNbr
,  WorkScheduleRuleName
,  EmploymentPct
,  WeeklyHourQty
,  MonthlyHourQty
,  PartTimeInd
```

```
  , LastModifiedDate
  , LastModifiedByName
  , DataOrigin
  )

-- First get Legacy-only records (i.e. don't overlap with SAP R/3 data
--     at all)
SELECT
    L.PersonnelNbr
  , L.FromDate
  , L.ToDate
  , L.SequenceNbr
  , L.WorkScheduleRuleName
  , L.EmploymentPct
  , L.WeeklyHourQty
  , L.MonthlyHourQty
  , L.PartTimeInd
  , L.LastModifiedDate
  , L.LastModifiedByName
  , 'Legacy' AS DataOrigin
FROM   dbo.LTWorkSchedule AS L
WHERE NOT EXISTS (    SELECT    *
                      FROM   dbo.STWorkSchedule AS S
                      WHERE  S.PersonnelNbr = L.PersonnelNbr
                      AND    S.FromDate      <= L.ToDate )

UNION

-- and get any Legacy records that overlap with SAP R/3 data, and de-
--     limit the record to the day before the SAP R/3 record takes effect
SELECT
    L.PersonnelNbr
  , L.FromDate
  , DATEADD(DAY,-1,S.FromDate) AS ToDate
  , L.SequenceNbr
  , L.WorkScheduleRuleName
  , L.EmploymentPct
  , L.WeeklyHourQty
  , L.MonthlyHourQty
  , L.PartTimeInd
  , L.LastModifiedDate
  , L.LastModifiedByName
  , 'Legacy-Delimited' AS DataOrigin
FROM   dbo.LTWorkSchedule AS L
    INNER JOIN dbo.STWorkSchedule AS S
      ON S.PersonnelNbr = L.PersonnelNbr
      AND S.FromDate BETWEEN DATEADD(DAY, +1,L.FromDate) AND L.ToDate --
if tie on FromDate, don't include legacy record
```

(continued)

```
WHERE NOT EXISTS (    SELECT    *
                      FROM      dbo.STWorkSchedule AS S2
                      WHERE     S2.PersonnelNbr   = S.PersonnelNbr
                      AND       S2.FromDate       < S.FromDate   )

UNION

-- and get all SAP R/3 records
SELECT
    S.PersonnelNbr
,   S.FromDate
,   S.ToDate
,   S.SequenceNbr
,   S.WorkScheduleRuleName
,   S.EmploymentPct
,   S.WeeklyHourQty
,   S.MonthlyHourQty
,   S.PartTimeInd
,   S.LastModifiedDate
,   S.LastModifiedByName
,   'SAP R/3' AS DataOrigin
FROM  dbo.STWorkSchedule AS S

GO


/********** Add Primary Key constraint ******************/

ALTER TABLE dbo.ITWorkSchedule
    ADD   PRIMARY KEY CLUSTERED (PersonnelNbr, ToDate,
        FromDate, SequenceNbr)
GO

/* eof */
```

Since SAPTrans is refreshed nightly, I-SAPTrans must be built nightly.

Once integration is complete, the HRDW build can be simplified to pull from one source.

Current System

HR Data Warehouse Build Overview

The HRDW is complex: it contains relation data structures, point-in-time snapshots of data based on current and future dates, and summary and detail information about people's HR history. It is used in one form or another by a large user community and data from this system finds its way into many systems within Microsoft.

Many of the HRDW's published data elements are based on time-sensitive data, so many data sets must be rebuilt nightly. Code determines which data sets to build when time is at a premium. Depending on which data sets are produced, the entire build process can take 6 - 14 hours.

As part of a nightly batch process, the HRDW is rebuilt more or less from scratch, because historical data can change and business rules require that changes be calculated from current data. Data used in the build process comes from SAP R/3, external systems, legacy systems, and caches of information maintained by the user groups and the production support community. The data is merged into useful structures and provided to user communities in publications.

The majority of the build process is executed within Microsoft's batch processing environment, except for a small portion of the publication process that is executed ad hoc by users. The build process is governed largely by an internally written SQL Server-based application known as Data Genie. It executes several processes concurrently, selecting the next task to execute based on predecessor/successor information stored as metadata.

Source data is imported through database dump-copy-load (DCL) processes, flat file imports, and ad hoc updates to operation data stores.

Each data structure is populated through the use of stored procedures (preferred) or SQL scripts.

Data is published through database DCL processes, flat file extracts, and by automatically mailing query result sets to specific user groups.

Microsoft Batch Processing Environment (PCB-DASH)

Microsoft HR executes thousands of batch processes through this environment daily, either on a scheduled or ad hoc basis. PCB-DASH (an internally developed tool) extends the functionality of batch (MS-DOS-like) programming and provides an administrative utility to monitor the progress of batch processes.

HR Data Warehouse Build Engine (Data Genie)

Created as part of the initial HRDW design effort, Data Genie contains metadata that describes the dependencies between build process tasks. The build at the time of this writing contains roughly 750 tasks, each of which has at least one predecessor and one successor. Based on these dependencies, Data Genie submits one or more concurrent tasks, tracks task progress and provides valuable metrics about each step of the build process. Data Genie is entirely data-driven, which allows significant changes to the batch process to be made without affecting a single line of code.

Source Data Import

Source data comes from several systems. Much of it is imported at the beginning of the build process but there are also dependencies on external systems, several of which perform nightly processing that prevents scheduling a time for data to be available. In these cases, code determines whether to wait for the data or to use data from the previous evening. Additional source data is captured as part of the data refresh process.

Microsoft IT has written a utility that extracts data from SAP R/3 and stores it in flat files. The build process waits for the creation of a specific file (known to be the last file) and then copies all data files to the build server. The batch process uses the SQL Server **bcp** utility to import the data into the **staging** database. Because data files are in tab-delimited character format and include some information that **bcp** cannot process (right-hand minus signs, dates that contain all zeros and occasional invalid numeric data), data is put in import tables as character strings, then stored procedures convert it and populate tables that were created using proper data types.

The HRODS database was defined to track non-SAP R/3, non-legacy operational data (such as domain mapping tables). Users control its data. A copy of it is dump-copy-loaded to the build server.

The Tombstone project (described earlier and currently underway) is simplifying the legacy data import process by retiring redundant systems and eliminating unnecessary legacy processing and dependencies.

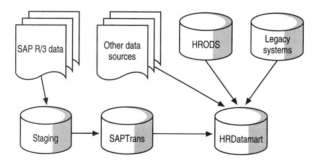

Figure 9.9   Simplified data flow diagram.

Data Refresh Process

The data refresh process uses about 500 scripts and stored procedures, each executed in predefined sequence to populate the database. The sequence of execution is important not only because of dependencies on previously populated tables but because data sets must be made available to external systems at different times during the evening. The Data Genie utility manages these dependencies.

Data from the STAGING database and HRODS database are merged into a set of data objects within the SAPTrans database. This data set is in a largely normalized format suitable for building the Feedstore data sets, but it lacks some necessary legacy system data.

SAPTrans is used as a base set of data that is merged with data from the legacy systems to populate tables within the HRDataMart database.

Data from external systems is imported as the external systems complete their processing.

Publication Process Overview

For this document, the publication process has been simplified to include only the major elements. Strictly speaking, all published data sets are built within the HRDataMart database. The Feedstore team publishes several sets of data from the HRDataMart that are used in automated and ad hoc processes.

The HRDataMart database contains several logical sections:

- **CPIT.** The current point-in-time tables contain a current snapshot of HR data.
- **MPIT.** The monthly point-in-time tables contain a snapshot of HR data based on a programmed calendar or fiscal month end date.
- **History.** These tables show each employee's Microsoft HR history. This data is used by the HR Online application
- **Archive.** These tables contain views of each employee's history as it looked at the end of each fiscal month. The archive tables contain several months' worth of data.

The publication process provides data from these logical sections to several users:

- **Feedstore.** The HRDW build process executes batch processes that create views on the CPIT and MPIT tables. These views are used to export data sets that are used by the Feedstore team (which is a secondary publication mechanism).
- **HR Online.** The HR Online application is fed through a DCL process that moves the HRDataMart database to a number of publication servers. The HR Online application is written so that it can query against multiple databases. The nightly batch processing updates each publication server separately; this allows users 24 X 7 access to data.
- **Information Desktop.** The Information Desktop application uses CPIT and Archive data. It resides on one of the HR Online publication servers.

Technical Environment

HR Data Warehouse Environment

The HRDW team maintains separate environments for development, testing, and production. Their configurations are similar but there are two unavoidable differences: it is impossible to reproduce user activity on the publication servers, and batch processing failures will cause down time and therefore timing changes.

Hardware and Software Configurations

Each configuration consists of three servers:

- **A Build Server.** A Compaq Proliant 5500 with 4 200 MHz processors, 640 MB of memory. It runs Windows NT 4.0 and SQL Server 7.0. The HRDW databases occupy about 17.5 G, some of which is required for dump device files.

- **Publication Server 1.** Similar in configuration to the build server, this also hosts MS Reports and the MS Reports load balancing components. Databases occupy about 24 G (none of this is used by dump devices). Publication servers require more space because they house data components that are not part of the HRDW build process but are still necessary (such as archived data sets).

- **Publication Server 2.** Similar in configuration to the build server, this also hosts MS Reports, IIS 4.0, and OLAP Server. HRDW databases require about 6 G (none of this is used by dump devices). This server is not used as a storage location for legacy data and archived data sets.

Tools of the Trade

Microsoft Tools

Microsoft tools and applications are used whenever possible; if necessary, third-party or internal tools are used for special tasks. A sample of the commonly used tools include:

- Visual Source Safe
- SQL Server
- Windows NT
- Internet Information Server
- Visual Studio
- Office
- Project

- Outlook/Exchange
- OLAP Services
- Access

Internal Tools

Some tools needed to be developed to support Microsoft's internal IT environment:

- **PCB-DASH.** This is the backbone of the Microsoft batch-processing environment. The IT production support team uses it almost exclusively for batch processing purposes.
- **MS Reports.** This is an ad hoc query generator built as a VB 6 ActiveX extension to Excel. It makes it straightforward for users to generate complex queries, use the results to populate Excel pivot tables, Excel spreadsheets, or Access pivot tables, and modify queries to view different slices of the data.
- **RAID.** This is a database used to manage information about bugs and project-related issues.

Feedstore

To support or extend SAP R/3 functionality, Microsoft uses a number of client-server systems that typically have separate databases and operate independently. The Feedstore was developed to keep data in these systems consistent by serving as a data warehouse for feeds. Publishing systems such as the HRDW provide commonly needed information (such as personnel data) to the Feedstore as one or more denormalized, **bcp**-formatted tables. Each night, after a set cutoff time, subscribing systems can pick up feeds as part of their nightly process. The Feedstore also maintains security.

Project-Specific Tools

- **HRDW Data Dictionary.** The HRDW development and test teams use this Microsoft Access-based tool to maintain information about data transformations that must occur as part of the build process. The information is entered early in the software development process.
- **Data Genie.** The build engine used to maintain the HRDW batch processes, this contains metadata (describing the relationship between HRDW data objects) used to schedule the execution of build process tasks. Using the metadata to determine dependencies, Data Genie can schedule up to 10 separate command streams to run simultaneously.
- **Audit Genie.** This sub-system schedules audit queries after the nightly build process has completed. Reports generated by the queries are made available to the appropriate users daily for data cleanup purposes.

External Tools

The primary third-party tool is ERWin, an entity relationship modeler from PLATINUM Technologies used to perform data model development tasks.

Operations Infrastructure

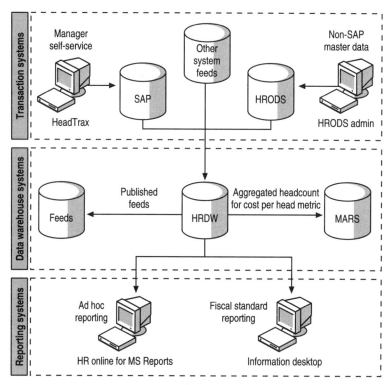

Figure 9.10   Transaction systems.

Here are descriptions (including logical disk partition sizes) of the configurations for the nightly build and two publication servers.

Build Server

- 4 Pentium Pro 200-MHz Processors
- 640 MB RAM
- SQL Server 7.0
- Windows NT 4.0 (SP4)

Build server partitions.

Logical drive	Partition	Directories needed
C	System	This partition belongs to MCSS
D	SQL and system DBs	D:\SQL
E	User database dumps	E:\SQL\BAK
F	Log dumps	F:\SQL\TRAN
G	Batch processing	N/A
H	Data devices	H:\SQL\DATA
O	Log devices	O:\SQL\DATA
T	**tempdb** devices	T:\SQL\DATA

Build server logical disk partition sizes.

C$	FAT	2000	D$	NTFS	2048
E$	NTFS	20464	F$	NTFS	6093
G$	NTFS	2092	H$	NTFS	16372
O$	NTFS	4148	T$	NTFS	4049

Publication Servers

Pub1

- 4 Pentium Pro 200-MHz Processors
- 640 MB RAM
- SQL Server 7.0
- Windows NT 4.0 (SP4)

Publication server Pub 1 partitions.

Logical drive	Partition	Directories needed
C	System	This partition belongs to MCSS
D	SQL and system DBs	D:\SQL
E	User database dumps	E:\SQL\BAK
F	Log dumps	F:\SQL\TRAN
G	Batch processing	N/A
H	Data devices	H:\SQL\DATA
O	Log devices	O:\SQL\DATA
T	**tempdb** devices	T:\SQL\DATA

Publication server Pub 1 logical disk partition sizes.

C$	FAT	2000	D$	NTFS	2001
E$	NTFS	36000	F$	NTFS	7000
G$	NTFS	2034	H$	NTFS	28654
O$	NTFS	8200	T$	NTFS	4140

Pub2

- 3 Pentium Pro 200-MHz Processors
- 512 MB RAM
- SQL Server 7.0 with OLAP Services
- Windows NT 4.0 (SP4)

Publication server Pub 2 partitions.

Logical Drive	Partition	Directories needed
C	System	This partition belongs to MCSS
D	SQL and system DBs	D:\SQL
E	User database dumps	E:\SQL\BAK
F	Log dumps	F:\SQL\TRAN
G	Batch processing	N/A
H	Data devices	H:\SQL\DATA
O	Log devices	O:\SQL\DATA
T	**tempdb** devices	T:\SQL\DATA

Publication server Pub 2 logical disk partition sizes.

C$	FAT	2044	D$	NTFS	2001
E$	NTFS	20464	F$	NTFS	6001
G$	NTFS	2184	H$	NTFS	16372
O$	NTFS	4200	T$	NTFS	4037

Security Model

The team used a business-driven security model document to clarify the business needs for securing access to HR data.

Topics Covered by the Security Model

- Profiles of expected users of the *HR Online* tool.

- Model definition and business rules for granting user access to data.

- Description of client-side data viewing security mechanisms, including features currently available in MS Reports, as well as change requests submitted to the MS Reports team.

- Description of server-side data access security mechanisms, including row-level and column-level security, and data transmission encryption.

- Description of the user administration approach. This includes the organizational model for maintaining security settings, and a walkthrough of user administration tasks.

Security Model for HR Online

The security model for *HR Online* describes how data access decisions will be made, and how security permissions will be assigned. In general, the security model is based on need to know. Its definitions are based on the "User Profile Analysis" presented above. Basically it:

- Identifies the **data subject areas** (groups of fields with similar security requirements) to which the various roles require access

- Categorizes groups of users by the **role** they play

- Identifies the **data view restrictions** (limitations on the groups of people a user can view) that apply to the various roles and data subject areas

The security model expresses data access business rules in a matrix that combines the defined roles, data subject areas, and view limitations. It is shown after the definitions below.

Data Subject Area Definitions

This security model defines useful data subject areas—groups of fields that are generally used together, and that have similar security restrictions. For example: the *Pay Scale Level* and *Salary* fields could be grouped together in a data subject area titled *Compensation*.

The data subject areas for the initial rollout of *HR Online*:

- **Non-Confidential.** A catch-all subject area for all data fields not considered sensitive within the company: *name*, *work phone*, and *work location*.

- **Current Base Pay.** Current base pay rate information. Fields include: *hourly pay rate*, *annual salary amount*, and *weekly work hours*.

- **Rewards & Recognition (non-stock).** All data related to an employee's compensation and review and reward results. This subject area does not include stock option grant award information, which means it does not include payroll information, which includes stock exercise activity. Fields include *annual salary*, *review rating*, *review bonus*, and *signing bonus*.

- **Stock.** All data related to an employee's stock option grants: *grant amount*, *grant price*, and *grant date*.

- **Payroll.** US payroll results that are returned from Microsoft's domestic payroll vendor: *year-to-date regular earnings*, *year-to-date bonus earnings*, *vacation balance*, and *overtime hours*.

- **Personal.** Private information associated with people at Microsoft: *home address, home phone, emergency contacts, social security number*, and *birth date*.

- **Diversity.** Sensitive information including *gender*, *ethnicity*, and *veteran status*.

Role Definitions

The roles in the security model map directly to the user profiles listed in the section above. Grouping users by role allows control of specific types of information based on a user's need to know. It also reduces administration costs because permissions can be granted to groups of users with common needs, instead of user by user.

These roles, based on the analysis of user profiles above, were proposed for the initial implementation of *HR Online*. They are listed from largest to smallest based on expected membership.

- HR Generalist, HR Administrative Assistant, HR Manager, HR Assistant
- U.S. Recruiter
- HR Data Administrator (HRIC & Regional System Specialist, super HR Operations user)
- Executive Assistant
- Internal Resource Specialist
- Compensation Analyst
- LCA User (Paralegal, Corp. Attorney)
- Recruiting Assistant
- HR Director
- Tool Administrator (HR Management Reporting/ABS Support Analyst)
- CS Staffing Specialist

- Benefits Administrator
- U.S. Payroll Administrator
- Stock Administrator
- Non-Confidential (A/P Specialist)

Data View Restrictions

Because users often need to know only certain data in a subject area, data view restrictions control which parts of the area a user can view. They apply only in the context of a data subject area. For example, HR Assistants can see compensation data only for groups they support, but they can access non-confidential data for any group. Here are the restriction categories:

All Data

- **Definition.** No data view restriction. The user can view data for all employees and contingent staff.

- **Implications.** The simplest and quickest to implement, maintain, and support, because there is no security logic to apply.

Approved Microsoft Companies

- **Definition.** The user must have a business reason to access SAP R/3 company data, but can view data for all employees and contingent staff within allowed SAP R/3 Companies. The set of approved companies could include ALL SAP R/3 Companies.

- **Implications.** Users must be mapped to SAP R/3 Companies.

Peer Exclusion (All Except HR, All Except LCA)

- **Definition.** The user can see data for the entire company except for people within the user's organization (most commonly Human Resources), as defined by a set of cost centers.

- **Implications**. Cost center lists (HR, LCA, etc.) must be maintained, and query performance is affected significantly.

CS Only

- **Definition.** The view of the data is restricted to contingent staff only.

- **Implications.** Requires additional views in the datamart and additional perspectives in *HR Online for MSR*. Performance would not be significantly degraded, but it increases system complexity (by adding views and perspectives) and makes the system more costly to maintain.

Bringing It All Together: Security Model Business Rules

The subject area security matrix was created using data subject areas, roles, and data view restrictions. The defined combinations represent the business rules for data access, and form the basis for the security mechanisms built into the *HR Online* reporting tool.

Roles are arranged in the matrix from *most* data access to *least*.

Restricted Data Access Security Model

The restricted data access model represents an approach where the data is more tightly secured from unauthorized access. The need-to-know presumption still applies, so users have access only to data that is needed for their jobs (based on relevant companies and peer exclusion rules). Some hypothetical examples of how this might be done are listed below:

Data subject area.

Role	Non-confi-dential	Current base pay	Rewards (non-stock)	Stock	Payroll	Personal	Diversity
Compensation Analyst	All Data	All Data	All Data	All Data	All Data	All Data	(no access)
Benefits Administrator, Security Analyst	All Data	(no access)	(no access)	(no access)	(no access)	All Data	(no access)
Recruiting Assistant	All Data	(no access)	(no access)	(no access)	(no access)	(no access)	Approved Companies All Except HR

Benefits and drawbacks of the selected security model.

Benefit	Drawback
Limits data access based on a business need to know. Reduces reliance on the honor system.	More complicated and expensive to implement.
Greater flexibility: Once the more complex data view restriction mechanisms are built, they can be re-used for future roles.	Higher cost to maintain and support.

Benefit	Drawback
	More costly to maintain when changes are made to the underlying reporting system, due to the greater complexity of the security model.
Reduced reliance on auditing to verify compliance.	Slower query performance due to extra security logic.
Ability to restrict specifically, down to a database row or column.	Row-level restrictions often confuse users, who don't understand why they are not seeing every row of data. This results in confusion, distrust, and a higher support burden.

Security Model Implementation Aspects

A small OLTP database was implemented to maintain each user's security settings. It tracks the user's network login, user role, and pertinent row-level restrictions. This information is used during the nightly refresh process to build the security tables used to control the rows returned to the user at run-time. This OLTP was constructed during the SHARP project and is maintained by application support personnel. It must be kept up-to-date: lapses can lead to security loopholes.

 Row-level security is very costly in terms of maintenance and query run time. Query system complexity would be greatly reduced if column-level security was sufficient.

What Worked?

After spending two years designing and implementing the HRDW and datamart infrastructure, the HR IT group has had success with (and will continue) the following practices.

Data Warehouse

A data warehouse is worth the significant, ongoing investment necessary to design and implement it. It enables a number of key capabilities that Microsoft HR has come to take for granted:

- Elimination of manual record-keeping systems and all their associated overheads.

- Ability of non-IT personnel to generate ad hoc reports.

- Reduced cost in generating standard reports—the bulk of the analysis logic is contained in the data warehouse design.

- Speed with which business questions can be posed and answered.
- Higher level of trust in report results.
- Reduction of "my numbers are different than yours" types of problems.
- Source for feeds of HR data to non-HR systems.
- Query capability that does not bog down OLTP systems.

Full Nightly Rebuild and Publishing

Except for persistent snapshots of data and fixed legacy data, such as fiscal month-end views, it continues to make sense to rebuild the data warehouse and datamarts from scratch nightly. One reason is that the interrelatedness of HR data would significantly increase the complexity of the build code to manage real-time, incremental updates. Source systems would have to be modified or configured to provide transactions on a real-time basis, and complicated code would have to be written to fit the transaction into a number of related data records. A second reason is that there is no compelling need to do otherwise: the nightly processing window leaves room to do it, at least one publication server is kept up at all times, and the business does not require fresher data.

Run Multiple Processes Simultaneously (Data Genie)

To meet nightly processing deadlines the system uses a lot of parallel processing. This is possible because most tasks in the data warehouse-build process are I/O-bound. By defining a metadata database with task dependencies and CPU needs coded, it is possible to write a series of procedures (Data Genie) that run between one and ten processes at any given time. On a multi-processor, enterprise-caliber server, this significantly reduces build times by tapping more system horsepower.

Load Balance Across Publication Servers to Provide 24 x 7 Uptime

Load balancing allows the system to be scaled to accommodate any level of query activity. It also allows the team to take individual publication servers down for refresh without any impact on ongoing query activity.

Rely on Metadata-Driven Processes to Simplify Implementation and Maintenance of Functionality

The data warehouse team used metadata-driven tools to simplify coding in the reporting (MS Reports), auditing (Audit Genie), and batch processing (Data Genie) environments. Despite the higher level of abstraction, the data-driven approach made it easy to make environment changes without extensive coding and testing. Further, adding functionality can be as simple as modifying the requisite tool or adding fields to the metadata to support it. It is not necessary to change code in a large number of procedures.

Another benefit of the metadata-driven UI (MS Reports) is that it allows testing to focus on the back end, where it is most effective.

Use Production-Caliber Environment for Development and Testing

The team found it impossible to simulate the production environment or to diagnose production problems successfully without duplicating the environment in development and testing. For HR data, a standard data subset is inadequate and more trouble than it is worth. However, other teams building sales and financial data warehouses have found this a useful approach.

Since testing and development use full production datasets, they require a production-caliber server to keep development and test build times reasonable. (Builds that take 8 hours on a production quality server might take 3 days on a single processor server with less memory.)

Finally, with systems as complex and parallel as a data warehouse, production problems may result from previously unknown interactions that do not occur on a non-production-caliber system. One example of this occurred when the team upgraded to a more powerful server in production to run the build process. It ran processes faster and at different rates, so some processes ran together for the first time, immediately exhibiting unexpected dependencies that caused problems. Without similar hardware, these problems could not be duplicated in the test or development environments. Tests had to be conducted in the production environment—something you want to avoid at all costs. The faster hardware has also accomplished more work between checkpoints and overflowed previously adequate transaction logs.

The use of a production-like environment allows the team to put a new release into production in 1-2 days: the previous average was 1.5 weeks.

The test or development environment must have *at least* one server that is configured the same as a production server.

Run Regular Builds in the Project Team's Development Environment at Least Weekly

Microsoft's product groups routinely run builds each night. This has proven useful in product development but it comes at a price. The project team has determined that this would be a good policy to follow in the IT environment as well.

The big advantage is simple: frequent builds keep an IT development environment close to a known working version. Although developers do not check in their code until they are sure it will run successfully, builds still break. When this happens, the closer the failed build is to a known working build, the easier it is to isolate what went wrong.

Recognize That Testing Is a Critical Project Function and Plan for It

The testing function on a data-warehousing project has three unique challenges: justification, staffing, and coverage.

The team must justify to management and to business counterparts the value that a testing team can provide. Like all software manufacturers, Microsoft has long realized that testers are critical if you want to ship quality products. But elsewhere, especially where the programmer/analyst staffing model dominates, this may take work.

The team must figure out how to staff itself by attracting testers that understand what testing is all about and have developer-caliber SQL Server skills. This can be hard in a world where demand for testers outstrips supply, and where many view testing as a stepping-stone to development. To find and acquire people who could be developers but prefer to be testers, the team:

- Moved away from the old model of staffing each project with testing contractors when it is time to bring on the test team. This is too late to start the acquisition effort.

- Increased the ratio of employees to contractors, to improve continuity and quality.

- Identified and trained people who have the aptitude and the desire to make good testers.

To meet the coverage challenge, the team must figure out how to test for unexpected consequences of functionality changes across the entire data warehousing system and the many variations of testing required to adequately model security, special build conditions, etc. The team addressed this by:

- Using automated table-compares against previous, known-working build results to test for unexpected consequences outside of the tables affected by a functionality change.

- Moving towards processes that are metadata-driven rather than hard-coded.

- Investing in the documentation and maintenance of business rule documentation and field mappings.

- Automating the setup process for code drops and builds, so that setup and build combinations can be kicked off and run unattended.

- Looking at ways to create sanitized production-like build environments where running a build can provide results for development, testing, and production support.

- Using testing automation to simplify regression of current bugs, fixed bugs, and new functionality.

- Using automated test scripts and testing readiness reviews to catch drops that are not ready to go to testing—preventing a waste of testing time.

- Packaging functionality into projects where the same approach to testing can cover all functionality. For instance, if a technical release includes upgrading to SQL Server 7.0, modifying the build process, and re-architecting a portion of the data warehouse—all of these can be tested through table-compares against the previous release results databases.

The Microsoft Solution Framework (MSF) Model Works Well

When it comes to the complexity and rigor of an ongoing data-warehousing project, the separated-role project team model works better than a programmer/analyst model. Data warehousing projects require that numerous highly skilled people each study and understand the DW and its infrastructure, after which they can specialize on a set of skills and a slice of that knowledge base. Testers, for instance, require different skills than developers and they approach the data warehouse from a very different perspective: developers focus on functionality, testers on functionality *and* all the other things that might be affected by it.

What Could Have Worked Better?

Separate Datamart DB(s) from the Data Warehouse DB

The current data warehouse is a combination data warehouse and datamart. By trying to do two things at once, this arrangement has failed (as often happens) to do either well. The data warehouse needs more normalized tables and a structure more convenient for some processing; the datamart needs more perspectives structured as star schemas, not as very wide, denormalized tables. Query performance is less than optimal.

The team plans to migrate to a classical data warehouse/datamart structure, wherein the data warehouse is normalized and multiple datamarts are composed of perspectives built as star schemas.

Insulate the Warehouse from Bad Input Data

The initial data warehouse design significantly underestimated the amount of bad data (data that was incomplete, incorrect, or did not follow business rules) that the system would have to deal with. In practice, the team has had to retrofit the build process with all kinds of scrubbing logic and audit reports in order to protect it from breaking (a major headache for the production support team) and to get the data corrected in the source systems.

The team's mandate is to *publish data*—even if it doesn't follow business rules. The build process must be protected, but users need to see data even if it's wrong (maybe especially if it's wrong). Consider an example: a manager's record is found to break the build process somehow, so it is removed. That fixes the build problem, but it creates cascading problems: for one thing, all of that manager's direct reports now are without a manager, and since it is a business rule that workers must have managers, it would seem that you now have to remove the direct reports' records.

So as the team re-architects the system, it will allow the inclusion of bad data and continue to provide comprehensive auditing reports. Data integrity is still crucial, and the team is considering ways to have more data items validated when they are entered. For example, if a required field is not filled in, an *unknown* value can be assigned to that field from the domain table.

While correcting data by assigning default values or figuring out the correct value using some algorithm just perpetuates the error in the source systems, sometimes the decision is forced. Suppose a person's cost center does not exist in the cost center table. To maintain referential integrity in the data warehouse (and not "lose" this record under certain join conditions) the developer must either substitute an *unknown* value for the cost center in the person's record or add a placeholder cost center record in the cost center table for the currently *unknown* cost center.

Create a Persistent Legacy Data Warehouse with a Structure Similar to the Production Data Warehouse

The team found that in the short term it was impractical to convert legacy data and insert it into SAP R/3, so it created a legacy data warehouse with business rules applied and in a format similar to (the same as, if possible) the comprehensive data warehouse. The team has worked to dynamically merge legacy data with SAP R/3 data to create the datamart tables. This has created a maintenance burden—due to the complexity of the resulting code—and a performance burden on each nightly build.

While doing a one-time conversion to a legacy data warehouse is a sizeable investment—six person-years in this case—it should pay for itself over time in lower maintenance costs and a shorter, simpler, less error-prone nightly build process.

Use Star Schemas as the Basis for All Datamart Reporting Perspectives

Most of the datamart reporting tables are very wide (lots of attributes) and denormalized. One table for example has 182 attributes in it. In contrast, Information Desktop tables were created as star-schemas with one fact table linked to multiple dimension tables.

Experience shows that star schemas perform better in a SQL Server query environment. When you process star schemas with the SQL Server 7.0 OLAP Services engine, and query the resulting cube using OLAP Services, performance is orders of magnitude faster (multi-minute Transact-SQL queries resolve in a few seconds using OLAP Services).

Consolidate Reporting Systems

During the SHARP project SAP R/3 conversion, the tight schedule impelled designers to leave the existing reporting system for legacy data and implement a new reporting system (the data warehouse) for SAP R/3 data. Unhappily this has meant that users creating reports sometimes had to use both systems and then combine the results. So a task that used to take them five minutes took twenty.

End-user demands required the HRDW team to reverse the earlier decision (made by the SHARP project team) to maintain separate reporting systems.

Were the team to do this again, it would recommend accomplishing this as part of the ERP system implementation project, rather than waiting for a more convenient time.

Design the Data Warehouse/Datamart to Optimize Maintainability

Data warehousing systems require constant, extensive maintenance. Over time the HRDW project team has grown to 30+ team members to deal with:

- Interfaces with 24 other systems and groups in Microsoft
- Demands for new functionality
- New versions of the systems and tools (SQL Server, OLAP Services, MS Reports, Windows NT, Office, etc.)
- New hardware and configuration opportunities
- Increased nightly processing demands

Thus the code must stand up to constant maintenance. Some factors which will increase the maintainability of the code are:

- Development standards
- Clean architectures
- Consistent commenting of code
- Data-driven designs
- High-quality design documentation

Simplify the Security Model

The extensive SHARP project security model significantly increased the development, testing, production support, and training costs. Mostly this is because the security business rules were implemented using column-level *and* row-level security in order to guarantee as much as possible that online users could not access information that they did not have a business need to view.

Column-level security is straightforward. Depending on their information needs, different users get to see different sets of columns. This is easy to implement, to support, and (for users) to understand.

Row-level security on the other hand is more difficult on all counts. Users' roles in the organization dictate what they can see of the organization. If they are responsible for one division, they may not be able to see records concerning other divisions. The SHARP implementation used a person/cost-center table, which contained a list of all cost-centers that a person was allowed to see, to limit the rows that a person could see by joining it to each view. Here are the costs of this approach:

- Queries take significantly longer to process.

- A data entry function is required to maintain the permissions table both initially and with cost-center changes.

- Two people with slightly different jobs can run the same reports and come up with different answers.

- A person may have full access to summary statistics, but drilling down to the detail records may show only a subset of the summary records.

- Users who do not understand inconsistencies which derive from the security model will often call for support.

- Development and testing of new functionality becomes more difficult, because of the combinations of scenarios (column-level and row-level) that have to be tested.

The team would prefer to abolish row-level security in favor of a combination of training and expected professionalism.

Create Clear Documentation, Including Business Rules, of Mapping Between Source and Publication Data

Getting business rules right is one of the most difficult challenges of a data warehousing project. Keeping them right and passing on the knowledge effectively over the years of the project life is also difficult. The original SHARP implementation was rushed because of a tight schedule, and the team was forced to assume that the project people would retain the knowledge, and that the team could play catch-up later. But within a year, most of the people had gone on to other jobs within the company, leaving the team with the job of re-architecting a system without sufficient knowledge of fundamental business rules. This was a hard lesson, and overtime is being invested now to document this information.

Use Multiple Processes for the Transformation of Data from SAP R/3 to the Warehouse

The team considers that it missed an easy opportunity to begin processing data files as soon as they've been dumped. Instead the nightly build does not begin to process the first data file until all the data files have been dumped out of SAP R/3. This can be corrected by determining the internal process dependencies and adding them to the processes managed by Data Genie so that they can be executed in parallel.

Limit External Interfaces to the Datamart Stars and Only if Necessary to the Warehouse Itself; Source All Reporting from the Same Stars

Because history perspectives were not included in the data warehouse until almost a year after its introduction, many reports and data extracts were written against source databases further up the chain. Thus to change system architecture the team has had to take into account all of those reports and extracts, either eliminating or rewriting them. If the initial plan had produced a comprehensive data warehouse and limited external users to using one or more datamarts, there would now be clear external interfaces that were independent of whatever plumbing came before them in the processing.

Project Structure and Management Concepts

Project Team Organization

Like most of the IT organizations within Microsoft, the business unit IT group uses a slightly modified version of the Microsoft Solution Framework (MSF) roles and responsibilities matrix. This divides the project team into five functional areas with different responsibilities:

- **Product Management** is responsible for customer communication, gathering business rules requirements, prioritizing requirements, project rollout, and training.

- **Program Management** is responsible for the overall project, for the project budget, and for the functional design, which includes the logical data model.

- **Development** is responsible for the physical system architecture, for the physical data model, and for writing and debugging the code used in the UI, database, and batch streams.

- **Test** is responsible for designing the test plan, test scenarios, and test cases. It runs test cases and guides the team in determining when the application is ready to release.

- **Production Support** is responsible for managing the operational environment, releasing new software into production, and diagnosing and solving problems with production systems.

Each function has a lead on the project team; together, the leads form a team of peers that manages the project. Lead program managers have overall and budgetary responsibility for the project, so they are typically first among equals in this team. While leads have responsibility for given project areas, other team members help the leads and are the primary reviewers of each lead's deliverables.

While this approach may seem less efficient than the competing programmer/analyst model, experience has shown that it produces a better-designed and higher-quality product at production release.

The test team, composed of people whose only focus is testing and who are trained in its disciplines, is perhaps the primary reason for this improved quality. Limiting the developers to unit testing and assigning the detailed and integration testing to a test team, ferrets out many more bugs. While the leads cooperatively determine which bugs will be fixed or deferred in an ongoing bug-triage process, this separation of roles allows far more bugs to be found and fixed before release than normally are found in testing under the programmer/analyst model.

While the data warehousing reporting team includes 30+ members, the maintenance and enhancement work are divided into smaller projects with typically 5-10 people on each. While individual projects come and go, the level of effort invested in supporting and expanding the data warehouse and reporting systems remains relatively constant.

Project Method

Due to the complexity of the enhancement work and the fact that it is typically incremental to existing functionality, the primary project method is a *waterfall* variant with project cycles of between 2 and 3 months.

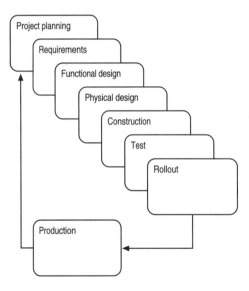

Figure 9.11   Project method.

Product management creates production change requests (PCRs) and scopes them for effort hours by program management and development. These are kept in a database and when a project is formed, the relevant PCRs define its scope.

Once the project is set up, functional specifications are developed for each of the PCRs and broken down into technical requirements, which are entered into a database. The requirements specify the functionality to be produced and are used by the development team to produce code and test scenarios, and by the test team to produce test cases. Test scenarios and cases are directly linked to these technical requirements and this becomes the basis for later testing coverage and testing status reports.

Throughout this process, business rules are captured and documented in a separate database. This is crucial to the success of the data warehousing effort, because without explicit documentation of business rules there is no consensus on what the data actually means or how it can be used.

While there are a number of documentation points in this process, the standard is still *just enough.* Too much documentation is just as bad as not enough. It is really a matter of quality, not quantity.

RAD Projects

When designing reporting systems or large pieces of functionality, Microsoft uses an iterative or RAD process. This varies from the waterfall approach only in that the requirements are broken down into feature sets in which the functional design, development, and some testing are done iteratively until consensus is reached. Often users are brought directly into the design meetings to facilitate the process.

Reviews

Just enough also works with reviews. The reviews necessary in each project cycle vary in depth, breadth, and manner of review according to the needs of the specific project (for example, low impact reviews are often done in e-mail). The following reviews are typically held:

- **PCR or requirements.** What is the scope of the project and does it make sense?
- **Functional specification.** Are the requirements covered by the functional specification?
- **Technical specification.** Does the technical specification completely describe functionality?
- **Physical design.** Are there holes in development's design?
- **Code.** Does the code meet design requirements? Does it meet standards? Is it implemented in the best way?
- **Test Plan.** What is the overall testing strategy for this project?
- **Test Scenarios.** What will be tested and what is the priority of the test scenarios? This provides an opportunity for development and program management to highlight areas and assess their relative risks.

- **Test Cases.** Do the test cases correctly test the relevant scenarios?
- **Testing Readiness.** Is the proposed drop from development to testing ready to go?
- **Production Readiness.** Is the code ready to be dropped to production?

Risk and Issue Management

The size of the effort makes it advisable to track issues and risks in a database and to review progress against them on a weekly basis. Any project team member can add risks or issues to the database; they are prioritized and assigned in a weekly meeting of program managers. The *priority 1* risks and issues are reviewed weekly in a meeting of all project leads.

People, Project Team Structure, and Strategy

The HRDW team operates as a team of peers. Program management, developers, testers, production support, and product management each report to their own function managers. A separate project manager (chosen from among the program managers) is responsible for each project for the group. There are usually two or three projects running for the HR Data Warehouse at any time. Project team members report directly to their functional manager but have their work directed by the project manager.

Lessons Learned

Train Project Members on Your ERP UI

Project members trained on the SAP R/3 UI had an easier time understanding the underlying database. This should hold true for any ERP.

Allocate Appropriate Time Up Front for Planning and Architecture

Everybody knows that sufficient planning pays off in shorter project times and higher quality deliverables. Nevertheless, there are always plenty of factors that seduce teams with a tight deadline, go-for-it approach. Resist the temptation to get started until you really know what you want to accomplish and how you will do it. Figure out where you want to go and how you want to get there before you start assigning checkpoints and a maximum trip time.

Assemble an Experienced Team

Insofar as it is possible, assemble a team of high-quality people that have worked together, and who understand the business, the current (legacy) system, and data warehousing issues in general. Building a good data warehouse is tricky. The more skills and knowledge the people have, the better the resulting design. The better the design, the easier it will be to train people on it. Collaboration is a must; if you know going in that the team members can work well together, you mitigate a lot of risk.

Convert Legacy Data into the ERP If At All Possible

On the SHARP project, converting legacy data into SAP R/3 would have required solving all the legacy data mapping problems as part of the implementation effort. This would have been a big hit, but it would have saved the project team from ever having to focus on legacy data issues again. As it turned out, maintaining the dual sourcing has increased costs and production problems. Conversion also solves the problem of how to correct historical information when you shut down your legacy systems—it's in the ERP.

If You Can't Convert Legacy Data, Build a Legacy Data Warehouse

If you decide not to load legacy data into the ERP, build a legacy data warehouse as part of the initial project. This is a significant effort, but an important one, because the team will inevitably lose people who know about the legacy systems. If you don't at least build a warehouse you increase long-term maintenance costs. The warehouse leaves you with the problem of how to correct historical information, but it solves many of the others.

Never Let People Access Source Databases for Reporting

Letting people use source databases for reporting undermines many of the benefits of data warehousing and almost always increases maintenance and support costs. Instead define the datamarts and (only if necessary) the data warehouse as the only external interfaces that people can use. This at least insulates the reporting systems from changes in the source systems, build processing, etc.

Value the People on the Project Team

Initial data warehousing projects often require skilled people to put out incredible efforts to bring in a very complicated project under deadline pressure. It is easy to burn people out. It is also easy to treat it as just another project. However, retaining people is key to the continued success of the data warehousing effort.

Make sure that you value the people on the project team and that you show it. Celebrate their accomplishments. Reward them in ways that are meaningful to them. Give them an incentive to stick around once the initial project is complete.

Don't Drive Architectural Design from Short-Term Deliverables

In the SHARP project a great deal of effort was focused on supporting the needs of the transition period. Instead of having a few people employ manual processes to produce data during the period, a great deal of effort was invested in programmatic solutions. In retrospect, this was effort that would have been better spent elsewhere.

Don't Defer History Reporting

Historical reporting is fundamental to any organization. If you don't plan for it in the initial implementation, people will prevent you from shutting down the previous systems, will write reports against source databases—will do whatever they have to do to get at historical information. No matter what people commit to, this will happen.

Glossary

Tools/Systems

- **SAP R/3.** The SAP R/3 enterprise application system.
- **RAID.** A Microsoft internal bug and issue tracking utility
- **MS Reports.** A Microsoft internal ad hoc query and reporting tool, results from which can be inserted in Excel PivotTables or spreadsheets, or in Microsoft Access tables.
- **Feedstore.** A Microsoft internal system that acts as a distribution point for common data, feeds as a way of synchronizing data between numerous distributed systems.
- **PCB-DASH.** A Microsoft tool that extends the functionality of batch—MS-DOS-like—programming and provides an administrative utility to monitor the progress of batch processes.
- **ERWin.** A data-modeling tool published by Platinum Technology, Inc. (http://www.logicworks.com)

Data Warehouse Project Terms

- **HRDW.** The Human Resources Data Warehouse and (as this term is used) all the reporting systems associated with it.
- **STAGING.** The database into which SAP R/3 data is initially placed.
- **SAPTRANS.** The database into which normalized and scrubbed SAP R/3 data is placed.
- **DATAMART.** The database into which feed and reporting tables are placed.
- **CPIT.** The current point in time view.

- **MPIT.** The month-end point in time view.

- **SHARP.** The project acronym: implementation of **SAP** R/3 for Microsoft's **HR** business unit.

- **HRODS.** A supplemental data source for data not available from any other system.

- **Build.** The code that rebuilds the data warehouse and datamarts from the source databases. Synonymous with *nightly processing*.

Other Terms

- **ERP.** Enterprise application system such as SAP R/3, PeopleSoft, BAAN, etc.

- **CS.** Contingent staff.

- **MCSS.** A Microsoft IT subgroup that provides critical support for servers and Windows NT within the Microsoft production environment.

C H A P T E R   1 0

MS Sales Data Warehouse

*By Joyce Behrendt,
Channel
Measurement,
Microsoft
Information
Technology Group*

MS Sales is the data warehouse solution used to track and control products sold by a variety of sources (distributors, resellers) in different forms (standalone or included in product suites). It has to collect, store, and make available enormous ranges of data collected from a variety of sources around the world. To serve its users, it has to have a functional logic that makes the data quickly and accurately accessible for standard and ad hoc reports.

The Solution in Focus

As in any data warehouse design, performance is a crucial factor. The challenge facing the MS Sales development team was to make timely, consistent, and accurate data available for users with divergent needs, *and* boost the performance levels of the original system. The resulting design shows how design techniques can meet the various challenges presented by the nature of the data and how they can build in features to ensure acceptable performance. It is based on Microsoft SQL Server 7.0 on Windows NT. Its segmentation of functionality addresses the requirements imposed by the nature and sources of data, and allows specific tasks to be tuned and optimized.

What You'll Find in This Chapter

- A discussion of the MS Sales data warehouse solution that moves from high level (basic business characteristics) to low level (specific design tactics).

- Design analysis that examines how the nature of the business case (capturing world-wide sales data for analysis) drove implementation of warehouse and datamart functionality.

- Explanations of optimizing techniques for replication, threading, restartability, partitioning, indexing, aggregation, and querying.

- Code samples for specific components.

- An overview of server hardware requirements.

- A discussion of project team organization and the importance of development environments.

Case Overview

MS Sales provides finance, sales, marketing, and product groups an integrated view of world-wide Microsoft product sales including point of sale (Microsoft, distributors, and resellers) and customer data. The advantages of using a data warehouse for this kind of data are obvious: categories such as items, points of sale, time spans, regions, and so on lend themselves to aggregation and querying.

But each application of warehouse technology presents challenges, as this case shows. Usually these have to do with the nature of the data to be collected, stored, and studied. In the case of MS Sales, the first challenge is scope—Microsoft sells many different products and versions around the world. Scope is further complicated by the complexity of the distribution channel—customers do not simply walk into a Microsoft store and buy a product; they also buy through distributors and through resellers, some of which report sales data quickly and completely, some of which do not. Then there is bundling—it would be relatively simple to track sales of Microsoft Excel if it were always sold separately, but it is also sold as part of Microsoft Office.

This chapter begins by discussing the MS Sales functional design, then moves on to discuss the data factory (where data transformation is handled) and the datamarts (the relational tables holding data). Each of these sections explains the basic setup, then defines components, then examines optimization techniques. The rest of the chapter discusses the general system architecture, the project team and its processes, and the design, development, and testing environments and techniques. Current methods and performance are sometimes compared to the earlier version of the system to show how the new design alleviated some issues and extended system usefulness.

Functional Design

This section discusses specific functional areas of the MS Sales design, stressing how the sources and nature of the data collected from the distribution channel are depicted in the data's hierarchical arrangement. Subsequent sections move deeper into warehouse design specifics.

Distribution

The distribution channel is arranged this way:

Microsoft → Distributor → Reseller → End Customer

Distributors and resellers report on sales, customers, and the inventory on hand for that week, and Microsoft account managers use that information to control the amount of inventory in the distribution channel. With solid information, it is possible to keep enough inventory on hand to meet demand, but not so much that products end up unsold and returned. Using MS Sales, account managers can focus on single distributors for specific weeks, see what they purchased from Microsoft, how many units they sold, and how many units are still in inventory at the end of the week. For example:

	Units Purchased	Units Sold	On Hand Inventory
Product A	12	14	2
Product B	5	11	3

Summarization

MS Sales allows sales to be summarized meaningfully for online analytical processing (OLAP). Account managers can query: "What is the total revenue of Microsoft Office products purchased by large organizations for each month in the current fiscal year?" Each sales transaction identifies the buying and selling organization, the product, date, and measures such as *UnitsSold* and *Revenue* (*UnitsSold* X *UnitPrice*). Each inventory transaction identifies the holding organization as well as the product, date, and *QuantityOnHand*. MS Sales' taxonomy (classification) allows users to query the fact tables using the basic dimensions such as *organization*, *product*, *geography*, and *time*. Figure 10.1 shows the hierarchy.

Organization

- Assign an organization type such as *distributor, reseller, end customer*.
- Classify end customer organizations by size into small, medium, and large organizations based on number of employees.
- Associate parenting relationships from a retail outlet up to its headquarters.

Product

- Identify products sold as a bundle with other products.
- Identify a distribution type of the product, such as *retail, academic,* or *not for resale*.
- Identify a product line hierarchy. *Stock keeping units* (SKUs) can be rolled up into a *product family*, which can be rolled up into a *product unit*, then into a *business unit*, and finally into a *product division* (the highest level).
- Pricing information allows managers to calculate revenue as *number of units sold* times the *unit price*.

Geography

■ Lower geography assigns a sales *subdistrict* based on U.S. postal codes. Subdistricts roll up into sales *districts* into sales *regions*, and into *subsidiaries*.

■ Upper geography rolls up *country*, which is a required attribute for each organization in MS Sales, into *subsidiary*, into *subregion*, into *region*, and into *area*.

Time

■ Sales date rolls up into fiscal week, into fiscal month, into fiscal quarter, and into fiscal year.

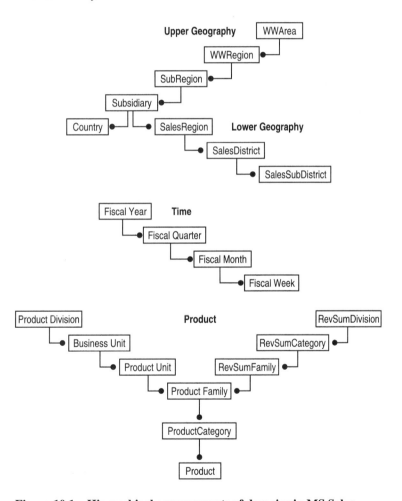

Figure 10.1   Hierarchical arrangements of domains in MS Sales.

Functional Components

MS Sales consists of four functional components: *operational data system*, *warehouse*, *factory*, and *datamarts* (each explained in more detail in the sections below). Here is an example of data flow through the components:

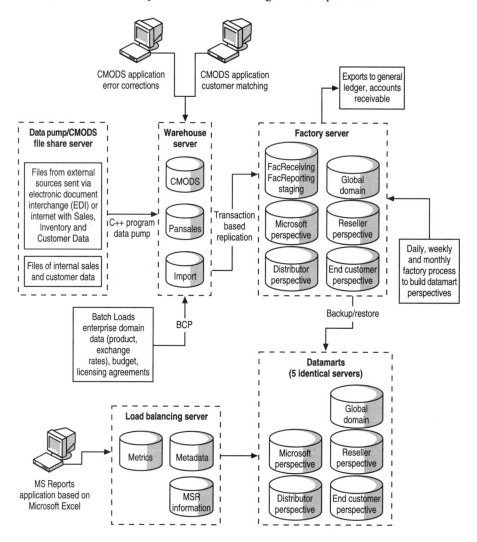

Figure 10.2   MS Sales functional process.

Operational Data System

The Channel Measurement Operational Data System (CMODS) loads sales, inventory, and customer files into MS Sales. To ensure data quality and consistency, the data pump checks for required fields, validates part numbers against the Microsoft master parts list, standardizes customer information, and tries to match the customer to the existing records to prevent duplication. Rejected rows are stored in a database where users can use an error correction application to match part numbers or customer records manually.

The data pump resides on a server dedicated to loading and validating the sales, inventory, and customer files. There are no SQL Server databases on this server. The data pump is written in C++, runs as a Windows NT service, and runs about 20 parallel threads. Domain tables, such as country and product, are loaded into memory. Validation of the sales records occurs against these domain tables, which are loaded into a C array. The arrays are reloaded from the domain tables periodically throughout the day, or when an event such as loading new product data into the warehouse triggers a reload. It is much faster to validate the sales files against the array in memory than by performing lookups in the database. To standardize the customer name and address information, the data pump passes the records through a third-party application before generating a match code and attempting to match the customer record to existing records. A CMODS database resides on the warehouse server and stores file tracking information as well as rejected records. The error correction application was written in Visual Basic. All components were written internally.

Each month, approximately 1500 reporting sources submit files totaling over 5,000,000 rows of sales and inventory, from which 60,000 new organizations are created. The reporting sources—distributors, resellers, and internal billing systems—submit text files through electronic document interchange (EDI) or submit text or Excel files through a Web site.

Warehouse

The warehouse databases are designed to store data efficiently and to allow quick inserts and updates. To speed inserts and updates, the tables are normalized and have a minimum number of indexes. This speeds row insertion by affecting as few pages as possible. For example, each day, several loads insert between 10,000 and

500,000 rows into the sales tables, and there are about 10,000 inserts and updates to customer information, usually one row at a time by numerous users working simultaneously. The indexes are mostly on primary and foreign keys to facilitate simple lookups and audit queries.

Normalizing the tables means that an update needs to occur in only one place. For example, if you change a subsidiary to roll up into a different region, you need to update only the subsidiary's *region* attribute. Another advantage of normalized tables is that they store more rows on a page and thus are kept as narrow as possible. When the optimizer scans pages, it has fewer pages to deal with.

All tables have an integer primary key (usually defined as an identity property) that is incremented by SQL Server when the row is inserted. If a code value uniquely identifying the row exists, it is implemented as an alternate key with a unique index. An integer column as a foreign key is more efficient than storing wide-character codes in the child table. For an example, see the Sales100 table in Figure 10.3 on page 352.

The MS Sales 1.0 system used character code values as primary keys and foreign keys, and as a consequence inserts and joins were very slow. The new design keeps row sizes as narrow as possible. Sometimes, however, a **tinyint** (a 1-byte integer from 0 through 255) was used in the original system as a primary key, and the new system's need for values greater than 255 forced the developers to change that datatype everywhere it existed. This was time consuming and it shows the practicality of being generous when choosing datatypes, rather than incurring extensive code and table change labor to increase numeric datatypes after the design is complete.

Set Processing

The new design also uses set processing whenever possible, which is faster than row-by-row operations in the warehouse. The new design still, however, updates or inserts one row at a time in the Organization, OrganizationAddress, and OrganizationTranslation tables. (See Figure 10.3 below.) Why here? Because the data pump and user CMODS Error Correction tasks create a lot of contention with these tables, and set processing would not work as well. For example, this arrangement works better when users change the organization referenced by one translation in order to get rid of a duplicate organization record:

```
BEGIN TRANSACTION
   UPDATE OrganizationTranslation
   SET    OrganizationID = @NewOrganizationID
   WHERE  OrganizationID = @OldOrganizationID

   DELETE OrganizationAddress
   WHERE OrganizationID = @OldOrganizationID

   DELETE Organization
   WHERE OrganizationID = @OldOrganizationID
COMMIT TRANSACTION
```

In these cases, single-row operations lock fewer resources (either rows or pages) than a set operation, and this reduces blocking. Another aid is vertical partitioning of the Organization and OrganizationAddress tables, which creates a one-to-one relationship between them. This creates two tables in the same database, which is created on one file group. This allowed developers to put less-frequently used columns (such as localized names and address columns that store DBCS characters) into a separate table. The process inserts a row into the Organization table, captures the new identity value using @@**identity**, then uses that new OrganizationID to insert a row into the OrganizationAddress table.

Relational Design

One of the central tables in the warehouse database is the OrganizationTranslation table. It stores one row for each SourceOrganizationId and ReportedOrganizationID. When a customer purchases from several resellers, the sales are reported in each data feed and tagged with a customer number assigned by the reseller. For example, reseller OfficeLand reports a sale of 10 copies of Windows NT Workstation to PlaneCo (customer number 432), and reseller OfficePlanet reports selling 20 copies of Windows NT Workstation to PlaneCo (customer number 55689). The two records are stored in the OrganizationTranslation table, but are associated with only one *organization* record for PlaneCo. If an account manager queries: "How many copies of Windows NT Workstation did PlaneCo buy in October?" the answer is 30.

Based on the organization name, country, and other attributes, users can determine that there should be only one organization record, and can then update the OrganizationId in the OrganizationTranslation table. No changes have to be made to the sales transactions. The data pump has an algorithm to generate match codes based on the organization attributes and then can auto-match the organization without user intervention. This is an efficient way to eliminate duplicate organization records. In the datamarts, end customer purchases can be summarized up to the Organization level.

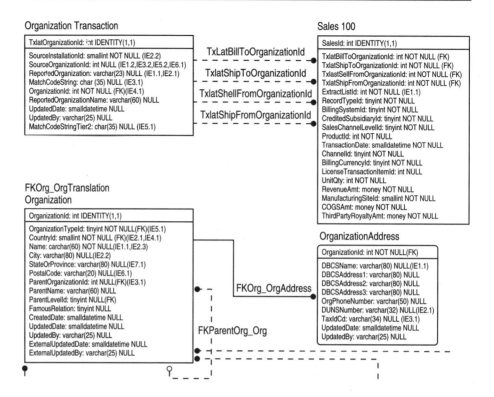

Figure 10.3   MS Sales relational design.

Factory

This server takes the normalized warehouse data (such as Organization, Sales, and Product), applies numerous business rules and data transformations, then populates the reporting tables. Data transformation is done by SQL statements in stored procedures and is automated.

In many systems, reporting tables contain summary data, but the MS Sales datamarts actually explode rows (some examples follow). Three million rows of sales transactions may end up as six million. Attributes are assigned to these derived transactions and some derived revenue is stored in separate columns.

Data Transformation

This section explains the various transformations performed on data and provides some sample code to show how. The transformations, which ensure that specific relationships and characteristics are reflected in the data, are performed in the

Factory. At the end of this section, some Factory-specific optimizations are discussed. The next section (on datamarts) continues the optimization analysis.

Attribute Inheritance

Many end customers classified as large, medium, or small organizations have a parenting structure. For example, SuperCola is a parent of the JuiceDrink company. So JuiceDrink's purchases can be rolled up and viewed as SuperCola's purchases at the headquarters level. The parenting structure allows three levels. If a given organization at the lowest level does not have certain relations defined, it inherits them from the immediate parent. Examples of relations are *Account Manager*, *Customer Segment*, or *Vertical Market*. This fill-down feature keeps data consistent with relationships between entities. It is relatively simple to create. The code below is a very simplified version you can try.

```
/*
** Create two tables and populate with sample rows
*/

DROP TABLE OrgGrouping, Organization, OrgInherited
GO
set nocount on

Create table Organization
 (OrgID int not null
 ,ParentOrgID int null)

insert into Organization select 100, 200
insert into Organization select 200, 300
insert into Organization select 300, 400
insert into Organization select 400, NULL
insert into Organization select 600, 200

Create table OrgGrouping
  (OrgID int
  ,AccountManagerName varchar(20) NULL
  ,PrimaryVerticalMarketName varchar(20)NULL )

insert into OrgGrouping select 100, 'Fred','Banking'
insert into OrgGrouping select 200, 'Gino','Insurance'
insert into OrgGrouping select 300, 'Ed','Accounting'
insert into OrgGrouping select 400, 'Kiko','Accounting'
-- Notice that OrgID 600 has no Org Grouping so it will inherit
   these from its parent.
```

(continued)

```
/****
-- Results in OrgInherited - 'Fill Down' feature
OrgId       AccountManagerName  PrimaryVerticalMarketName Pass
-----------  -------------------- -------------------------  -----------
400         Kiko                Accounting                0
300         Ed                  Accounting                1
200         Gino                Accounting                2
100         Fred                Accounting                3
600         Gino                Accounting                3
****/


---------------------------------------------------------------
-- Start filling the table from the highest parent on down.
-- First insert all unparented orgs (highest levels)
---------------------------------------------------------------
SELECT O.OrgId
      ,AccountManagerName = coalesce(G.AccountManagerName, 'Unknown')
      ,PrimaryVerticalMarketName =
          coalesce(G.PrimaryVerticalMarketName, 'Unknown')
      ,Pass = 0
INTO OrgInherited
FROM Organization O
LEFT OUTER JOIN OrgGrouping G
          ON O.OrgID = G.OrgID
WHERE ParentOrgID is null  -- defines highest level parent

-- Index
CREATE INDEX IX1UOrgInhAttHold ON OrgInherited (OrgID)
      WITH FILLFACTOR = 100

DECLARE @Pass tinyint, @rows int
SELECT @Pass = 1
SELECT @rows = 1
---------------------------------------------------------------
-- Loop around until we run out of children (0 rows inserted)
---------------------------------------------------------------
WHILE @rows <> 0
BEGIN

  INSERT INTO OrgInherited
      (OrgID
      ,AccountManagerName
      ,PrimaryVerticalMarketName
      ,Pass )
SELECT O.OrgID
    -- Inherited attributes.  If child AcctMgr is null, use parent.
    ,AccountManagerName =
        coalesce(G.AccountManagerName, P.AccountManagerName)
    -- Inherited attributes.  Always use parent
    ,PrimaryVerticalMarketName = P.PrimaryVerticalMarketName
```

```
        ,Pass = @Pass
   FROM Organization  O
   LEFT OUTER JOIN OrgGrouping G -- Child
             ON O.OrgID = G.OrgID
   JOIN OrgInherited P              -- Immediate Parent
     ON O.ParentOrgID = P.OrgID
    AND P.Pass = @Pass - 1  -- only go up one level up at a time.
    SELECT @rows = @@rowcount

    SELECT @Pass = @Pass + 1

END
```

Unbundling

This process transforms a sale of a bundled product, such as Microsoft Office, into a sale for each component, such as Microsoft Excel and Microsoft Word. The percentage of revenue to be allocated for each of the components is maintained in allocation tables. A query against Microsoft Excel, for example, can thus show all sales, including copies sold as part of Microsoft Office.

The code below shows the transformation from the bundled product to the component products. The ProductComponent table is unique on each parent and component product combination. This is a one (or none)-to-many relationship, so it uses an outer join. The revenue is multiplied by the allocation percentage.

```
Select
    S.SalesDateId
   ,S.TxlatShipToOrganizationId
   ,S.TxlatSellFromOrganizationId
   ,ProductId    = isnull(C.ComponentProductId,S.ProductId)
   ,UnitQty  = convert(decimal(14,2),(S.UnitQty
          * isnull(C.ChildQuantity,1)))
   ,RevenueAmt  = convert(money, (S.RevenueAmt
                    * (isnull(C.RevenueAllocationPercent,100.0)
                       /(convert(float,100.0)))))
INTO    ##BundledSales
FROM    SegmentedSales  S
LEFT OUTER JOIN ProductComponent C
  ON C.ParentProductId = S.ProductId
 AND  C.ParentProductDistTypeId = 4694    -- As-Shipped Bundles
```

Non-Reporting Outlets

Not all resellers report their sales to end customers, even though they buy Microsoft products from distributors. By assuming that the reseller does not itself consume the product, MS Sales can then assume that *reseller purchases* = *reseller sales*. This avoids the problem of missing information, by allowing the system to create the sales transactions to default end customers for known non-reporting resellers (NRO). A stored NRO allocation table determines which other attributes to apply to the transaction and a percentage of the revenue. In each subsidiary, this table is maintained by financial analysts familiar with the reseller transactions. They can store allocation at either a detail or summary level.

In the query below, the ##NROFinalSales table contains sales from distributors to known non-reporting resellers. This statement performs left outer joins to both the detail and summary allocation table and uses the percentages in the detail allocation table to calculate per-product revenue. If there is no join to the detail allocation table, the statement uses the summary allocation table. Because allocation tables contain the percentages used in the multiplication of the UnitQty and other amount columns, one sales record for $100 may end up as two $50 sales to end customers.

NROAllocation (summary).

RevSum Category ID	Subsidiary ID	Partner Sub SegmentID	Customer SubSegment ID	Default Txlat Org ID	Percentage
221	1	10	251	35688	.48
221	1	10	262	35689	.52
221	1	11	250	45587	.52
221	1	11	251	45588	.28
221	1	11	262	45589	.20

```
INSERT <column list>
SELECT
 U.SalesDateID
,U.CreditedSubsidiaryID
,3                              -- Becomes Sold-thru transaction
,ISNULL(N.TxlatOrgID, N2.TxlatOrgID)-- ShipTo from NRODistrict
,OrganizationTypeId = 7              -- All ShipTo Orgs are Type EndCust
,TxlatShipFromOrganizationId =
    U.TxlatShipToOrganizationId      -- Selling from original ShipTo
,U.ProductID
,51  -- Literal for NRO Trans
,U.UnitQty       * ISNULL(N.Percentage, N2.Percentage)
,U.ActualLicenseCnt * ISNULL(N.Percentage, N2.Percentage)
,U.SecondaryLicenseCnt  * ISNULL(N.Percentage, N2.Percentage)
,U.RevenueAmt       * ISNULL(N.Percentage, N2.Percentage)
,U.TOrgSubSegmentId      --  Use TOrgPartnerSubSegment from SellOut Trans
,ISNULL(N.TxlatOrgID, N2.TxlatOrgID)
,U.TxlatShipFromOrganizationId
,U.SalesSubDistrictOptionValue
  FROM ##NROFinalSales U
  LEFT OUTER MERGE JOIN NROAllocationDetail N
    ON N.RevSumCategoryID = U.RevSumCategoryId
   AND N.SubsidiaryID     = U.CreditedSubsidiaryID
```

```
      AND N.LicenseTypeId     = U.LicenseTypeId
      AND N.PartnerSubSegmentId = U.TOrgSubSegmentId
   LEFT OUTER JOIN NROAllocationSummary N2
      ON N2.RevSumCategoryID =
         CASE WHEN N.RevSumCategoryID IS NULL THEN U.RevSumCategoryId
         END
      AND N2.PartnerSubSegmentId = U.TOrgSubSegmentId
      AND N2.SubsidiaryID = U.CreditedSubsidiaryID
   WHERE N.RevSumCategoryID IS NOT NULL
      OR N2.RevSumCategoryId IS NOT NULL
```

Factory Optimization

The factory process can take three hours or three days depending on how many months of sales have to be processed. The initial MS Sales 3.0 factory design was entirely a single-threaded batch process, but volume and complexity increases since 1996 impelled several changes to shrink the total run time so that reports could be published on time.

Replication

The initial design, implemented in SQL Server 6.0, required that the warehouse database be backed up and restored to the factory server just before running the factory process. This was practical when the database was only a few GB and the factory was run weekly. When SQL Server 6.5 transaction replication became available, it was implemented as a transport mechanism, allowing new sales, inventory, and organization records to be sent to the factory as they are added or changed in the warehouse.

Every article (in MS Sales, articles are always at the full table level) that is to be published is persistently stored in the Publication table. The MS Sales development team wrote stored procedures that can drop one or more articles and then re-add them. (This was included to automate change and update procedure. It is explained more fully below.) When an article is re-added, a new complete snapshot is taken of the publishing table, the table on the subscribing database is dropped and recreated, the data is bulk copied in, and all indexes on the table are created. This method required no major changes with the implementation of SQL Server 7.0, which also supports continuous replication.

The example code below unpublishes an article. The **StopPublishingArticle** stored procedure executes the SQL Server 7.0 system stored procedure **sp_DropArticle** for all tables with a PublishIND = 0.

```
UPDATE publication SET PublishIND = 0
WHERE tablename in ( 'BillingSystem')

EXEC @rc = StopPublishingarticle
```

This example code below publishes an article. The StartPublishingArticle stored procedure executes the SQL Server 7.0 system stored procedure sp_AddArticle for all tables with a PublishIND = 1.

```
UPDATE publication SET PublishIND = 1
WHERE tablename in ( 'BillingSystem')

FXFC @rc = StartPublishingArticle
```

These automated scripts are used because:

- Columns are added to tables and new tables are added to the warehouse frequently, as new features are implemented. For example, changing the sales tables to eliminate two unused columns and to add a new column to track cost of goods sold amounts (COGS) required manipulating 132 sales tables (one sales table for each month) representing about 20 GB of data. The automated scripts make it possible to propagate the same changes in an unattended batch mode requiring little manual intervention and downtime.

- When several hundred thousand rows are added to the sales tables or mass updates affect several hundred thousand rows, it is often faster to unpublish the affected table, perform the updates, then take a new snapshot. When these set operations are performed on the warehouse, replication sends one row at a time to the factory; the bulk operation in native SQL Server mode (used by the snapshot) is faster than sending one insert at a time.

- Occasionally data on the subscribed table does not match data on the published table. The first step in the factory process is to perform replication validation. If any tables are found to be different, then a snapshot is initiated. The factory waits for this to complete, then checks again, and begins the normal factory process only when the validation is successful. If the validation is still unsuccessful on the third try, the operations team is paged. All of this happens without user intervention.

In SQL Server 6.5, the MS Sales development team wrote custom scripts to recreate indexes by reverse-engineering the scripts from the published table after the snapshot was applied. The team also wrote custom scripts to audit the data between the published and subscribed databases using remote procedure calls, and based the comparison on a sum of UnitQuantity and RevenueAmt in the sales table. SQL Server 7.0 automatically creates indexes and performs **sp_article_validation** as part of its feature set. These are not full-text indexes, because most of the data is numeric or short-name columns.

Multi-threaded Processing

The factory process takes a parameter that tells it how many months of sales to process. In daily mode, it processes either the current month or the current and prior month. The first release of MS Sales 3.0 processed one month at a time. To shorten factory process duration, several instances of the sales processes were run in parallel. In testing, the Performance Monitor %Processing Time counters showed that on a four-processor server no more than four threads of concurrent activity was practical—adding more threads slowed down all processes. To support parallel instances of the sales procedures, the developers changed the processes to accept an instance number of 1, 2, or 3. Another independent process operates on inventory transactions. All work tables have the instance number appended to the name.

At the beginning of the factory job, all the months to be processed are stored in a table. As each independent thread is started, it picks up a month to be worked on and updates a status field in that table to *in progress*. The second thread picks up the next month, and so on. As each thread completes, it updates the status to *done* for that month. When all months are done, the rows are deleted from this table to create space for the next time the factory job runs.

Because of this concurrency and the number of temporary tables needed, I/O is distributed by means of a 6-GB **tempdb** striped on two drives. The **staging** database stores all the procedures and intermediate work tables; it is about 45 GB striped on four drives and has a 5-GB transaction log. These intermediate tables remain populated until just before the next time the process runs, to facilitate troubleshooting.

Restartability

The factory process can take many hours, even days, and it would be disastrous if a last-hour problem required a restart from the beginning. If the batch job executes a stored procedure and it cannot connect to the server or the procedure is disconnected, the batch job automatically retries three times. If it fails on the third try, the operations team is paged. This allows for completion in many instances, and, in others, for timely intervention that can avoid losing the processing already completed.

There are other tables (aside from the one that holds a row for each month to be processed). One holds each step that must be completed to transform the sales transactions (and it would be possible to create another that holds steps within a single process). A status column for each process is updated to *complete* when the process finishes running. If the job restarts after running partially, it executes the same processes but it uses the table to avoid rerunning ones that have already completed. Any process tagged *complete* in the table's status column is not run. Once all steps in the process are done, the rows are deleted from this table so that it is initialized for the next run.

Here is the table. The instance number added to the name of each procedure allows parallel processes to be restarted independently.

Procedures needed to transform sales transactions.

Process	Status
BuildNROTransactions1	Complete
BuildUnbundledSales1	Complete
DetermineLandedAttribution1	Started
PopulatePartitionedSalesTables1	Pending
BuildNROTransactions2	Complete
BuildUnbundledSales2	Started
DetermineLandedAttribution2	Pending
PopulatePartitionedSalesTables2	Pending

Datamarts

The MS Sales datamarts consist of relational tables in a SQL Server 7.0 database. To design the tables, developers used report prototypes from business users throughout Microsoft to make sure the system would capture every data point that the business wanted to see: Revenue Amount, Units Sold, Product, Subsidiary, Customer Name, Postal Code, TransactionDate. The team also designed hierarchical structures for areas such as product lines, geography, and time (see "Relational Design" below), and an organization taxonomy so that classification was clear and consistent. A dictionary of this type is a good idea when you are designing a system that classifies entities (in this case organizations) in many different ways.

The team used input from business users, the MS Reports application team, operations, and development to design the physical datamarts—the first step in the system design process. Query performance was a major factor. For frequently run summary reports, quicker response was required, so pre-aggregated tables were created by the factory process. Designers also knew that most queries would run on the current three months of detail data, so data that is four months or older is summarized to monthly granularity and actual invoice dates are eliminated.

Study of business requirements also showed that certain hierarchies must change only at month end, not during the month, to keep revenue from shifting during the month. To handle this, updates to the hierarchy in the warehouse are allowed, but the factory process inserts only new domain values—it does not update the foreign key or parent of a child in the lower level of the hierarchy until month-end processing.

A project is currently underway to implement SQL Server 7.0 multidimensional OLAP (MOLAP) for summary reports. Detail reports at the part number or customer level will still rely on the relational tables (ROLAP), but MS Reports will be enhanced to allow the data to be retrieved from MOLAP and then allow drill-through capability to get detail data from ROLAP.

Relational Design

This is a simplified view of the Sales fact table and some related dimensions in the Reseller perspective. Every sales table in the data marts has a *Central Figure* organization. In this case, the central figure is the selling organization, or reseller. It is generally desirable to eliminate joins, and this has been accomplished here by denormalizing some hierarchical relationships, and placing the primary keys on the fact table and the primary dimension tables (Seller Organization, Buyer Organization, Product and Subsidiary). These are used for aggregating the data on the fly. In a final step before returning results to the Excel pivot table, the intermediate table is joined to the domain tables (such as Area below) to fill in the name columns.

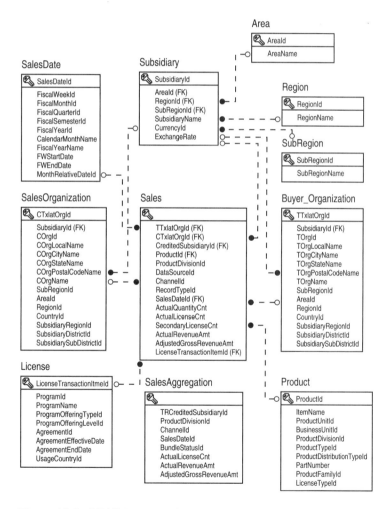

Figure 10.4   MS Sales star schema.

Optimization Techniques

Partitioning Strategy

From experience, designers realized that partitioning the data into multiple databases and multiple tables optimizes data movement, transformation, and querying. It is easier to put together smaller packages than to filter out subsets of data from large tables.

Partitioning examples.

Partitioning strategy	Explanation
Horizontal partitioning by organization type Databases: Microsoft Distributor Reseller End Customer	There is a database for each report type based on the seller's organization type. The fact tables (sales, purchases, or inventory) in each of these databases contain sales from the corresponding organization type. Since each of these represents different segments of the distribution channel, the sales transactions must be broken up to avoid double-counting the revenue.
Horizontal partitioning by Time—Fiscal year Databases: MicrosoftCurrent Microsoft1999 Microsoft1998 DistributorCurrent Distributor1999 Distributor1998	Each of the databases is further partitioned by fiscal year. The 'current' database contains the current and prior month of sales. This is done because current data changes daily, historical data much less often. The current databases are small (about one GB) and can be backed up and restored to the reporting servers very quickly. At the end of a fiscal month, the current fiscal year is reprocessed and those databases are copied to the reporting server. About three to four times a year, all history is reprocessed and all databases are copied out to the reporting server—which takes about three days to run. A restatement is always performed after the end of the fiscal year.
Horizontal partitioning by Time—Month Tables: FM111RSLSALSL00 (September) FM112RSLSALSL00 (October) FM113RSLSALSL00 (November) FM111RSLSALSL00_FOrg FM111RSLSALSL00_TOrg	Each sales table within each reporting database is partitioned by fiscal month. At the left, the 3-digit number following *FM* represents the FiscalMonthId. A domain table of fiscal months indicates the start and end date, calendar month name, calendar year, and fiscal year. The remainder of the intelligent table name indicates Reseller (RSL) Sales (SALS) at the detail level (L00). The MS Reports metadata layer encodes this information when formulating the SQL query. There are buyer organization and selling organization tables by month that have an extension such as "_FORG" (from organization or seller), "_TORG" (to organization or buyer). These contain only organizations that had sales

Partitioning strategy	Explanation
	or purchases for that month. This allows queries joining these tables to be very fast. An early attempt used a single organization table that had all attributes and rows (about 5,000,000 wide rows), but the performance was too slow. The final domain partitioning strategy takes up more disk space, but enables more satisfactory query performance for users.

Aggregations

One physical summary table was created for each fact table at the most often used aggregation. This eliminates the part number and customer number level detail and summarizes up to the ProductDivision and Subsidiary level. For one month, the row reduction went down significantly from 3,017,803 to 111,845 rows. The row size of the aggregation layer is also considerably smaller because it now has fewer columns. Data pages were reduced from 28,470 in the detail table to 583 for the aggregation.

MS Reports uses the metadata to decide if the aggregation table can be queried based on the columns and filters selected by the user. The metadata uses an aggregation table if all columns in the select list and join clause are present in the aggregation table definition. If a specified column (such as PartNumber) is not available in the aggregation layer, the metadata uses the detail table instead.

Other aggregations are done on the fly, based on the level of detail selected by the user. The designers decided not to create other physical aggregations, because it would take too long to build them and they would occupy too much space.

Indexes

As a rule, all primary key and foreign key columns are indexed. These are the columns that typically are used to join tables and apply restrictions. Primary keys and foreign constraints are not created in the datamarts because the tables are populated only by batch processes and not by user interaction.

When system analysis showed that a geographical attribute at the lowest level, SubsidiarySubdistrictID, appears in most queries as both a restriction and a join column, a clustered index was created on this column in the fact tables and in the domain table to improve performance.

There are not many covering indexes or multiple column indexes on the reporting tables. The designers plan to use the Index Tuning Wizard in SQL Server 7.0 to run a workload of queries, and possibly identify some covering indexes.

Query Techniques

To query the monthly partitioned sales tables, MS Reports generates a script with one query per month of data that the user wants. For instance, it creates 12 queries to return sales for an entire year. In the first set of queries, only foreign key ID values are selected from the fact table. Once the data is summarized to the level of detail specified by the user, a final join is made to the domain tables for name columns such as ProductDivisionName or FiscalMonthName. This keeps the intermediate results tables narrow, resulting in faster performance and smaller memory usage for the group by operation.

Here is the SQL generated by MS Reports:

```
/* Create Work Tables */
CREATE TABLE
MSRQueryResults..joycebe31332
(
RevSumDivisionID int null,
PricingLevelID tinyint null,
FiscalMonthID smallint null,
RevSumCategoryID int null,
d_RslrPurchaseAdjAmount money null
)

CREATE TABLE
MSRQueryResults..joycebe31332Final
(
RevSumDivisionID int null,
PricingLevelID tinyint null,
FiscalMonthID smallint null,
RevSumCategoryID int null,
d_RslrPurchaseAdjAmount money null
)
 GO

/* Query #1 */
INSERT INTO
MSRQueryResults..joycebe31332
SELECT
J.RevSumDivisionID,
J.PricingLevelID,
L.FiscalMonthID,
J.RevSumCategoryID,
SUM(convert(money,((A.ActualRevenueAmt/AG.ExchangeRate) +
(A.AdjustedGrossRevenueAmt/AG.ExchangeRate))))
FROM
Reseller1999..TPM3RSLPURSL01 A,
GlobalDomain..ManagementReporting J,
GlobalDomain..SalesDate L,
GlobalDomain..ExchangeRate AG
WHERE
A.ManagementReportingID = J.ManagementReportingID AND
```

```
A.SalesDateID = L.SalesDateID AND
A.SalesDateID = AG.SalesDateID AND
 (
AG.CurrencyID = 15 AND
A.TRCreditedSubsidiaryID = 1 AND
A.ChannelID = 1 AND
A.SalesDateID  IN(52,53,54,55))  AND ( A.TRCreditedSubsidiaryID IN (
1,3,4,6,44,45,46,47,48,50,52,53,70,71,94,95,43,102,96,97,98,99,101,51,49
))
GROUP BY
J.RevSumDivisionID,
J.PricingLevelID,
L.FiscalMonthID,
J.RevSumCategoryID
 GO


/* Query #2 (Same query but from a different month) */
INSERT INTO
MSRQueryResults..joycebe31332
SELECT
J.RevSumDivisionID,
J.PricingLevelID,
L.FiscalMonthID,
J.RevSumCategoryID,
SUM(convert(money,((A.ActualRevenueAmt/AG.ExchangeRate) +
(A.AdjustedGrossRevenueAmt/AG.ExchangeRate))))
FROM
ResellerCurrent..TPM1RSLPURSL01 A,
GlobalDomain..ManagementReporting J,
GlobalDomain..SalesDate L,
GlobalDomain..ExchangeRate AG
WHERE
A.ManagementReportingID = J.ManagementReportingID AND
A.SalesDateID = L.SalesDateID AND
A.SalesDateID = AG.SalesDateID AND
 (
AG.CurrencyID = 15 AND
A.TRCreditedSubsidiaryID = 1 AND
A.ChannelID = 1 AND
A.SalesDateID  IN(40,41,42,43,44))  AND ( A.TRCreditedSubsidiaryID IN (
1,3,4,6,44,45,46,47,48,50,52,53,70,71,94,95,43,102,96,97,98,99,101,51,49
))
GROUP BY
J.RevSumDivisionID,
J.PricingLevelID,
L.FiscalMonthID,
J.RevSumCategoryID
 GO
```

(continued)

```
INSERT INTO
MSRQueryResults..joycebe31332Final
SELECT
RevSumDivisionID 'Rev Sum Division',
PricingLevelID 'Pricing Level',
FiscalMonthID 'Fiscal Month',
RevSumCategoryID 'Rev Sum Category',
SUM(d_RslrPurchaseAdjAmount) 'Rslr Purchase Adj Amount'
FROM
MSRQueryResults..joycebe31332
GROUP BY
RevSumDivisionID,
PricingLevelID,
FiscalMonthID,
RevSumCategoryID

DROP TABLE MSRQueryResults..joycebe31332
 GO


/* Retrieve Results Query */

SELECT
   RD0.RevSumDivisionName 'Rev Sum Division',
   PL0.PricingLevelName 'Pricing Level',
   FL0.FiscalMonthName 'Fiscal Month',
   RC0.RevSumCategoryName 'Rev Sum Category',
   d_RslrPurchaseAdjAmount 'Rslr Purchase Adj Amount'
FROM
   GlobalDomain..RevSumDivision RD0,
   GlobalDomain..PricingLevel PL0,
   GlobalDomain..FiscalMonth FL0,
   GlobalDomain..RevSumCategory RC0,
   MSRQueryResults..joycebe31332Final WorkTable
WHERE
   WorkTable.RevSumDivisionID *= RD0.RevSumDivisionID AND
   WorkTable.PricingLevelID *= PL0.PricingLevelID AND
   WorkTable.FiscalMonthID *= FL0.FiscalMonthID AND
   WorkTable.RevSumCategoryID *= RC0.RevSumCategoryID
 GO
```

A similar approach is used to create ad hoc reports: users position the cursor inside a Transact-SQL script or stored procedure to query each table, then append the results to a work table. For more complex ad hoc reporting, temporary skinny tables (having only the needed columns and rows) can be created, then joined to the large fact tables to get data rows into another work table for further manipulation.

Nulls

Datamarts have no null values. Instead, a 0 is used for the primary key value with a name of *N/A* or *Non Specific*. This avoids performing outer joins. For example, an account manager is an optional attribute of an organization in the warehouse. An associative entity called OrganizationAccountManager stores OrganizationId and AccountManagerID. The organization table in the datamarts, however, has an AccountManagerID non-null column. The factory process that builds the organization table defaults AccountManager to 0 if there is no row in the OrganizationAccountManager table for that OrganizationID. The AccountManager domain table has an AccountManagerID of 0 with an AccountManagerName of *N/A*.

Basically, this simply makes things clearer for users. Many don't realize they need to perform outer joins when a foreign key column is nullable, and this helps them avoid getting a result set with rows missing. Similarly, when an amount column has no value attached, it defaults to 0 because users prefer to see a 0 instead of null in Excel pivot tables.

Usage Analysis

MS Reports stores statistics about datamart table and column usage in a table called MSR_LOG. This table provides statistics such as:

- Average query time for the previous week.
- Which tables were involved in queries that took more than ten minutes.
- Which columns were used to filter rows in queries that took more than ten minutes. (These may indicate an index is needed.)
- Which fields have not been queried in the last six months. (These are candidates for removal.)
- How many other queries were running at the time as the subject query.

Here is a description of the columns in the MSR_LOG table.

MSR_LOG table.

Column_Name	Data_Type
LoginName	varchar(25) not null
LogDate	datetime not null
SQLText	text not null
TimeQuery	float not null
TimeRetrieve	float not null
TimeFormat	float not null
ActiveUsers	smallint not null

(continued)

Column_Name	Data_Type
ActiveQueries	smallint not null
TablesUsed	varchar(50) not null
FieldsSelect	varchar(255) not null
FieldsFilter	varchar(255) not null
CreateTypeCode	smallint not null
StatusCode	smallint not null
TempTableRows	int null
ReportType	varchar(50) null
SPIDSUsed	tinyint null
OutputType	tinyint null
TimeResolve	float null
LoadBalancing	smallint null
InsertCount	smallint null

Architecture

MS Sales has a distributed architecture. It runs 24 x 7 to load and process world-wide sales data. Data received in the morning often can be reflected in the datamarts by the afternoon. Because data volumes increase exponentially and enhancements are constantly being added, the design, code, and architecture are continually evaluated in search of ways to enhance performance.

The factory server was recently upgraded from a Compaq 5500 to a DEC alpha, because testing showed that this would reduce factory run times by about 30%. This change was made possible when the system was upgraded to SQL Server 7.0, which can back up and restore databases (this is how datamart databases are moved from the factory server to the datamart server) between the Intel and alpha platforms.

How MS Sales activity is distributed across servers.

Server	Hardware	Activity
Data pump server	Compaq 4 200 MHz processors 2 GB memory	The data pump service (executing on this server) continuously sweeps file shares to find sales and inventory files sent from the distributors, resellers, and Microsoft billing systems. It validates the product and customer information in the sales files against domain tables loaded into memory from the warehouse SQL Server database. A sales file can contain anywhere from 100 - 100,000 records. The data pump runs as a Windows NT 4.0 service and is multi-threaded to take advantage of all four processors.

Server	Hardware	Activity
Warehouse server	Compaq 4 200 MHz processor 2 GB memory 396 GB of raw disk space and 86 GB of database space	This server has SQL Server 7.0 installed and contains the normalized, standardized, and valid warehouse sales, inventory, and customer data. Domain loads, such as product, are scheduled throughout the day. These are Windows NT batch files that call the SQL Server bulk copy program (**bcp**) utility to import data, ISQL.EXE to execute stored procedures, and then perform file handling routines such as copy, delete, and rename. The data pump inserts valid data into the warehouse database on this server and inserts the rejected rows into a holding database where users can use the error correction application on the data. Business analysts run many ad hoc reports to audit sales. Processing on this server transforms data and creates new data based on rules. Although most data transformation is done in the factory server, some data in the warehouse needs to be derived and stored permanently without risk of recalculating the sales for closed fiscal years. The transformation is done by stored procedures and the data is stored in relational tables in the warehouse database. A SQL Server 7.0 distribution database resides on the warehouse server and replicates all warehouse data to the factory server. Three other servers subscribe to subsets of the warehouse.
Factory server	DEC alpha 4 533 MHz processor 2 GB memory 1.03 Terabytes (TB) of raw disk, 240 GB of database space	This server also has SQL Server 7.0 installed. A batch process executes a series of stored procedures that transform the warehouse data into the reporting tables in datamart databases; it is copied out from there to the datamart servers. The batch process is a Windows NT batch file that calls ISQL.EXE to execute stored procedures. Data transformation is done entirely by the stored procedures. The batch process spawns four parallel threads to maximize throughput. At the end of the factory process, the reporting databases are regularly backed up and restored onto each of the five datamart servers.
Datamart servers	Compaq 4 200 MHz processor 2 GB memory	The datamart servers are the target of all OLAP activity in a set of SQL Server 7.0 databases. Users query the data with MS Reports or by ad hoc methods using Microsoft Access or Microsoft SQL Server Query Analyzer. Three of the servers participate in load balancing by MS Reports. One of the other datamart servers is dedicated to users in a specific department and is used to generate and refresh some standard Excel spreadsheets using MS Reports in unattended mode. The Excel spreadsheets are copied out to file shares in the subsidiaries using Windows NT file replication.

Project Team

All requirements gathering, development, and testing are done in house. The team collaborates on decisions. The MS Sales system is so widely distributed that the team must review and manage changes to make sure that a change to one area does not adversely affect another. The MS Sales project team contains these groups:

- Business analysts
- Analysts
- Development
- Test
- Production support

The business analyst team has about 20 members and is separated into smaller teams responsible for sales through Microsoft, through the channel (resellers and distributors), and taxonomy (classification of organization attributes and hierarchies). Analysts work with other departments such as the Sales and Marketing, Finance, and Product groups. The channel sales team works with distributors and resellers who report sales information, and is responsible for data quality and user training on reports. Team members are assigned responsibility for specific subsidiaries.

Business analysts often travel to Microsoft subsidiaries to gather requirements and conduct training. Subsidiary personnel occasionally visit Microsoft corporate headquarters.

Presently, two analysts write requirements documents based on input from the business analysts, and from analysts and users in other Microsoft departments. No single method is defined, but there is a requirement template that indicates each area that could be affected. Within each area, there are several statements that describe the requirement. After the high-level requirements are agreed upon with the business users, a requirement hand-off meeting is held, during which the analyst describes the features to business analysts, development, test, and production support.

The development team starts working on the detail design based on the requirements and notes taken from the requirements hand-off meeting. Because some batch processing is very complex, flow charts are created or updated to facilitate a walkthrough of several use cases (see the flowchart below). The design document contains tables that help visualize data input, transformation, and output, and snapshots of the proposed table changes shown in an entity relationship diagram. Other sections include:

- **Operational changes.** This section lists new jobs to be scheduled, file shares to be created, databases that need to be expanded.

- **Table changes.** This also includes descriptions of needed indexes, primary keys, foreign keys, other constraints and permissions.

- **View changes.**

- **Stored procedure changes or new procedures.** Each stored procedure has a description, summary of steps, parameters (optional and required), and pseudocode

- **Batch job changes.**

- **Change script steps.** After a substantial set of table changes, it may be a good idea to recreate all stored procedures, views, triggers, and permissions. This section helps plan the best order in which to execute the steps.

- **Data conversion.** This section identifies whether an initial set of rows should be inserted into new tables, how data should be converted for existing tables where columns are being added or removed, and whether new values need to be added to operational tables.

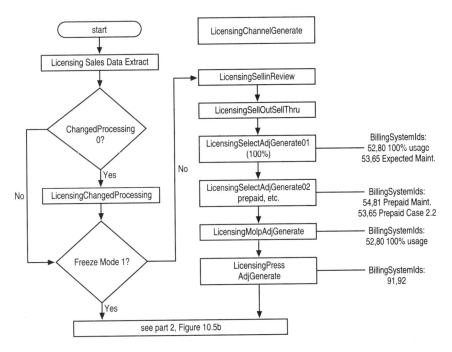

Figure 10.5a   Sample flow chart used in design process for new features (part 1).

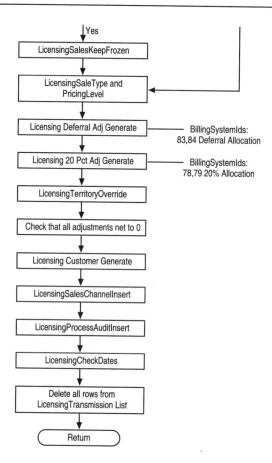

Figure 10.5b   Sample flow chart used in design process for new features (part 2).

Once the detail design is complete, the business analysts, analysts, test, and production support teams meet for a design review, walking through all the changes. Changes may be made to the design before actual coding has begun. Once the code is complete, the same group meets for a code review, using a code printout and a process flowchart.

When the requirements are complete, the test team creates a test plan, then refines it based on the design and code reviews as well as interviews with the business analysts and production support team. The test team organizes a pre-test review, reconvening the teams involved in the requirements and design process. When testing is complete, the test team holds another meeting to review bugs found and to discuss any outstanding bugs. The business analysts may choose to have the build released to user acceptance testing (UAT) even though some minor bugs still exist.

The production support team manages the UAT and the production environments. The team helps pursue MS Sales' two primary goals: lights-out processes (automated, no manual intervention) and on-time publishing (there usually are tuning enhancements in the works). The team also monitors all production servers for availability, missed delivery goals, usage, disk space, job failure rates, runtime statistics, bugs found in production, and builds applied to production. They compile metrics and report to the entire team each week.

Development Environment

In addition to the production environment, MS Sales maintains three full-sized development, test, and user acceptance environments in which to develop and test code. This is a considerable expense, but management agreed to purchase the additional hardware to ensure that data quality and delivery goals are met before new features are put into production. For example, no data export should take more than two hours to run, but if the export code is developed and tested on small data sets, it is difficult to predict how long it will take in production. Then too, the factory data transformations are so complex that the development environments must be loaded with current production data so that every scenario can be tested thoroughly. You cannot ensure referential integrity if you test relational database features against small data subsets.

Development

The development team uses several servers to upgrade software, restore databases from production, and to prototype, develop, and create database upgrades. The servers are in the same building where the team resides so that each developer can have experience installing and troubleshooting Windows NT, SQL Server, and other MS Sales software. During the SQL Server 7.0 beta, the team had to run SQL Server 7.0 in the Visual C++ debugger in order to set break points and capture diagnostic information useful to SQL Server development. The development team is often the first to install early beta versions of Microsoft server software and give feedback to the product development teams. After the team achieves a required degree of stability on the test servers, it upgrades the other MS Sales test environments for a final round of testing before releasing the change into production.

The development team also develops and tests components before releasing code to the test team.

Testing

The test team has a more integrated environment than the development team. They use it to:

- Ensure that database change scripts work properly and do not corrupt existing data.
- Test feature enhancements based on requirements and detail designs.

- Create failure conditions and verify that processes correctly roll back and restart from where they left off.

- Regression-test all processes, including those that did not receive changes. Sometimes a change in one component has an unexpected effect in a downstream component. There are so many imports, exports, and data transformations across all MS Sales components that the dependencies are not always obvious at design time.

- Test the end-to-end process: receiving files, validating data, warehouse transformations, replication to the factory, and running the factory to apply business rules and build reporting tables for the datamart.

Software Acceptance Testing

For the SQL Server 7.0 beta testing, the software acceptance team was called in to install the datamart databases on one of their servers, run a custom multi-user simulation program that executes a query workload (taken from the production datamarts), and capture the run time and row counts for each query. They ran a baseline test in SQL Server 6.5, then ran it again in SQL Server 7.0. Working closely with the SQL Server development team to make sure that SQL Server 7.0 ran as fast or faster than SQL Server 6.5, the team reran the workload after each new build of SQL Server. By the time SQL Server 7.0 was released, the performance was 43% better than the SQL Server 6.5 baseline.

User Acceptance Testing (UAT)

The production support team administers this environment. Once the test team has signed off on a build, the production support team performs the UAT on it. Business owners specify which loads and processes they want run in this environment, then the production support team audits and validates the test results and works with other departments for data loads and/or exports to ensure that the integration works as expected. When a new version of the data correction application or a new reporting application is produced, the team runs it for the first time in this environment. Invariably, bug fixes and enhancements are needed before the feature is installed in production. The development team makes the changes and drops an incremental build which goes through test and then to UAT. These changes are merged once the set of features has been signed off and approved for production.

C H A P T E R   1 1

Data Warehouse Management Infrastructure: MetaEdge

By Juan Jose Ortiz and Li-Wen Chen, MetaEdge Corp.

Designing a very large database or data warehouse system requires that you carefully assess needs, then make many decisions on infrastructure, components, relationships, as well as numerous considerations of data size, treatment, storage, and so on. Besides influencing performance, design decisions of this type also influence the maintenance of the system after it is moved into production, and, in many ways, its scalability and extensibility.

The Solution in Focus

MetaEdge, a Microsoft Certified Solution Provider (MSCP), developed a data warehouse management solution using Microsoft Repository and integrated metadata layers. Using object-oriented technology to build an object metadata model on top of a relational metadata store, this solution allows:

- Applications to communicate with the common repository without regard to its internal relational design

- Management software to use the model to manipulate metadata elements and coordinate data exchange with metadata sources

- Decision-support applications or presentation layers to request elements transparently

Besides environment transparency in a distributed metadata architecture, an object metadata model also provides resiliency to deal with dynamic relationships and complex interactions among metadata "objects." Building object models on top of metadata repositories fosters data distribution across the information technology (IT) infrastructure by shielding applications and users from underlying storage structures, and makes it possible to build a knowledge management infrastructure based on object models, metadata management, and presentation of data with multiple views.

What You'll Find in This Chapter

- Discussions of object, space, backup/recovery, and metadata management in large database systems.

- Explanations of components and functional areas: how they work and interact.

- Strategies for avoiding design problems, optimizing performance, and tuning.

- Suggestions for making design and implementation decisions.

- An extended treatment of metadata that begins with basic information and proceeds through design characteristics and culminates in a discussion of how to use metadata to manage a data warehouse effectively and efficiently.

- Sample code for metadata management procedures, showing how to define part of the open information model for physical layout storage, populate one of the repository objects in the storage information model, etc.

Case Overview

This chapter discusses the challenges facing designers of very large databases (VLDBs) and data warehouses. These systems are typified by huge amounts of data (between 110 GB and 10 TB) and by complex logical structures involving numerous entities and modifications. Challenges arise from these characteristics in the form of requirements for more complicated object management, more sophisticated backup and recovery strategies, and, especially, more carefully planned and implemented infrastructures for managing metadata. This chapter works through these areas, defining the problems and offering recommendations. It also takes a look at a technical architecture built on Microsoft Repository that uses metadata to drive data warehouse administration.

Object Management

Using current relational database management system (RDBMS) technology system developers now can implement VLDB and data warehouse systems—systems holding between 100 GB and 10 TB of data—although several types of major challenges remain. The first type has to do with operation and maintenance: typically, RDBMS-based implementations require the database administrator (DBA) to manage a large number of objects, including data files, file groups, tables, indexes, views, stored procedures, etc. This requires performing numerous tedious tasks that can result in errors, especially when performed manually. The second type of challenge concerns storage requirements for object space management. A third type concerns change management: because a typical VLDB or warehouse contains many objects, unauthorized and/or unintended changes to it must be detected.

This section discusses how data warehouse object management should address these challenges.

Hierarchical/Grouping Mechanism for Managing Many Objects

A typical data warehouse may have hundreds of tables (and associated indexes, views, file groups, data files, etc.) and numerous logical relationships (hierarchical and grouping in most cases) between sets of objects. For administration purposes, it is more convenient to act on a group of related objects than on one object at a time. This tactic is practical only if groups are hierarchically arranged, but since each data warehouse embodies different business requirements and characteristics, the hierarchy must fit the warehouse's structure. There is no single best hierarchy or grouping scheme.

To see how the number of objects can grow dramatically in a warehouse environment, consider a telecommunications company's marketing data warehouse with this structure:

Fact tables

- Billing
- Payment
- CallDetail
- CustomerActivity

Dimension hierarchies

- Customer > Account > Subscription
- Country > Region > State > City
- Equipment Vendor > Category > Model
- Channel Group > SalesOffice > Agent
- Year > Month > Week > Day

If you create aggregate tables for combinations of the following dimension elements

- All Customers, Customer, Subscription
- Channel Group, Agent
- Region, City
- Month, Week, Day

then you create 36 tables. (See the aggregate matrix example below.)

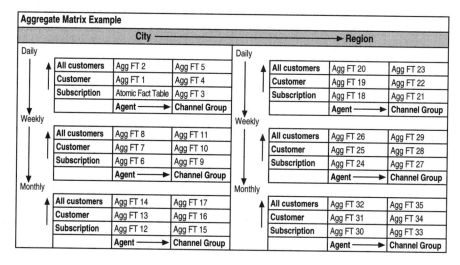

Figure 11.1   Data warehouse aggregate table sample.

If you partition the table by month and plan to store 24 months of history, the total number of tables grows to 864. Each table will have at least two indexes, for a total of 1728.

For this example, you can group tables, indexes, views and other objects this way:

- By partition (Jan99, Feb99, Mar99…)
- By subject area (Customer, Billing, Payment, CallDetail…)
- By filegroup (atomic data file group, aggregate data file group …)

This leads to a hierarchy of groups and objects, such as:

> year > monthly partitions > subject area> filegroups > tables & indexes

or

> subject area > monthly partitions > filegroups > tables & indexes

In SQL Server, a filegroup is defined as a named collection of one or more data files. All data and objects in the database (tables, indexes, stored procedures, triggers, and views) are stored within data files. Filegroups allow files to be grouped for administrative and data allocation purposes. For instance, table and index data can be associated with a specific filegroup, which means that all their pages will be allocated from the files in that filegroup. It also means that you can improve performance by allocating filegroups to different disk drives, and that you back up and restore individual files or filegroups instead of the entire database.

To complete this design you need to include other database management related objects (such as transaction logs and trace files) under their own groups.

Naming Convention

A standard naming convention is produced in the early design stage and followed through the entire data warehouse implementation and life span. It ensures that the names of objects created in or deleted from a data warehouse on a regular basis follow predictable patterns. With a pattern, you can create templates and reuse them to generate programs and objects.

Objects in the same group should share naming conventions, and a validation mechanism must be in place to detect and flag violations. A convention can stipulate, for instance, that all objects belonging to a particular partition group must share the same partition type in their names. Attributes that can be shared in objects' names include group, table type, partition type, and object type. An example is shown below.

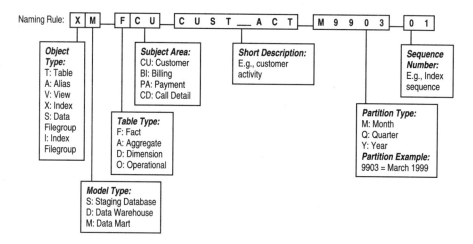

Figure 11.2   Naming convention example for database objects.

Metadata management tracks and controls modifications to naming conventions. Modifications are neither desired nor frequent but they are sure to occur over time, arising from something as simple as an expansion of the business model, or from something as complex as the merger of two companies and the integration of their systems. A good object management plan should allow you to alter database object-naming conventions to make room for new requirements.

You should publish naming conventions in multiple media (online, user manuals, etc.) and make them available to new DBAs, new application developers, and new employees. Revise the conventions periodically to keep them updated.

File Systems and Directory

Separate and properly sized file systems keep object management independent of other operating system and RDBMS resources. Back up and restore file systems separately so that the object management system can assist the RDBMS backup and recovery procedures.

The file system stores data definition language (DDL) statements, programming scripts, stored procedures, event log files, and other types of files. Directory levels in the file system should match the hierarchical and grouping design of database objects and offer extended description to the standard naming convention. It is also important to break the directory into two isolated areas: one for production versions of files and the other for development. This allows you to impose tighter security for production systems, but somewhat looser security for testing and development environments. Make it a regular maintenance procedure to find and remove irrelevant subdirectories and temporary files. Here is an example:

File directory layout sample.

Directory level	Directory layout
First	C:\data_warehouse
Second *(system areas)*	\production, \testing
Third *(database names)*	\database1, \database2, \database3, …
Fourth *(general file categories)*	\ddl, \log, \program, \dmp, …
Fifth *(partitions)*	\199901, \199902, \199903, …\
Sixth *(subject areas)*	\billing, \payment, \calldetail, \customer_activity
Seventh *(filegroups and database objects)*	\filegroups, \tables, \indexes, \views, \users, \stored_procedures, \triggers, …
Eighth (file types)	\sql_file, \script, \dump_files, \log_files, …

Object Creation

In a typical data warehouse, new objects are created and old objects are removed and archived. Archiving can be automated but it must be controlled efficiently. For instance, consider a sales tracking database keeping sales records for two years, with records partitioned by month. At the end of every month a new table is created to store that month's data, and the table with the oldest month of sales records is removed and archived to tape.

Space management is a major challenge of object creation, and this requires considering the number of database objects. Although the early design phase projects future growth, it is better to add storage space as it becomes necessary than to buy a lot of storage right off. Besides, storage technology often requires upgrades, and you can control these costs by holding off on large initial investments. For more details, see the "Space Management" section below.

Object Obsolescence

You can automate the removal and archiving of old database objects, but truncating and disposing of data impose some administrative burden: you have to save the objects' related files such as structured query language (SQL) script files and log files to inexpensive media, then delete the objects. Tie this process to the backup and recovery design and implementation. It is difficult to "undelete" data, but you have to support it to some degree.

Object Validation and Correction

In a database with many objects, it is difficult to detect some problems:

- Are any objects that should be in the database missing?
- Are any objects in the database that are not supposed to be there?

- Are there objects for which definitions have been changed by accident or by unauthorized users?
- What is the change history for database objects?

The object management infrastructure should support both automatic and ad hoc validation. You need to implement validation reporting and a correction plan (or scripts). Object validation tends to use few system resources, so frequent validation does not affect system performance, but validation for hundreds of objects may create a strain. For example, validating index column sequence for over a thousand indexes could slow down the RDBMS over the several hours it requires.

Object correction is another challenge. In the first few years of production, it is not rare for the data warehouse specification to be changed frequently. Staff changes can also introduce inconsistency in database objects. Correcting inconsistent, inaccurate, or invalid objects can be time consuming and difficult. For example, different indexing requirements for data loading, online analytical processing (OLAP) analysis, and data reorganization can require the validation of a large number of indexes (over a 1000 in the example above). You have to monitor their uniqueness, column sequence, and existence very closely and periodically validate them to deliver consistent performance to users. For another example, views become invalid when their scripts do not reflect changes to the names of tables they reference. This may not cause serious problems, but it creates maintenance overhead.

Space Management

Estimating disk space requirements is tricky in data warehousing projects. Original estimates often need to be adjusted once the physical design indicates more realistic space requirement and management needs. This section offers some considerations that can improve your accuracy.

Filegroup Sizing

SQL Server offers two types of filegroups:

- **Default filegroup.** This contains the primary data file and any other data files not allocated to any specific filegroup. The primary file contains all of the database system tables. A database can have only one primary file.
- **User-defined filegroups.** These can specify non-system tables and indexes. You can back up and restore individual filegroups and you can place them on separate disks.

The default filegroup must be large enough to hold all system tables and any tables not allocated to user-defined filegroups. System table size depends on the number of objects (they add rows whenever a new database object such as a table or index is added), on the number of users, and on other system information, but still is very small when compared to the warehouse. You should store large non-system data objects such as tables and indexes on separate (that is, user-defined) filegroups, and, as part of a sound recovery strategy, on separate disks as well.

The filegroup space requirements defined in the design phase are adjusted as pieces of the data warehouse are built. Column quantities and widths in warehouse tables hardly change, but changes in the number of rows can increase space requirements significantly. To estimate an accurate initial table size:

1. Calculate the total number of bytes in a row and then find the number of rows that fit in a data page. (In other words, 8060 bytes/page divided by the bytes/row.)

2. Divide the approximate number of rows in the table by the number of rows contained in each data page.

The result equals the number of pages that are needed to store the table. Filegroup size depends on the number of tables and indexes stored in it. To find the best way to allocate tables and indexes to filegroups, you have to understand the database structure, data source transactions, and hardware configuration.

Index Space Sizing

The indexing mechanism, which determines the index space requirements, also undergoes constant adjustments as the system is built and it is yet another challenge in a data warehouse project. During the design phase, find the answers to these questions:

- How many indexes are needed?
- How many columns are in each index?
- What is the column sequence?
- What are the OLAP indexing requirements?
- What are the data loading indexing requirements?

Indexing requirements can change after the system has been rolled out into production, which not only makes it harder to size index space but can lead to inconsistent indexes, which in turn add maintenance overhead. In a typical data warehouse implementation, indexes commonly consume more disk space than tables do. You need to understand how new indexes will affect performance so that you can balance space requirements against performance gains. To do this, use the SQL Server 7.0 Tuning Wizard to analyze representative samples of normal database activities (in SQL scripts) to determine an optimal indexing strategy. With the Tuning Wizard you can:

- Find the best mix of indexes for a given database workload, by using the query optimizer to analyze the workload's queries.

- Analyze the effects of proposed changes, including index usage, distribution of queries among tables, and query performance.

- Find ways to tune the database for a small set of problem queries.

- Customize the recommendation by specifying advanced options such as disk space constraints.

Bitmap Indexing

OLAP applications are query-intensive, usually querying a set of rows in a certain range of particular keys, unlike traditional online transaction processing (OLTP) applications, which usually query a specific row. A bitmap index is a stream of bits, each relating to a column value (columns with low cardinality are good candidates) in a single row of a table. Since data warehouses (unlike OLTP systems) usually store the static data and have lower insert, update, and delete activities, the overhead involved in updating a bitmap index is acceptable. Because bitmap indexes are highly compressed when they are built on low cardinality columns, they offer significant space saving as well as dramatic performance improvement, sometimes using only 1 percent of the space of the B-tree index (the tree structure for storing database indexes in which each node contains searchable ranges of key values that link to data records). A column's degree of cardinality is the number of its unique values compared to the total number of rows in the table. If it is less than 0.1 percent, it is an ideal candidate for a bitmap index.

SQL Server 7.0 does not yet support bitmap indexing, but it offers techniques to compress data files and to reorganize index pages so that they contain an equally distributed amount of data and free space. SQL Server 7.0 OLAP Services enhances performance by allowing you to store data in either relational or multi-dimensional format.

Full-Text Indexing

A full-text index, which keeps track of significant query words and where they are located, is commonly used with text search engines, which normally look for text data that matches a specific combination of words or phrases. This kind of search is very useful in OLAP systems since data warehouses keep text descriptions about entities such as products (brand, style, color, etc.) and customers (company names, sales reps, etc.). SQL Server 7.0 stores full-text indexes in the file system, but administers them through the database. Administration starts by building full-text catalogs and registering tables and columns within the catalog. You have to plan the placement of full-text indexes carefully for tables in full-text catalogs. If you are indexing a table that has millions of rows, assign it its own full-text catalog. Full-text index space requirements depend on the number of text fields to be indexed and their size.

Transaction Log Sizing

Think for a moment:

- How many times have you needed to move transaction log backups around to make room for new transaction log backups in a large data warehouse?
- How many times has the database stopped because the transaction log disk drive was full?

These situations cause serious productivity problems in the data warehouse, but they can be avoided if you size transaction log files correctly. Unfortunately, even though you can carefully estimate transaction log size in the design stage, tuning it in production requires some guessing. In a typical situation, the transaction log needs to be sized to hold an entire daily/weekly batch data loading process. (Note that transaction log files cannot be part of a filegroup.)

To avoid running out of space, SQL Server can increase disk space for the transaction log automatically, but transactions stop if the disk fills up. You need to set alerts that notify you when the transaction log size has reached a high percentage of available space. To keep the log at a reasonable size, you can back it up frequently with the **truncate_only** option, which clears the log by removing inactive (committed) transactions, but you cannot use a truncated transaction log for database recovery. For more details see the "Backup and Recovery Strategy" section, below.

Transaction log size mostly depends on backup frequency, database size, and transaction volume. In a data warehouse system, the loading process generates an extensive amount of log activity. Rule of thumb: size the amount of data in daily/weekly batch data loading and allocate a slightly larger space for the transaction log. You must also allocate disk space for the transaction log backup. SQL Server's **select into/bulkcopy** option allows a database to accept non-logged operations. Although certain changes are always logged, this option helps conserve log space during bulk load operations because non-logged operations speed up performance by not writing details on the modified data to the log. As with **truncate_only**, you can't perform data recovery if you use this option because the log does not completely list the data that would have to be added. You can recover data only from a full or incremental database backup.

You can monitor transaction log activity with SQL Server Enterprise Manager or Windows NT Performance Monitor.

Loading File Sizing

Data warehouse systems contain batch-collected data (typically an ASCII format flat file) that is transferred from OLTP systems. It is normally held in a staging area until it can be loaded and should not be removed from there until it has been successfully loaded. You can estimate the amount of this data (daily, weekly, or monthly) but to estimate how much extra room you need in the staging area before loading it you have to take several situations into account. You will need extra storage if the warehouse system suffers from hardware or operating system problems, if the RDBMS has stopped, or if the backup system is not working. For example, a 1-TB data warehouse at a telecommunications company has allocated more than 100 GB of staging area space.

Spare Space

You can require tens of GBs of spare space for **tempdb** when you have several multi-GB atomic data tables, and even more if you want to keep spare data files to serve urgent data file additions.

Space Allocation and Space Recycling

Put atomic data (table/index) and any table/index with several hundred MB of data in their own filegroups. When large entities are in independent filegroups, it is easier to make tables, create indexes, drop, monitor, reorganize, back up, and recover. Aggregation tables/indexes of one particular week or month can share one filegroup, because they are usually smaller and can always be re-created.

Backup and Recovery

Data warehouse backup and recovery require totally different approaches than are applied to smaller databases. To help you create a strategy, this section starts with goals, and then covers major techniques for achieving them. Generally, you want to balance database availability, performance, and recoverability.

Backup and Recovery Goals

- **Design for resiliency.** A major goal is to keep the database running in spite of some hardware failures. If the database does not go down, it does not have to be recovered.

- **Back up with minimal impact to database availability and performance.** Another goal is to back up when there is minimal interference from database processing operations and to avoid taking the database off-line whenever possible.

- **Detect potential problems early.** A backup strategy should incorporate an automated monitoring mechanism to detect potential problems as early as possible. It should monitor backup problems as well as recovery opportunities to ensure speedy recovery and minimize database downtime. Use the SQL Server Transact-SQL RESTOREVERIFYONLY command to make sure a backup set is complete and that all volumes are readable, and use SQL Server Profiler to monitor events such as errors, opened cursors, Transact-SQL statements, database connections, and stored procedures.

- **Recover all data under any circumstances.** Design backups to cover all recovery scenarios: user errors, loss of data in memory, loss of data files, loss of transaction log, loss of the whole database, and disaster. Outline, document, and test all recovery scenarios.

- **Recover quickly and effectively.** When you have to recover, bring the database on-line as quickly as possible, using tested procedures and incorporating the most efficient methods.

Backup and Recovery Strategy

Prevent a Single Point of Failure

A single point of failure means that a single component failure can result in total system failure. In terms of backup and recovery strategy, it means you cannot recover from a failed component if you have only one backup and it is unusable. To prevent a single point of failure you need some sort of storage redundancy.

Guard against single points of failure in the database and in the backups. Reinforcing critical objects in the database (through operating system mirroring or multiplexing) reduces the probability that the database will go down in the first place. Taking multiple backup copies of the database and the transaction log insures that you can recover from any media failure, even if one of the backup copies is unreadable.

Triple mirroring involves setting up enough disks so that each can be mirrored three times. This provides better redundancy and allows you to keep a backup copy resident on disk. It is fairly common and highly desirable for mission-critical databases, but in a data warehouse environment there is too much data to triple-mirror all database files, so it is used only for critical data files.

Design the Database for Enhanced Recoverability

Because it takes longer to back up and recover large objects, you should consider partitioning large *logical* tables into smaller, more manageable *physical* tables. This allows you to back up and recover individual objects more quickly, and to load, update, and perform maintenance on partitioned tables in parallel. A partitioning scheme usually is determined during the physical database design phase.

Also during design, you should consider isolating volatile objects (objects that are updated frequently) based on processing requirements. The fewer objects in read-write mode at any one time, the faster the back up and recovery.

Design Applications for Enhanced Recoverability

Application design, specifically for batch update and load processing, determines recovery speed after a database crash. As transactions get larger, they decrease database operation speed and increase database recovery time. To ensure quick recovery, design all non-utility batch update jobs with frequent commits and for checkpoint restartability. This shortens recovery time, because checkpoint restart logic allows the application to pick up where it left off rather than from the beginning.

In some situations (short updates performed on temporary tables, etc.) it is better to update tables quickly without any commits; in others (non-logged operations performed in data loading, etc.) it is better to refresh a whole table with no logging rather than performing frequent commits. You can identify these cases during the table load/update design phase.

Develop a Physical Backup Method

There are three types of physical backup: full database, differential, and transaction log. In SQL Server, you can perform any of these while users continue to work with the database, although some activities such as creating a database or index are restricted, and non-logged operations conflict with the backup process.

Full database backup

- Backs up original files and records their locations.
- Captures database activities that occur during the backup process.

The backup contains:

- Schema and file structure.
- Data.
- A portion of the transaction log that contains all database activities since the start of the backup process. SQL Server uses this to ensure data consistency when the backup is restored.

Full database backups are practical for small databases. In VLDB environments, it is better to use individual file or filegroup backups. Common examples are table partitions by month, in which a new filegroup is created when a new month's transactions are loaded. You can create indexes in the same filegroup, then back up the filegroup. Backing up a new table partition and indexes together facilitates recovery because to recreate an index SQL Server requires all base table and index files to be in the same condition they were in when the index was first created.

Differential backup

- Backs up the parts of the database that have changed since the last full database backup.
- Captures database activities that occur during the backup process.

This is smaller and takes less time to complete than a full database backup. If you take frequent differential backups, you stand to lose less data than if you take less-frequent full backups. Differential backups allow you to restore a database only to the time that the differential database backup was created, not to the exact point of failure (this requires transaction log backups). A common plan is to create several transaction log backups after each differential database backup to supplement it.

Transaction log backup

- Backs up the transaction log from the last successfully executed BACKUP LOG statement to the end of the current transaction log.
- Truncates the transaction log up to the beginning of its active portion (from the point of the oldest open transaction to the end of the log) and discards the inactive portion.

You have to perform a database backup before recovering a database with a transaction log backup.

Combinations of differential and transaction log backups are ideal for frequently updated databases. In a data warehouse system, most tables are updated only during the daily/weekly batch load process, so it is efficient to perform individual file or filegroup backups after the loading process. If some files need to be modified after the loading process, use frequent transaction log backups; otherwise, make the filegroups read-only to prevent updates and speed recovery.

Exploit the Read-Only File/Filegroup Feature

You can reduce backup and recovery times and save backup resources by keeping as many tables in read-only mode for as long as possible, although this complicates the processing environment.

The benefits of read-only tables are:

- You need to take data file/filegroup backups only once—you don't need additional backups. This significantly reduces resource consumption because most data warehouse fact tables rarely need changes once they are loaded. If you leave data files (or filegroups) in read-write mode, they need to be backed up.
- Recovery savings are also significant with read-only filegroups because you don't have to apply any transaction logs to read-only tables: read-only filegroups can be restored from backups, they do not need to be rolled forward.

To implement the read-only feature effectively you should work closely with the application team to integrate the load/update processing tightly with the data file/filegroup status switching mechanisms. The ideal sequence of events, called *just-in-time* status switching, is:

1. The data file/filegroup is normally in read-only mode
2. When it is ready to get updated or loaded, it is switched to read-write
3. The load or update takes place
4. Immediately after the update/load processing completes, it is switched back to read-only
5. The data file/filegroup is then backed up
6. The cycle repeats

This technique is highly efficient for both backup and recovery, because the affected objects are backed up at just the right time so that the backup contains all the database changes required for up-to-the-minute recovery. Properly designed, this should work most of the time for most data warehouse tables.

The best scenario is to back up a data file/filegroup after the load/update has completed and after it has been turned to read-only mode. If you can't switch the status after several attempts, take a backup of the data file/filegroup in read-write mode for insurance, then keep trying until you get a read-only backup or until the next update cycle begins.

With SQL Server you can put data warehouse tables that must not be modified in a filegroup, then use the ALTER DATABASE command to mark it read-only. You can then back up and restore the filegroup without recovering transaction logs.

ALTER DATABASE command syntax:

```
ALTER DATABASE database
{ MODIFY FILEGROUP filegroup_name filegroup_property}
```

Values for *filegroup_property*.

Value	Description
READONLY	Specifies that the filegroup is read-only. Updates to its objects are not allowed. Only users who have exclusive access to the database can mark a filegroup read-only. You cannot make the primary filegroup read-only.
READWRITE	Reverses the READONLY property, enabling updates. Only users who have exclusive access to the database can mark a filegroup read-write.
DEFAULT	Specifies that the filegroup is the default filegroup for the database. A database can have only one default filegroup. When you make a filegroup the default, the default property is removed from any other filegroup that was the default. CREATE DATABASE makes the primary filegroup the initial default filegroup. New tables and indexes are created in the default filegroup if no filegroup is specified in the CREATE TABLE, ALTER TABLE, or CREATE INDEX statements.

Design Data Files for Quick Recovery

In a backup and recovery scheme, data files can be classified as **switchable** or **non-switchable**. A switchable data file can be turned to read-only and often follows a fixed processing schedule known as cycle processing (for example: daily update, monthly loads).

Data files can be marked switchable if they are updated and loaded only for a small percentage of time in their cycle; for instance, between 9 – 11 PM in a 24-hour cycle, or the first few days of the month in a monthly cycle. These files are backed up on demand, after their cycle updates are complete and following the *just-in-time* procedure described above.

A non-switchable data file always stays in read-write mode because it is updated randomly and unpredictably. These files are backed up on a fixed schedule (daily, etc.), during off-peak hours to minimize resource contention. Back them up frequently: the more recent the backup, the faster the recovery.

Optimize Checkpoint Processing

Checkpoints provide a consistent version of the database at regular intervals and help minimize recovery time after a failure. They play a significant role in a backup and recovery strategy. If you monitor the database checkpoints and assess database performance, you can more accurately estimate how long it will take to get the RDBMS back after a database crash.

To augment the automatic checkpoint, perform manual checkpoints at key events:

- At the completion of a cycle processing (monthly loads, daily updates, etc.). This ensures that all database changes are externalized onto the data files and that you will have to apply only a minimum of logs during recovery.

- Before any database shutdown. This accelerates the shutdown process and minimizes start-up problems. This extra step can help you bring down the database quickly and consistently.

At a checkpoint, SQL Server ensures that all transaction log records and modified database pages are written to disk. When SQL Server is restarted, the recovery process for each database rolls forward a transaction only when it is not known whether all the data modifications in the transaction were actually written from the SQL Server buffer cache to disk. A checkpoint forces all modified pages to disk, so it represents the point at which the startup recovery must start rolling forward transactions.

When using transaction log backups, do not set the **trunc. log on chkpt.** database option to TRUE. At each checkpoint, this truncates the transaction log and does not back up the truncated part.

Customize Backup and Recovery Scripts

To integrate the database management system seamlessly with the media management tool, you often have to develop extensive customized scripts. If you design scripts so that they can hook up easily with other tools, you maximize automation of processes that:

- Invoke and monitor backups for all data files as required
- Interface with load/update processes
- Monitor and manage the transaction log backup
- Monitor database events
- Invoke checkpoints at key events
- Invoke backups for system tables
- Generate reports on backups
- Generate reports for recovery analysis

A good backup utility tool for VLDB systems should provide:

- Efficient handling of the read-only feature
- Automated handling of status switching
- Automated support for multiple backup copies of transaction log backups
- Recovery analysis

Automate Monitoring

Implement automated monitoring of database problems such as:

- Checkpoint problems
- Transaction log problems
- Data corruption

You need to detect existing and potential problems as early as possible. When your backup strategy depends heavily on the read-only feature, you should develop an automated monitoring procedure to ensure that all read-only data files/filegroups are backed up after they are turned to read-only. (For more details, see the "Read-Only File/Filegroup" section, above.) You should also monitor the latest backup copy of all data files to make sure you have the most recent backup copy: the more recent the copy, the faster the media recovery.

Use the Windows NT Performance Monitor and the SQL Server Profiler to monitor database events, backups, error logs, transaction logs, and system performance variables, to create monitoring alerts, and to perform trend analysis. You can also create applications that use SQL Server Profiler extended stored procedures to monitor SQL Server database systems.

Develop Test Database and Recovery Scenarios

To ensure the quickest possible recovery, support DBAs need to know how to handle various recovery scenarios. You should develop scenarios that test these areas:

Backup

- System files
- Read-only data file/filegroups
- Read-write data file/filegroups
- Transaction logs

Recovery

- From loss of system files
- From loss of transaction log
- From loss of transaction log backup copy
- From read-only data file/filegroup
- From read-write data file/filegroup
- From loss of the whole database
- Point-in-time

Plan for Disaster Recovery

Although disaster recovery requirements vary, keeping multiple backup copies is usually a good idea. At predetermined intervals (weekly, for instance) create a tape copy of all database backups and appropriate transaction logs and store it offsite. In a worst case, you can use this copy to rebuild the database within a few days.

Summary of Backup and Recovery Tips

- Prevent a single point of failure in the online files as well as the backups through
  - Hardware mirroring
  - System files
  - Transaction logs
  - Data files/filegroups
- Develop file and filegroup physical backups for recovery
- Partition the VLDB to facilitate backup and recovery tasks
- Minimize backup and speed up recovery with the read-only feature
- Back up index filegroups: it is faster to recover than to rebuild
- Use checkpoints at key events to minimize startup/shutdown problems
- Gather information for recovery analysis

- Keep data file/filegroup read-only as long as possible
- Monitor SQL Server regularly for existing or potential problems
- Integrate all tools and automate procedures
- Develop a test database and test scenarios
- Provide for disaster recovery with multiple backups and offsite storage

Metadata Management Infrastructure

In a data warehouse context, metadata (data about data) represents all the information needed and all the rules applied to run operations. It is a catalog of each component's contents and functions.

Metadata Types

Back-office operations have a different set of metadata than front-office operations. Every tool has its own catalog to control operations within its execution domain. Most data warehouses have three types of metadata:

- Semantic
- Technical
- Operational

Semantic

Semantic (business) metadata describes business processes. A byproduct of the warehouse design phase, it specifies:

- System description
- Application design

System description metadata identifies source and target systems. Source system information comes from the analysis of operational source systems, data dictionaries, and associated applications; target system information comes from data dictionaries and case tools. Metadata in this subject area includes data models, table names, indexes, and size and mapping information between source and target systems.

The **application design** is derived through analysis of data source systems, business user requirements, business rules, and company policies (security, etc.). The metadata for the design comprises business dimensions, hierarchies, business measures, security policies, and other elements. OLAP tools and middle-tier software use this information to deliver data to business users in the right format and under the right business semantics, shielding them from the complexity of SQL or programming languages. Here is a list of elements for each subject in the semantic metadata.

Semantic or business metadata.

Application design	System description
Object definitions (dimensions, entities, relationships)	Data source analysis
Dimensional hierarchies	Mapping between source and target systems
Business measure formulas	Table names, size, indexes and aggregation level
User roles and permissions	Entity domain values
Data access security rules	Data granularity
Subject areas	Amount of history
Naming conventions	Data owner
	Data location
	Data currency

Technical

Technical metadata describes jobs, execution programs, and extraction, transformation, loading (ETL) rules for data processing. Jobs and programs are built during the warehouse project development phase. The derived technical metadata includes job names, tasks, programs, parameters, input files, version control, aggregation paths, and attribution rules.

There are two types of execution programs:

- Programs already created without metadata design
- Programs that are metadata driven (use a metadata engine to generate programming code)

For both types, you can use a reverse-engineering product that scans program modules and captures their logic to recreate the metadata contents of executable objects. For programs already created, this process captures all program names, locations, execution parameters, descriptions, and the accessed objects during execution. For metadata-driven programs it creates these elements *and* the source code for generated modules.

In a data warehouse environment, batch jobs perform data extraction and loading during the quiet operation period—normally at night, when users have logged off. Two types of jobs run in this batch execution window:

- External jobs. These run outside the database and perform extraction, transport, and transformation (ETT) processing.
- Internal jobs. These run within the database and perform aggregation, database object manipulation, and backup routines.

Jobs are triggered at a specific time by the system scheduler or by events (for instance, in a sequence of job dependencies). Trigger procedure information is technical metadata. In general, technical metadata elements address job execution or transport/transformation. Here are some of the elements in these subjects.

Technical metadata.

Job execution	Transport and transformation
Job name and description (tasks and programs)	Transformation rules
Job type (source, extract, load)	Source-to-target data movement process
Estimated execution time	Aggregation paths
Program name, parameters, and code	Table attribution rules
Program version, author, and owner	Data quality procedures
Input file names	
Triggers and alerts	

Operational

Operational metadata describes system performance. When the project implementation phase brings the data warehouse into production, data processing becomes another IS routine task and the warehouse (like any other production system) generates statistics that administrators can use to track performance and identify bottlenecks. Operational metadata captures these statistics, which are mostly generated in back-office operations such as source data compilation, extraction, and loading. Other statistics come from front-office operations such as query request processing and data delivery, and are gathered by OLAP servers, operating systems, and other middle-tier software.

Operational metadata concerns:

- Operation management. Information about job execution and other management procedures.

- Scheduling and automation. An operation schedule that describes job sequences, dependencies, and timing of operations stored in the system scheduler.

Combined, these areas provide a performance dashboard that allows you to monitor the system, identify bottlenecks, and react promptly in case of trouble. Here are the subjects and elements of the operational metadata.

Operational metadata.

Operation management	Scheduling and automation
Date and time of job start and end	Job scheduling
Number of rows processed	Job dependencies
Number of rows rejected	Operation sequence
Job completion status	Data transport process
Error reporting and notification	Operation cycles
Statistics on database usage	Space management automation
Statistics on OS resource usage	Change management versioning
Statistics on OLAP server activity	Data retention and archiving
	Backup and recovery schedule

In large database environments, the number of jobs, tasks, and programs make automation an unavoidable choice for operation management. Common automated tasks are data movement, loading, space management, backup, recovery, archiving, and table/view creation.

Metadata Sources

During the warehouse design and development phases, most of the semantic and technical metadata is generated or entered manually by data modelers, architects, and programmers. Over time, more system components can be automated, and new vendor tools may become available to help generate and store different kinds of metadata elements. Common metadata sources include:

- COBOL copy books/JCL
- Scripts and DDL statements
- RDBMS data dictionary
- Event logs
- Manually created metadata
- ETL tools
- OLAP tools
- CASE tools

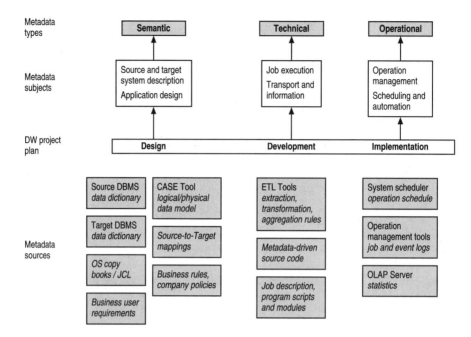

Figure 11.3 Metadata overview.

A SQL Server 7.0 data warehouse has a set of system databases containing semantic metadata (such as table names, index names, file locations, and database user permissions) and operational metadata (such as job schedules and alerts). These represent a SQL Server catalog of database objects and configuration settings used by administrative tools such as SQL Server Enterprise Manager. Programmers can manage objects in the catalog using the SQL Data Management Object (DMO) API. This can be used in combination with other SQL Server services to deliver a complete solution for metadata-driven, warehouse administration (discussed later in this chapter).

SQL Server systems have four system databases:

- **master.** This records all system level information: login accounts, system configuration settings, the existence of all other databases, and the location of the primary files that contain the initialization information for user databases.

- **model.** The template for all databases created on the system. When a CREATE DATABASE statement is issued the model is copied in as the first part of the new database (the rest is filled with empty pages).

- **msdb.** SQL Server Agent uses this to schedule alerts and jobs, and to record operators.

- **tempdb.** This has no metadata, but it holds all temporary tables and temporary stored procedures. It provides the temporary storage needed, for example, when SQL Server generates work tables.

Metadata Integration

Metadata is essential for data warehouse administration, but often it is contained in proprietary structures. Without a standard mechanism for metadata interchange, elements are duplicated across several vendors' metadata repositories, synchronization becomes a problem, and operation control is hampered. Metadata integration and synchronization across environments has become a major hurdle in data warehouse technology, and industry leaders in The Meta Data Coalition (MDC—http://www.MDCinfo.com) are driving a common metadata interchange specification.

Think of semantic, technical, and operational metadata as conceptual layers with elements physically stored in different locations. One way to integrate them is to use middle-tier management software to connect distributed metadata stores to a common repository accessible to administrators through the central administration console.

A repository offers:

- Single point of access to all metadata layers: semantic (business), technical, and operational

- Centralized control of user profiles

- Synchronization of changes

- Version control

- Environment transparency

Access to all metadata layers enables centralized warehouse administration. Centralized control of user roles, views, and privileges, enables interface independence—the system can be deployed to different GUIs ranging from browser clients to executive information systems (EISs) and desktop applications. Users can upgrade systems or switch GUIs without affecting their user profile. This strengthens security control.

An integrated metadata framework facilitates synchronization and change propagation. Synchronization ensures data consistency across metadata sources that share elements. For instance, table names can be redundantly stored in CASE tools, data dictionaries, and OLAP servers. Metadata is dynamic, and a repository provides better version control when new business requirements, new platforms, and changes of data sources or business rules affect the contents in one or more metadata layers. Repository management software tracks changes and controls new object versions after they occur.

Finally, environment transparency allows tools and applications to share metadata. In distributed heterogeneous environments, object-oriented technology can help create a transparent development environment. A common repository with *distributed object-oriented technology* offers:

- **Cross platform operation.** Metadata in different tools may be scattered over several operating system platforms, so it's critical to simplify access to it wherever it is.

- **Scalability.** Distributed-computing allows software architects to configure the system in a high-scalability model.

- **Object services.** A common object-oriented repository enables object retrieval, addition, and manipulation. These services support external applications and simplify their logic.

- **Language independence.** Integrating metadata usually involves different platforms, operating systems, engineers, or projects. Object-oriented technology isolates developers from these variables, giving them more flexibility in programming languages.

- **Distributed environment transparency.** Integrating sources provides useful business intelligence to users and insulates them from the heterogeneity of distributed computing.

- **Standards compliance provides modularity and reusability.** Distributed object technology provides binary object interoperability, which increases the degree of modularity possible in software engineering and allows more extensible solutions. Reusability reduces development and implementation time.

Microsoft Repository, which is an object-oriented repository sitting on top of a SQL Server database, can help achieve these goals. Object models in the repository are called open information models (OIMs) and provide interfaces based on component object model (COM) architecture. The repository supports multiple standards such as Unified Modeling Language (UML) and Extensible Markup Language (XML).

MetaEdge, a Microsoft Certified Solution Provider (MSCP), developed a data warehouse management solution using Microsoft Repository. It is described below. Figure 11.4 shows the solution's integrated metadata layers.

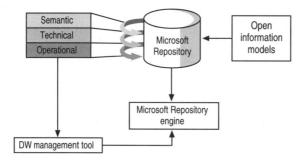

Figure 11.4   Integrated metadata layers.

Metadata Technical Architecture

When you consider a metadata technical architecture, you can take either of two approaches. The first uses a central repository to store all relevant warehouse metadata, eliminating cross-platform obstacles and speeding up search and retrieval. Synchronization is the big challenge in this approach: data warehouse environments evolve constantly, so changes are frequent, and all metadata changes have to be propagated to the repository.

The second approach also uses a central repository, but it does not store *all* metadata. Instead it stores *non-distributed* metadata, which is generated manually or imported from unstructured data sources such as spreadsheets and text, and *connections to distributed* metadata, which is found in proprietary structures from vendor tools and can reside on any remote system. In this approach, changes to distributed metadata are not propagated to the central store, because elements are retrieved dynamically over the connection. When you request a metadata element, middle-tier management software locates its source and retrieves the element, usually with a software tool API for communicating with other tools and external applications. This approach reduces synchronization efforts and improves data consistency. Environment transparency is the big challenge in this approach.

Both approaches require these components (Figure 11.5):

- Administration console
- Management software for integration
- Metadata common repository (or central store)
- Metadata model

The metadata model is inherent in the common repository. It can be an object model or a relational database model. In a distributed metadata architecture, a pure relational central store does not provide the flexibility needed for environment transparency because external applications need to parse the relational structure to request or update metadata elements. For instance, if an application has to access a set of records it needs to know table names, column names, data types, and other information; if it connects to multiple sources, it needs to know the location of each source. If multiple applications are accessing multiple sources in an enterprise system, an abstraction layer is essential to provide transparent access to any set of records located anywhere in the system.

This is where object-oriented technology comes in. With it, you can build an object metadata model on top of a relational metadata store: applications can communicate with the common repository without regard to its internal relational design, management software can use the model to manipulate metadata elements and coordinate data exchange with metadata sources, and decision-support applications or presentation layers can request elements transparently. In short, an object metadata model can provide environment transparency in a distributed metadata architecture.

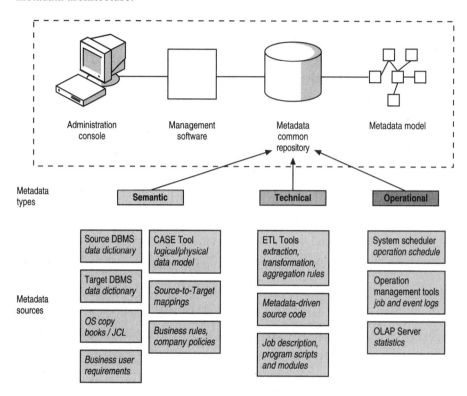

Figure 11.5   Schematic of metadata technical architecture.

An object metadata model also provides resiliency to deal with dynamic relationships and complex interactions among metadata "objects." In an object-oriented framework, objects carry methods and properties that facilitate their use. In fact, the object metadata model can support higher-level abstraction layers, which further enable conceptualization of new objects or groups of objects with new methods and properties. For instance, two objects such as dimension members *customer* and *account* are grouped together with a third object, *customer-account relationship*, to form a higher-level object called *customer hierarchy*. One new method of the *customer hierarchy* object is "drill down" from customer level to account. Figure 11.6 shows some metadata sample objects and Figure 11.7 shows an object view of metadata.

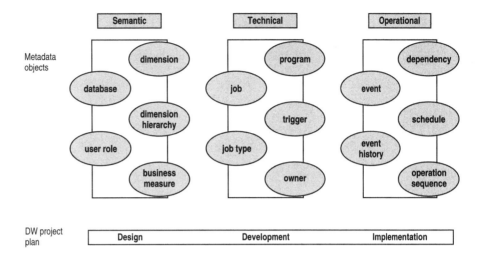

Figure 11.6   Sample metadata repository objects.

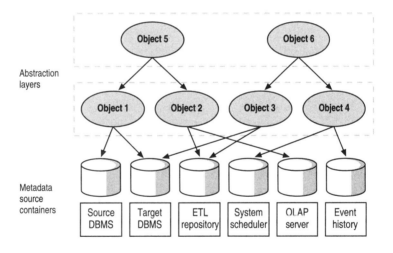

Figure 11.7   Object view of metadata.

Knowledge Engineering

From the object view presented in Figure 11.7, you can extend the set of metadata source containers to include virtually any enterprise information source. Data is found in relational, multi-dimensional, or proprietary structured repositories such as metadata repositories, data warehouses, and datamarts. These represent only a small fraction of corporate knowledge compared to the amount of unstructured data found in text files, spreadsheets, e-mail servers, and corporate Web pages. Fortunately, with the emergence of standards such as XML, unstructured data actually becomes easier to search and retrieve because of the standard metadata content added to it. XML makes metadata a key for sharing information.

Object models on top of metadata repositories foster data distribution across the information technology (IT) infrastructure by shielding applications and users from underlying storage structures. This increases the production and use of knowledge.

Figure 11.8 summarizes the main goals of the metadata technical architecture, and its role as foundation for knowledge engineering (KE). In general, KE relies on a four-step cycle:

1. Search by browsing a catalog of available data
2. Identify data sources by metadata access to the data warehouse design
3. Find context by metadata access to the business rules
4. Deliver information to the user

The cycle starts and finishes when a user triggers a decision-making process that involves search and execution of one or more queries. During execution, metadata helps determine the currency and location of the requested data. Then the retrieved data set is presented within a business context defined by dimensions, hierarchies, and business measures.

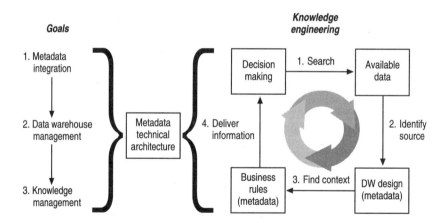

Figure 11.8   Metadata technical architecture as foundation for knowledge engineering.

Figure 11.9 shows a technical view of a KE architecture that encompasses a COM/DCOM (distributed COM) object layer surrounding a set of core modules that provide metadata access as well as features such as security control and information delivery. This shows how corporations can build a knowledge management infrastructure based on object models, metadata management, and presentation of data with multiple views.

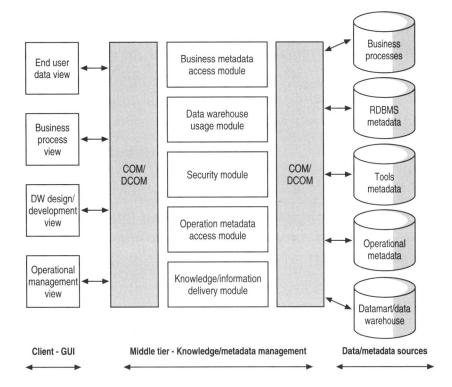

Figure 11.9 **Knowledge engineering architecture.**

Metadata-Driven Warehouse Administration

This section describes how to implement a warehouse administration system with the metadata architecture components just described. It proposes a data warehouse technical architecture with one layer targeted to data processing and another to warehouse management. Then it describes how to use open information models (OIMs) to build a metadata repository. It gives an example of how to build one of these models, including design and programming code, then describes how DTS Designer and OLAP Services capture metadata. It then provides some sample code that reads metadata to retrieve a database object, and concludes by addressing some technical requirements not supported by the common repository but needed for an enhanced design.

A data warehouse technical architecture gives developers an overview of the major components needed for data storage and processing. It represents a logical view and does not necessarily match all physical components such as servers or network connections. The technical architecture proposed below includes data processing and other components that facilitate overall system administration. It uses the latest technology offered by SQL Server 7.0 and the metadata management tool from MetaEdge. One of its key benefits is a symbiotic environment from back-office operations to front-office data delivery that speeds up the implementation process by reducing the system integration effort but that is flexible enough to accommodate other vendors' solutions by providing an open metadata interface. You need to determine which components will best fit your needs and existing resources.

The proposed architecture includes these software components:

- SQL Server 7.0
- SQL Server Data Transformation Services
- SQL Server Agent Services
- Microsoft Repository
- Management tool from MetaEdge
- Universal Management Console

SQL Server is the RDBMS engine. It hosts the data warehouse and the metadata common repository, and offers services to perform multiple administrative tasks: Data Transformation Services (DTS) for back-office tasks such as data extraction, transformation and loading, and Agent Services (AS) for alert management, notification, job execution, and replication management.

Another essential component, Microsoft Repository, acts as a universal database store. It is wrapped with an object-oriented layer that allows it to store: executables and source code for software development, database descriptions and interface definitions from applications and tools, and different kinds of objects or components. In a data warehouse context, it is also a common metadata repository. It stores semantic, technical, and operational metadata within object models (called OIMs) that physically represent relational database schemas. Each offers a set of interfaces that encapsulate methods and properties to describe different objects. Applications can request and manipulate objects through these interfaces without regard for the underlying database schema. Microsoft's COM architecture provides the object layer's foundation, adding a standard interface for communications across heterogeneous environments.

Another component is MetaEdge's metadata management tool, which interacts with the Microsoft Repository engine and SQL Server services to support operations such as data movement, loading, and delivery. It does this by implementing a set of open information models geared toward warehouse management. The table below shows the main tasks performed and the SQL Server services they involve.

Management tasks.

Task group	Services	Tasks
Physical database administration	SQL Server Distributed Management Objects	Table partition maintenance, data summarization control, table index and table view maintenance, RAID configuration, space management, and database object administration
Operation management	SQL Server Agent and Data Transformation Services	Initial/incremental load processing, system scheduler and event management, performance monitor, backup, recovery, and archiving
Data delivery	SQL Server OLAP Services and Decision Service Objects	OLAP cube creation, information delivery mechanism, administration of OLAP objects such as dimensions, hierarchies, etc.

The administration tool is the Universal Management Console. It contains a set of snap-ins from Microsoft Management Console (MMC)—a shared user interface for Microsoft BackOffice server management. The shared console provides a convenient and consistent environment for administration tools: SQL Server Enterprise Manager, OLAP Manager, and the metadata management tool. It provides a single point of access for general system administration.

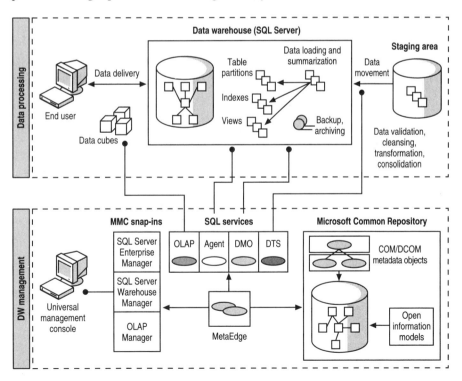

Figure 11.10   Technical architecture for metadata-driven warehouse administration.

Figure 11.10 shows a concise overview of each component in the data warehouse architecture. The upper layer presents the data processing pieces and the lower one presents the management elements. Both layers continue to be built up throughout the data warehouse lifecycle and you have to understand how they interact so that you can see how to integrate the system with its pivotal components—information models and the common repository. Understanding this requires a closer look at the architectural design.

This architecture can satisfy common decision support needs and can be integrated with multiple data sources. It describes a star-schema data warehouse served by a relational staging database where data cleansing and transformation take place, along with meaningless key generation and the consolidation of conformed dimensions. The data warehouse itself can contain different subject areas, and these can be physically stored in a distributed fashion. In this case, each subject area is a dependent datamart connected to a bus architecture that enables an enterprise warehouse system. Such advanced design is built incrementally with the metadata management infrastructure under the data processing layer. For simplicity, this example assumes that the architecture involves only one subject area (*marketing*) and the small data cubes delivered to users would represent marketing reports.

This provides enough background detail to move on to the construction process of both the data warehouse and the metadata repository. Figure 11.11 highlights the interaction between the metadata common repository and the milestones during warehouse construction. Information models play a key role in this interaction, and they must be designed before warehouse construction can begin so that metadata can be captured from the beginning. The figure shows the evolution of a warehouse system through the project phases. At the bottom of the figure, you can see the building process for the metadata common repository: information models are designed and built for selected steps in the warehouse construction layer. These design steps provide the basic metadata for warehouse management. They are common to any data warehouse solution, so information models can be defined in advance. Microsoft Repository offers a set of pre-built information models, described in the table below.

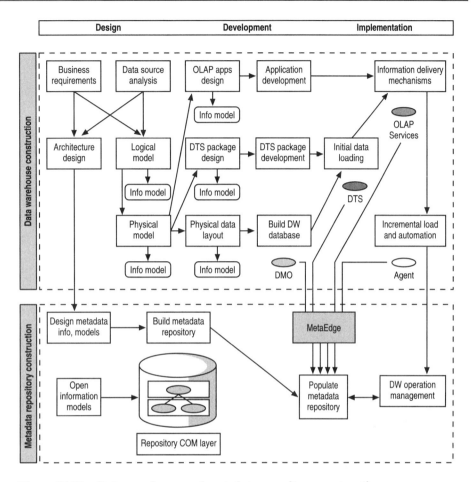

Figure 11.11   Data warehouse and metadata repository construction.

Microsoft Open Information models.

Open Information Model	Description
UML	Unified Modeling Language. The most abstract model, this helps to analyze, design and visualize software artifacts.
UMX	UML extensions.
CDE	Component descriptions. Used for COM architecture development.

(continued)

Open Information Model	Description
COM	Component Object model. Also used for COM development.
DBM	Database model. Used to describe and store database schemas at the level of SQL standard.
DTM	Datatype model. For defining datatypes.
GEN	Generic. Subject-area independent model.
SQL	Microsoft SQL Server. Database model specialized for SQL Server.
OCL	Oracle. Database model specialized for Oracle.
OLP	OLAP model. Used for OLAP application design.
DTS	Data Transformation Services model. Used for DTS package design.

Of interest here are the models in bold (**SQL**, **OLP**, and **DTS**), which store different pieces of metadata. The SQL model stores logical and physical data models (descriptions of tables, columns, keys, and other database objects). The OLP model stores the OLAP application design (dimensions, dimension elements, hierarchies, facts, and other information used by the data delivery mechanism and OLAP Services). The DTS model stores information about packages that contain job tasks, dependencies and scheduling information. These models can be defined in advance, before being populated, much the same way as the warehouse database is built before being loaded, and you can map metadata across these models. For instance, suppose a fact table contains columns for a set of dimensions and a set of facts, that the dimension columns map to particular levels in dimension hierarchies, and that the table is loaded by a specific job with scheduled frequency. (See Figure 11.12 for a similar dimensional matrix.) Using the Universal Management Console, you can define these mappings or higher-level metadata.

Figure 11.11 shows that the information model needed to store the database physical layout must cover filegroup names, locations, and transaction logs, and could also include RAID system configuration and I/O device configuration. Figures 11.13a and 13b present the two pieces of the information model design: the first shows database objects, the second shows storage objects (covering the database's physical layout).

Hierarchy level			
E		Year	
D		Quarter	
C		Month	
B		Date	
A		Timestamp	

Atomic level of data stored			Company Wide	All Products	Vendor
			Region Key	Category Key	Brand
			Location Key	Product Key	Product Key
Dimension change			A-B	A-B	
Keeping change history?	N	N	Y	Y	N

Figure 11.12   Sample multidimensional model and associated job matrix.

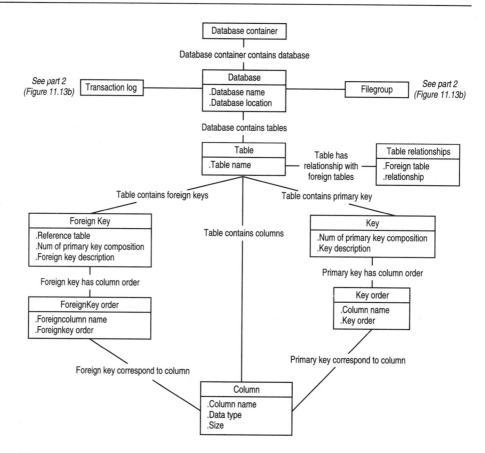

Figure 11.13a   Database information model (part 1).

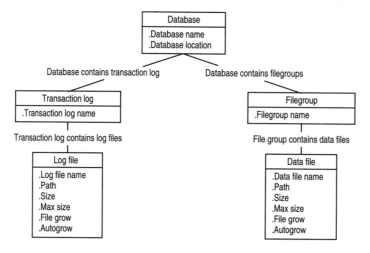

Figure 11.13b   Database information model (part 2).

The following example code defines part of the open information model for physical layout storage (referred to as "CCDW storage TIM" in the code). To create the information model, the code uses Type Information Model objects such as classes, interfaces, methods, and properties. Microsoft Repository uses the same structure to store information models. For more information see the *Microsoft Repository Programming Guide.*

```
Public Const IDatabaseContainer_IFACEID = "{53f618be-c2b1-11d2-b311-0060089cfbc8}"
Public Const Database_CLSID = "{53f618bf-c2b1-11d2-b311-0060089cfbc8}"
.................
'----------------------------

Sub Main()
  ' Create the Repository object
  Dim Repos As New Repository
  ....................
        Set RootObj = Repos.Open("SERVER=" + Server + ";DATABASE=" + DBName, "repos",
"repos")
  ....................

  call BuildTIM(RootObj, "CCDW Storage TIM", DBName, CCDW_STR_MODEL)

  ' Build the Simple Database TIM
Public Function BuildTIM(Root As RepositoryObject, strTIMTitle As String, DBName As String,
Model As Integer) As Boolean
  BuildTIM = True

  ' Get the interface to create the type library
  Dim IManageReposTypeLib As IManageReposTypeLib
  Set IManageReposTypeLib = Root.Interface("IManageReposTypeLib")

  ' Check if the type lib for Simple Database TIM already exists
  Dim ReposTypeLibs As ITargetObjectCol
  Set ReposTypeLibs = IManageReposTypeLib.ReposTypeLibs
  If HasTypeLib(ReposTypeLibs, strTIMTitle) Then
    Dim msg As String
    If DBName = "" Then
      msg = "The default repository already contains a tool information model named "
    Else
      msg = DBName + " already contains a tool information model named "
    End If
    MsgBox msg + strTIMTitle + ".", , "Error"
    BuildTIM = False
    Exit Function
  End If

  ' Create a new Repository Type Library
  Dim TypeLib As ReposTypeLib
  Set TypeLib = IManageReposTypeLib.CreateTypeLib(OBJID_NULL, strTIMTitle, TypeLib_LIBID)
```

(continued)

```
    ' Create the various repository system definitions
    BuildInterfaceTIM Root, TypeLib, Model
    BuildClassTIM TypeLib, Model
    BuildRelationshipTIM TypeLib, Model
    BuildPropertyTIM Model
End Function


' Create interface definitions
' Stored the created interface definitions in a VB collection to be used later on
Sub BuildInterfaceTIM(Root As RepositoryObject, TypeLib As ReposTypeLib, Model As Integer)
    If (Model = CCDW_STR_MODEL) Then
      gIFaceDefs.Add TypeLib.CreateInterfaceDef(OBJID_NULL, "IDatabaseContainer",
IDatabaseContainer_IFACEID, Nothing), "IDatabaseContainer"
      ' Make ReposRoot implements IDatabaseContainer interface so that it provides
      ' root level access to all databases defined in the repository.
      AddInterfaceToReposRoot Root, gIFaceDefs("IDatabaseContainer")
      gIFaceDefs.Add TypeLib.CreateInterfaceDef(OBJID_NULL, "IDatabase", IDatabase_IFACEID,
Nothing), "IDatabase"
      gIFaceDefs.Add TypeLib.CreateInterfaceDef(OBJID_NULL, "IDatafile", IDatafile_IFACEID,
Nothing), "IDatafile"
      gIFaceDefs.Add TypeLib.CreateInterfaceDef(OBJID_NULL, "ITable", ITable_IFACEID,
Nothing), "ITable"
      .....
    End If
End Sub


' Create class definitions, add interface to class
Sub BuildClassTIM(TypeLib As ReposTypeLib, Model As Integer)
    Dim ClassDef As ClassDef

    If (Model = CCDW_STR_MODEL) Then
      Set ClassDef = TypeLib.CreateClassDef(OBJID_NULL, "Database", Database_CLSID)
      ClassDef.AddInterface gIFaceDefs("IDatabase")

      Set ClassDef = TypeLib.CreateClassDef(OBJID_NULL, "Table", Table_CLSID)
      ClassDef.AddInterface gIFaceDefs("ITable")
    End If
End Sub


' Create relationship definitions and the collection objects
Sub BuildRelationshipTIM(TypeLib As ReposTypeLib, Model As Integer)
    Dim RelDef As RelationshipDef, RefColDef As CollectionDef
    Dim lFlags As Long

    If (Model = CCDW_STR_MODEL) Then
      Set RelDef = TypeLib.CreateRelationshipDef(OBJID_NULL,
"DatabaseContainerContainsDatabases")
      lFlags = COLLECTION_NAMING Or COLLECTION_NAMESUNIQUE
      Set RefColDef = gIFaceDefs("IDatabaseContainer").CreateRelationshipColDef(OBJID_NULL,
"Elements", DispatchID, True, lFlags, RelDef)
```

```
     Set RefColDef = gIFaceDefs("IDatabase").CreateRelationshipColDef(OBJID_NULL, "Root",
DispatchID, False, 0, RelDef)


    ' Database contains Table
    Set RelDef = TypeLib.CreateRelationshipDef(OBJID_NULL, "DatabaseContainsTables")
    lFlags = COLLECTION_NAMING Or COLLECTION_NAMESUNIQUE Or COLLECTION_PROPAGATEDELETE
    Set RefColDef = gIFaceDefs("IDatabase").CreateRelationshipColDef(OBJID_NULL,
"Element3s", DispatchID, True, lFlags, RelDef)
    Set RefColDef = gIFaceDefs("ITable").CreateRelationshipColDef(OBJID_NULL, "Database",
DispatchID, False, 0, RelDef)
  End If
End Sub

' Call PopulatePropValues to create the property def objects of the interface
' and set the property values
Sub BuildPropertyTIM(Model As Integer)

  If (Model = CCDW_STR_MODEL) Then
    PopulatePropertyValues gIFaceDefs("IDatabase"), "Name", "String"
    PopulatePropertyValues gIFaceDefs("IDatabase"), "Location", "String"
  End If
End Sub

' Create the property def objects of the interface and set the property values
' IFaceDef - interface definition object
' strProp - name of property definition
' strDataType - datatype of property definition
' lSize - size of datatype, apply only to string
Sub PopulatePropertyValues(IFaceDef As InterfaceDef, strProp As String, strDataType As
String, Optional lSize As Variant)
  Dim PropDef As PropertyDef

  If IsMissing(lSize) Then lSize = 255

  ' Set the various values based on datatype of a particular property
  Select Case LCase(strDataType)

  Case "string"
    Set PropDef = IFaceDef.CreatePropertyDef(OBJID_NULL, strProp, DispatchID, SQL_C_CHAR)
    PropDef.SQLType = SQL_VARCHAR
    PropDef.SQLSize = lSize
    PropDef.SQLScale = 0
  End Select
End Sub
```

This example populates one of the repository objects in the storage information model.

```
Public Function RepBuildDatabase(CommonObj As Object, RepObj As
RepositoryObject, RepObj1 As RepositoryObject, DatabaseName As String,
DatabaseLocation As String) As RepositoryObject
    Dim Database As RepositoryObject

    Set Database = CommonObj.CreateReposObject(CommonObj.CCDWStrTypeLib,
"Database")
    Database("IDatabase").Name = DatabaseName
    Database("IDatabase").Location = DatabaseLocation

    RepObj("IDatabaseContainer").Elements.Add Database, DatabaseName
    RepObj1("IInformationModel").Element1s.Add Database, DatabaseName
    Set RepBuildDatabase = Database
End Function
```

This example retrieves the metadata from one of the repository objects in the storage information model.

```
'--------------------------------------------------------------------------
'   Repproject: Retrieve storage model
'
'--------------------------------------------------------------------------
Public Function RepGetTableCol(RootObj As RepositoryObject) As ITargetObjectCol
   Set RepGetTableCol = RootObj.Interface("IDatabase").Element3s
End Function

Public Function RepGetDatabaseServer(Database As ITargetObjectCol, I As Integer) As String
   RepGetDatabaseServer = Database(I).Interface("IDatabase").Location
End Function

Public Function RepGetDatabaseName(Database As ITargetObjectCol, I As Integer) As String
   RepGetDatabaseName = Database(I).Interface("IDatabase").Name
End Function

Public Function RepGetDatabaseObject(Root As RepositoryObject, ObjName As String) As Object
   Set RepGetDatabaseObject = Root.Interface("IDatabaseContainer").Elements(ObjName)
End Function
```

This example drives the repository population and retrieval functions described above.

```
Sub Main()
   Set RootObj = CommonObj.Connect2Repository(Repos, Server, DBName, userid, passwd)

   .....
```

```
  Set DatabaseSource = obj.RepBuildDatabase(CommonObj, RepRoot, InformationModelSource,
"CCDWTestDB", "conan")
  Set TranslogSource = obj.RepBuildTransLog(CommonObj, DatabaseSource, "dummy")
  .....
End Sub


Sub BuildTables()

  Set TableSource = obj.RepBuildTable(CommonObj, DatabaseSource, FilegroupSource,
ComponentSource1, "Customers")
  .....



' Read the meta information stored in CCDW Project model
Sub RetrieveStorageModel(objectName As String)
  Dim DatabaseSource      As RepositoryObject
  Dim TableSource As RepositoryObject
  Dim FileGroupCol As ITargetObjectCol
  Dim FilegroupSource As RepositoryObject

  Dim TableCol As ITargetObjectCol
  Dim KeyCol As ITargetObjectCol

  Set storageobj1 = CreateObject("ccdwmodel.Repstorage")

  'On Error GoTo RepositoryFail

  ' --------------- -----------------------------------------------------------
  ' get Database Object based on Object Name
  Set DatabaseSource = storageobj1.RepGetDatabaseObject(RootObj, objectName)
  ' get TableCol from Database Object
  Set TableCol = storageobj1.RepGetTableFDbCol(DatabaseSource)

End Sub
```

Of course, you can create new information models for steps found at a more detailed level than those shown in Figure 11.11. With these models in place, you can capture metadata in different ways; for instance, using graphical interfaces such as the Universal Management Console and DTS Designer. The UMC allows you to build database objects or design OLAP applications; DTS Designer allows you to build DTS packages. You can also enter metadata manually, or capture it from external tools via the COM object communication layer. The section below reviews how metadata is captured from DTS and OLAP Services.

DTS Designer in SQL Server 7.0 is the graphical tool for creating and editing packages. It provides features for saving package metadata and data lineage information to Microsoft Repository, and for linking those types of information. A DTS package is a self-contained description of all the work that must be performed as part of a transformation. You can store catalog metadata for databases referenced in a package, and accounting information about the package version history of a particular data row in a datamart or data warehouse.

When you save DTS package information into the Microsoft Repository, you can save metadata about the source and target databases referenced in the package: primary keys, foreign keys, column type, size, position, scale, nullability, and indexes. You can also save data lineage information. DTS allows you to determine the source of any piece of data, and the transformations applied to it. You can track data lineage at the package and row levels of a table, and capture a complete audit trail of data transformation and package execution information in the data warehouse. When you save a package, version information is linked to lineage data, allowing you to track:

- Changes to the package metadata, such as changes to data columns and keys

- Which package version produced a particular set of transformations

DTS Designer uses its own information model to structure package metadata and data lineage information and save it to Microsoft Repository.

Microsoft SQL Server OLAP Services creates a repository to store metadata for multidimensional objects such as cubes, dimensions, hierarchies, etc. By default, this "OLAP Services repository" is a Microsoft Access (.MDB) database on the computer where OLAP Services is installed. You can use the Migrate Repository Wizard to migrate this repository to a SQL Server (.MDF) database on the same or another computer.

After the metadata repository has been built and populated, you can modify or expand any piece of the architecture without major design overhauls. For instance, it is common to find different needs for OLAP presentation layers. Finance analysts may prefer Excel as a front-end for data delivery, and marketing analysts may prefer a graphical tool. You can add presentation layers by integrating with OLAP services, that is, without dealing with database connections. You can also add a subject area to the data warehouse. Although this requires some design and development effort, the information delivery mechanisms do not need to deal with new table or column names. In addition, as warehouse usage grows, Agent Services will monitor the system and feed data back into the metadata repository, where you can run statistical usage reports to plan changes and better allocate existing resources.

Here is some Microsoft Visual Basic code to retrieve metadata information from the repository in order to create a new table using SQL Distributed Management Objects (SQL-DMO)—a collection of objects encapsulating SQL Server database and replication management, and used to build applications.

The code has a reading part and an execution part. The reading part includes two steps:

1. Reading interfaces (repository database object interface and table object interface)
2. Reading table definition and saving it into a temporary variable

The execution part consists of reading the table information from the temporary variable saved in the first part, and creating the table using SQL-DMO.

 The code assumes that the information model defined in Figure 11.13a, part 1, exists in the repository.

```
//
//    get the database repository object interface
//
HRESULT getDatabaseObj(IRepositoryObject * m_pIRootObj, BSTR dbname, IDispatch **ppIDb)
{

        CIfacePtr<IDispatch>                      pInterface ;
        CIfacePtr<ITargetObjectCol>               pDbCol;
        CIfacePtr<IRepositoryObject>     pPCObj;
        DISPID dispid_dbs ;
        DISPID dispid ;
        OLECHAR  *Dbs_str  = L"Elements";

        CComVariant                                      sComVar;
        CRepVariant                                      sRepVar;

        HRESULT hr = S_OK;
        USES_CONVERSION;

        // for ReportError
        m_pIRootObj->get_Repository(&pIRepository);

        m_pIRootObj->get_Interface(CVariant("IDatabaseContainer"),&pInterface);


        //
        pInterface->GetIDsOfNames(IID_NULL, &Dbs_str, 1,
               LOCALE_USER_DEFAULT, &dispid_dbs);

        // get database collections
        get_RepTargetObjCol(pInterface, dispid_dbs , &pDbCol);
        pDbCol->get_Item(CVariant(dbname),&pPCObj);

        // get the interface IDatabase
```

(continued)

```
        pPCObj->get_Interface(CVariant("IDatabase"),ppIDb)

        return S_OK;
}

//
// get the table repository object interface
//
HRESULT getTableObj(IDispatch *pIDb, BSTR TabName, IDispatch **ppITab)
{

        CIfacePtr<IDispatch>                    pInterface;
        CIfacePtr<ITargetObjectCol>        pTabCol;
        CIfacePtr<IRepositoryObject>    pPCObj1;

        HRESULT                                              hr;
// status

        DISPID dispid_Tabs ;

        OLECHAR  *szPropE3 = L"Element3s";                      // db contains tables

        BSTR                                    sName;
// Any BSTR
        CComVariant                             sComVar;
        CRepVariant                             sRepVar;
// Used to retrieve any variant

        *ppITab = 0;
        USES_CONVERSION;

        pIDb->GetIDsOfNames(IID_NULL, &szPropE3, 1, LOCALE_USER_DEFAULT, &dispid_Tabs);

        // get the table collection
        get_RepTargetObjCol(pIDb, dispid_Tabs, &pTabCol);

        //
        // Search for tables with input table name (key)
        //

        pTabCol->get_Item(CVariant(TabName),&pPCObj1);

        pPCObj1->get_Name(&sName);

        pPCObj1->get_Interface(CVariant("ITable"),ppITab);

        return S_OK;

}
//
```

```
//      get the table definition from repository and save it to ptab
//
HRESULT RepGetTabInfo(IRepositoryObject * m_pIRootObj, BSTR dbname, BSTR TabName, TabInfo
*ptab)
{
        CIfacePtr<IDispatch>        pIDb;
        CIfacePtr<IDispatch>        pITab;
        CIfacePtr<IDispatch>        pICol;
        CIfacePtr<ITargetObjectCol>            pColCol;
        CIfacePtr<IRepositoryObject>          pPCObj;
        OLECHAR  *szPropE3  = L"Element3s";     // column collection
        OLECHAR  *szdtype= L"Datatype";
        DISPID  dispid_Cols,dispid;
        long   ncols;
        CComVariant                    sComVar;

        .
        .
        .

        // get the database repository object interface
        getDatabaseObj(m_pIRootObj, dbname, &pIDb);

        // get the table repository object interface
        getTableObj(pIDb, TabName, &pITab);

        // get the column collection
        pITab->GetIDsOfNames(IID_NULL, &szPropE3, 1, LOCALE_USER_DEFAULT, &dispid_Cols);
        get_RepTargetObjCol(pITab, dispid_Cols, &pColCol)

        pColCol->get_Count(&(ptab->nCols));

        ptab->cols = new ColInfo[ptab->nCols];
        memset(ptab->cols, 0, (ptab->nCols)*sizeof(ColInfo));

        for (long i=0; i < ptab->nCols; i++){

           pColCol->get_Item(CVariant(i+1),&pPCObj);

           // column name
           pPCObj->get_Name( &sName  );

           ptab->cols[i].Name = SysAllocString(sName); // column name

           pPCObj->get_Interface(CVariant("IColumn"),&pICol);

           //column data type
           pICol->GetIDsOfNames(IID_NULL, &szdtype, 1, LOCALE_USER_DEFAULT, &dispid);
           get_RepProp(pICol,dispid,&sComVar);
```

(continued)

```
            ptab->cols[i].Type = SysAllocString(sComVar.bstrVal);

            // more column properties
                    .
                    .
                    .

      }
      return S_OK;
}
//
//
//     Read the table infomation from repository and
//     create the table using sql-dmo
//
HRESULT CreateTable(IRepositoryObject * m_pIRootObj, BSTR srvname, BSTR dbname, BSTR
TabName)
{

        ...
        LPSQLDMODATABASE pSQLDatabase ;
        LPSQLDMOSERVER pSQLServer ;
        LPSQLDMOTABLE pTable;
        LPSQLDMOCOLUMN* apColumns;
        HRESULT         hr = NOERROR;
        TabInfo         tab;

        LPCLASSFACTORY  pIClassFactory1=NULL;     // columns
        USES_CONVERSION;

        // get the table information from repository
                RepGetTabInfo(pIDb, TabName, &tab);


        // connect to the SQL-Server

                hr = CoCreateInstance(CLSID_SQLDMOServer, NULL, CLSCTX_INPROC_SERVER,
                            IID_ISQLDMOServer, (void **) &pSQLServer);


                pSQLServer->Connect(srvname,L"sa",L"") ;

                hr = pSQLServer->GetDatabaseByName(dbname, &pSQLDatabase);

                apColumns = new LPSQLDMOCOLUMN[tab.nCols];
                memset(apColumns, 0, tab.nCols * sizeof(LPSQLDMOCOLUMN));

           hr = CoGetClassObject (CLSID_SQLDMOColumn, CLSCTX_INPROC_SERVER,
                        NULL, IID_IClassFactory, (void**) &pIClassFactory1);
```

```
        for (long i =0 ; i< tab.nCols; i++) {

                hr = pIClassFactory1->CreateInstance(NULL, IID_IUnknown,
    (void**) &(apColumns[nCol]));

                hr = apColumns[nCol]->SetName((tab.cols[nCol].Name));

                // Data type

                hr = apColumns[nCol]->SetDatatype((tab.cols[nCol].Type));

        }

        hr = CoCreateInstance(CLSID_SQLDMOTable, NULL,
    CLSCTX_INPROC_SERVER, IID_ISQLDMOTable, (void**) &pTable);

        // set the table name
        pTable->SetName(TabName);

        // add the columns to the table
        for (i = 0; i < tab.nCols && SUCCEEDED(hr); i++)
         hr = pTable->AddColumn(apColumns[i]);


    // setup other table properties

        .
        .
        .


        // add table to the database
        hr = pSQLDatabase->AddTable(pTable);

        return hr;
```

This shows how to read metadata from the repository and perform tasks via DMO or other SQL Server services such as DTS, OLAP Services, or Agent Services. The example creates a table with SQL-DMO from a table definition stored in the repository. You could do the same thing using Transact-SQL, but the method in the example capitalizes on the metadata repository's integrated approach between objects. For instance, the creation of a large fact table includes partitioning information as well as an indexing strategy. Other fact tables will include information about the aggregation level across dimension hierarchies at which they summarize data. You can combine all this information with usage statistics captured from the OLAP Server to tune performance based on new indexes and new aggregate tables.

SQL Server 7.0 integrates metadata for OLAP Services and DTS into the repository. Microsoft has also created an open information model for database objects (the DBM model). However, when you are building a data warehouse, these information models are still missing from the Microsoft Repository:

- A model for physical data layout, including disk array layout, physical database layout, etc.

- A model for operational metadata, including job management, scheduling, tasking, event management, etc.

- A model for information delivery, such as cube creation, cube delivery destination, reports delivery destination, etc.

- A model for warehouse management, such as aggregation management, partition management, data mart management, etc.

In the design and development stages, there are some integration issues:

- SQL Server provides DMO and name space objects, which provide a good interface for data warehouse management, but they cannot put metadata directly into the repository. This can complicate things because users usually prefer to plan the whole database before physically creating it.

- Microsoft Visual C++'s ActiveX Template Library (ATL) smart pointer to COM still cannot be easily integrated into repository COM objects written in Visual Basic.

Scalability

Scalability includes the ability to grow incrementally and to maintain consistent performance as the system does so. Field experience shows that data in most large data warehouse implementations doubles in the first year of operation, through increased granularity, new subject areas, and longer history retention. To maintain performance with growth, the design needs to cover parallel processing and partitioning.

Parallel Processing

Warehouse data volume is likely to grow continuously, and as it does it challenges the hardware and software environment. Parallelism is one of the most efficient methods for dealing with this.

Because the data warehouse involves intensive I/O and processing of large volumes of data, it must be operated at the highest possible degree of parallelism. A range of technology exists to make this possible. Database engines include parallel features for querying, loading, and indexing. Hardware and operating system architectures permit configuration for high degrees of parallelism in distributed computing, symmetric multiprocessing (SMP), massively parallel processing (MPP), clustering architectures, multiprocessing, multi-threaded processing, asynchronous, and parallel I/O architecture.

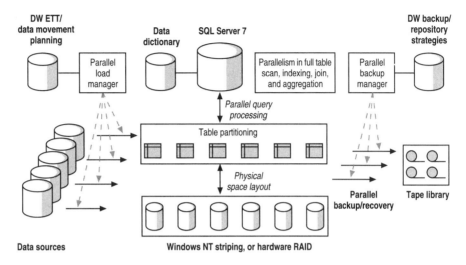

Figure 11.14   Parallel processing architecture.

You can apply parallel processing in most aspects of the data warehouse environment. Tasks such as load processing and query execution can benefit extensively from parallel processing techniques such as intra-query parallelism, which speeds up query execution by overlapping scans, joins, and sorts.

In general, combining parallel processing with partitioned data should yield the best performance results. MetaEdge has introduced a parallel processing architecture for the SQL Server data warehouse driven by the Parallel Load and Backup managers. This architecture (shown in Figure 11.14) covers these processes:

- Parallel data extraction and loading
- Intra-query parallelism
    - Table partitioning, Windows NT disk striping, or disk array RAID
    - Star query and star indexing
    - Hash join, etc.
- Parallel backup and recovery
    - Data file/filegroup backup, differential backup
    - Multiple streaming, multiple threaded I/O

Partitioning

Hardware Partitioning

Common-sense disk partitioning tries to configure disks for the best throughput when every disk functions and for minimum impact when a disk fails. The disk partitioning strategy affects database I/O performance, and operation procedures in the production environment. Here are some guidelines for VLDB partitioning:

- Configure RAID-5 (RAID-S) or equivalent devices for all data files that will turn read-only after a while.

- Configure some write-intensive disks with RAID 0+1 for transaction logs and temporary filegroups.

- Choose synchronous write cache in the controllers for a RAID-5 set.

- Choose a big stripe-block size, that is a multiple of I/O block-size. For example, use 8 KB for database block size and 128 KB for stripe block size.

- Check hardware I/O specifications. Controllers can handle only so many disks; don't over configure.

- Be aware of the overall traffic between the array (of all disks) and the host via SCSI or fiber channel interfaces.

- Complete mirroring and re-silvering for VLDB.

Database Partitioning

- Select a partitioning key. *Time* is a common key because the time dimension is always used as a constraint and it facilitates maintenance (you can drop the last monthly partition in the warehouse after a new month's data is loaded). Indexing and backup need to be done only once on the new partition.

- Analyze alternative strategies. Strategies can favor one set of queries over others. For instance, partitioning by time will benefit queries that scan and compare data for this month versus the same month last year, but will not help queries that look at particular products throughout the whole year.

- Avoid hot spots. A given partition can become a hot spot if a disproportional number of queries run against it. Because *time* is often used as a partition key, the hot spot tends to be the most current period. It also tends to move around, showing up in a different storage location when a new current period enters the system. You can remove these by disk-striping the area, but this approach can hinder the benefits of parallel querying and have other undesirable effects.

- Consider disk failures. If you have a 1.1-TB disk farm you can probably expect one disk outage per month. You can assign partitions to disks so that a disk failure takes out only a single partition, leaving surviving partitions available, but this remedy prevents queries against a single partition from scaling, due to the limited I/O.

- For best performance, optimize the physical layout of individual partitions so that each is scanned in parallel, and each has the best possible I/O throughput to query servers. To avoid I/O bottlenecks, spread each partition over a number of disks.

CHAPTER 1 2

Microsoft MARS OLAP Services Implementation

By Chris McKulka, Finance Information Technology

After the Microsoft MARS (Management reporting System) data warehouse had been in place for several years, the decision was made to improve and extend its functionality.

The Solution in Focus

This goal was achieved by adding OLAP reporting capabilities. The project required only 11 weeks, during which one full-time developer, one part-time systems analyst, and one part-time tester added Web-based OLAP reporting capabilities to the existing data warehouse by implementing one server based on Microsoft SQL 7.0 OLAP Services and one based on Microsoft Internet Information Server (IIS). The effort developed a new user interface that mirrors almost all of the previous system's ad hoc query and income-reporting functions.

This was much faster and cheaper than a full-scale data warehouse design and deployment, and it improved performance: running in parallel, the OLAP and legacy systems now take 4 – 5 seconds to execute ad hoc queries that used to take 30 minutes. Canned reports have shrunk from 10 – 30 MB to 170 K. When the design is fully deployed, some servers and processes will no longer be necessary; removing them will further reduce database administration and information technology (IT)-maintenance costs.

What You'll Find in This Chapter

- A discussion of how OLAP processing can be added to a data warehouse to improve performance and extend functionality.

- A description of the evolution of MARS (Management Reporting System) showing the various databases it uses and how its original capabilities were supplemented and extended through a transitional configuration to the (not yet complete) final version.

- An extended discussion of OLAP Services: what they added to system functionality and how they were implemented.

- Details on querying in the new system, showing how OLAP Services improved data retrieval and manipulation.

Case Overview

For two and a half years, Microsoft financial analysts used the Management Reporting System (MARS) data warehouse and report generator to create profit and loss statements (P&Ls), balance sheets, and other internal, statutory, and tax reports. As so often happens, however, data grew significantly as time went by, and performance declined. And as users developed needs for more than income and sales data, MARS grew into a larger data warehouse, including human resources, project accounting, and budget data.

To speed up report- and query-generation and reduce maintenance costs, Microsoft added online analytical processing (OLAP) reporting capabilities to the data warehouse. Besides solving the performance problem, this also demonstrated the speed with which Microsoft's OLAP technology can be deployed in an enterprise data warehouse. In 11 weeks, one full-time developer, one part-time systems analyst, and one part-time tester added Web-based OLAP reporting capabilities to the existing data warehouse by implementing one server based on Microsoft SQL Server 7.0 OLAP Services and one based on Microsoft Internet Information Server (IIS). They also built a new user interface that mirrors 95 percent of the previous system's ad hoc query and income-reporting functions.

While this may seem a significant amount of time and effort, it was much faster and cheaper than a full-scale data warehouse design and deployment. More important, it solved the problems that were bothering MARS users. Running in parallel, the OLAP and legacy systems now take 4 – 5 seconds to execute ad hoc queries that used to take 30 minutes. Canned reports have shrunk from 10 – 30 MB to 170 K. Information is available in ad hoc queries and in preformatted, publication-quality profit and loss (P&L) reports (stored as Excel files). Once the remaining, lower-priority functions are implemented, redundant servers and processes can be removed to further reduce database administration and information technology (IT)-maintenance costs.

The system's 1,100 users fall into three categories: financial analysts, high-level managers, and department administrators. In each category, some users access the system over the local LAN and others use the WAN.

- **Financial Analysts**, the system's most frequent users, track budgets, compare projected costs to actual costs, find and explain variances in project costs, and make ad hoc queries for decision support.

- **High-level managers** are controllers, general managers, and executives who run entire divisions and businesses within divisions. These users often require summary data rather than details, so they often view P&L reports in Microsoft Excel and only occasionally use the Web interface for queries.

- **Department administrators** use MARS to generate reports about specific Microsoft cost centers. Before the OLAP Services implementation, they executed queries with MS Reports (an internal Visual Basic-based tool). Now they use the Internet Explorer Web-display technology enhanced with the Microsoft Office 2000 Web Components.

Scope and Goals

Over time, MARS began to fail to meet the needs of financial analysts, high-level managers, and department administrators because ad hoc query responses were too slow and Excel-based P&L statements took too long to open. Both problems were worse for international users querying over the WAN.

To reduce query times and shrink P&L report file sizes so they open faster, developers replaced the old query and reporting interface and added an OLAP Server. This did not affect back-end data modeling, which was already in place and was considered successful. They also developed two ways to reduce database administration and IT-maintenance costs: reduce the number of servers to maintain (especially redundant report generators, which are more prone to crashes than other servers in the system) and make it easier to create new views of existing data. (Details are in the section "Future System (OLAP Only)" below.)

MARS Architecture

MARS presents data from SAP on a server running SQL Server 7.0 and several online transaction processing (OLTP) data sources based on SQL Server 6.5 and 7.0. The data sources range in size from .5 GB to 85 GB.

- **SAP.** General Ledger, Fixed Assets, Statutory and Balance Sheet (85 GB).

  Reporting functionality: MARS provides the ability to report on summary level expenses and revenue more quickly and easily than SAP alone.

- **Alfred.** A SQL Server database that allocates expenses to sales channels and product units. Alfred administrators create allocation rules that implement Microsoft accounting policies. For instance, the cost of supporting Microsoft's local area network might be allocated to business units based on headcount (1.5 GB).

  Reporting functionality: MARS only.

- **MS Sales.** Detailed sales and revenue data stored on multiple SQL Server-based servers (60 GB).

  Reporting functionality: Full revenue reporting functionality at a very granular level. Revenue data is in MARS at a summary level.

- **Rigel.** Converts and posts MS Sales (see Chapter 10) data to the general Ledger datastore on SAP (1.5 GB).

  Reporting functionality: MARS only.

- **Human Resources Data Warehouse (HRDW).** Human resources data from SAP and legacy systems (3.0 GB). (See Chapter 9 for a discussion of this solution.)

  Reporting functionality: Full reporting functionality from an HR perspective. Native reporting functionality does not meet the needs of the finance community so this data is brought into Mars and manipulated.

- **HeadTrax (HTX).** A Web-based front end to the HR data stored in SAP. Users (Microsoft managers) can review the status of every person and position in the organization, change attributes of current people and positions, and open new positions (1 GB).

  Reporting functionality: Limited. HTX is designed to be a transaction system—a role it fills very well. Mars provides finance-focused reporting.

- **Feedstore.** Certain sets of data are used widely throughout Microsoft—lists of companies, products, ISO currency codes, exchange rates, etc. Originally, each system negotiated a feed with the publishing system, but users chose different publishing systems and formats, leading to inconsistent sets of domain data and massive duplication of effort. The Feedstore was created to provide a single source for each of the widely used data sets (48 GB).

  Reporting functionality: MARS and the many other Feedstore subscribers at Microsoft. No native reporting functionality.

- **Budget WorkBench (BWB).** Budget planning data. Managers use BWB to specify their future resource needs and revenue expectations (4 GB).

  Reporting functionality: Full. Data is sent to MARS to be allocated (via Alfred) and presented in standard management P&Ls.

- **On Target.** Project-cost and time-entry data. About one-third of Microsoft employees use this to capture the amount of time they spend on particular projects. The data is compared to budget plans (0.5 GB).

  Reporting functionality: Limited published reports. MARS reporting.

By collecting and reconciling these data sets, MARS makes it possible for users to create queries suited to their purposes. For example, individual OLTP systems let managers view and report on cost and employee-count data individually, but MARS lets them use data from departments other than their own to analyze costs per employee and to compare planned and actual costs.

Original System

The original MARS back-end consisted of several OLTP data sources. Stored procedures on a Microsoft SQL Server 7.0-based server (the **processing** SQL server) scrub data from the OLTP sources to create unified data representations. For example, MARS users can bring data from HTX and the HRDW together with SAP expense data to derive a metric called **Cost per Head** (HC—head count) and use MARS's month-by-month history of headcount data to compare HC to expenses over time. Before MARS, users could not get historical HC data from the HR systems because this was not a key HR view.

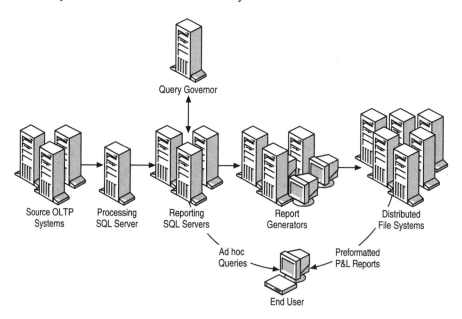

Figure 12.1   Original MARS implementation.

Three **reporting** servers based on Microsoft SQL Server 7.0 support ad hoc queries and pass data to the multiple **report generators** needed to service the request volume. When new data is posted each night to the reporting SQL Server computers, the report generators open stored Excel P&L reports, refresh them with new data, then save them to distributed file servers around the world. The query governor caches queries and results; this allows users to send queries, disconnect from the LAN while the query runs, then re-connect to retrieve the results.

The querying tool was MS Reports (MSR), an internal Visual Basic-based application. It composed structured query language (SQL) code based on fields the user dragged into the query-design area of the UI, sent SQL statements to the data store, and logged query statistics to the MSR Server database. This was one source of unacceptable query response time: MS Reports had to create a large number of SQL statements in order to pull data from the database. Another source was the formatted P&L reports: they were huge Excel files that often contained data not pertinent to users' queries. While performance was slow over the LAN, it was much worse for international users over the WAN: their most trivial queries required minutes to complete and typical reports took an hour to open.

A third source of performance problems was replication. MARS originally used Windows NT File Replication Services to copy roughly 140 15 – 20 MB preformatted P&L reports from Microsoft's headquarters in Redmond to the company's 11 international data centers during the financial month-end close. This placed a significant processing and transfer load on the network.

Note   OLAP provides vastly superior performance over the WAN—almost equivalent to LAN performance, according to tests. Strictly speaking, this was not an MS Reports issue, but a SQL Server one because queries written in MS Query, a pre-SQL Server 7.0 utility, deliver poor WAN performance compared to OLAP. OLAP improves WAN performance in two ways. First, it queries only for data the user is actually looking at, rather than bringing back a huge set out of which the user needs only a small percentage. OLAP reduces total query and data transport times (presuming the user needs only some of the block of SQL data, which is typical) by issuing very small, fast queries instead of one large query. Second, OLAP uses a more efficient format to send data back to the client.

Current System (Migrating to OLAP)

Developers concluded that OLAP Services could alleviate the problem even if the migration temporarily increased system complexity, as shown in Figure 12.2.

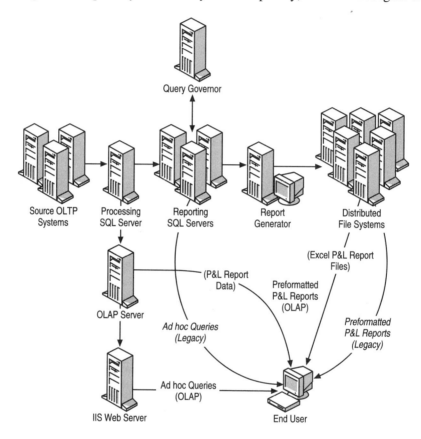

Figure 12.2   Current MARS implementation.

In this transitional stage, the original and OLAP-enabled versions of MARS operate in parallel, so that both systems are available for users for queries and reports. As you can see by comparing Figures 12.1 and 12.2, the system still contains the query governor and the components directly beneath it (source OLTP systems, processing SQL Server, reporting SQL Server computers, report generators and distributed file servers). When the OLAP-enabled system is completed it will mirror all functions of the original system, allowing for removal of the distributed file servers, query governor, and redundant report generators.

The OLAP environment requires only one report generator because querying and reporting functionality are distributed to the OLAP and IIS Web servers. The OLAP data server has four 400-MHz Intel Xeon processors and 2 GB RAM. It is based on Microsoft SQL Server 7.0 OLAP Services. Each night it receives 200,000 rows of data from the processing SQL Server and copies the data to each of the two active **virtual cubes**. Virtual cubes allow disparate data to be presented in one view. For example, MARS uses virtual cubes to present *budget dollars*, *actual dollars*, *budget headcount*, and *actual headcount* in one consolidated view. This concept is explained in the section "Database Administration and IT Maintenance" below, and shown in Figure 12.5. The OLAP data server also provides users with data they request through the Web page. Users retrieve the Web page from the Web server, but data is sent to them directly from the OLAP Server.

This transitional stage retains the equipment from the original system. These components will be removed when migration is complete:

- **File servers.** These allow P&Ls to be "pushed" to locations closer to users, to reduce WAN impact. Extra file servers will no longer be needed because the OLAP P&Ls are so small there is no need to move them closer to users.

- **Report generators.** These refresh the P&Ls daily to reduce the amount of query activity SQL Server has to support. In the original system, the report generators pre-ran queries so that users could open P&Ls and immediately go to work, rather than waiting up to five minutes for the P&L to refresh. Report generators will no longer be needed because users can refresh OLAP P&Ls so quickly that there is no need to refresh them ahead of time.

- **Reporting SQL servers.** These support user ad hoc queries. In the original system, the user base is partitioned: domestic users on Server A, international users on Server B. This is ineffective in that it often leads to one server being over-utilized while the other is idle. These extra servers will no longer be needed because one OLAP server can handle the entire load.

- **Query governor.** This limited each user's queries to keep any one user from saturating the system, and allowed users to submit a query, disconnect from the LAN, and come back later for the results. It will no longer be needed because three-second OLAP queries obviate the need for both of these functions.

Future System (OLAP Only)

In the final stage, the MARS OLAP implementation will remove servers and processes that are not needed in a pure OLAP system. As you see in Figure 12.3, this will reduce the system complexity introduced in the transition stage:

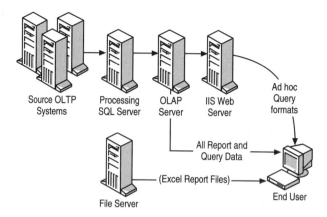

Figure 12.3   Planned MARS implementation (OLAP only).

It will also increase efficiency. A single OLAP server will service all local and worldwide users. It removes the need for distributed file servers, reporting SQL servers, the report generators, and the query governor. Distributed file servers become unnecessary because the single P&L report file server in Redmond can serve users around the world. It stores Excel-based P&L report sizes ranging from 170 – 350 K—much smaller than the 15 – 20 MB files previously required—that can be distributed quickly over the WAN to client computers, where they are quickly populated with data from the OLAP Server. Clients download only new data, not the report template; rather than download the entire template every night, they now can download it only when it changes. The extra reporting servers are no longer needed to view the P&Ls once they have been refreshed. The query governor is no longer needed to control loading and temporary connection because queries are so much faster.

Database Administration and IT Maintenance

Database administrators support MARS in four ways: they ensure a supply of data, set up reports, process data into star schemas, and create OLAP cubes. The OLAP Services implementation has little or no effect on the first two functions because they're based on back-end processing. The last two functions, however, depend on defining **perspectives**, which are filters that save time by presenting groups of users with data they're likely to need. For example, the *Channel* perspective creates data tables of product names, geographic regions, revenue and expenses by time period. For the original MARS implementation, database administrators had created 18 perspectives, each with different access restrictions, for the MS Reports query tool. Users chose perspectives from a drop-down list.

After studying system use, the implementation team found that it could retain about 2/3 of MARS's functionality by implementing the top two perspectives (*Channel* and *Consolidated*) and relaxing security requirements. To create functionality better adapted to OLAP, the team decided to replace these two perspectives with virtual cubes that incorporate logical (physical) cubes for actual and budgeted amounts, using the same data in the original perspectives. Since MARS users were already familiar with the perspective concept, the implementation team carried the nomenclature over to the new system. In the new query interface, users specify a *perspective* rather than a *cube*, even though they are now accessing a virtual cube. (This may seem inconsequential, but it eliminated training effort and ensured that users would quickly adapt to the new system and use it.) When the OLAP Services design is fully implemented, the database administrators plan to create additional virtual cubes that mirror the rest of the old system's functions.

An immediate advantage is that virtual cubes can be defined in about half the time it took to define perspectives. Taking the long-range view, cubes require about half as much maintenance, leading the team to expect savings from reduced administration time. Microsoft's Information Technology Group (ITG) also expects to save money: the new system will require maintenance of fewer servers because the new system discontinues P&L report replication to distributed file servers and eliminates the need for redundant report generators.

OLAP Services Implementation

The MARS implementation team created a proof of concept in two days, demonstrating the performance gain MARS achieved with Microsoft SQL Server 7.0 OLAP Services. During the next three weeks, the team built a demonstration OLAP system that included 90 percent of the proposed functionality. For the next eight weeks, the team implemented more functions, incorporated feedback from users, automated data processing, created installation documentation, and tested and tuned the implementation.

No team members had experience with OLAP Services before this project. The full-time developer was a skilled Visual Basic and SQL developer and was familiar with the MARS data warehouse, for which Microsoft SQL Server 7.0 provides OLAP Services.

In the original system, the 1.5 - 2-second latency rate per request/response round-trip on the WAN (typical in large WANs) increased the time required to retrieve query results. Building queries with MS Reports was difficult because it required so many trips back to the Redmond servers. Even basic queries took minutes to formulate and display a complete response. Like death and taxes, latency is a fact of life, so the team knew it had to reduce the number of request/response round trips and the amount of information sent per query. They could do this by substituting desktop browser technology and Office 2000 Web Components (OWC).

OWC was crucial in delivering this solution. It integrated seamlessly with the new system (all designers had to do was point the OWC to the server and the cube of interest) and was very fast (due to highly efficient MDX). Here is all the code that was needed to configure the OWC after it was embedded in the Web page and given the ID **PTable**:

```
PTable.ConnectionString = "Provider=MSOLAP;" & _
                "Data Source=MarsOLAP1;" & _
                "Initial Catalog=Mars OLAP Chan;"
PTable.DataMember       = "Channel"
PTable.ActiveView.AutoLayout
```

How is the amount of data reduced? Because using SQL Server 7.0 OLAP Services and client-side Office 2000 Web Components allowed users to focus the data returned by each query. For drill-down requests (detail data to support a summary) OLAP returns only the child data points that underlie the summary data point. The original system *displayed* only the data on which the summary was made, but it *returned* all data at the next lower level of detail. For example, if a user requested sales data for Hungary, the system returned sales data for all of Eastern Europe but displayed only the data for Hungary. This was why reports were so huge. For the same query, the OLAP Services system returns only the sales data for Hungary, resulting in a smaller data package. (For detailed information, see the SQL Server 7.0 OLAP Services white paper, available at http://www.microsoft.com/sql.)

MARS Data Model

An OLAP data model presents information as cubes, which consist of descriptive categories (dimensions) and quantitative values (measures). The OLAP implementation draws data from the existing MARS data warehouse, which prepares data for analysis by extracting it from operational systems, cleansing, validating, and summarizing it, then organizing it in star schemas. Star schemas, which link central fact tables to related dimension tables, were chosen over snowflake schemas for the original MARS data warehouse design because stars have fewer table links, which usually improves query performance. (The original design uses snowflake joins in a few cases where they improve query speed or where straight star joins are impractical. See Figure 12.4 for an example.)

So the OLAP team began with the existing star schemas. To map them to the OLAP data model, the developer used the Cube Wizard (a component of the OLAP Manager snap-in to the Microsoft Management Console). It provides a drag-and-drop user interface with which you can translate pre-built star and snowflake schemas to OLAP cubes (or virtual cubes). When the Cube Wizard opened for each new cube, the developer chose a fact table, defined measures for it, then specified a dimension table and type (standard or time), and, if necessary, which joined columns should be linked. Installing OLAP and prototyping the first cube took only a few hours.

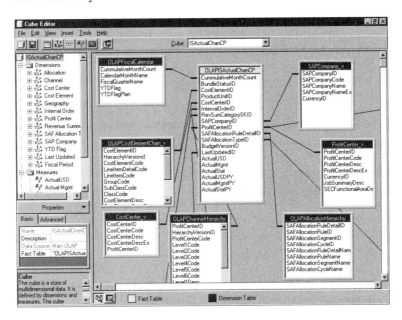

Figure 12.4   Sample design schema from the MARS data warehouse.

After the virtual cubes were designed, the developer opened each virtual cube individually for editing in OLAP Manager, and used the **Cube Roles** dialog box to create one role each for the *Channel* and *Consolidated* virtual cubes (corresponding to the top two perspectives for MARS queries). Cube roles define which users or Windows NT user groups can access and query data in the cube. Database administrators can query any data using the cube-browser tool in OLAP Manager, but roles must be set up to allow client-side query tools to access cubes. The *Channel* virtual cube contains only sales and marketing information, so the developer assigned more people and user groups to that role than to the *Consolidated* virtual cube, which contains all information in the data warehouse, including some that is sensitive.

The *Channel* virtual cube combines two physical cubes: one with *budget* data and one with *actual* data. The *actual* cube has three partitions: *prior year (PY)*, *current year closed fiscal periods (CY)*, and *current year open periods (CP)* and forecast.

Virtual cubes allow you to combine disparate datasets (such as *actual* and *budget*) and include any dimensions that the two datasets have in common. Partitions allow you to break a huge dataset into chunks (partition it). In MARS, this allows the separation of *PY*, *CY*, and *CP* into different partitions. This design offers some significant benefits:

- OLAP allows the partitions to be sourced from different tables.
- The partitions can be processed at different times, allowing for advantageous scheduling. All partitions are processed early in the night, while the SQL and OLAP servers are waiting for data from source systems. This processing incorporates user hierarchy changes made during the day. The *CP* partition is reprocessed later in the night, after data is received from SAP. Because CP is relatively small its processing time is short, so refreshing the OLAP data has minimal impact on processing.

Figure 12.5 shows the physical cubes (partitions) that make up each logical cube.

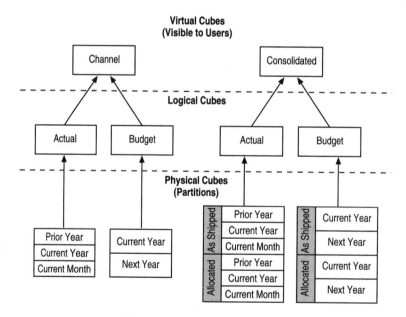

Figure 12.5   Physical cube partitions of logical cubes.

Minimizing Data Explosion

Data grouping (called pre-aggregation) has obvious benefits. By building in associations between certain types of data, the system installs a logic that expedites and focuses queries and reports. But any strategy has its limits: excessive pre-aggregation can cause data explosion—a dramatic term for using too much disk space by doing too much grouping. OLAP Services provides tools for evaluating how much an aggregation will improve performance so that you can assess proposed changes and identify the point at which storage growth starts to outstrip performance gains.

MOLAP Storage

The developer chose to store partitions in multidimensional OLAP (MOLAP) because it offered greater speed than either relational OLAP (ROLAP—which provides multidimensional analysis of data, aggregates, and metadata stored in an RDBMS) or hybrid OLAP (HOLAP—which provides simultaneous multidimensional analysis of data in multidimensional and relational databases). MOLAP also resulted in data sets that are smaller than the original fact tables on the SQL Server 7.0-based servers.

Although HOLAP is normally faster than ROLAP, and in many cases equal to MOLAP, HOLAP performance depends on the level of detail requested in a given query. To ensure consistent performance, MARS uses MOLAP over HOLAP. When aggregations were stored in HOLAP, 15 users simultaneously sent queries to the database and informally noted response times. Some of the queries caused OLAP Services to access non-aggregated data stored in the relational database, dramatically slowing response times. Users had no way of knowing which data were aggregated, so these slow downs were inexplicable and appeared arbitrary.

This shows the potential limitations of test formulation. In this instance, users with more information might have found the solution acceptable. One way to resolve this problem in HOLAP mode is by adding more aggregations to the cube, using the Usage-Based Optimization Wizard (see the "Usage-Based Aggregation" section below).

Pre-Aggregation

Aggregates, which hold pre-computed totals, can improve query response times. MARS developers used the Storage Design Wizard to specify MOLAP as the aggregation storage method on the OLAP Server and to specify the number of aggregates. The wizard, a component of OLAP Manager, allows developers to set either the maximum storage size of the aggregates (regardless of performance gain) or the percentage of the possible performance gain (regardless of storage size). Performance increases as storage size increases, but the point at which storage growth outstrips performance gain varies with each data warehouse. The team found that it is a good idea to start with no aggregations and add them as needed to achieve performance gains. MOLAP is so fast that the cost of aggregates can often outweigh their benefit.

OLAP Services analyzes the OLAP metadata model and determines the optimum set of aggregations from which all others can be derived so that OLAP Services can get non-aggregated data from a few existing aggregate values rather than having to scan the entire dataset.

Because database size was secondary to the project's primary goal of improved performance, the development team decided to specify a percentage of the possible performance gain. This involves specifying a slight performance gain (1 or 2 percent) then testing the system to see if performance is acceptable. If it is, then that figure represents the percentage at which aggregate storage size is the smallest and performance is acceptable. The developers tested the MARS system with a 2-percent performance gain. At that level, most queries to the 6-million-row dataset took less than four seconds, which was acceptable performance. (Generally, specifying a higher percentage gain will not have much affect on datasets smaller than 100 million rows, several times larger than the current MARS dataset.) For more information on this topic, refer to the "OLAP Services White Paper" found at http://www.microsoft.com/sql/70/gen/olap.htm.

Usage-Based Aggregation

In addition to specifying an aggregation percentage, the implementation team plans to employ usage-based aggregation. The computed aggregation function of SQL Server 7.0 OLAP Services is based on mathematical models that may or may not correspond to actual usage patterns. The usage-based model studies patterns to determine the most effective aggregation scheme for a specific, operational system.

During the first six weeks of production, the team examined the query logs to identify queries that took longer than five seconds. They then used the Usage-Based Optimization Wizard (a component of OLAP Manager) to create usage-based aggregations. First they specified the criteria to identify queries that should be optimized (queries that took longer than five seconds) then instructed OLAP Services to create a new set of aggregations for the most-frequently-sought queries. If users report slow performance for specific queries, the team can re-examine the logs and search for solutions.

User Access to MARS Query Data

The MARS implementation team developed a Web-based UI that helps users design and issue useful OLAP database queries. The UI also allows users to view summaries of detail data and data that underlies them. The Web UI offers functionality similar to that of MS Reports but is much faster.

The MARS Web-based query client is an .ASP page residing on the system's Web server and accessed over the intranet. The query client uses the PivotTable Office Web Component, a control that runs in a browser. It allows users to analyze data by sorting, grouping, filtering, outlining, and pivoting. Office 2000 Web Components can query and display data from a spreadsheet range, a relational database such as Microsoft Access or SQL Server, or any OLAP data source that supports the Microsoft OLE DB for OLAP interface. In this implementation, it queries and displays data from the OLAP Server.

User computer requirements are Microsoft Internet Explorer Version 4.01 (or later) running on any version of Windows 9x or Windows NT, 16 MB of RAM, any Intel 486 or Pentium Processor, or any DEC alpha processor. These are also requirements for the Office Web Components, the collection of COM controls for publishing spreadsheets, charts, and databases to the Web. Users must have a Microsoft Office 2000 license, but the productivity suite does not have to be installed on the client machine. When a user who hasn't installed the Office 2000 Web Components browses the page, Internet Explorer (IE) detects this and downloads the components from the corporate Office installation server. IE grabs the .CAB file from the codebase URL, checks the digital signature, and if the user agrees, unpacks and installs it using the Web Installer control, which drives the Windows Installer.

The Data Source Office 2000 Web Component is the reporting engine behind the PivotTable component. It uses Microsoft Active Data Objects (ADO) to manage communication with the OLAP Server and determines what database records are available for display on the page. For example, if a data access page displays customers and orders, the data source component retrieves the order records for the customer being displayed, and sorts, filters, and updates those records in response to user actions.

Multi-Tiered Query Caching

The MARS OLAP implementation uses server-side and client-side query caching to speed up queries. The caching system is possible because of close interaction among the PivotTable and Data Source components running on the client machine and OLAP Services running on the OLAP Server. The OLAP Server caches user queries as well as data, making it possible for OLAP Services to answer some queries by using previously cached data rather than accessing the disk. For example, if one user requests sales data for January, February, and March, then another user asks for first-quarter data, OLAP Services can summarize January through March data from RAM faster than it can pull a first-quarter summary data from disk.

The PivotTable Service on the client machine supports the PivotTable and Data Source components, and brings many OLAP Server caching capabilities to the desktop. (The service requires 2 MB of hard disk space and 500 KB of RAM, in addition to RAM for cached data.) The PivotTable Service determines how to answer a user request as quickly as possible and eliminate redundant network traffic. This is possible because OLAP Services sends cube metadata to the client cache the first time a user queries a particular cube. For example, if a user requests sales data for January, February, and March, the PivotTable Service holds the results in RAM. If the user then requests sales data for the first half of the year, the service requests only April, May, and June data, recognizing that it already has the data for the first three months. This reduces both the amount of data on the network and the number of request/response round-trips.

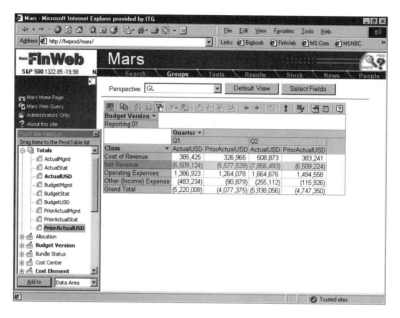

Figure 12.6   Query result.

Once the PivotTable Service has loaded the requested data into the client computer's RAM and displayed the result via the browser's PivotTable Component, users can interact with the table in two ways. They can drag additional fields from the **PivotTable Field** list (which appears in its own window) or they can summarize or view data point details (by double-clicking the column or row or the data point with which they want to interact). The client-side PivotTable Service determines the fastest way to access the requested data then displays the result. This allows users to quickly "drill down" on underlying detail or summarize detailed data.

Conclusion

This implementation was so successful that it was quickly decided to use the new system to support the entire budgeting reporting process, which is so time sensitive and critical, that the decision represents an overwhelming vote of confidence from Microsoft Finance and ITG.

Replication Implementation

Replication: the final frontier—well, not quite in terms of *how* your organization can implement SQL Server 7.0, but it is central to designing and deploying enterprise-scale distributed database applications. No doubt your organization will go into the twenty-first century striving to create and maximize a digital nervous system—using digital information to make better and faster business decisions—and whatever design you use, system availability will be crucial. So far, this book has presented several ways to boost availability, and at the core of every solution lies replication. This section examines the performance and reliability issues you need to consider when designing a replication infrastructure (Chapter 13) and best practices you can use to deploy it (Chapter 14).

CHAPTER 13

Creating a Replication Design

Contributed by Jeff Rogers, MCS—New York

This chapter looks at numerous tactics you can use to create a replication strategy. Replication is essential in a distributed database environment, but large-database systems by their nature present special challenges: distributed data sources and users, tables that must be maintained and synchronized, user groups with different needs and dependencies. There are plenty of options, and all of them have advantages and trade-offs. It is important to understand them when creating a replication design—especially insofar as they affect performance and data consistency.

What You'll Find in This Chapter

- Descriptions of the six types of SQL Server replication: their advantages and disadvantages with respect to system design, how they can be combined, and their requirements and limitations.

- Basic questions you can ask about users, types of information, and system characteristics to identify what you need to replicate and how to do it.

- Extensive discussion of bidirectional replication, which is enhanced and simplified by new options in SQL Server 7.0.

- Ideas for tuning a replication process to meet performance and scalability goals.

What Replication Does

The discussion that follows uses terminology based on a publication metaphor to stress the flow of data in the replication process. The primary database (from which changes are replicated to other databases) is referred to as a **publication**, or the **Publisher** when it is sending data; any database receiving replicated data is referred to as a **Subscriber**; an **article** is a table or stored procedure that is published (replicated).

Distribute Data to Other Sites

Replication can distribute data to locations closer to users. For example, a company may replicate data from its headquarters in New York to a branch office in London so users there can quickly access a local copy of the data. This reduces network traffic and increases transaction speed for users in London. Replicating data from an online transaction processing (OLTP) system to a dedicated reporting server keeps CPU-intensive reporting activity from interfering with transactional activity.

Combine Data from Multiple Sites

Replication can combine data from several locations to widen the scope of the data available for reports. For example, local branch-office databases can be published to a central database at corporate headquarters so that reporting and analysis can be performed on all corporate data. This topology is often referred to as a **central Subscriber**.

Provide Data Redundancy

Replication can copy data (although not schema, configuration, or security changes) from a primary database to a backup database (often called a "warm backup") for use if the primary database becomes inaccessible. Because it usually is preferable to have more than data, it is more common to copy transaction logs to the backup server. See "Using Standby Servers" in Microsoft SQL Server Books Online for more detail.

Support Mobile Users

Replication can provide mobile users with a local copy of the data that they can later synchronize with a central database.

Overview of Replication Technologies

SQL Server has six replication types, each of which offers different advantages and limitations. Significant capabilities of each type are compared in the table below and discussed in more detail throughout the chapter. See SQL Server Books Online for detailed descriptions of architecture, requirements, and setup procedures.

Snapshot replication. This periodically captures the current data at a given instant and sends it to a Subscriber, replacing the entire replica.

Transactional replication. This marks selected transactions in the Publisher database transaction log for replication, then distributes them asynchronously to Subscribers as incremental changes.

Replication of the execution of stored procedures. A variation of transactional replication, this replicates the execution of a stored procedure rather than its individual data changes. It is especially efficient for replicating maintenance-oriented operations that affect many rows.

Immediate-updating Subscribers. A variation on snapshot and transactional replication: an update at the Subscriber is immediately reflected at the Publisher by a trigger on the Subscriber's table that initiates a two-phase commit protocol. The Publisher then uses transaction replication to update other Subscribers.

Merge replication. Using triggers to track row changes, this compares the state of each row at the Publisher and Subscriber and reconciles differences. Built-in data reconciliation provides a high degree of site autonomy, making this a good choice for mobile users who need to update while disconnected from the network.

The table below summarizes the methods' characteristics. Some clarifying notes (marked by references in the table) are provided below.

SQL Server replication type overview.

Type	Site autonomy	Guaranteed transactional consistency	Bidirectional replication	Dynamic filtering (see note 1 below)	Vertical filtering	Supported on Desktop Edition
Snapshot	Yes	Yes	No	No	Yes	Yes
Transactional	Possible (see note 2 below)	Yes	Possible (see note 4 below)	No	Yes	No (see note 5 below)
Replication of the execution of stored procedures	Possible (see note 2 below)	No (see note 3 below)	Possible (see note 4 below)	N/A	N/A	No (see note 5 below)

Type	Site autonomy	Guaranteed transactional consistency	Bidirectional replication	Dynamic filtering (see note 1 below)	Vertical filtering	Supported on Desktop Edition
Transactional with immediate-updating Subscribers	No	Yes	Yes	No	Yes	No (see note 5 below)
Snapshot with immediate-updating Subscribers	No	Yes	Yes	No	Yes	Yes
Merge	Yes	No	Yes	Yes	No	Yes

Notes on the table:

1. Dynamic filtering uses an intrinsic function such as the Subscriber's **suser_sname()** as part of a filter clause. With dynamic filters you can replicate different data from a single publication to each Subscriber based on the Subscriber's user ID, which is much simpler than defining a separate publication with a static filter for each Subscriber. For more information see "Dynamic Filters" in SQL Server Books Online, and the "Filtering with Merge Publication" section, below.

2. Site autonomy for transactional replication usually requires that the Subscribers be read-only or that data be logically partitioned between sites so that each data element is modified by only one site. You can, however, build nonpartitioned bidirectional transactional replication by including custom conflict-resolution code in stored procedures. See "Implementing Nonpartitioned, Bidirectional, Transactional Replication" in SQL Server Books Online.

3. The replication mechanism does not guarantee transactional consistency when replicating the execution of stored procedures. See "Option: Replicating the Execution of Stored Procedures" in SQL Server Books Online.

4. See the section on bidirectional transactional replication, below.

5. The Desktop Edition of SQL Server can be a Subscriber to a transactional publication but cannot act as a transactional Publisher.

Questions for Gathering Basic Information

One way to work through the design of a replication solution is to ask questions that can help clarify important issues. Topics such as bidirectional replication, filtering, and synchronizing are discussed more fully later in this chapter and in Chapter 14.

Is Bidirectional Replication Required?

There are five methods for implementing bidirectional replication. Advantages and disadvantages are touched on in the next few questions and discussed more fully later in the chapter.

- Merge replication
- Transactional replication with immediate-updating Subscribers
- Snapshot replication with immediate-updating Subscribers
- Transactional replication with data partitioning between sites
- Transactional replication using stored procedures with conflict resolution logic

See the section "Bidirectional Replication" later in this chapter for a more detailed discussion of each of these options.

Will Subscribers Be Mobile Users Running Windows 9*x*?

The Desktop Edition of SQL Server that runs on Windows 9*x* does not support transactional replication, so merge replication is the only option for implementing bidirectional replication for mobile users running Windows 9*x*. You can use transactional, merge, or snapshot replication to replicate read-only data to Windows 9*x* Subscribers. (The Desktop Edition of SQL Server can subscribe to a transactional publication.)

Can Bidirectional Replication Partition Data Between Subscriber and Publisher to Avoid Conflicts?

In bidirectional replication, data partitioning eliminates replication conflicts by defining a group of rows that each site owns and that it alone can modify. Sites treat rows owned by other sites as read-only. This is usually implemented by including a column in the published table that identifies which site owns each row.

Regardless of which bidirectional transactional replication method you use, it is a good idea to partition the data between replicating sites to avoid conflicts.

Will the Subscribers Doing Bidirectional Replication Be Continuously Connected to the Publisher over a Highly Reliable Network?

The replicated table at the immediate-updating Subscriber can be modified only when a connection can be established to the Publisher because a trigger on the table has to initiate a two-phase commit protocol with the Publisher.

How Many Subscribers Will Be Involved in the Replication Scenario?

Pull Subscribers (running the Distribution or Merge Agent on the subscribing server rather than the distribution server) minimize the load on the distribution server and work best for large numbers of Subscribers. Consider allowing anonymous Subscribers so that each Subscriber does not have to be registered and tracked at the publishing server. See the "Pull and Anonymous Subscribers" section at the end of this chapter for more details.

How Large Are the Published Tables?

Synchronizing large tables requires time and network bandwidth. See the synchronizing section in the Chapter 14 for tips on decreasing the amount of time required for synchronization.

How Many Data Modifications Occur Against the Published Tables Each Hour?

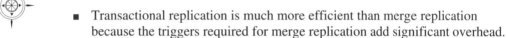

Two points related to replicating large numbers of transactions:

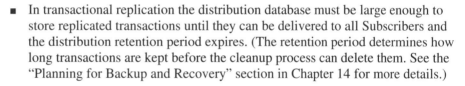

- Transactional replication is much more efficient than merge replication because the triggers required for merge replication add significant overhead.

- In transactional replication the distribution database must be large enough to store replicated transactions until they can be delivered to all Subscribers and the distribution retention period expires. (The retention period determines how long transactions are kept before the cleanup process can delete them. See the "Planning for Backup and Recovery" section in Chapter 14 for more details.)

How Quickly Do Transactions Need to Be Replicated to Other Sites?

In high transaction-rate environments, transactional replication has significantly lower overhead and latency than merge replication. In low to moderate transaction-rate environments, either method can provide latency as low as a few seconds. You can minimize latency by scheduling the Merge or Distribution Agents to run continuously.

How Will Replication Affect Transactional Consistency?

Merge replication's conflict resolution prevents it from guaranteeing transactional consistency, but you can overcome this by partitioning the data between sites to eliminate conflicts. Standard transactional replication guarantees transactional consistency but does not resolve conflicts.

See the white paper "Replication for Microsoft SQL Server 7.0" for a detailed discussion of transactional consistency. (Go to http://www.microsoft.com/sql/ and look under "Mobile Computing.")

Do Subscribers Need a Subset of the Rows in the Published Tables?

If it is not necessary to publish all rows in a table to all Subscribers, you can filter out some of the rows (called **horizontal partitioning**). This minimizes the amount of data transmitted across the network, stored in the replication system tables, and stored in the Subscriber database, but it slows down the Log Reader Agent in transactional replication and the Merge Agent in merge replication.

See the "Performance and Scalability Issues" section later in this chapter for more on filtering.

Do Subscribers Need All of the Columns in the Published Tables?

Transactional and snapshot replication allow you to select which published table columns you want to replicate (called **vertical partitioning**). This can decrease the amount of data transmitted across the network and stored in the subscribing databases.

SQL Server 7.0 merge replication does not support vertical partitioning.

Bidirectional Replication

In SQL Server 6.5, if you could not partition data between sites, implementing bidirectional replication required a lot of custom coding to handle conflicts and control loopback. SQL Server 7.0 simplifies this with two new options (*merge replication* and *immediate-updating Subscribers*). Another option (*subscription loopback detection*) even simplifies bidirectional transactional replication.

The options and issues discussed in this section can help you select the best option for your replication environment.

Partition Data Between Sites When Possible

Partitioning defines a group of rows so that only one site can change them. Ownership usually is indicated in a column in the published table. For example, you could include a *branch ID* to indicate which branch created and owns the record. Partitioning avoids conflicts, which is always preferable to incurring the overhead and administrative burden of resolving them.

Bidirectional Replication Using Merge Replication

Merge replication is usually the simplest bidirectional method because it includes a built-in conflict resolution mechanism that you can base on priority, time, or a value you customize.

One downside is that it uses triggers on the published tables, and the overhead these add to each transaction makes this method slower than transactional replication. Another is that it does not guarantee transactional integrity because it replicates net changes at the row or column level, and they are rejected if they conflict with changes made at other sites. You can avoid this by using partitioning.

See the white paper "Replication for Microsoft SQL Server 7.0" for a detailed discussion regarding transactional consistency. (Go to http://www.microsoft.com /sql/ and look under "Mobile Computing.")

Bidirectional Replication Using Immediate-Updating Subscribers

Using the immediate-updating Subscribers option you can implement transactional or snapshot bidirectional replication. A trigger in the replicated tables at the Subscriber site detects modifications and starts a two-phase commit with the Publisher.

Transactions are applied at the Publisher using stored procedures that determine if the modification at the Subscriber will conflict with any prior modifications at the Publisher. Thus, even though the actual datatype for the Subscriber replicated table is binary, the table must have a timestamp column in which to insert the value of the Publisher's timestamp field. If the stored procedures find that changes have been made at the Publisher since the Subscriber received its last copy of the changes via the normal asynchronous transactional replication, the transaction is rolled back at both Subscriber and Publisher.

Because the transaction is replicated to all other Subscribers using the normal, asynchronous transactional or snapshot mechanism, there is some latency.

One major limitation is that an immediate-updating Subscriber site can modify the replicated tables only if the publishing site is available to participate in the two-phase commit, so this option is inappropriate when users must be able to update the Subscriber even when the network or publishing database are unavailable.

Another consideration is that the two-phase commit protocol adds overhead to modifications initiated at the immediate-updating Subscriber, making this option unsuitable when a very high rate of transactions occurs there.

See "Immediate Updating Subscribers" in SQL Server Books Online for more information.

Bidirectional Replication Using Transactional Replication with Partitioned Data

It is fairly easy to implement bidirectional transactional replication if you can avoid conflicts by partitioning the data between sites so that only one site can update any given row. Set up all sites as Publisher *and* Subscriber of the replicated table(s).

Note   You cannot use this option for sites that run Windows 9*x* because the Desktop Edition of SQL Server cannot act as a transactional Publisher.

When using bidirectional, transactional replication you need to deal with replication loops (transactions initiated at a site get replicated back to it). For example, the diagram below shows an insert transaction initiated at site A. The transaction is replicated to Site B, which then tries to replicate the insert back to Site A, but the Distribution Agent reports a duplicate key error because the row already exists at Site A.

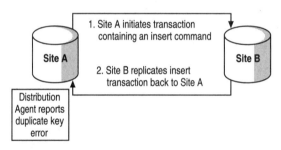

Figure 13.1   Example of replication looping.

To stop replication looping you have to set the subscription *loopback_detection* option by calling the **sp_addsubscription** stored procedure. You cannot set this through SQL Server Enterprise Manager.

Note   SQL Server Books Online incorrectly indicates that the published table must have a timestamp column to use the subscription *loopback_detection* option. It does not, but it does have to have a timestamp column to use the immediate-updating Subscriber option.

Figure 13.2 shows bidirectional, transactional replication between three sites. The replication scenario is organized in a hub-and-spoke topology, meaning that all data flows through a central site (Site A). There is no direct connection between

Sites B and C. The example uses the *loopback_detection* option to avoid replication loops. Note that data is partitioned between sites to avoid conflicts. Rows in boldface are owned by the site; rows in normal typeface are treated as read-only.

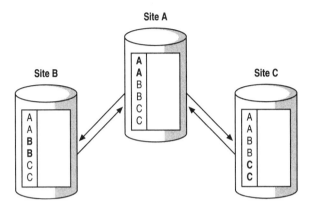

Figure 13.2   Bidirectional transactional replication with partitioned data.

Bidirectional Replication Using Transactional Replication with Conflict Resolution Logic

If you cannot logically partition data between sites you can still implement bidirectional replication using transactional replication if you write custom stored procedures that apply changes to the Subscribers and handle conflicts. This can be tricky to implement correctly because you must consider all possible conflict scenarios and handle them appropriately.

Here is the procedure:

1. Set up each site as a Publisher of the replicated table(s).

2. Set up each site as a Subscriber to the replicated table(s). When defining the subscriptions use the loopback detection option so that transactions initiated at a Subscriber aren't replicated back to it.

3. Create custom stored procedures that apply changes to the Subscribers and handle conflicts.

See the "Implementing Nonpartitioned, Bidirectional, Transactional Replication" topic in SQL Server Books Online for implementation details.

Potential Conflicts in Bidirectional, Nonpartitioned, Transactional Replication

You need to analyze each application to determine which conflicts can occur and how they should be handled. The information in this section can help you understand the types of conflicts that could occur in your replication environment.

As you'll see, a large variety of conflicts can occur, and building logic to handle all of them can be complex. One way to simplify the conflict resolution logic is to restrict the types of activity at each site so that you avoid certain categories of difficult conflicts. For example, you can make the restriction that no sites are allowed to update the key value of a row, or you can define straightforward rules regarding which site wins a conflict.

The table below shows the results of some replication actions. It is based on a scenario in which Sites A and B have just been synchronized and the operations at each site are modifying the same row. The third column shows the result of replicating the operations. Notes referenced in the table are provided below.

Potential replication conflicts.

Modifications at Site A	Modifications at Site B	Result of replication
Case 1. Insert row 1	Insert row 1	Duplicate key error. Distribution Agent stops until error is resolved.
		(See note 1 below)
Case 2. Update row 1 field a	Update row 1 field a	Data state of row diverges between two sites if field a is updated to different values at each site
		(See note 2 below)
Case 3. Update row 1 key field	Delete row 1	Data state of row diverges between two sites
		(See note 3 below)
Case 4. Update row 1 field a	Update row 1 field b	Data state of row converges to the same field values at both sites, but each site made the update without knowing about the update at the other site.
		(See note 4 below)
Case 5. Update row 1 (any fields)	Delete row 1	Delete takes precedence over update; Site B never sees the update from Site A
		(See note 5 below)
Case 6. Delete row 1, insert row 1	Delete row 1	Data state diverges between two sites
		(See note 6 below)
Case 7. Delete row 1, insert row 1	Update row 1 key field	Data state diverges between two sites
		(See note 7 below)
Case 8. Delete row 1, insert row 1	Update row 1 non-key field	Data state diverges between two sites
		(See note 8 below)

Notes on the table:

Case 1. Sites A and B both insert a record with the same key value.

Without conflict resolution logic, the Distribution Agent reports a duplicate key error and stops. It cannot be restarted until an administrator intervenes to resolve the problem.

Case 2. Sites A and B update the field to a different value.

Even without conflict resolution logic, the Distribution Agent does not report an error because both sites' update commands execute successfully when replicated to the other site. However, the data state of the row diverges between the two sites unless you include custom logic in the replication update stored procedure.

After replication, Site A has the updated value from Site B, and Site B has the updated value from Site A, but the two sites will never converge to the same value for that field. Note that the data state diverges only if both sites update the same field.

Case 3. Site A updates a key field; Site B deletes the row.

The data state of the row diverges between the two sites unless you include custom logic in the replication update and delete stored procedures. After replication, Site A has the row with the updated key value and Site B does not have the row at all.

Case 4. Site A updates a field; Site B updates a different field in the same row.

The Distribution Agent does not report an error because the commands at both sites execute successfully when replicated to the other site. Because each site updates the row without having seen the update from the other site, this can cause a logical conflict for some applications.

Case 5. Site A deletes a record; Site B updates that same record.

The Distribution Agent does not report an error because both Site A's delete and Site B's update execute successfully when replicated to the other site. Because Site A never sees Site B's replicated update, this can cause a logical conflict for some applications.

Case 6. Site A deletes a row, then inserts a row with the same key value; Site B deletes the row.

The data state of the row diverges between the two sites unless you include custom logic in the replication stored procedures. After replication, Site A does not have a row 1 as a result of the delete replicated from Site B. Site B has a row 1 as a result of the insert replicated from Site A.

Case 7. Site A deletes row 1, then inserts a row
with the same key value; Site B updates the key field of row 1.

The data state of the row diverges between the two sites unless you include custom logic in the replication stored procedures. After replication, Site A has a version of row 1 with the updated key field as a result of the update replicated from site B, but Site B has two versions of row 1: one with the original key value, and a second with the updated key value. This is because the delete replicated from Site A does not delete any rows at Site B because the key value for row 1 changes at Site B before the delete is replicated.

Case 8. Site A deletes row 1 then inserts a row
with the same key value; Site B updates a non-key field of row 1.

The data state of the row diverges between the two sites unless you include custom logic in the replication stored procedures. After replication, Site A has a version of row 1 that reflects the update to the non-key field, and Site B has a version that does not reflect the UPDATE to it.

Requirements and Limitations

Replicating Between Servers with Different Character Sets

A **character set** (also called a code page) is a set of 256 letters, numbers, and symbols. The printable characters in the first 128 values are always the same; the last 128 characters (also called extended characters) differ between character sets. The default character set for SQL Server versions 6.0, 6.5, and 7.0 is 1252 (also called ANSI, ISO 8859-1, or Latin 1 character set).

Replication between servers configured to use different character sets can cause data corruption if the data contains extended characters. The character codes themselves replicate correctly, but they are interpreted differently on SQL Servers configured with different character sets. For example, the symbol ` is stored as the extended character code value 130 on a server running the 1252 character set. When that character is replicated to a server running the 850 character set, the code is displayed as the character é.

 SQL Server 7.0 interprets any columns defined with data type **nchar**, **nvarchar**, or **ntext** as Unicode data—use this capability if you have to replicate between different languages.

See "Character Set" in SQL Server Books Online for additional information.

Replicating Between Servers with Different Sort Orders

A sort order is a set of rules that determines how character data is compared, how result sets are collated, and when compared characters are considered equal. The sort orders available depend on the character set.

Replication between servers using the same character set but different sort orders can run into problems when evaluating filter criteria. For example, suppose Server A and Server B both use the 1252 character set, but A uses dictionary sort order (case-insensitive) and B uses binary. The publication has a horizontal (row) filter with the condition "district = 'Northeast.'" A row in the *district* column with the value NORTHEAST is replicated on A (where NORTHEAST = Northeast) but is not replicated on B (where NORTHEAST ≠ Northeast).

You can use the stored procedure **sp_helpsort** to see which character set and sort order a SQL Server has been configured to use.

See "Sort Order" in SQL Server Books Online for more information.

Foreign Keys

When publishing tables with foreign key constraints you can choose whether to include the constraint in the definition of the article (the database subset to be replicated). You should include it to enforce referential integrity at the subscribing sites if they modify the published tables (bidirectional replication); you can often exclude it if the replicated tables are read-only at the Subscriber sites (because referential integrity is enforced at the publishing site).

If you include the foreign key constraints in the publication you should also include the tables they reference. Replication can fail if the article definition includes a foreign key constraint but not its referenced tables.

Foreign Key NOT FOR REPLICATION Option

Used with foreign key constraints, the NOT FOR REPLICATION option offers two advantages. First, when it is set at the Subscriber, it improves transactional and merge replication performance by allowing SQL Server to forego validation (because the option indicates that the reference was validated at the site where the user made the change).

Second, the foreign key NOT FOR REPLICATION option allows transactional replication to handle deferred updates to a table referenced by a foreign key at the Subscriber. (A deferred update is when a row update is changed into a row delete followed by a row insert.) When the updated column is part of a unique or clustered index, SQL Server performs an update as a deferred update—the Distribution Agent replicates the delete and insert commands to the Subscriber (rather than the original update). The problem occurs when the Distribution Agent tries to execute the delete half of the delete-insert pair against a Subscriber table that is referenced by a foreign key constraint. The replicated delete command fails with an error message indicating that the delete conflicts with the foreign key constraint.

For example, suppose a foreign key constraint on *Child_Table* in the subscribing database references *Parent_Table*, which is subscribed to a transactional publication. An update executed against *Parent_Table* in the publishing database is replicated to the Subscriber as a delete-insert pair but the delete fails against *Parent_Table* in the subscribing database if it attempts to delete a row referenced by a row in *Child_Table*. The Distribution Agent reports the failure and will not replicate any subsequent transactions until an administrator resolves the problem.

To avoid the problem, use the NOT FOR REPLICATION option in the foreign key constraint definition on the child table at the Subscriber. The option prevents SQL Server from checking that foreign key constraints are enforced when executing commands from the replication Distribution Agent. (The foreign key constraint is still enforced for commands from other users.)

Rule of thumb: always use the NOT FOR REPLICATION option when defining foreign key constraints that reference replicated tables in a subscribing database.

See "CREATE TABLE (T-SQL)", "CREATE TRIGGER (T-SQL)" and "Use the Not for Replication Option on the Identity Property" in SQL Server Books Online for more information.

Replication and Sequential Row ID Values

Replication complicates the task of defining unique row ID values across multiple sites. The replication scheme must avoid conflicts between row IDs at different sites. Three ways to do this are described below.

Use GUID (Globally Unique Identifier) Values

SQL Server 7.0 has a new data type called **uniqueidentifier** that holds a globally unique identifier (GUID). You can set up a table to automatically generate new GUID values by defining the column with the NEWID() function as the default value.

GUIDs are guaranteed to be unique across all sites and there is an endless supply, but they are long, non-sequential numbers that are difficult for users to read or use in a query, for example: 6FA2E608-D03A-11D2-A413-0080C72CF4DB.

Combine a Sequential ID with Another Value to Create a Unique Combination

For example, combining an identity column with a site ID creates a composite primary key that is unique across all sites within a replication scenario. If you do this, the identity column must be defined with the NOT FOR REPLICATION option so that replicated rows maintain their identity value.

There are two additional issues that apply only when using transactional replication to publish a table with an identity property. First, the .SCH file that is used to create the table at the Subscriber will not include the identity property even if the published table has one. You must edit the .SCH file to add the identity property (with the NOT FOR REPLICATION option) or initialize the table at the Subscriber manually. (The .SCH file is created by the Snapshot Agent and placed in the \Mssql7\Repldata directory.)

Second, INSERT statements executed at the Subscriber must include a column list when the subscribing table includes an identity property with the NOT FOR REPLICATION option. The default mechanism for transactional replication is to apply the transactions at the Subscriber using the **sp_MSins_<table_name>** stored procedure, but this procedure's INSERT command does not use a column list. You can customize the stored procedure so that the INSERT statement includes a column list, or you can configure the publication to replicate the INSERT command (rather than a call to the stored procedure) and define the publication with the *use column names in the SQL statements* option.

Assign Ranges of Sequential ID Values to Each Site

This common solution gives each site a predetermined range of ID values. Ranges can be assigned automatically (using identity columns) or calculated with code in the front-end application, a stored procedure, or a trigger. Ranges must not overlap, of course.

If you use an *Identity* column for this method, set its seed to the minimum range value and define a check constraint to make sure it is not incremented beyond the maximum range value.

If you use the **identity** property and the CHECK constraint or trigger, you have to use the NOT FOR REPLICATION option to disable them when data is entered by replication. This permits rows to maintain their ID when replicated to other sites.

See "Planning for Replication" in SQL Server Books Online for more information.

Performance and Scalability Issues

This section discusses performance and scalability issues you should take into account when designing replication. It does not explain in detail how to set up replication; it simply supplements information in Microsoft SQL Server Books Online (especially "Replication Model", "Enhancing Performance" and "Filtering Data to Improve Efficiency") and the white paper "Replication for Microsoft SQL Server 7.0." Review these sources before making any design decisions.

Replication Mechanisms

Transactional vs. Merge Replication in a High Transaction-Rate Environment

Transactional replication generates less processor overhead than does merge replication, so in high transaction-rate environments it generally achieves higher throughput. The Log Reader Agent reads the Publisher's transaction log, finds transactions marked for replication, then copies them to the distribution database. Not much processing is required so there is little CPU overhead.

Merge replication uses triggers in each row or column of the published tables to capture changes and record them in the merge system tables (also in the published database). Processing trigger code adds significant CPU overhead in high transaction-rate environments.

Consider Snapshot Replication for Large Tables with a High Level of Data Volatility

A bulk copy process utility (**bcp**) can move large amounts of data to SQL Server Subscribers much faster than transactional or merge replication, so snapshot replication can be the fastest way to synchronize a large table when a large percentage of its data has changed.

 Rule of thumb: if more than 30% of the rows in a large table have been modified since the last synchronization, replicating a snapshot of the entire table may be faster than replicating the data changes using transactional or merge replication.

There is a drawback. The Snapshot Agent on the Publisher places a shared table lock on all published tables while bulk copying data. This ensures a consistent snapshot but prevents users from modifying the table, although they can still query it. On the Subscriber, the Distribution Agent also requires exclusive access to published tables while it refreshes the data.

Transactional Replication via Execution of Stored Procedures

SQL Server 7.0 allows you to replicate the *execution* of stored procedures rather than the data changes resulting from them. This can dramatically improve efficiency in situations where a single SQL statement executed against the Publisher is decomposed and replicated as multiple operations at the Subscriber. In these and similar circumstances, it is more efficient to re-execute the procedure at the Subscriber, rather than replicate the changes created by the execution.

For example, a single UPDATE statement affecting 10,000 rows might be replicated as 10,000 single-row update operations, each of which has to be stored in the distribution database, transmitted across the network, and executed on the Subscribers. This is because SQL Server performs operations against individual rows, so it records the operation as a series of 10,000 delete operations in the Publisher's transaction log. The transactional replication Log Reader Agent scans the log and replicates a DELETE command for each delete operation. This same is true for INSERT statements.

It can be worse when updates affect columns that are part of the key for a unique or clustered index. SQL Server breaks these into a delete-insert pair of operations, so if the update modifies the primary key for 10,000 rows in a published table, 10,000 delete operations are replicated, followed by 10,000 insert operations.

To see what is actually replicated, execute the **sp_browsereplcmds** stored procedure in the distribution database to see a readable result set of the replicated commands stored there.

You can avoid these inefficiencies by modifying the published table with stored procedures, then replicating their execution. For example, you can create a stored procedure called **sp_my_delete** that deletes rows from the published table, then include it in a transactional publication. When you execute it **sp_my_delete**, only a single call to that stored procedure is replicated to Subscribers regardless of how many rows it deletes.

You must replicate stored procedures carefully. One potential problem is that the stored procedure may yield different results when executed at different Subscribers or the Publisher, if, for example, a table modified or referenced in the stored procedure has different data at different sites.

See "Option: Replicating the Execution of Stored Procedures" in SQL Server Books Online for more information.

Filtering

When you plan and implement replication, you should make sure that, whenever possible, Subscribers receive only necessary data. This minimizes replication traffic and can help enforce business rules that dictate which data subsets are available to each Subscriber.

Filtering can accomplish this but it involves a performance trade off. Filters create more complex query processing for SQL Server, so replication rates may be slower for filtered articles, although this additional overhead can be offset if there are significantly fewer rows to replicate than the total unfiltered data set.

Vertical Filtering in a Transactional Publication

Vertical filtering, which limits the columns replicated as part of an article, can increase performance by decreasing the amount of storage required in the distribution database and the amount of data transmitted when large character, text, or image columns are excluded from the publication. Best of all, it does not significantly affect performance.

Merge replication does not support vertical filtering under SQL Server 7.0, although you can work around this limitation by partitioning the table into two physical tables with a one-to-one relationship—one containing only the columns that need to be published and the other containing the rest.

Horizontal Filtering in a Transactional Publication

Horizontal filtering does impose a significant amount of overhead and thus decreases replication throughput.

The Log Reader Agent implements horizontal filtering in a transactional publication when it reads rows marked for replication from the Publisher's transaction log. For each row it reads from the transaction log, the agent must evaluate the filter criteria to see if the operation needs to be replicated. This decreases the agent's throughput.

Subscriber-Side Filtering with Transactional Replication

You can implement Subscriber-side filtering by using custom replication stored procedures instead of defining a filter condition in the transactional publication. This transmits all of the rows across the network, but on the Subscriber site the Log Reader Agent calls the stored procedure, which applies only changes that match the filter criteria.

Subscriber-side filtering avoids the overhead incurred when the Log Reader Agent compares every row against the filter criteria, but adds network overhead by sending all rows across the network. It therefore works best when few rows are filtered out and most rows would be transmitted across the network to the Subscriber anyway.

See "Using Custom Stored Procedures in Articles" in SQL Server Books Online for more information.

Filtering with Merge Publication

Merge replication uses three filtering concepts: subset filters, join filters, and dynamic filters.

Subset Filters

This is the simplest type: defining a subset filter clause for an article. The clause is similar to a *where* clause condition in a select statement and should be in the form **column_name = value_expression**.

Join Filters

Join filters (also called merge filters) define a cross-table relationship that is enforced during a merge (similar to specifying a join between two tables). The filter names two articles and specifies the join condition to represent the relationship between the two tables in them. The join condition is usually in the form: **Table1.Column = Table2.Column**.

Dynamic Filters

The filters described above are static and require a separate publication for each partition. This is fine if there are only a few partitions, but if numerous Subscribers require different partitions a lot of administrative overhead is required to set up and maintain a publication for each Subscriber.

To address this problem, merge replication supports *dynamic* filters—subset filter clause conditions that use a system function that is evaluated differently for each Subscriber during merge replication. The most common system functions used for this purpose are SUSER_SNAME() and HOST_NAME().

Physically Partitioning Data into Multiple Tables

For applications requiring maximum throughput, you want to minimize the rows delivered to each Subscriber, and you often can do this more effectively by developing natural partitions of the table than by using horizontal filtering. This avoids the overhead associated with resolving filter conditions but it can make schema maintenance more complex.

For example, three branch locations (A, B, and C) each own their own accounts but need read-only access to the other branches' activity. You can create a separate account table for each branch. Branch A publishes its activity to B and C and subscribes to publications from them. Applications at the branches can query account information with a view that uses *Union All* operators to present a single logical table. Union views are not updateable, so any data modifications must be made directly against the base table; they also generate overhead.

See "Fragmenting as an Alternative to Filtering" in SQL Server Books Online for more information.

Pull and Anonymous Subscribers

Use Pull Subscriptions to Support a Large Number of Subscribers

Pull subscription has two important features: it is administered from the Subscriber rather than the Publisher, and the Distribution or Merge Agent runs on the Subscriber rather than the distribution server. Push subscription works the opposite way.

For replication, one merge or Distribution Agent is created for each Subscriber to a published database and each task requires CPU time and other resources. Pull subscription is the best choice for large numbers of Subscribers, because it runs the Distribution Agent or Merge Agent on the Subscriber, so it requires fewer CPU resources at the distribution server. It also works well for mobile users because the Subscriber runs the Distribution Agent or Merge Agent and thus controls when changes are synchronized. The disadvantage is that it decentralizes replication management: each pull subscription must be created and scheduled from the Subscriber rather than the Publisher.

To decide between push and pull subscriptions, you have to weigh the convenience of centrally administered push subscriptions against the greater scalability of pull subscriptions.

Merge replication is much more CPU intensive than transactional, so while it may be practical to run a dozen concurrent transactional Distribution Agents on a single Distributor, running more than a few concurrent Merge Agents on it consumes significant CPU resources.

Anonymous Subscriptions Can Be Useful for Supporting Very Large Numbers of Subscribers

Anonymous subscriptions are pull subscriptions that do not register Subscriber information at the Publisher. In other words, the Publisher does not "see" anonymous subscriptions. They are useful when there are hundreds or thousands of Subscribers (as in Internet-based replication) and keeping track of them would simply be too cumbersome.

If anonymous Subscribers are defined, the distribution clean up task will not remove any distribution database information until the retention period expires, rather than removing it as soon as all Subscribers have received it. Anonymous subscriptions can cause more information to be retained longer in the distribution database.

Multiple Distribution Databases on a Central Distribution Server

With SQL Server 7.0 you can create multiple distribution databases on a single server and configure a single computer to act as the distribution server for multiple publishing servers. This can lead to excessive contention on the replication system tables, though, and it often is safer to create a separate distribution database for each publishing server.

A publishing server must be configured to work with only one distribution database. You cannot publish two databases on a single server and configure them to use different distribution databases.

C H A P T E R   1 4

Deploying Replication

By Jeff Rogers,
MCS—New York

The previous chapter looked at tactics you can use to create a replication strategy. This chapter extends the discussion into deployment, concentrating on functionality, advantages, and trade-offs. To configure replication you have to understand how to set up and control its various elements, and to do that you have to know something about how they work. These are covered first. Then synchronization is discussed in detail: how to tell when it has been accomplished, what to do when it hasn't. Much of this chapter emphasizes automating replication mechanisms, which is made easier by new features in SQL Server 7.0, although technical details on manual methods are also included because they serve as safety nets for some automated procedures and because in some circumstances they are superior. Also discussed is how to plan for backup and recovery—the natural conclusion, you might say, of the topic of replication.

What You'll Find in This Chapter

- Scripting, alerts and other replication topics: how they work and how to incorporate them.

- How to use stored procedures for automation.

- How to detect when the Subscriber is not synchronized with the Publisher and how to automate a response.

- How to automate synchronization and how to perform it manually—and the conditions that help you choose which to use.

- Tips to boost performance when loading data onto Subscribers.

- How to plan backup and recovery.

Configuring Replication

This section explains how to configure replication to improve manageability and reliability. It reviews some basic topics (discussed in more detail in Microsoft SQL Server Books Online) then provides more detailed advice on using SQL Server 7.0's new Subscriber validation feature.

The discussion uses terminology based on a publication metaphor to stress the flow of data in the replication process. The primary database (from which changes are replicated to other databases) is referred to as a **publication**, or the **Publisher** when it is sending data; any database receiving replicated data is referred to as a **Subscriber**; an **article** is a table or stored procedure that is published (replicated).

Scripting

SQL Server 7.0 simplifies the scripting of publications, articles, subscriptions, and other replication configuration settings. You can now script the installation or removal of replication, or the creation or removal of individual publications and their subscriptions. This can be useful for backup and recovery, and for automating setup when you have numerous servers with an identical replication configuration (although you still have to edit server names before running a replication script on different computers).

Alerts

Alerts, which can be set to respond to normal replication events as well as error conditions, can help create a robust replication environment. SQL Server 7.0 has eight pre-configured alerts that respond to important replication events. They are disabled by default. To activate them:

1. Configure the system message to be logged to the Windows NT Application Event Log.
2. Define the action to be taken.
3. Enable the alert.

SQL Server 7.0 pre-configured replication alerts.

Alert name	Message number	Message format
Replication: Agent custom shutdown	20578	Replication: Agent custom shutdown
Replication: Agent failure	14151	Replication-'%s': agent '%s' failed. '%s'
Replication: Agent retry	14152	Replication-'%s': agent '%s' scheduled for retry. '%s'

(continued)

Alert name	Message number	Message format
Replication: Agent success	14150	Replication-'%s': agent '%s' succeeded. '%s'
Replication: Expired subscription dropped	14157	The subscription created by Subscriber '%s' to publication '%s' has expired and has been dropped
Replication: Subscriber has failed data validation	20574	Subscriber '%s' subscription to article '%s' in publication '%s' failed data validation.
Replication: Subscriber has passed data validation	20575	Subscriber '%s' subscription to article '%s' in publication '%s' passed data validation.
Replication: Subscription reinitialized after validation failure	20572	Subscriber '%s' subscription to article '%s' in publication '%s' has been reinitialized after a validation failure.

For more information on defining replication alerts, see "Monitoring Replication Alerts," "Managing SQL Server Messages," and "Defining Alerts" in SQL Server Books Online.

Inactivity Threshold

The inactivity threshold allows you to monitor the health of agents by checking that all agents with a running status have logged a history message within a specified period. If one has not, error 14151 is raised. It sends a message to an operator or takes any other action you define when you enable it.

You set the inactivity threshold through the Replication Monitor in SQL Server Enterprise Manager. It is implemented by the **Replication Agents Checkup** job, which runs the stored procedure **sp_replication_agent_check** based on the **heartbeat_interval** parameter (equal to the inactivity threshold). The procedure looks at each running agent and raises a 14151 error for any agents that have not logged a history message within the heartbeat interval.

Agent Profiles

Each replication agent is associated with an agent profile, which lists the parameters it uses when it runs. Profiles are are easy to modify (using system stored procedures) and a single profile can be used by multiple agents. For example, you can modify an agent profile to turn on the **-validate** option and all Merge Agents associated with that profile will perform a synchronization validation the next time they run. (See the "Verifying that Publisher and Subscriber are Synchronized" section below.)

Each agent also contains a set of command-line parameters you can view or modify using SQL Server Enterprise Manager. Command-line parameters for an agent take precedence if they conflict with agent profile parameters.

Here are the system stored procedures you can use to modify agent profiles. (See SQL Server Books Online for details.)

- **sp_help_agent_profile.** Displays a list of profiles.
- **sp_update_agent_profile.** Changes the profile associated with a specific agent.
- **sp_add_agent_profile.** Creates a new agent profile.
- **sp_drop_agent_profile.** Drops an agent profile.
- **sp_help_agent_parameter.** Displays the list of parameters for a specific profile.
- **sp_add_agent_parameter.** Adds a parameter and its value to an agent profile.
- **sp_change_agent_parameter.** Changes a parameter of an agent profile.
- **sp_drop_agent_parameter.** Drops a parameter of an agent profile.

These system tables store information for the agents, jobs, and profiles. (See SQL Server Books Online for details.)

- **distribution..MSsnapshot_agents**
- **distribution..MSlogreader_agents**
- **distribution..MSdistribution_agents**
- **distribution..MSmerge_agents**
- **msdb..MSagent_profiles**
- **msdb..MSagent_parameters**
- **msdb..sysjobs**
- **msdb..sysjobsteps**

Verifying That Publisher and Subscriber Are Synchronized

SQL Server 7.0 has a new inline validation capability that allows you to check data synchronization, in most cases without stopping replication. It can compare Publisher and Subscriber rowcounts (relatively fast) or rowcounts *and* checksums (takes longer). This can be useful:

- After recovering the publishing, distributing, or subscribing database
- When using a manual process to initialize the Subscriber
- When verifying that data has been replicated correctly

To help you plan and automate the process and interpret the results, here are the steps SQL Server uses to validate a transactional publication:

1. The validation process starts with a call to **sp_article_validation** or **sp_publication_validation** (which calls **sp_article_validation** for every article in the publication).

2. **Sp_article_validation** calls **sp_table_validation** on the published table and saves the values returned for the rowcount and checksum of the published table.

3. **Sp_article_validation** posts a call to **sp_table_validation** in the Publisher transaction log and passes the rowcount and checksum values from step 2. The normal transactional replication mechanism sends the **sp_table_validation** to Subscribers, validating them at the point when they should have the same data the Publisher had in step 2.

4. **Sp_table_validation** raises a system message indicating the success or failure of the validation check at the Subscriber. (These are different system messages than the 20574 or 20575 system messages raised in the next step.)

5. The Distribution Agent raises the 20574 system message if the validation fails and 20575 if it passes, and posts related information to the **msdb..sysreplicationalerts** table. The Distribution Agent itself does not fail: it records a warning in SQL Server Enterprise Manager **Session Details of the Distribution Agent** log. You can read it by double-clicking on a history displayed in the **Distribution Agent History** window.

Steps SQL Server uses to validate a merge publication:

1. The validation process starts when the Merge Agent is run with the **–validate** parameter set to 1 (for rowcount only) or 2 (for rowcount *and* checksum). (See "Replication Merge Agent Utility" in SQL Server Books Online for more information on settings.)

2. The Merge Agent runs **sp_table_validation** against the Publisher and Subscriber and compares the selected values.

3. **Sp_table_validation** agent raises the 20574 system message if the validation fails and 20575 if it passes, and posts related information to the **msdb..sysreplicationalerts** table. The Merge Agent itself does not fail: it records a warning in SQL Server Enterprise Manager **Session Details of the Merge Agent** log. You can read it by double-clicking on a history displayed in the **Merge Agent History** window.

Automating a Response to Validation Failure

To automate a response to the validation process:

- Enable the pre-configured alert for message ID 20574 that fires when validation fails.

- Configure that alert to take an appropriate response: notify an operator or run a job to resynchronize the Subscriber.

See "Automating a Response to an Alert" in SQL Server Books Online for information on using the **msdb..sysrreplicationalerts** table to automate alert responses.

You can also set up mechanisms to automatically validate Subscribers periodically. The mechanism is different for transactional and merge publication methods, and different for Merge Agents that run continuously.

To periodically validate Subscribers to a transactional publication, you create a job that runs **sp_validate_publication** on a schedule (for example, every night at 1:00 a.m.).

To periodically validate a Subscriber to a merge publication where the Merge Agent is not continuous, you can create a job that uses **sp_change_agent_parameter** to change **–validate** to 1 or 2 at some time (say, 1:00 a.m.) and another job to re-set **–validate** to 0 when the check has been run.

To periodically validate Subscribers to a merge publication where the Merge Agent runs continuously, you have to set the **–ValidateInterval** parameter to how often, in minutes, the Subscriber should be validated (default 60). For example, to validate every 24 hours, set **–validate** to 1 or 2 and **–ValidateInterval** to 1440. (See "Replication Merge Agent Utility" in SQL Server Books Online for more settings information.)

Blocking Caused by Validation Process

The rowcount and checksum values for a given table are calculated by calling **sp_table_validation**, which guarantees accuracy by placing a shared table lock on the table while it calculates values. The rowcount-only mode usually is faster, reducing the amount of time the table is locked.

Sample Execution Times

The table below shows some sample times for running **sp_table_validation** on a single table. Tests were performed on a machine with 2 Intel 333 MHz Pentium II processors, 500 MB of RAM and 1 9-GB SCSI hard drive. Note the large difference in total execution time for both modes (rowcount-only and rowcount + checksum) when the table is already in the data cache. If the table has to be read into cache during the check, then disk I/O becomes the limiting factor, so total execution times are the same for both modes, although CPU utilization still is higher for the rowcount + checksum mode.

Sample run times for sp_table_validation on a single table (in seconds).

Table Size	Table in Data Cache		Table not in Data Cache	
	rowcount-only	rowcount + checksum	rowcount-only	rowcount + checksum
100,000 rows, 5 MB	< 1	< 1	< 1	< 1
1,000,000 rows, 50 MB	1	4	5	5
5,000,000 rows, 250 MB	3	22	30	30

Validating Bidirectional Transactional Replication

Sp_publication_validation may detect spurious errors for bidirectional transactional scenarios, including scenarios that use immediate-updating Subscribers, when modifications at the Subscriber cause its rowcount and checksum values to differ from the Publisher. (See the description of the validation process earlier in this section.)

To validate Subscriber synchronization reliably you have to stop all Subscriber modifications (except those caused by replication) during validation—that is, from the time **sp_publication_validation** is run at the Publisher until the **sp_table_validation** call has been replicated and executed at the Subscriber.

If the Subscriber passes validation, the distribution task issues message 20575. You can enable the pre-configured alert for this message as a trigger to re-start modifications at the Subscriber.

Additional Issues with Synchronization Validation

- The validation process excludes text and image columns when calculating checksum values.

- For the checksum to be valid, the table must be structured identically at the Publisher and the Subscriber: the same columns in the same order, the same data types and lengths, and the same NULL/NOT NULL conditions.

- Checksum validation cannot be used with vertically filtered articles because the Subscriber has only a subset of the Publisher's columns, which results in different checksum values.

- Floating-point values can cause checksum differences if character mode **bcp** is used to synchronize the Subscriber, because there are small, unavoidable differences in precision when converting between a floating point number and the number's character string representation. You can avoid this by using native-mode **bcp**, or by using a numeric or decimal datatype instead of floating-point. Character-mode **bcp** is used whenever the publication has heterogeneous Subscribers.

- To ensure that checksum values are accurate, the table at the Publisher should be created using a single CREATE TABLE statement rather than a CREATE TABLE statement followed by an ALTER TABLE statement to add a column. The two methods cause slight differences in the table's internal structure, which can result in different checksum values even when the data is identical. To make sure the internal table structures are identical, compare the offset column values for each table in the **syscolumns** table.

New Subscribers must be initialized with the schema and data of the published tables. This can be done automatically by the replication agents or manually by the administrator. You determine which method will be used when you create the subscription. If you create it using the wizard, you can select whether you want to initialize the data and schema at the Subscriber. If you use a stored procedure to create the subscription, set the procedure's **sync_type** parameter to either **automatic** or **none**.

Synchronization

This section begins by reviewing the automatic synchronization process and offers performance tips. Next it discusses situations in which you might want to initialize the Subscriber manually and shows how to initialize merge and transactional Subscribers manually. Then it discusses tools you can use to load data on the Subscriber and suggests performance enhancements.

Automatic Synchronization Process

Automatic synchronization involves two basic steps: the Snapshot Agent prepares the initialization files, and another agent (the Merge Agent for merge replication, the Distribution Agent for snapshot or transactional replication) applies the initialization files to the Subscriber. Normal replication cannot take place until both steps are completed.

The Snapshot Agent prepares the initialization files, which consist of script files and data files. Script files are used to create the Subscriber replicated tables and stored procedures, and other Subscriber-side objects necessary for the replication process. Data files are created with the **bcp** utility, and are used to populate the Subscriber data tables. Both types of files are placed in the *Mssql7\Repldata* directory on the distribution database.

Another agent (Merge Agent for merge replication, Distribution Agent for snapshot or transactional replication) initializes the Subscriber by applying the script and data files there. It uses script files to create the tables and other objects, then populates them, usually by importing data from data files using **bcp**. But **bcp** is not used in two cases. When non-SQL Server Subscribers are initialized, the table is populated using a series of single-row INSERT statements generated from the **bcp** data file created by the Snapshot Agent; when Subscribers are synched to a merge publication with a dynamic filter, the Merge Agent extracts data directly from the published tables and inserts it at the Subscriber using single-row INSERT statements.

Here are some hints for improving automatic synchronization performance.

- **Nonlogged Bulk Load.** Automatic synchronization uses **bcp** to load data into Subscriber tables. By default, **bcp** logs every row copied, and this slows down the **bcp** process and fills up space in the transaction log. You can alleviate this by using **bcp** in nonlogged mode (although operations such as space allocations are still logged). To use nonlogged mode, these conditions must be met:

  - The database option **select into/bulkcopy** must be set to **true**.

  - The target table must either have no indexes, or, if there are indexes, then the table must not have any rows when the bulk load operation starts.

  - The target table must not be part of a publication although it can be a subscribed table.

  - The TABLOCK hint must be specified either in the **bcp** command or by using the **sp_tableoption** to set the **tablock on bulk load** option.

- **Use Native Format bcp Files Whenever Possible.** The Snapshot Agent can create **bcp** files in either native or wide-character (Unicode) formats. Wide-character files (two bytes per character) can be more than four times larger and they take longer to produce and to apply on the Subscriber.

  You determine the format when you define the publication. If you use the Create Publication Wizard and you select that all Subscribers are running SQL Server, the Snapshot Agent will create native-format **bcp** files, otherwise it will create wide-character files.

  If you use stored procedures to create the publication, you set the **sync_mode** parameter of the **sp_addpublication** or **sp_addmergepublication** stored procedures to either **character** or **native**. Non-SQL Server Subscribers are not allowed if the publication is created with the **native** option.

  Use wide-character format files only when you know there will be non-SQL Server Subscribers. If you have to replicate a large table to a mix of SQL Server and non-SQL Server Subscribers, you can synchronize the Subscribers with manually generated **bcp** files to avoid the overhead of using wide-character format files for all Subscribers.

See the "Manual Synchronization" section (next) for details.

- **The Database Should Be Large Enough To Hold the Fully Populated Replicated Tables.** This prevents costly expansion during synchronization.

- **Increase the QueryTimeout Values for the Distribution or Merge Agents.** This may be necessary when synchronizing large publications or merge publications with dynamic filters. Add the parameter **-QueryTimout <value>** to the agent's command line in the **Replication Monitor** section of SQL Server Enterprise Manager. (See "Replication Distribution Agent Utility" and "Replication Merge Agent Utility" in SQL Server Books Online for a detailed syntax definition.)

Here are some tips specific to Subscriber initialization of merge publications:

- **Add *rowguid* Column to the Published Table before Initializing a Merge Publication.** If there isn't a *rowguid* column in the merge published table, the Snapshot Agent will add one when it runs the first time. This can take a while for large tables, extending the Snapshot Agent's run time.

- **Install SQL Server Service Pack 1 or Later Before Using Merge Publications with Dynamic Filters.** SQL Server Service Pack 1 includes significant Subscriber initialization enhancements for merge publications with dynamic filters. Without them, Subscriber initialization can be extremely lengthy for any article with a published table containing more than a few thousand records. (See the "Filtering with Merge Publication" section in Chapter 13 for information on filters.)

- **Avoid Automatic Synchronization of Merge Publications with Dynamic Filters for Subscribers with Large Partitions of the Published Data.** The time required to initialize a Subscriber to a merge publication with a dynamic filter increases dramatically along with the number of rows in the Subscriber's partition of the publication. This is a problem only if the publication uses a dynamic filter (one using an intrinsic function such as **suser_sname()** in the filter clause).

  For example, if a published table has a total of 300,000 rows, but only 2,000 rows fall in the partition of Subscriber A, then automatic synchronization might take only a few minutes to initialize Subscriber A with those 2,000 rows. But if 100,000 rows fall in A's partition, it might take hours. You may need to initialize Subscribers manually when more than a few thousand rows fall within their partition. (This figure is a rough estimate; you should conduct tests to determine how long Subscriber initialization will take in your replication environment.)

  See "Manual Synchronization" below for more details.

Manual Synchronization

There are circumstances in which it is faster and more efficient to handle synchronization manually, for instance if you have to:

- Initialize a Subscriber with a 10-GB table. Rather than allow SQL Server to use the standard, single **bcp** process to populate the table, it may be faster to segment the data file into multiple files and then use multiple bulk insert processes to load the table in parallel.

- Initialize a Subscriber with a 100-MB table when the Subscriber is connected via a slow dialup network link. It may be faster and more reliable to copy the data file to a tape or CD, take it to the Subscriber, and load it manually.

- Replicate all of the tables and stored procedures in a database to a remote location either for redundancy or load distribution purposes. To initialize the Subscriber, it might be faster and simpler to back up the published database and load the backup at the Subscriber.

- Synchronize a Subscriber to a merge publication with dynamic filters. Initializing Subscribers to a merge publication that includes dynamic filters can take a very long time if the filter passes more than a few thousand rows to that Subscriber. It may be dramatically faster to manually bulk copy the appropriate data from the Publisher to the Subscriber.

- Replicate to a Subscriber that already has the necessary schema and data. In this case you can bypass Subscriber initialization altogether.

Steps to Manually Synchronize a Merge Subscriber

Here are the steps required to synchronize a merge Subscriber manually. They are explained below.

1. Create the new subscription with the manual synchronization option.
2. Run the Snapshot Agent.
3. Create and load data into the replicated table at the Subscriber.
4. Run the Merge Agent against the new Subscriber.

Step 1: Create the new subscription with the manual synchronization option.

You can create the subscription using either the SQL Server Enterprise Manager or the **sp_addmergesubscription** stored procedure (set the **sync_type** parameter to **none**). Modifications to the published table are not recorded for replication until the Snapshot Agent runs and creates the merge triggers on the published tables.

Step 2: Run the Snapshot Agent.

The Snapshot Agent:

1. Adds a *rowguid* column to the published table if one does not already exist.
2. Creates a nonclustered index on the *rowguid* column if one does not already exist.
3. Adds triggers used to track data changes to the published tables.
4. Creates various script files in the *Mssql7\Repldata* directory.
5. Creates **bcp** data files for the published tables (unless the publication includes a dynamic filter).
6. Creates **bcp** data files for several of the merge system tables.

The Snapshot Agent creates the **bcp** data files for the published tables each time it runs, regardless of whether there are any new subscriptions to the publication and even if subscriptions were created with the **no_sync** option. This can be time consuming for large publications, so it is a good idea to run the Snapshot Agent only when a new subscription needs to be synchronized.

Step 3: Create and load data into the published table at the Subscriber.

It is important to include a nonclustered index on the *rowguid* column of the published tables, but the index should be created after data is loaded into the table.

See the next discussion for issues related to populating the published table.

Step 4: Run the Merge Agent against the new subscriber.

The Merge Agent:

1. Adds triggers that track data changes to the published tables on the Subscriber.
2. Creates merge system tables in the subscribing database.
3. Populates the merge system tables using the **bcp** files created by the Snapshot Agent in step 1.
4. Replicates to the Subscriber any modifications that have occurred at the Publisher since the **bcp** files for the merge system tables were created in step 1.

Step 4 is very important. Merge uses the data in the merge system table to determine which data modifications to apply to the Subscriber, so the data in the merge system tables must be in sync with the data in the published tables. To guarantee this, the data to populate the published tables and the merge system tables must be extracted from the Publisher at the same instant. If the data in the merge system tables and published tables are not in sync, then some data may never be replicated to the Subscriber or there may be an attempt to re-replicate existing data to the Subscriber, causing conflicts.

The Merge Agent automatically populates the merge system tables using the **bcp** files created by the snapshot agent in step 2, so you must populate the replicated tables with data extracted from the Publisher at the same instant that the Snapshot Agent was run in step 2. The obvious solution is to use the **bcp** files that the Snapshot Agent generated for the published tables in step 2.

Steps to Manually Synchronize a Transactional Subscriber

Here are the steps required to synchronize a transactional Subscriber manually. They are described below.

1. Place a shared table lock on the published tables to block data modifications.
2. Copy data for synchronization out of the published tables.
3. Create the new subscription with the **manual** synchronization option.
4. Release the shared table lock on the published tables.
5. Create and load data into the published tables on the Subscriber.
6. Create stored procedures used to apply replicated data changes to the Subscriber.
7. If the Subscriber is configured as an immediate-updating Subscriber, add triggers to support two-phase commit back to the Publisher.

Step 1: Place shared lock on the published tables.

There must be no transactions against the published tables between the time that data for synchronization is copied out of the published tables in step 2 and the time that the new subscription is created in step 3. Transactions are marked for replication starting when the new subscription is created with the manual option, so any transactions that occur between steps 2 and 3 are not replicated to the Subscriber.

You can prevent transactions from occurring between steps 2 and 3 by placing a shared table lock on the published tables. Use these commands:

```
begin tran
select * from <published table name> (tablock, holdlock) where 0=1
```

The table lock is maintained until you commit the transaction (step 4).

Steps 1 and 4 are unnecessary if you know that there will be no transactions against the published tables.

Step 2: Copy data for synchronization out of the published tables.

Use **bcp**, DTS, or another method to copy data out of the published table.

Step 3: Create the new subscription with the *manual* synchronization option.

You can create the subscription using either the SQL Server Enterprise Manager or the **sp_addsubscription** stored procedure (set the **sync_type** parameter to **none**).

Transactions against the published tables are marked for replication in the Publisher's transaction log as soon as the subscription is created.

Step 4: Release the shared table lock on the published tables.

Release the shared lock by committing the transaction started in step 1 with the COMMIT TRAN statement.

Step 5: Create and load data into the published tables on the Subscriber.

See the "Tools and Tips for Loading Data on the Subscriber" section (next) for details.

Step 6: Create stored procedures used to apply replicated data changes to the Subscriber.

SQL Server 7.0 transactional replication by default uses three stored procedures to apply inserts, updates, and deletes to the Subscriber: **sp_MSins_<table_name>**, **sp_MSupd_<table_name>**, and **sp_MSdel_<table_name>**, where **<table_name>** is the name of the published table.

For manually synchronized subscriptions, you must create these stored procedures at the Subscriber. There are two ways to create them. The first is to copy them from another Subscriber (the default procedures are identical for all Subscribers to the same article). If the article has no other Subscribers you can copy them from a Subscriber to different article and modify the stored procedure name (to match the format above) and the table name (referenced in the text of the stored procedure).

You can also create them by extracting their code from the *<table_name>.sch* file. This file is created by the Snapshot Agent and is normally in the *\Mssql7\Repldata* directory. The catch is that the Snapshot Agent creates this file only when there is a new automatic synchronization subscription, so to use this method there must be at least one other subscription defined with automatic synchronization.

Step 7: Add triggers to support two-phase commit back to the Publisher.

Immediate-updating Subscribers need three triggers in each published table to initiate the two-phase commit when clients modify the Subscriber tables: **trg_MSsync_ins_<table_name>**, **trg_MSsync_upd_<table_name>**, and **trg_MSsync_del_<table_name>**, where **<table_name>** is the name of the replicated table.

The triggers are fairly complex, and their code differs from one Subscriber to the next, even for the same replicated table. There is no easy way to get scripts to create the triggers because the scripts are never saved to a file. For an automatic subscription, the distribution agent runs three undocumented stored procedures to create the triggers: **sp_MSscript_sync_ins_trig**, **sp_MSscript_sync_upd_trig**, and **sp_MSscript_sync_del_trig**. Running these is probably the best option for getting a script to create the triggers.

Below are sample calls to the stored procedures to create the three trigger scripts along with the declarations for the stored procedure parameters. The sample calls were traced with the SQL Server 7.0 Profiler tool. The stored procedures exist in the **master** database, but should be run from the context of the Subscriber database.

Note   These procedures are *undocumented*, and can change at any time without notice.

Insert Trigger:

```
sp_MSscript_sync_ins_trig 1328059817, [JBR4], [pubs],
[trg_MSsync_ins_employee], [sp_MSsync_ins_employee_43], [dbo], [null],
[msrepl_synctran_ts], null

sp_MSscript_sync_ins_trig
    @objid          int,
    @publisher      sysname,
    @publisher_db   sysname,
    @trigname       sysname,
    @procname       sysname,
    @proc_owner     sysname,
    @identity_col   sysname = NULL,
    @ts_col         sysname = NULL,
    @filter_clause  nvarchar(4000)
```

Update Trigger:

```
sp_MSscript_sync_upd_trig 1328059817, [JBR4], [pubs],
[trg_MSsync_upd_employee], [sp_MSsync_upd_employee_43], [dbo], [null],
[msrepl_synctran_ts], null, 0x0100

sp_MSscript_sync_upd_trig
    @objid          int,
    @publisher      sysname,
    @publisher_db   sysname,
    @trigname       sysname,
    @procname       sysname,
    @proc_owner     sysname,
    @identity_col   sysname = NULL,
    @ts_col         sysname = NULL,
    @filter_clause  nvarchar(4000),
    @primary_key_bitmap  varbinary(4000)
```

Delete Trigger:

```
sp_MSscript_sync_del_trig 1328059817, [JBR4], [pubs],
[trg_MSsync_del_employee], [sp_MSsync_del_employee_43], [dbo], [null],
[msrepl_synctran_ts], null, 0x0100

sp_MSscript_sync_del_trig
    @objid          int,
    @publisher      sysname,
    @publisher_db   sysname,
    @trigname       sysname,
    @procname       sysname,
    @proc_owner     sysname,
    @identity_col   sysname = NULL,
    @ts_col         sysname = NULL,
    @filter_clause  nvarchar(4000),
    @primary_key_bitmap  varbinary(4000)
```

Tools and Tips for Loading Data on the Subscriber

Here are three tools you can use to load data manually at the Subscribers and some tips for using them.

- **bcp** utility and the BULK INSERT statement

- Data Transformation Services (DTS)

- Database backup and restore

bcp and BULK INSERT

- **The new SQL Server 7.0 BULK INSERT statement is significantly faster than bcp.** The new Transact-SQL statement BULK INSERT is similar to **bcp** in that they both bulk copy data into SQL Server from files. BULK INSERT, however, is faster because it runs as part of the SQL Server process (in process) while **bcp** runs in its own, separate process space (out of process). You still need **bcp** to bulk copy data out of a table, but the BULK INSERT command provides better performance when bulk copying data into a table.

- **Nonlogged bulk load.** Nonlogged bulk load operation (either **bcp** or BULK INSERT) can be several times faster than a fully logged bulk load operation and helps keep the transaction log from filling up. These are the conditions for nonlogged mode:

    - The database option **select into/bulkcopy** must be set to **true**.

    - The target table must either have no indexes, or, if there are indexes, then the table must not have any rows when the bulk load operation starts.

    - The target table must not be part of a publication.

    - The TABLOCK hint must be specified either in the **bcp** command or by using the **sp_tableoption** to set the **table lock on bulk load** option.

- **Drop all nonclustered indexes before starting the bulk insert.** It takes many times longer to bulk copy data into a table when the table has one or more nonclustered indexes. It is much faster to bulk copy the data into the table without any indexes and then build the indexes after the bulk copy is complete.

- **Use the ORDER hint to load a table with a clustered index when the data file is in clustered index order.** SQL Server 7.0 **bcp** and BULK INSERT have an ORDER hint you can use to bulk insert data quickly into a table that has a clustered index, but only if the data in the data file is already ordered by the clustered index key. If it is not, then it is significantly faster to bulk insert the data into the table with no clustered index and add the clustered index after the bulk copy.

- **Use parallel bulk inserts on SMP computers.** If you have an SMP computer, you can significantly improve performance by running multiple bulk insert sessions in parallel. SQL Server 7.0 can even run multiple bulk insert operations to populate a single table, if these conditions are met:

  - The database option **select into/bulkcopy** must be set to **true**

  - The table must not have any indexes

  - The TABLOCK hint must be specified in either the **bcp** or BULK INSERT command, or the table option **table lock on bulk load** must be set to **true**

Parallel bulk inserts into a single table should have separate, segmented input files so that each bulk insert can read from a separate file.

Example:

You need to create and populate ten tables at a Subscriber: eight are small (fewer than 10,000 rows each), one is medium (1,000,000 rows), one is relatively large (5,000,000 rows).

The Subscriber is a large reporting server on an SMP computer with eight processors. To create and populate the ten tables, seven concurrent sessions can be started, leaving one processor free to handle interactive user requests.

The first session runs a script to create and populate all eight of the smaller tables, a second session creates and populates the medium table, and the four other sessions load the large table in parallel.

The medium and small tables are created with the clustered index in place before the tables are loaded. The ORDER hint is specified for each of the BULK INSERT statements for each of these tables (so all these tables' data files must be ordered by the clustered index key). Here is an example of the BULK INSERT command:

```
Bulk insert medium_table from e:\medium_table.bcp with (tablock,
order)
```

There will need to be four separate, segmented data files for the large table—one for each of the four BULK INSERT statements used to populate it. The clustered index on the large table is created after the table is loaded.

All nonclustered indexes are created after the tables have been populated.

Data Transformation Services (DTS)

There are two ways to use DTS to initialize Subscribers manually: use the DTS Import or Export Wizards to transfer objects and data from one database to another, or use the DTS Designer to build a comprehensive package that coordinates all necessary custom tasks.

The DTS Import and Export wizards allow you to select a group of tables and other objects to transfer from one database or server to another. The wizards are similar to the **Database/Object Transfer** function in the SQL Enterprise Manager in SQL Server version 6.5 or SQL Server 6.0 Transfer Manager, but they are more sophisticated in that they allow you to add custom transformation and data mappings to the transfer process. After using the wizards you can run the resulting DTS package immediately, or save the package and run it later.

The DTS Designer is more free-form than the wizards. You can use it to set up a package that functions like a batch control system, or you can set up workflows in which one step depends on one or more previous steps, or steps execute in parallel. To build a package you define the components needed to execute the necessary steps, then define precedence constraints so that the tasks execute in the correct order. You can control how many processors DTS uses to execute tasks with the **Limit the maximum number of tasks executed in parallel** property.

Here are some of the DTS components that might be used in a Subscriber initialization package. When creating the package's custom tasks, take into account all the **bcp** and BULK INSERT recommendations above.

- *Execute Process* tasks that run the **bcp** utility to copy data from publishing tables to data files.
- *Execute SQL* tasks to create the destination tables and other objects in the subscribing database.
- *BULK INSERT* tasks to bulk insert data from the data files into the destination tables.

Database Backup and Restore

One way to synchronize data at a Subscriber is to back up either the publishing database or another subscribing database, then restore the backup to the Subscriber. This can be a useful method when you publish all or most of the data in a large database.

Doing this requires using a couple special options: **with replace** (to confirm that you really do want to restore from the backup of another database) and **with move** (to restore the .MDF, .NDF, and .LDF files to the appropriate locations). See "Restore (Transact-SQL)" and "Copy Database" in SQL Server Books Online for more details.

There are two major drawbacks to this method. First, the Subscriber gets a copy of all backed up data on the database, so this method is not ideal when the Subscriber needs only some of the data. Second, some Subscriber-side objects necessary for replication will not exist on the Subscriber after restoring from backup—either because they did not exist in the database that was backed up or because the restore process did not restore them. The restore process detects when a database is restored from the backup of a different database, and does not restore certain replication-related system tables, stored procedures, and triggers. This behavior is necessary to prevent possible problems, but it complicates the use of backup and restore to initialize a new Subscriber. It is an issue only when restoring from the backup of another database: when restoring from a backup created from the same database, all replication related items are restored.

No merge system tables or merge triggers (to record data modifications on the subscribed tables) are restored when loading the backup of a merge Subscriber or Publisher to a different database. However, these objects are created and populated the first time the Merge Agent runs against that new Subscriber, even if it was created for manual synchronization.

The three replication stored procedures used to apply changes to a transactional Subscriber do not exist on the publishing database, and you have to create them if you initialize the Subscriber by restoring from a backup of the Publisher: **sp_MSins_<table_name>**, **sp_MSupd_<table_name>**, and **sp_MSdel_<table_name>**, where **<table_name>** is the name of the published table. These procedures do exist on other Subscribers to the same publication and are restored when initializing one Subscriber by restoring from the backup of another Subscriber. Methods for creating these procedures are discussed in the "Steps to Manually Synchronize a Transactional Subscriber" section on page 486.

Immediate-updating Subscribers use three triggers on the subscribed table to initiate the two-phase commit back to the Subscriber when changes are made at the Subscriber: **trg_MSsync_ins_<table_name>**, **trg_MSsync_upd_<table_name>**, and **trg_MSsync_del_<table_name>**, where **<table_name>** is the name of the replicated table. The code for these differs slightly from one Subscriber to the next, even for the same replicated table. Because they are different on each Subscriber, the restore process excludes them when restoring from a backup of another database. You will need to create the triggers manually if you manually synchronize an immediate-updating Subscriber. Methods for creating them are discussed in the "Steps to Manually Synchronize a Transactional Subscriber" section on page 486.

Planning for Backup and Recovery

Recovery Strategy for Merge Replication

The recovery strategy for merge replication is relatively simple:

- Schedule periodic backups of the publishing and subscribing databases
- When a database is lost, recover from backup and run the Merge Agent

The Merge Agent uses normal merge replication to bring a recovered site back into sync with the other sites. The only data that will be lost is data that originated at the site being recovered and was not yet replicated when the database went down.

For example: Site A and Site B use merge replication. For recovery purposes it does not matter which is Publisher or Subscriber. If Site A is lost, you recover Site A from backup and run the Merge Agent. It compares the generation history for each row at Site A with its corresponding row at Site B. If a row at Site B is more recent than a row at the recovered version of Site A, the agent replaces the Site A row with the Site B row. When the Merge Agent is done, Site A is identical to Site B.

Recovery Strategy for Transactional Replication

Developing a recovery strategy for transactional replication is somewhat complex. From a planning point of view the simplest option is to resynchronize after recovering a site involved in replication, but this can take a long time for large publications. You can develop a recovery strategy that does not always require resynchronization, but to understand when you can avoid resynchronization, you have to understand how transactions move from the Publisher to Distributor to Subscriber.

Dependencies to Consider When Recovering Transactional Replication

Transactions are replicated from the Publisher to the Subscriber in two stages: the Log Reader Agent moves transactions from the Publisher to the Distributor, then the Distribution Agent moves them to the Subscriber.

Pointers at each stage track which transactions have been replicated. The pointer from the Distributor to the Publisher tracks which transactions have been read from the Publisher's transaction log. The pointer from the Subscriber to the Distributor tracks which transactions have been distributed to the Subscriber. If either of the pointers is invalid after restoring a database from a backup, subscriptions must be recreated and data resynchronized.

In SQL Server 7.0 each transaction is identified by a timestamp value that is generated when the transaction is written to the Publisher's transaction log and is maintained throughout the replication process. (SQL Server 6.*x* used job IDs to track replicated transactions.) You can view the transaction log operations and associated timestamps by running the statement DBCC LOG('<DATABASE NAME>').

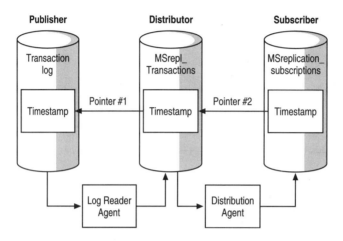

Figure 14.1   Timestamp pointers in transactional replication.

Pointer #1 (from Distributor to publishing database)

The distribution database records the timestamp (also known as the LSN or log sequence number) of each replicated transaction that is read from the Publisher's transaction log. These are recorded in the **MSrepl_transactions** table in the distribution database. The largest timestamp is the last scanned transaction. When the Log Reader Agent starts, it gets this timestamp from the table, then uses it as a starting point and scans forward through the Publisher's transaction log.

If the last scanned transaction is not present in the Publisher's transaction log (which may happen when recovering either the publishing or distribution database) the Log Reader Agent may fail. (See the next section.)

Pointer #2 (from Subscriber to distribution database)

Each Subscriber records the timestamp of the last replicated transaction in its **MSreplication_subscriptions** table. When the Distribution Agent starts, it gets the timestamp from the table, queries the Distributor's **MSrepl_transactions** table for any transactions with a larger timestamp, and replicates them to the Subscriber.

Recovering the Subscribing Database

To design a recovery strategy for the subscribing database you have to:

- Schedule periodic backups of the subscribing database
- Set the "minimum retention period" for the distribution database to be at least as long as the period between subscribing database backups

The "minimum retention period" of the distribution database determines how long transactions must remain in the distribution database before the cleanup process can delete them. The default is 0 hours, meaning that they can be deleted as soon as they have been replicated to all Subscribers that need them.

For example, if you back up the subscribing database every 24 hours, then you should set the minimum retention period to be at least 24 hours. If you need to recover from backup taken 24 hours earlier, the last 24 hours of transactions will still be in the distribution database for re-replication.

If you set the retention period to 24 hours and you recover the Subscriber from a backup taken 48 hours earlier, then transactions that occurred between 24 and 48 hours ago probably will have been deleted from the distribution database and will not be re-replicated to the recovered Subscriber. The Distribution Agent will not report any error in this situation; it will simply re-replicate any transactions that are still in the distribution database.

Recovering the Distribution Database

To design a recovery strategy for the distribution database you have to:

- Schedule periodic backups of the distribution database
- Coordinate the backups of the publishing database's transaction log with the backups of the distribution database

After recovering the distribution database, the Log Reader Agent will fail if pointer #1 (the timestamp of the last transaction scanned in the Publisher's transaction log) is no longer valid. When the distribution database is recovered, pointer #1 is also recovered to an earlier time (the time that the distribution database was backed up).

For pointer #1 to be valid after recovery, the last scanned transaction at the time that the distribution database was backed up must still be in the Publisher's transaction log. This means that the Publisher's transaction log cannot have been truncated since the last time the distribution database was backed up. By default the transaction log is truncated each time you back it up. You can avoid truncation by using the NO_TRUNCATE option in the BACKUP LOG statement.

For example, if you back up the distribution database every four hours, then the Publisher's transaction log should be backed up and truncated just before the distribution database backup. The Log Reader Agent should be stopped while the backups are being done. To automate this process you could create a job with these steps:

1. Stop the Log Reader Agent so that no transactions will be read from the Publisher's log.
2. Back up and truncate the transaction log.
3. Back up the distribution database.
4. Restart the Log Reader Agent.

You can back up the transaction log more frequently than the distribution database, but be sure to use the NO_TRUNCATE option.

Rule of thumb: do not use the **trunc. log on chkpt.** database option if you want to recover the distribution database without re-synchronizing all publications.

Recovering the Publishing Database

To design a recovery strategy for the publishing database you have to:

- Schedule periodic, coordinated backups of the publishing *and* distribution databases
- Develop a custom method to extract data from the Subscriber(s) that may not be present in the recovered publishing database

Pointer #1 will almost always be invalid after recovering the publishing database from an earlier backup, and this will cause the log reader to fail. In other words, the log reader scans the distribution database, and the last transaction recorded there usually will not exist in the Publisher's log if the Publisher has been recovered from an earlier backup. To overcome this you also need to restore the distribution database to the same point (or slightly earlier) than the publishing database.

After you restore the publishing database, the Subscribers will most likely have more recent data than the Publisher. To synchronize them, you need to devise some method of extracting data from the Subscriber(s) and inserting it into the Publisher. For example, if a published table has an incrementing ID column, then you could extract all rows from the Subscriber's table for which the ID value is greater than the largest ID value in the Publisher's table.

APPENDIX

Upgrading from
SQL Server 4.21*x* to SQL Server 6.5

By Manuel Martinez and Larry Barnes

If you are currently using Microsoft SQL Server 4.21*x* and you want to upgrade to SQL Server 7.0, your options are somewhat limited. Because of the many database structural changes between SQL Server 4.21*x* and SQL Server 6.*x*, you cannot upgrade to SQL Server 7.0 directly from SQL Server 4.21*x*: You must first upgrade to SQL Server 6.5 and then to SQL Server 7.0.

There are other options, but not many, and whether any of them are suited to your circumstances will depend on the number of servers you need to upgrade and the data contained in the databases. For example, if your SQL Server 4.21*x* databases are not huge, you can remove SQL Sever 4.21*x*, install SQL Server 7.0, and then rebuild the databases. This is seldom practicable. You can also consider leaving some databases on SQL Server 4.21*x* on a separate server, and accessing them with interim methods until the data becomes outdated or it can be brought over to the new system. If you want to transfer data only, you may be able to use Microsoft Data Transformation Services (DTS) and upgrade directly to SQL Server 7.0.

But if you need to bring over *all* SQL Server 4.21*x* database objects, then you must upgrade to SQL Server 6.5 first. This chapter captures the collective experience of numerous information technology (IT) consultants and the processes defined in the Microsoft Solutions Framework (MSF) to help you deploy SQL Server 6.5 on your system. It is a complex undertaking, best approached systematically, with an understanding of the phases entailed in the overall project, an efficient distribution of tasks and responsibilities, and all appropriate planning completed at each phase (envisioning, planning, and deployment).

Note   On terminology: SQL Server versions 4.2a and 4.2b were designed for OS/2; versions 4.2 and 4.21 were designed for Windows NT. Throughout this chapter, the term 4.2*x* is used to refer to these versions, although the discussion is concerned primarily with Windows NT systems.

Initiate the Upgrade Process

A successful upgrade project begins with an envisioning phase, which includes developing an enterprise vision statement and deployment scope document, creating a high-level conceptual design, and conducting a high-level risk assessment.

Write the Vision Statement

The vision statement should clearly explain the reasons for upgrading and broadly describe expected outcomes. It should include business, fiscal, and functional objectives, and input from the project sponsor, management, upgrade team leader, and other members appointed to the project team. The statement should:

- Specify results that will be achieved. (For example, which databases and applications will be converted.)

- Identify benefits. (For example, increased productivity using database applications.)

- Establish realistic outcomes based on company resources and project parameters.

- Set a realistic time frame, based on resources and circumstances, to achieve specific goals. (For example, project will commence on X date and complete on Y date.)

The vision statement documents the database environment and provides the basis for the scope document, conceptual environment diagram, and high-level risk assessment. Build in as much detail as you can; you will refer to it throughout the upgrade project.

Define the Project Scope

The project scope expands the vision statement with specific details, including the business case for deployment, features, resources, and scheduling. Use it as a guide for deploying the upgrade process and establishing the project's limits. Keep it to three pages or less and make sure it identifies:

- **Business goals, requirements, and constraints.** Vendor applications that don't support SQL Server 6.5, customized code that is not yet upgraded to support SQL Server 6.5, etc.

- **Assumptions.** Identify hardware resources that need testing, check the availability of targeted databases, etc.

- **Critical dates.** Identify start/end dates, time dependencies, etc.

Address these areas while defining the project's scope:

Databases

- Which ones run on SQL Server 4.21*x*
- Reasons they haven't been upgraded
- Importance to the organization
- Visibility within the organization (how widely used)
- Ownership: administrators, users, departments
- Hours they are open for business use
- Estimated sizes
- Number of stored procedures (regular and complex)
- Number of triggers (regular and complex)

Maintenance, Backup, and Recovery

- Backup and recovery plan
- Database backup and maintenance schedule

Servers

- Which ones host databases
- General configurations (CPU, memory, disk space, and so forth)
- Microsoft Windows NT versions
- Upgrading or replacement plans
- Ownership: system managers

Applications

- Which ones access servers
- Importance to the organization
- Which were developed in-house (size, who maintains them)
- Third-party products (support of SQL Server 6.5 or vendor plans to support it, whether vendor is still in business)

Clients

- Classify client computers in terms of business function, operating system (including version, CPU, memory), geography, or network systems. This simplifies client configuration issues later.
- Applications used by client groups

Project Time Frame

- Project start/complete dates

Resources

- Project budget
- Staff members available for team roles (database administrator, system manager, operations manager, application developer, testers)

Add this information to the sample worksheets in the section "Document the Database Environment," below.

Create a High-Level Conceptual Design

Use the vision/scope findings to diagram the interrelationship of the SQL Server database environment, applications, and users. Create two diagrams: one representing applications that access enterprise databases, and one showing which groups of users access the databases. Figure A.1 is a sample application view, Figure A.2 a sample user view. Each outlines the hardware and Windows NT Server version supporting the databases.

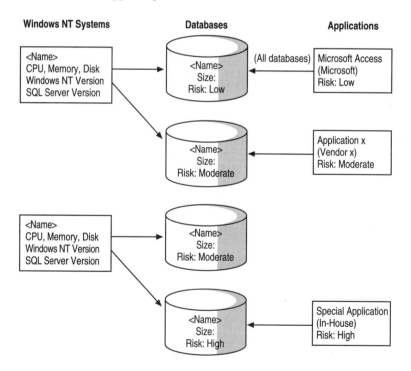

Figure A.1   Application view of a conceptual design highlighting systems, databases, and applications.

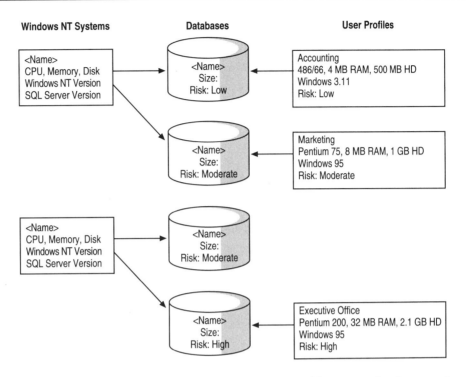

Figure A.2   User profile view of a conceptual design with systems, databases, and user groups.

Conduct Initial Risk Assessment

The sample designs above show a *risk* rating. You should identify and assess risks before you move forward to create the logical design. Look at financial constraints, limiting factors, the level of vision/scope support from various business units, inconsistencies in the project, and ways to mitigate risks. Use the elements in the table below to define and assess each factor:

Risk assessment categories.

Category	Description
Risk Impact	Three levels of application development and project integration risk impact—low, medium, and high.
Low	Risks not critical.
	Can delay (but not interrupt) the upgrade process.
	Mitigation not immediately needed; the team can wait until a later date (within weeks of identifying the risk).

(continued)

Category	Description
Medium	Risks can be critical.
	Can interrupt part of the upgrade.
	Mitigate medium-impact risks within several days of being identified.
High	Risks are critical and can jeopardize the project.
	Risks will interrupt part, or all of the upgrade.
	Mitigate high-impact risks immediately. The SQL Server upgrade planning process should stop until the team resolves these risks or structures the plan around them.
Risk Probability	A percentage that indicates the likelihood that the risk will occur. Used with risk impact levels to determine the risk resolution priority level.
	For example: A high-probability, high-impact risk should be dealt with immediately. A low-probability, low-impact risk will likely have very little impact and can be deferred.
Risk Description	The risk description contains two parts:
	A *brief description* of the risk and how it affects the process. For example: "The helpdesk hotline requires extended access to the helpdesk application and database."
	A *detailed description* of how the risk affects the project. This helps find ways to mitigate it. For example: "The Helpdesk is open for business M-F 6 a.m. – 9 p.m. EST and Saturday 10 a.m. – 5 p.m. EST. The application HLPDSK.EXE accesses the Helpdesk databases, which contain the database objects with SQL Server 6.5 reserved keywords. The SQL Server upgrade must have minimal impact on the Helpdesk during business hours. (4/3)"
	[The date (4/3) tells when the team documented the risk; this helps tracking and research.]
Owner	Risks typically apply to a particular task or aspect of a project. The owner is the group most closely affected by the risk or responsible for accomplishing tasks associated with it. In the Risk Description example, the group in charge of the helpdesk application owns this risk.
Date	Date the risk was first identified.
Mitigation	Detailed description of how to resolve or minimize the risk, providing alternatives that can involve a change in the project plan and procedures. For example: "To minimize the risk of overloading the Helpdesk during business hours, SQL Server upgrade will begin Saturday, May 3rd at 6pm. This allows for the maximum amount of time to implement and test the upgrade. (4/3)"

Category	Description
	"The helpdesk database and application will undergo unit and system testing on a separate test system. The upgrade team will develop test scripts that a helpdesk user team, including a customer service representative and supervisor, and department manager, will approve. (5/1)"
	[The dates in parentheses document when the upgrade team established a mitigation plan during a risk assessment meeting—not a proposed date for the action. In the project plan, include due/completion dates for action items.]

The initial risk assessment can be filled out at the same time as the database environment worksheets (see the section "Document the Database Environment," below). Here is an example of a risk assessment using the defined risk categories:

Example of an initial risk assessment.

Impact	Probability	Risk Description	Owner	Date	Mitigation
High	25% (Low)	Some applications will be heavily affected by the SQL Server 6.5 semantic differences.	Applications team	mm/dd	The planning process includes review of all current applications and identification of any issues and their resolution.
High	45% (Med.)	Human resource allocation: IT group does not have the time to support the project. Other responsibilities prevent full commitment.	Project management team	mm/dd	The schedule includes backup personnel to share responsibility with team members and complete tasks. Regular communication needed to facilitate staff.
High	5% (Low)	Project requires a business sponsor to ensure that upper management supports the upgrade plan.	Project management team	mm/dd	Identify a business sponsor during the first few days of the project, and determine the sponsor's responsibilities.

(continued)

Impact	Probability	Risk Description	Owner	Date	Mitigation
High	5% (Low)	Some workstations have insufficient hardware or need re-configuration. Replacing equipment increases the project budget.	Applications team	mm/dd	Isolate incompatible equipment and resolve. Increasing the total cost of ownership (TCO) represents a high-priority issue.
High to moderate	5% (Low)	Sufficient staff with the right technical skills required for project. Lack of expertise can increase time to complete the upgrade.	Project management team	mm/dd	Evaluate project team expertise, and identify and recruit best members.
Moderate	10% (Low)	Project needs more upper management support. Executive management needs to attend status meetings.	Project management team	mm/dd	Secure business sponsor. Communicate project status to executive management.

Define the Project Structure

Assembling everything you have learned this far, develop the upgrade project process. This entails creating a project team and structure (see Chapter 1, "The Right Team and the Right Skills"), developing training plans, and preparing a communications plan.

Training and Reference Materials

Training for Microsoft SQL Server 6.5 and Windows NT Server 4.0 is important, especially if the user base has no experience with earlier releases. Sources of training information available from Microsoft include:

- Microsoft Certified Professional (MCP) training (http://www.microsoft.com/mcp/)
- Training and MCP certification (http://www.microsoft.com/train_cert)
- Microsoft Press books (1-800-MSPRESS [677-7377] or visit the Web site at http://mspress.microsoft.com/).

Include time, personnel, and budget for identifying and obtaining resources, scheduling training classes, and buying reference materials. For current information and resources, refer to the Microsoft Web page at http://www.microsoft.com/search/. Also see the list of references and tools in the section "More Information" at the end of this chapter.

Create a Communications Plan

Communicating progress to team members and users helps coordinate project activity and control expectations. Whenever possible, use media accessible to all parties—e-mail, Web pages, corporate publications, or public folders. The communications plan should help users understand the status of the SQL Server upgrade and its impact, specifically:

- How much disruption users will go through (collectively and individually). Explain anticipated downtime for databases and applications.

- What database objects conflict with Microsoft SQL Server 6.5 reserved keywords and the new names for these database objects.

- How users upgrade their computers to the latest version of SQL Server client software. How new applications will be installed on clients.

Gather Information for Selecting Installation Type

This section describes the information you need to complete the conceptual database environment and to determine the upgraded database environment in detail. Use the findings to determine the upgrade type, the tasks it will require, and its associated risks (all of which are described in later sections). Perform another risk assessment at this point to deal with changes in business, organizational, and technical issues.

Information Needed

Gather information in these areas to help determine the upgrade tasks required:

Systems
- What are the detailed current system configurations?
- Are the database systems under-powered? Run Windows NT Performance Monitor (Perfmon) to gauge CPU, memory, and disk utilization.
- Do the database systems need to be upgraded or replaced?
- Which hardware should be replaced?

- What test systems should be added to the configuration?
- Which new systems will be in place to support the upgraded databases?

Databases

- What are the detailed characteristics of each database?
- What changes are required to upgrade database objects?
- What semantic changes are required in database-stored procedures and triggers?
- What is the scope of the backup and recovery process? How reliable is this process?
- How critical and visible is each database to the organization?
- Are there organizational or ownership issues associated with each database?
- Can the database be taken offline and, if so, for how long?

Applications

- Which changes are required to upgrade the application?
- What are the upgrade issues involved for this application?
- How critical and visible is each application to the organization?
- What are the organizational or ownership issues associated with each application?
- Can the applications be taken offline and, if so, for how long?

Client environments and user profiles

- What are the different classes of client environments?
- What are the hardware and software configurations for these environments?
- What procedures are required to upgrade the client configurations?
- How many users are in each user class?
- Which departments are they from?
- How active are the users?
- What is the risk to the upgrade if there are problems in converting these users?

There's no hard-and-fast rule about when to gather information. Some information (on hardware, for instance) may be readily available during the envisioning phase; other information may not be available until the planning phase.

Document the Database Environment

To understand the existing database environment and the new systems that have to be put in place, create diagrams to display the test systems and databases required, and the applications and user classes that access these databases. Use the sample worksheets to provide the detail behind the high-level diagrams. They include a column indicating the project phase during which the information should be collected: E=Envisioning, P=Planning, and D=Deployment.

Worksheet for system information.

Item	Value	Purpose	Phase
Hardware			
System			
Vendor		Background, sizing	E/P
CPUs		Performance	E/P
Memory		Base requirement, performance	E/P
Disk configuration:			
• System			
• SQL Server data			
• SQL Server log files		Performance, reliability	E/P
System drive: free disk space		Install or upgrade requirement	P
System bus		Performance	E/P
System manager group		Logistics, risk assessment	E
Other item: (specify)			
System software			
Windows NT version		Reliability, base requirement	E/P
Server type		Performance	E/P
Network transports		Background	E/P
Multiple SQL Server directories? (check Libpath)		Potential upgrade issue	P/D
Other item: (specify)			
SQL Server			
Version		Base requirement, reliability	E/P
Database administrator group		Logistics, risk assessment	E
SQL Server transports		Logistics, client installation	E/P

(continued)

Item	Value	Purpose	Phase
Master database size		Base requirement	E/P
Free **master** database space			
• Upgrade > 7 MB?			
• Large enough for **tempdb** to be created?			
(check model size)		Potential upgrade issue	P/D
Model database size		Potential upgrade issue	D
Open database parameter			
(must be > the total # of databases)		Installation requirement	D
Other item (specify):			

Worksheet for database information.

Item	Value	Purpose	Phase
Type (line of business or decision support?)		Risk assessment	E
Visibility (high, medium, or low)		Risk assessment	E
Availability (for example, M-F, 9 AM–6 PM)		Logistics	E
Backup		Risk assessment	E/P
Last recovery test date		Risk assessment	E/P
Database administrator group		Logistics	E
Database size		Install or upgrade requirement	P/D
Database log size		Install or upgrade requirement	P/D
Other item: (specify)			

(continued)

Item	Value	Purpose	Phase
Configuration parameters			
Memory		Potential Upgrade issue	P/D
Character set (use **sp_helpsort** to find the current value along with the current sort order)		Upgrade issue	P/D
Sort order		Upgrade issue	P/D
Estimated/actual stored procedure, trigger, view count		Scope potential database modifications	P/D
Other item: (specify)			
Applications (enter the applications accessing this database)		Logistics, risk assessment, defining project scope	E/P

Worksheet for application information.

Item	Value	Purpose	Phase
Vendor (if none, state "In-house")		Risk assessment	E
Visibility (high, medium, or low)		Risk assessment	E
Development manager group		Logistics, risk assessment	E
Supports SQL Server 6.5?		Risk assessment	E/P
Operating system		Logistics	E/P
Database API (dblib/ODBC)		Install or upgrade requirement	E/P
Source code available?		Risk assessment	E/P
Development team exists?		Risk assessment	E/P
Application size (large, medium, or small?)		Risk assessment	E/P
Other item: (specify)			
User profiles (enter the user profiles for this application)		Logistics, risk assessment, defining project scope	E/P

Worksheet for user profile information.

Item	Value	Purpose	Phase
Organization		Logistics	E/P
Computer expertise (low, medium, or high)		Risk Assessment	E/P
Visibility in the organization (low, medium, or high)		Risk Assessment	E
Other item: (specify)			
Computer configuration			
Vendor CPU		Logistics / Deployment	E/P
Memory		Logistics / Deployment	E/P
Disk		Logistics / Deployment	E/P
Operating system		Logistics / Deployment	E/P
Network		Logistics / Deployment	E/P
Other item: (specify)			
Databases (enter the databases accessed by this user profile)		Logistics, risk assessment, defining project scope	E/P
Applications (enter applications executed by this user profile)		Logistics, risk assessment, defining project scope	E/P

Select the SQL Installation Type

After gathering detailed information on the database environment, determine the best installation type by considering requirements and constraints. There are four types of SQL Server installations:

- **Type 1.** Installing SQL Server 6.5 on a different computer.

- **Type 2.** Installing SQL Server 6.5 and Windows NT Server 4.0 on the same computer as SQL Server 4.21x and Windows NT Server 3.51. This approach enables dual booting of Windows NT 3.51 and Windows NT 4.0.

- **Type 3.** Installing SQL Server 6.5 side by side with SQL Server 4.21x.
- **Type 4.** Installing SQL Server 6.5 over the top of SQL Server 4.21x. This installation type is the riskiest because the SQL Server 6.5 back-out plan requires additional work.

Note   This section deals only with the databases and systems. Application and client conversion issues are addressed in the sections "Convert Databases and Applications" on page 526 and "Install SQL Server 6.5" on page 535.

Type 1: Install on a Different Computer

The recommended upgrade method is to install Microsoft SQL Server 6.5 on a different computer than SQL Server 4.21x.

Advantages:

- **Minimum impact.** Besides extracting the system object scripts and bulk copy program (**bcp**) data files from the SQL Server 4.21x computer, the new database environment does not affect the current environment. Testing on the new computer does not affect the current configuration. The back-out plan is designed to address any issues that occur during the upgrade process and has no effect on the existing database server.
- **Performance and storage capacity.** Many SQL Server 4.21x installations reside on the computers where the software was originally installed. Hardware advances and price decreases have produced a new range of Windows NT database computers that are more powerful and affordable.
- **No back-out impact.** Restoring the existing configuration is not an issue with this installation.

Disadvantages:

- **Price.** Although the price for CPU, disk, memory, and bus technologies are decreasing, the cost of a new database system could be prohibitive.
- **Setup costs.** This approach requires additional hardware, software, and resources to oversee the installation.

In most cases, the advantages of minimal impact, a separate test environment, and an upgrade to a state-of-the-art database system outweigh the price of a new system and the allocation of a team member to oversee the process. However, if logistical and internal obstacles prohibit the purchase and installation of a new system, consider one of the remaining three installation types.

Different Computer

Production Computer

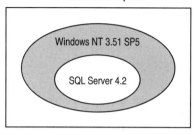

- Install Windows NT 4.0
- Install Windows NT 4.0 SP3
- Install SQL Server 6.5
- Install SQL Server 6.5 SP3
- Load 4.2 Database into 6.5

New and Test Computer

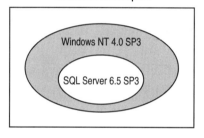

Figure A.3   Schematic of installation type 1.

Type 2: Install on a Different Operating System, Same Computer

Windows NT allows multiple operating systems to reside on one system, which means Windows NT Server 4.0 can be installed on a different operating system path than Windows NT Server 3.51 but remain on the same system. Then SQL Server 6.5 can be installed onto the Windows NT Server 4.0.

Advantages:

- **Price.** No new hardware is required.

- **Minimum impact.** Minimal collision between SQL Server 4.21x and SQL Server 6.5. Installing Windows NT and SQL Server has no effect on the existing SQL Server environment, so long as it doesn't override existing operating system and SQL Server directory structures (see "Type 3, Side-by-Side," below).

- **No back-out impact.** Restoring the existing configuration is not an issue.

Disadvantages:

- **System downtime.** SQL Server production databases are not available during upgrading or testing of the new operating system environment.
- **Disk resources.** Additional disk space is required.

Same Computer (Windows NT Side by Side)

Production and Test Computer

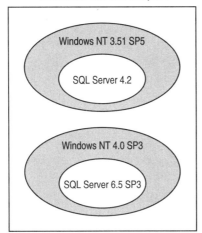

- Install Windows NT 4.0
- Install Windows NT 4.0 SP3
- Install SQL Server 6.5
- Install SQL Server 6.5 SP3
- Load 4.2 Database into 6.5

Figure A.4   Schematic of installation type 2.

Type 3: Install Side-by-Side on the Same Operating System

You can install SQL Server 6.5 on the same operating system as SQL Server 4.21*x*.

Advantages:

- **Price.** No new hardware is required.
- **Minimal system downtime.** Running both versions of Microsoft SQL Server on one system makes it possible to test SQL Server 6.5 while the SQL Server 4.21*x* system is running.
- **No back-out impact.** No need to restore the original configuration on back-out.

Disadvantages:

- **Performance and system resources.** Running SQL Server 4.21*x* and SQL Server 6.5 concurrently adds resource requirements to the system.

- **Run-time issues.** Both versions can run concurrently, but users may access the incorrect system if the environment is not configured properly.
- **Testing.** You must upgrade from Windows NT Server 3.51 to Windows NT Server 4.0 and re-run the verification test suites—Windows NT Server 3.51 is the only version that supports both SQL Server 4.21*x* and SQL Server 6.5.

SQL Server Side-by-Side

Production and Test Computer

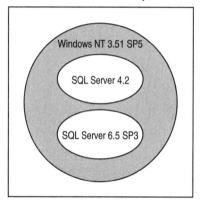

- Install SQL Server 6.5
- Install SQL Server 6.5 SP3
- Load 4.2 Database into 6.5
- Install Windows NT 4.0
- Install Windows NT 4.0 SP3

Figure A.5   Schematic of installation type 3.

Type 4: Install Over-the-Top

Over-the-top means upgrading directly to SQL Server 6.5 from SQL Server 4.21*x* and to Windows NT 4.0 from Windows NT 3.51. The back-out plan is to restore the previous state of the SQL Server 4.21*x* system.

Advantage:

- **Simplicity.** It is simplest method, provided that nothing goes wrong.

Disadvantage:

- **Complexity.** It becomes the most complex option if something goes wrong because all changes to the original SQL Server 4.21*x* environment must be reversed.

Over-the-Top

1. Production Computer

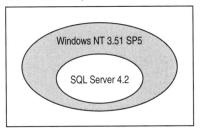

3. Production Computer After Windows NT Install

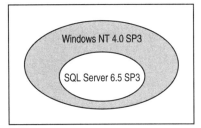

2. Production Computer after SQL Srv 6.5 Install

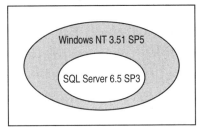

Test Computer

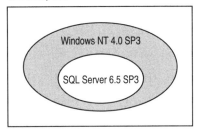

- Install SQL Server 6.5 over 4.2
- Install SQL Server 6.5 SP3
- Install Windows NT 4.0
- Install Windows NT 4.0 SP3

Test Computer
- Install Windows NT 4.0 and Windows NT 4.0 SP3
- Install SQL Server 6.5 SP3
- Load 4.2 Database

Figure A.6   Schematic of installation type 4.

Select Upgrade Options

After selecting an installation type, you must establish strategies for:

- Backup and recovery
- Back-out (according to installation type)
- Back-out for clients
- Database population

Select a Backup and Recovery Strategy

Use disk backups whenever possible to eliminate potential problems reading backups from tape. If you use tape backups for either SQL Server or Windows NT, verify that the tape dump can be loaded.

There are three options for backup and recovery:

Backup and recovery options.

Strategy	Description	Advantages	Disadvantages
SQL Server backup	Uses the SQL Server backup procedures to recover the databases. The databases should undergo full backups. To minimize risk, test the restoration procedure at regular intervals.	This is a known and tested strategy. Every SQL Server 4.21*x* database should have a reliable backup and recovery strategy. Backups from SQL Server 4.21*x* can be restored to the SQL Server 6.5 server, even if keyword incompatibilities exist.	Recovering the SQL Server master database requires the database administrator to take additional steps.
Windows NT file copy and backup of SQL Server device (*.DAT) files	Takes all SQL Server database files and copies or backs them up to a disk or tape. Database recovery is accomplished by copying the files back to their original directory trees.	Simplest of all recovery strategies.	Uses more disk space. This option is compatible only with the pre-upgrade SQL Server installation. Exercise caution, especially if the SQL Server services are on multiple devices and directories. Make sure all .DAT files are backed up.
SQL scripts and bulk copy	Saves all database metadata in script files. All data is stored in **bcp** files. Database recovery involves recreating the master database and applying master **bcp**s, as in syslogins. Databases and devices are recreated.	This is the most flexible option, because the data is stored in a database-independent format. It's the only option available when upgrading from one processor type to another (Intel to Alpha, for example) or when upgrading to a database with a different character set or sort order.	The most complex of the three choices. **bcp** operations occur on one table at a time. Some system tables will require **bcp** copies also. All metadata must be saved in scripts.

For more information, see SQL Server Books Online or "Backing Up and Restoring Databases" in the *MS SQL Server Administrator's Companion* available on Microsoft TechNet.

Select Back-out Strategy According to Installation Type

A back-out plan that restores the system to its original condition should be able to handle the worst-case scenario, which usually entails system and application disk failures. For example, the system administrator should be able to restore the system if a disk failure during installation leaves a mirrored disk configuration in an inconsistent state.

Of the four installation types, the only option that does not require back-out plan is installing SQL Server 6.5 on a new computer, Type 1. The remaining three installation types are listed below in decreasing order of back-out plan complexity:

- Type 4, installing SQL Server 6.5 over the top of SQL Server 4.21*x*
- Type 3, installing SQL Server 6.5 side by side with SQL Server 4.21*x*
- Type 2, installing SQL Server 6.5 and Windows NT 4.0 on the same computer as Windows NT 3.51 and SQL Server 4.21*x*

These SQL Server server-side objects are added or modified during the SQL Server 6.5 upgrade or installation and must be addressed by all back-out strategies.

- SQL Server 6.5 application files and directories.
- SQL Server installs all of its application files in a directory tree under a path specified by the user at installation time. The default directory is C:\Mssql or in the case of installation type 4 (over-the-top) C:\Sql.
- SQL Server converted databases, including the master database. By default, these databases exist underneath the SQL Server directory tree in the ...\data directory.
- SQL Server 6.5 registry entries. SQL Server stores its current configuration state in these Windows NT registry entries:

```
HKEY_LOCAL_MACHINE\SOFTWARE\Microsoft\MSSQLServer
HKEY_CURRENT_USER\SOFTWARE\Microsoft\MSSQLServer
HKEY_LOCAL_MACHINE\SYSTEM\CurrentControlSet\Services\MSSQLServer
HKEY_LOCAL_MACHINE\SYSTEM\CurrentControlSet\Services\SQLExecutive
```

Back-out Strategy for Over-the-Top Installation

This upgrade option requires the most complex back-out plan. You must assume that a failed installation might leave the SQL Server databases and application files in a state of limbo.

1. Run the SQL Setup Utility (SETUP.EXE) and select the **Remove SQL Server** option. The next screen asks if you want to remove the files from the Microsoft SQL Server 6.5 application directory tree. Before selecting this option, make sure that no SQL Server 4.21*x* devices are underneath this tree and that there is a valid backup of the SQL Server 4.21*x* databases.

2. Manually clean up directories and the Windows NT registry. Delete the SQL Server application directory tree, where the files related to the SQL Setup Utility still exist. Invoke the registry editor, REGEDT32.EXE, and remove any of the registry keys listed above that still exist.

3. If you chose to install SQL Server 6.5 files within the existing SQL Server 4.21x directory tree, restore the SQL Server 4.21x application directory tree.

4. Replace the SQL Server 4.21x application directory tree over the SQL Server 4.21x application directory tree.

5. Restore the SQL Server 4.21x databases (depending on the database backup strategy selected). The simplest method is to copy the SQL Server device files to disk or use Windows NT backup to save all of the SQL Server device files on tape. Copy the file to disk if you have the disk space available.

Back-out Strategy for Side-by-Side Installation

1. Run the SQL Setup Utility (SETUP.EXE) and select the **Remove SQL Server** option. The next screen asks if you want to remove the files from the SQL Server 6.5 application directory tree. Check the **libpath** system variable to ensure that you are referencing SQL Server 6.5 files and not SQL Server 4.21x files. Be careful not to delete the SQL Server 4.21x database devices.

2. Manually clean up directories and the Windows NT registry. Delete the SQL Server 6.5 application directory tree, where the files related to the SQL setup utility (SETUP.EXE) still exist. Invoke the registry editor, REGEDT32.EXE, and remove the registry keys listed above.

Back-out Strategy for Same Computer Installation

1. Run the SQL Setup Utility (SETUP.EXE) and select the **Remove SQL Server** option. The next screen asks if you want to remove the files from the SQL Server 6.5 application directory tree. Be careful about touching the separate Windows NT 3.51 and the SQL Server 4.21x directory trees, especially the SQL Server database devices.

2. Manually clean up directories and the Windows NT registry. Delete the SQL Server 6.5 application directory tree, where the files related to the SQL Setup Utility (SETUP.EXE) will still exist. Invoke the registry editor (REGEDT32.EXE), and remove the registry keys listed above.

Back-out Strategy for New Computer Installation

1. Run the SQL Setup Utility (SETUP.EXE) and select the **Remove SQL Server** option. The next screen asks if you want to remove the files from the SQL Server 6.5 application directory tree. Be careful about touching the separate Windows NT 3.51 and the SQL Server 4.21x directory trees, especially the SQL Server database devices.

2. Manually clean up directories and the Windows NT registry. Delete the SQL Server 6.5 application directory tree, where the files related to the SQL Setup Utility (SETUP.EXE) are located. Invoke the registry editor (REGEDT32.EXE), and remove the registry keys listed above.

Backing out SQL Server Clients

Backing out client software is not as critical as backing out server software because SQL Server 6.5 clients are backward compatible with SQL Server 4.21x. These procedures describe the back-out steps to use if there are problems between the new version of the client and the SQL Server 4.21x database.

Back-out 32-Bit Clients:

1. From C:\Mssql, run the SQL Server Setup Utility (SETUP.EXE) and select **Remove Client Utilities and all files**.

2. Run the registry editor (REGEDIT.EXE) to remove the remaining registry entry.

    `HKEY_LOCAL_Machine\Software\Microsoft\Mssqlserver`

3. Reinstall the SQL Server 4.21x client software.

Back-out 16-Bit Clients:

1. Delete the application directory tree where the SQL Server client software was installed.

2. Remove the SQL Server entries from the WIN.INI file.

3. Reinstall the SQL Server 4.21x client software.

Back-out MS-DOS Clients:

1. Remove the files copied from the \Clients\MSDOS installation directory.

2. Reinstall the SQL Server 4.21x client software.

SQL Server 6.5 Database Population Strategy

SQL Server 6.5 must be loaded with the SQL Server 4.21x databases after a successful installation. The three methods of accomplishing this are:

■ Installing SQL Server 6.5 and Windows NT 4.0 over the top of SQL Server 4.21x and Windows NT 3.51.

■ Loading SQL Server 4.21x dump files. This process is similar to the recovery process described in the section "Select a Backup and Recovery Strategy."

■ Running SQL scripts and **bcp**. This process requires a thorough understanding of the database metadata and data, including client-specific information stored in the master and syslogins.

Develop the Service Offering Document

The service offering document lists the tasks required to upgrade from SQL Server 4.21x to SQL Server 6.5 and, if necessary, from Windows NT 3.51 to Windows NT 4.0. The list of tasks may be the minimal amount of functionality required to start the upgrade; any additional functionality will be provided in subsequent upgrade "versions."

By implementing functionality in stages, you can keep the scope manageable and the delivery on schedule. When you have determined the functionality of a particular version, freeze it and save any further functionality requests for later versions. For SQL Server 6.5, determine which databases to convert, their conversion order, and the conversion order of associated applications.

Determine Activity Flow

To define the service offering:

- Start with a list of required tasks generated from the database environment design and installation type that you selected.
- Examine costs and potential risks for each requirement.
- Identify and place acceptable requirements in the service offering, so they become part of the project plan.
- After the service offering is agreed to, it should not be changed without agreement from all parties.

Identify Functionality

To determine functions and services, prioritize the entire list of items into groups and evaluate the implementation and support costs, starting with the highest. Separate the functions into these groups:

- Building the test environment
- Resolving SQL Server 6.5 incompatibilities
- Converting applications
- Installing servers
- Installing clients
- Testing after the upgrade

Specify Operational Constraints

Identify any operational constraints, such as database operational hours and important business milestones. When the deliverable functionality is agreed upon, it should be signed-off by the project manager, product manager, and other stakeholders.

Use an Installation Checklist

A checklist can help keep track of the upgrade process. Task explanations follow the sample below.

Installation Checklist.

Item	Value	Purpose
Choose one of the four installation options.		Pre-installation
User name Company name		Installation
Product ID		Installation
Licensing option • Per-server • Per-seat		Installation
SQL Server root directory • Free disk space > 60 MB • With Books Online > 75 MB		Installation
Master device size • 25 MB (required) • 40 MB or larger (recommended)		Installation
Character set • SQL Server 4.21x • SQL Server 6.5 (same recommended)		Installation
Sort Order • SQL Server 4.21x (default: binary order) • SQL Server 6.5 (dictionary order, case-insensitive)		Installation
Network Transports Check Windows NT transports; enable local named pipes if no networks are installed.		Installation
Auto-start • SQL Server • SQL Executive		Installation
SQL Executive user account Valid Windows NT domain account (Include the domain with the user name, as in domain/username.)		Pre-installation/ minimum requirement/ installation issue

Definitions of key checklist terms:

- **User name, company name, product ID.** The product ID is provided on the SQL Server CD case.

- **Licensing option.** Licensing includes per-server and per-seat options. Check SQL Server 6.5 license to determine the type of option purchased.

- **SQL Server root directory.** The drive and directory for the SQL Server root directory become the installation path where the setup program will place the SQL Server files. The default is C:\Mssql.

- **Master device size.** The space allocated to the **master** database device; the default and minimum size is 25 MB. If disk space is available, increase the **master** database device minimum to 40 MB to save time later if additional space is needed. Choosing the correct device size is not so critical with SQL Server 6.5 as it was with SQL Server 4.21x; SQL Server 6.5 allows you to expand and shrink devices as space requirements change.

- **Selected character set.** Try to keep the same character set and code page as the SQL Server 4.21x database. If you are using a SQL Server 4.21x dump for upgrading, the same character set and code page are required when moving to SQL Server 6.5. Note that the default code page and character set changes during the SQL Server 4.21x-to-6.5 setup process. If you are planning to use replication, the character sets of all participating servers must be the same.

- **Sort order.** It is important to select the correct sort order: the default for SQL Server 4.21x is *binary*, for SQL Server 6.5 it is *case-insensitive*.

- **SQL Server Books Online installed.** These require an extra 15 MB; installing them is highly recommended if you don't plan on upgrading beyond SQL Server 6.5. If you do plan on upgrading to SQL Server 7.0, then the online books may not be practical.

- **Auto-Start options.** Do you want SQL Server to start when Windows NT starts? Do you want SQL Executive (the SQL Server 6.5 scheduler) to start when Windows NT starts? SQL Executive is new to SQL Server 6.5 and is the scheduling mechanism you use to automate backups and replication schedules.

- **SQL Executive user account.** Choose the Windows NT account that you want the SQL Executive user context to start in. Your options are **LocalSystem** or an account that you specify. If you specify an account, make sure it's a Windows NT administrator account known to all SQL Server computers. If you plan to use replication, specify a Windows NT administrator account specifically for the SQL Executive. Replication uses trusted connections so the subscriber computer must recognize the SQL Executive user account as a valid Windows NT account.

Set up the Test Environment

A test plan is a critical project component, especially for high-risk ones with highly visible or very complex database applications. Organizations that depend on SQL Server 4.21x applications should upgrade to SQL Server 6.5 only if they can ensure the upgrade will not negatively affect targeted business applications, and this requires a test team and a test lab with the correct environment. Setting up a test environment includes installing and configuring test servers with SQL Server versions 4.21x and 6.5, and configuring test client computers. A test environment can also serve as a pilot for new servers that host SQL Server 6.5.

The test team should create a plan that thoroughly examines the new system, produces concrete results, is repeatable, and provides a method of detecting differences between test runs against the SQL Server 4.21x and SQL Server 6.5 environments. A good test plan includes:

- Identified applications, databases, and client environments
- Test environment configuration options for servers and clients
- Comprehensive test script
- Automated test run process
- Output capture and comparison utilities
- Ability to reproduce the environment to a known state
- Separate test servers
- Side-by-side installations
- Separate clients
- Clients on the test server
- Actual clients

Identify Test Target Objects

Incorporate information gathered from the database environment diagrams and the database environment tables into a test plan that answers these questions:

- What is the risk level associated with converting each database, application, and user profile? (Incorporate higher-risk items into the test environment; omit lower-risk items.)
- Is there any commonality between databases or user profiles? (Omit similar databases or user profiles.)

SQL Server 6.5 introduces many new reserved keywords, or database object names. As the project team converts SQL Server 4.21x databases to SQL Server 6.5, check for and remove keywords that conflict with reserved keywords in SQL Server 6.5. (The section "Convert Databases and Applications" on page 526 discusses this in greater detail.) The test environment should include an instance of the SQL Server 4.21*x* databases as well as an instance of SQL Server 6.5 databases. The test team can also save multiple versions of the SQL Server 6.5 test databases to track the changes required for the new database.

Define the Test Server Environment

After the test team identifies the test target objects, it specifies the hardware and software required to test them. The test lab should include test environments for SQL Server 4.21*x* and SQL Server 6.5. The team must also maintain a clean separation between the SQL Server 6.5 *test* environment and the SQL Server 4.21*x production* environment. The test team can choose to install multiple test servers: one test system operating on Windows NT 3.51 and SQL Server 4.21*x*, and another on Windows NT 4.0 and SQL Server 6.5. One computer can run both SQL Server 4.21*x* and SQL Server 6.5, simulating a same-computer or side-by-side installation.

Set up SQL Server 6.5 test computers so they match the four installation types (new computer, same computer, over-the-top, and side-by-side) and load test databases, either in a backup format or with copies of the SQL Server devices (.DAT files), SQL scripts, and bulk copy program (.BCP) files. Here are four test server environment scenarios:

- **Use the new production server as the test server.** The test servers use the end-state SQL Server 6.5 production hardware and software (an attractive option, considering SQL Server 4.21*x* server hardware technology may be out of date).

- **Identify a separate test server.** Using a separate test server rather than a current production server for testing separates the production and test environments. Install SQL Server 4.21*x* on the test server if it is infeasible to run the test scripts against the production server with SQL Server 4.21*x*. Configure the test server as closely as possible to the production one.

- **Use the existing production server as the test server.** If your organization doesn't want to buy test hardware, there are two SQL Server installation options:

  - Install Windows NT Server 4.0 on the same computer as Windows NT 3.51. This requires taking the production system down when testing, and risks disrupting the production environment while in test mode.

  - Install SQL Server 6.5 side-by-side SQL Server 4.21*x*. This risks accidentally damaging the existing production environment when it is in test mode, and requires the test team to direct clients carefully to the correct server instance.

- **Go directly to production.** This scenario works for minimum-risk upgrades—for example, upgrading a database that few users access or that is not critical to daily operations.

Define the Test Client Environment

Choose one of the three test client environment options:

- **Configure separate client computers.** This isolates the test and production environments, and allows the team to test a variety of client production environments. The team has to procure and configure client computers. Having separate computers for test clients is important if the client environments differ significantly from the server environments (Windows 3.1, Windows 3.11, or Macintosh, for example).

- **Place the client on the same computer as the test server.** This is suitable when the client or user profile risk is low, the clients are 32-bit applications, and testing client performance is not a primary goal.

- **Use existing client computers.** This works with friendly clients, when there is low risk and a short test period.

Create Test Scripts

The next step is to build test scripts, which is especially challenging when the applications accessing the SQL Server databases have sophisticated user interfaces. Such applications include those written by vendors, in-house programs written in C, and applications (such as Microsoft Access) written in fourth-generation language (4GL) tools. There are four methods for developing and invoking test scripts.

- **Generate SQL statements manually.** This requires a general understanding of how an end-user or application accesses the SQL Server database. It entails the least setup work, but allows the greatest margin for error.

- **Sample targeted user 4GL applications for representative SQL statements.** Use this method when applications access the database through ad hoc queries, reports, and 4GL tools such as Microsoft Access. Identify target users and interview them to determine the best SQL statements to include in the test suite.

- **Document application usage for complex environments.** Define the critical operations for identified applications. Document the scripts that users follow to use an application on SQL Server 4.21x and 6.5, then incorporate this information into test scripts users can execute while the test team observes the application-database interaction.

- **Capture inbound SQL statements.** Trap incoming SQL statements generated by an application to build an automated test script. This method works well with the previous method. An automated test suite doesn't require users and provides a base test that the team can modify to generate other scripts. Scripts can be entered directly into the ISQL command-line utility to generate SQL Server 4.21x and SQL Server 6.5 test output for comparison. This approach requires capturing SQL statements after each application modification and involves additional work.

Methods for capturing input test scripts:

- **SQLEYE (on SQL Server 4.21x only).** This tool uses the published SQL Server Open Data Services Service Provider Interface (SPI) to emulate SQL Server. As a pass-through utility, SQLEYE logs incoming SQL Server 4.21*x* information and calls the DB-Library to pass the information to the actual SQL Server.

- **SQL Trace (on SQL Server 6.5 only).** This incorporates SQLEYE functionality into SQL Server 6.5, allowing you to save captured SQL statements in script files. For more information, search SQL Server Books Online for *SQL Trace*.

- **DBCC trace flags.** Invoking DBCC TRACEON (4032) redirects incoming SQL statements to either the current client or the error log. For more information, search SQL Server Books Online for *trace flags*.

- **Modify the application code.** Modify the target application with hooks that capture SQL statements generated by the application.

SQLEYE and SQL Trace provide the cleanest output, but setting up SQLEYE requires some additional work. DBCC trace flags demand less setup work, but more work to capture output. Modifying application code requires the most work and frequently introduces errors.

Convert Databases and Applications

Before you can convert databases and applications in SQL Server 4.21*x* to SQL Server 6.5, you must identify and resolve keyword conflicts, and correct syntactic and semantic differences.

Keyword Conflict Resolution for Databases

SQL Server 6.5 uses a number of new reserved keywords:

```
AUTHORIZE
CASCADE
CROSS
DISTRIBUTED
ESCAPE
FULL
INNER
JOIN
LEFT
OUTER
PRIVELEGES
RESTRICT
RIGHT
SCHEMA
WORK
```

The CHKUPG65.EXE utility identifies existing database object names that conflict with SQL Server 6.5 reserved keywords, detects deleted database code stored in syscomments, and writes this information to an output file. Run the utility and review the report and resolve all keyword conflicts and issues with syscomments. For more information, see "Running the CHKUPG65.EXE Utility" in SQL Server Books Online.

Note   CHKUPG65.EXE was called CHKUPG.EXE in earlier versions of SQL Server, but the functionality is the same.

You must also manually modify all SQL Server system procedures—especially stored procedures and triggers—to reflect database object name changes. You can do this before or after upgrading to SQL Server 6.5. Recompiling stored procedures and recreating the triggers after upgrading to SQL Server 6.5, helps identify system procedures that need modification. Be sure to document all database object name changes and distribute them to the test team members and users.

You can also use the scanning tool, SQL65KWD.BAT, which uses Windows NT FINDSTR.EXE to find keywords to export all SQL Server database objects and procedures into ASCII script files. It can scan any ASCII file including SQL Trace and SQLEYE output, SQL Server output enabled through the DBCC TRACEON (4302) option, and application source code.

To use SQL65KWD.BAT, enter this command at the MS-DOS prompt:

```
sql65kwd %1 %2
```

where *%1* is the file to scan, *%2* is the file to receive the scan output.

Then enter the SQL65KWD.BAT file:

```
rem sql65kwd.bat %1 %2
rem %1 - File to search
rem %2 - File to output results to
findstr /I /N /G:sql65kwd.txt %1 > %2
```

This batch file tool also requires a keyword input file SQL65KWD.TXT:

```
ABSOLUTE
ACTION
ALLOCATE
ARE
ASSERTION
AT
AUTHORIZATION
BOTH
CASCADE
CASCADED
```

CASE
CAST
CATALOG
CHAR_LENGTH
CHARACTER
CHARACTER_LENGTH
CHECK
CLOSE
COALESCE
COLLATE
COLLATION
COLUMN
COMMITTED
CONNECT
CONNECTION
CONSTRAINT
CONSTRAINTS
CORRESPONDING
CROSS
CURRENT
CURRENT_DATE
CURRENT_TIME
CURRENT_TIMESTAMP
CURRENT_USER
CURSOR
DATE
DAY
DEALLOCATE
DEFERRABLE
DEFERRED
DESCRIBE
DESCRIPTOR
DIAGNOSTICS
DISCONNECT
DISTRIBUTED
DOMAIN
DOUBLE
END_EXEC
ESCAPE
EXCEPTION
EXPIREDATE
EXTERNAL
EXTRACT
FALSE
FETCH
FIRST
FLOPPY
FOREIGN
FULL
GET

```
GLOBAL
HOUR
IDENTITY
IDENTITY_INSERT
IDENTITYCOL
IMMEDIATE
INITIALLY
INNER
INPUT
INSENSITIVE
INTERVAL
ISOLATION
JOIN
KEY
LAST
LEADING
LEFT
LEVEL
LOCAL
MATCH
MINUTE
MONTH
NAMES
NATIONAL
NATURAL
NCHAR
NEXT
NO
NOCHECK
NULLIF
OCTET_LENGTH
OF
ONLY
OPEN
OPTION
OUTER
OUTPUT
OVERLAPS
PAD
PARTIAL
PIPE
POSITION
PRECISION
PRESERVE
PRIMARY
PRIOR
PRIVILEGES
READ
REFERENCES
RELATIVE
```

```
REPLICATION
RESTRICT
RETAINDAYS
RIGHT
ROWS
SCHEMA
SCROLL
SECOND
SERIALIZABLE
SESSION
SESSION_USER
SIZE
SOME
SPACE
SQLSTATE
SYSTEM_USER
THEN
TIME
TIMESTAMP
TIMEZONE_HOUR
TIMEZONE_MINUTE
TRAILING
TRANSLATE
TRANSLATION
TRUE
UNCOMMITTED
UNKNOWN
UPDATETEXT
USAGE
USER
USING
VALUE
VARYING
VOLUME
WHEN
WORK
WRITE
YEAR
ZONE
```

You can also use the SET QUOTED IDENTIFIER ON functionality to enclose keywords (including reserved keywords) in double quotes (" "). This feature (also in SQL Server 6.0) provides American National Standard Institute (ANSI) compatibility. If you use this feature, however, you must also quote the keywords in procedures and application code. Change keywords whenever possible to avoid modifying application code.

Keyword Conflicts in Applications

After modifying databases, you must also modify applications to eliminate object names that conflict with SQL Server 6.5 reserved keywords. Developers should review and scan application code and captured outbound SQL statements. Identifying semantic differences that escape this process requires detailed analysis of code, captured logs, or both.

Although the CHKUPG65.EXE utility (described in the section "Keyword Conflict Resolution for Databases" on page 526) detects reserved keywords on the server level, SQL Server 6.5 does not include a similar tool to detect keyword conflicts on the client level. The project team can use the tools briefly described below (see also the section "Create Test Scripts" on page 525):

- **Search application code with SQL65KWD.BAT.** The most direct method for detecting conflicts (see "Keyword Conflict Resolution for Databases").

- **Use SQLEYE.** Captures outbound SQL statements from SQL Server applications. SQLEYE uses the published SQL Server Open Data Services SPI to emulate SQL Server. As a pass-through utility, SQLEYE logs incoming SQL Server information and calls DB-Library to pass the information to the target SQL Server.

- **Invoke DBCC TRACEON (4032).** Another capturing tool, this redirects incoming SQL statements to either the current client connection or the error log.

- **Use SQL Trace.** Saves captured SQL statements in script files.

Correct Syntactic Differences

SQL Server 6.5 is SQL-92 compliant, so developers will have to rewrite and recompile some stored procedures. In SQL Server 4.21x, Transact-SQL syntax for some sub-queries and SQL statements, such as GROUP BY, are not SQL-92 compliant, and executing stored procedures containing these statements will cause SQL Server 4.21x syntax errors in SQL Server 6.5. To correct them, you must drop and re-create the offending procedure.

You can use trace flags (most notably flag 204) to instruct SQL Server 6.5 to revert to SQL Server 4.21x behavior, but you should do this only as a temporary workaround. Specific syntactic differences are listed below.

SQL Statement Will Not Run

- Columns must be in both the SELECT and GROUP BY clauses, unless they have been aggregated in the SELECT list.

- Modification of table aliases within a query.

- Tables and stored procedures prefixed with "##" refer to global, rather than local objects.

- Temporary tables can now be up to 20 characters long.
- Stricter parameter passing.
- Single and double quotes have different meanings based on the setting of SET QUOTED_IDENTIFIER.
- User-defined DATATYPE names.
- Extended procedures must be recompiled and re-linked.
- Null checks operate in runtime.
- New reserved keywords.
- ANSI style and "old" outer join syntax cannot be mixed in the same query.
- Conditional Compilation no longer available.
- Extended procedures created only in the **master** database.

SQL Statement Will Run with the Trace Flag Enabled

Setting DBCC trace flags to change SQL Server 6.5 behavior back to that of SQL Server 4.21*x* avoids syntax error messages such as:

- Error 204 (Disable SQL-92 behavior).
- Columns must be in both the SELECT and GROUP BY clauses, unless they have been aggregated in the SELECT list
- Order by items must appear in the SELECT list if DISTINCT is specified.
- Not specifying a column name with SELECT INTO or CREATE VIEW.
- SQL Server 6.5 doesn't allow nested aggregates.
- Error 110.
- Duplicate table names in FROM clause are treated differently.

Correct Semantic Differences

Finding all possible SQL Server 6.5 incompatibilities during this step is often not possible. A complete SQL language parser would be required to identify every instance where SQL Server 6.5 semantics change SQL Server 4.21*x* statement results. Comprehensive test scripts can ensure a successful upgrade. Specific semantic differences are listed below:

SQL Statement Runs but Returns Different Results

- Changes made to some system tables.
- Changes to system stored procedures.
- Queries.
- LIKE evaluates trailing blanks differently in fixed length strings.

- BETWEEN operator.
- DATEDIFF function more accurately reflects the number of "minute boundaries" crossed.
- Numeric constants with decimal value are represented as numeric, not float.
- Sub-queries introduced by a comparison operator such as " > ALL" will now evaluate to true when the sub-query returns no rows.
- Sub-queries now conform to ANSI Standard.
- Default NULLABILITY setting can be configured.
- CREATE TABLE, and ALTER TABLE.
- Primary key and foreign key implementation (SP_PRIMARYKEY, SP_FOREIGNKEY, SP_DROPKEY).
- Microsoft Distributed Transaction Coordinator can change the behavior of remote procedures.
- Remotely stored procedures.
- SELECT-INTO is now an atomic operation.
- RAISERROR error numbers minimum value has increased to 50,000.
- RAISERROR sets @@ERROR to zero if severity is ten or less.

Application Conversion Risk

You can delay application modification until after the SQL Server upgrade, but you may encounter cases wherein applications fail or return different result sets. You should defer modification when the risk of breaking an application is low, or when you cannot determine the full extent to which SQL Server applications access a database. For example, when users have developed Microsoft Access and Excel queries to download departmental data, it is difficult to identify all applications that access a database. Users can take care of the changes if you inform them of the new object names.

Assigning developers who have experience with the target applications minimizes the risk of converting the applications during the upgrade. If this is not possible, a comprehensive set of test scripts becomes much more important.

The goal is to maintain or improve application performance. Upgrading the server hardware and operating system can help. Measure existing application performance before and after upgrading in a controlled environment (a stand-alone environment, if possible). Although the majority of the modifications involve keywords, the open database connectivity (ODBC) changes to SQL Server 6.5 can affect application performance.

The issues to examine include:

ODBC Changes

- ODBC SQL Server driver has ARITHABORT turned on (default).
- ODBC 2.65 default behavior.
- Changes in ODBC drivers affect utilization of **tempdb**.
- Additional issues to look out for:

Database Administrator

- Changing sort order can affect application behavior.
- SQL Server 6.5 appends database dumps to devices (default) rather than overwriting the existing device.
- New installations write to root directory C:\Mssql (default).
- Fewer concurrent Win16 ISQL/w connections from a single client due to larger packet sizes.
- Removal of graphical SHOWPLAN.
- Objects can now be created in a transaction.

DB-Library

- VBSQL.OCX Replaces VBSQL.VBX

Test Applications

Testing should begin after the initial database and application conversion. Refer to the previous section "Set Up the Test Environment" for more details. Here is a high-level test sequence:

1. Run test scripts against original applications and save the results. If the application does not produce output you can use for comparison, write out the expected behavior.
2. Run a specific set of performance test scripts against original applications, save the results and use them later to contrast performance between the environments.
3. Determine the database object names and keywords that require modification.
4. Eliminate keyword conflicts in the SQL Server 4.21x database objects or upgrade to SQL Server 6.5 and modify the database objects.
5. Record these changes and communicate them to all constituents.
6. Modify applications to reflect the new database object names.
7. Modify applications to remove semantic differences. The first pass may not capture them all. Compare output results for validation.

8. Run specified test scripts against new applications and save results. This requires several steps:

    a. Run test scripts against applications to generate outbound SQL statements.

    b. Use the outbound SQL to produce result files.

    c. Compare SQL Server 4.21x and SQL Server 6.5 results. If different, investigate the differences and repeat the steps beginning with application modification. When the results are identical, move to the next activity, installing SQL Server 6.5.

9. Run performance test scripts. Ensure that the performance matches or improves in the new environment.

Install SQL Server 6.5

After careful planning and comprehensive testing, the project team can install SQL Server 6.5. Use the Installation Planning Checklist (see the section "Use an Installation Checklist" on page 521) as a guide for running a smooth installation.

Estimate System Downtime

Estimate required system downtime. Convert databases and applications during off-peak hours or on a weekend to minimize impact on users. Estimated downtime depends on how long it takes to:

- Back up the databases.
- Test for and resolve system object name conflicts.
- Perform the SQL Server 6.5 upgrade.
- Convert the database, which includes freezing the production database, resolving system object name conflicts, and loading the SQL Server 4.21x database to SQL Server 6.5.

Database size is the most significant factor in estimating system downtime. Here's a rule of thumb for estimating an over-the-top installation, Type 4:

- 1–10 gigabyte (GB) database takes less than six hours.
- 10 – 20 GB database takes 6 – 10 hours.
- 20 – 50 GB database takes 10 – 20 hours.
- A 50+ GB database can take over 24 hours.

Upgrade Task Checklist

This walks through the installation and upgrade process for each installation type:

Installation and upgrade checklist.

Step	Installation Type				Description
	New Computer	**Same Computer**	**Side-by-Side**	**Over-the-Top**	
1	x	x	x	x	Ensure that latest vendor Hardware Access Layers (HAL) are installed.
2	x	x	x	x	Install latest Windows NT 3.51 Service Pack 5. (Included on TechNet.)
3	x	x	x	x	Fill out Installation Planning Checklist.
4	x	x	x	x	Create a set of SQL scripts used to verify a successful SQL Server 6.5 upgrade. This step usually occurs as part of the test plan. *Don't omit this step if you upgrade without a test plan.*
5	x	x	x	x	Gather information to recreate databases and devices on the SQL Server 6.5 system.
					There should be no new databases after this step.
					For manual database and device creation, use the SQL Server 4.21x administrator utility to obtain:
					• Database size and space available for each database.
					• Device size and space available for each device.
					For automating the database and device creation, write a SQL script to create SQL Server 4.21x databases and devices, simplify the existing database/device relationships. Enforce a one-database-to-one-device relationship.
					The over-the-top upgrade requires this information to recreate the master SQL Server 4.21x database/device environment in case of installation failure.

	Installation Type				
Step	**New Computer**	**Same Computer**	**Side-by-Side**	**Over-the-Top**	**Description**
6	x	x	x	x	Check for SQL Server 6.5 keyword conflicts.
					Run CHKUPG65.EXE from the SQL Server 6.5 installation directory. This reports keyword conflicts and whether syscomments has any deleted source code. Restore any source code before continuing the installation.
					Use SQL Server Object Manager to dump the source code for stored procedures and triggers into a file. Use SQL65KWD.BAT to search the file for keyword conflicts.
7	x	x	x	x	Back up all SQL Server databases. Ensure there is a reliable backup of SQL Server 4.21*x* databases before renaming system objects.
					To ensure that your backup is sound, restore the backup to test databases. Bypass this step if you are confident of the back up and restore strategy, and both have been tested recently.
8		x	x	x	Back up the Windows NT registry files.
9		x	x	x	Back up the SQL Server directory tree.
10	Optional	Optional	Optional	x	Begin installation. Notify users of the SQL Server downtime. Freeze all SQL Server 4.21*x* databases. Shut SQL Server down and start it in single user mode.
					Note: Data in all upgrades other than the over-the-top option can be frozen later but this requires creating an additional copy of SQL Server 4.21*x* databases for resolving system object name conflicts. Remember that resolving the object name conflicts affects applications running against the production environment.
					Use **sp_configure** to temporarily double the open objects and lock parameters before the over-the-top installation.

(continued)

	Installation Type				
Step	**New Computer**	**Same Computer**	**Side-by-Side**	**Over-the-Top**	**Description**
11	Optional				Install Windows NT 3.51, Service Pack 5 and SQL Server 4.21*x* on the new computer.
					Rather than installing Windows NT 4.0 and loading the SQL Server 4.21*x* databases with the modified system object names, reproduce the existing environment on the new computer, and then perform an over-the-top upgrade. This option requires installing Windows NT 4.0 *after* SQL Server 6.5.
12	x	x	x	x	Eliminate all reserved word conflicts in the SQL Server 4.21*x* database object names, stored procedures, and triggers. Continue running **Step 6** until there are no more system object conflicts.
					Save the SQL commands used to modify SQL Server keywords and code: this documentation allows the team to reproduce any work if something goes wrong with the installation, and restore the backup copy of the SQL Server databases.
					If using SQL Scripts and the bulk copy program (**bcp**) to load the SQL Server 4.21x databases into SQL Server 6.5, eliminate conflicts now. Otherwise another option is to defer eliminating keyword conflicts until after the upgrade to SLQ Server 6.5.
13	x	x	x		Execute this step if you have not executed **Step 10** yet.
					Begin installation. Notify users of the SQL Server downtime. Freeze all SQL Server 4.21*x* databases. Shut SQL Server down and start it in single-user mode.
					Apply all system object name changes discovered in **Step 12**. Testing against a database other than the production one requires this additional work, but is worthwhile and can minimize production system downtime.

	Installation Type				
Step	**New Computer**	**Same Computer**	**Side-by-Side**	**Over-the-Top**	**Description**
14	x	x	x		Load the SQL Server 4.21*x* database to the 6.5 version. Use backup files, or a combination of **bcp**s for the data and the SQL Object Manager for the system objects and code.
15	x	x			Install Windows NT 4.0 and Service Pack 3 (highly recommended).
					Organizations using Windows NT 3.51 might postpone moving to Windows NT 4.0. **Note:** Project teams that choose **Step 11** execute this step after installing SQL Server 6.5.
					For the same-computer upgrade option only, reboot to Windows NT 4.0.
					Note: Installing a new version of Windows NT results in two Windows NT machine names: one for the Windows NT 3.51 system and one for the Windows NT 4.0 system (if both are members of a Windows NT domain).
					Naming decisions affect client access to the database.
16	x	x	x	x	Install SQL Server 6.5.
17	x	x	x	x	Check for a successful installation:
					Check the SQL Server installation log files.
					Reboot the computer if no errors were detected.
					Start SQL Server. Check the event viewer for errors.
					Start SQL/Executive. Check the event viewer for errors.
					Set the default network access. Invoke the SQL Client Configuration Utility within the SQL Server program group. Select the Net Library tab and set the default network from **Named Pipes** to the network stack used by the majority of clients accessing the server.

(continued)

	Installation Type				
Step	**New Computer**	**Same Computer**	**Side-by-Side**	**Over-the-Top**	**Description**
					Test DBLIB connectivity:
					• Register SQL Server into SQL Server Enterprise Manager by machine name [use the machine name, not (local)].
					• Click on the + to see if the SQL Server Enterprise Manager can access the server information.
					• If this fails, find out why and resolve.
					Test ODBC connectivity:
					• Run MS-Query.
					• Create a DSN and connect to SQL Server.
					• See if a list of table names is displayed.
					• If this fails, find out why and resolve.
18	x		x		Apply SQL Server 6.5 Service Pack 3. Reboot and execute **Step 17**.
19	x	x	x		Recreate the database and devices on SQL Server 6.5 manually or with the script file generated in **Step 6**. This is not necessary for over-the-top installations.
20	x	x	x		Restore the databases: If you used backup, restore all databases. If you used scripts and **bcp**: • Recreate system objects and systems procedures with the script generated in **Step 5**. • Use **bcp** to copy files created in **Step 14**.
21	x	x	x	x	Execute **Step 12**: If you deferred keyword conflict resolution until after the upgrade, do it now.
22	x	x	x	x	**Test:** Run the SQL Server Interactive SQL utility, ISQL/w, and the test SQL scripts created in **Step 4**. Run SQL scripts created for the test plan.

| | Installation Type | | | | |
Step	New Computer	Same Computer	Side-by-Side	Over-the-Top	Description
23	Optional		x	x	Install Windows NT 4.0 and Service Pack 3. Rerun **Step 22**.
24	x	x	x	x	Upgrade client environments to SQL Server 6.5.
25	x	x	x	x	Remove the single-user mode restriction for all databases.
26	x	x	x	x	Redirect all clients to the SQL Server 6.5 system if the new computer has a different Windows NT machine name, or if clients access the computer by the network address.
27	x	x	x	x	Verify that applications and ad hoc query tools can access the SQL Server 6.5 system and databases. Distribute the system object name changes to application developers and query users so that they can modify code and queries to conform to the system object name changes.

Upgrade Clients

Client upgrades fall into two categories:

- **Clients.** 32-bit, 16-bit (including Windows 3.1 and Windows 3.11), and MS-DOS

- **Database access layers.**
  - Low-level application programming interfaces (APIs): ODBC and DB-Library
  - Higher-level object interfaces: ActiveX Data Objects (ADO), Advanced Data Connector (ADC), Remote Data Objects (RDO), Data Access Objects (DAO), and Microsoft Visual C++ database classes.

Use the client software upgrade process for user profiles defined in the section "Document the Database Environment" on page 507.

Upgrade 32-Bit Clients

Hardware requirements for 32-bit client upgrades.

Hardware	Requirements
Computer	Refer to HCL compatibility list. For Intel, 80486 is the recommended minimum.
Minimum memory	16 MB (Windows NT), 8 MB (Windows 95)
Disk drive space	A minimum of 21 MB of free disk space for the installation, 11.1 MB for the installed files. Installing SQL Server Books Online on disk adds 15 MB. Running SQL Server Books Online from the CD-ROM adds 1 MB.
Operating system	Windows NT Server and Workstation version 3.5 or later, or Windows 95. (For Windows NT Server and Workstation, version 4.0 is highly recommended.)
Network software	Windows NT or Windows 95 installed software. BANYAN and PATHWORKS require additional software.
Network adapter	Select a Network Internet Card (NIC) from the Hardware Compatibility List for the Windows version you are using, available on TechNet.

The complete set of utilities installed on the client computer:

- **Bulk Copy Program (bcp).** Copies data to or from an operating-system file.
- **ISQL utilities.** ISQL/w and ISQL are used to enter Transact-SQL commands and procedures.
- **SQL Server Enterprise Manager.** Performs server and enterprise administration tasks.
- **SQL Security Manager.** Manages user accounts for SQL Servers that have security integration with Windows NT.
- **Configuration Diagnostics.**
    - **SQL Server Client Configuration Utility.** Determines which version of DB-Library is installed on a client and how to set up SQL Server connection information on a client. (Highly recommended.)
    - **Makepipe/Readpipe.** Tests whether network named pipes are working.

The utilities are installed in these directories under the SQL Server installation path specified in the client setup:

- \BINN (Windows NT-based client executable files)
- \DLL (Dynamic-link library files)
- \INSTALL (SQL Server Books Online files)

To install the 32-bit client, run the SQL Server SETUP.EXE program on the appropriate hardware directory (for example, E:\I386\SETUP.EXE, or E:\SQL65\I386\SETUP.EXE on the BackOffice 2.5 CD-ROM). The setup sequence prompts for the information provided in the following table. Use the table to plan client installation options.

Installation Parameters for 32-Bit Clients.

Parameter	Value(s)	Default Value(s)
SQL Server application device and directory		C:\Mssql
Recommended minimum user configuration of utilities		**bcp** ISQL/w SQL Server Enterprise Manager SQL Server Security Manager Configuration Diagnostics MS Query SQL Server Web Assistant MS DTC Client Support SQL Trace Utility
SQL Server Books Online		Install

Upgrade 16-Bit Clients

The 16-bit SQL Server client installation requires 15 MB of free disk space. After the installation, SQL Server consumes an additional 5 – 6 MB, or, if you are installing SQL Server Books Online, approximately 16.5 MB. Other hardware requirements are similar to those for earlier versions of SQL Server. The upgrade is a two-phase operation: installing SQL Server client and installing ODBC. To install the SQL Server 6.5 client, run \Clients\Win16\SETUP.EXE. The setup sequence prompts you to enter parameters; use the table to plan client installation options.

Installation Parameters for 16-Bit Clients.

Parameter	Value(s)	Default Value(s)
SQL Server application device and directory		C: \Mssql
SQL Server client applications		ISQL (640 KB) Client Configuration Utility (80 KB) SQL Server Books Online (12,640 KB)
Default Network		Named Pipes

If disk space is limited, disable SQL Server Books Online; you should keep the configuration utility and ISQL for diagnostic and troubleshooting purposes.

Upgrade MS-DOS Clients

SQL Server 6.5 does not provide a setup for MS-DOS based clients. To install the software, copy the files from the \Clients\MSDOS directory on the SQL Server CD-ROM into a \Sql60\Bin directory on the client. Add the \Sql60\Bin directory to the computer's executable path, or add an entry to AUTOEXEC.BAT to run the SQL Server client each time the client starts. To upgrade an existing client installation on an MS-DOS based computer, shut down any SQL Server client components and follow the steps for a new installation. To ensure a terminate-and-stay-resident (TSR) is not loaded, at the command prompt, type:

```
Enddblib
```

Upgrade Macintosh Clients

The SQL Server 6.5 installation does not contain software for upgrading Macintosh clients. Macintosh database connectivity depends on specific vendors and applications. Refer to the development environment or application documentation to learn more about the specific database access method used.

Update Database Access Layers

OLE-DB supports access to non-relational information stores and relational databases. You should use the ActiveX Data Object (ADO) Object Model for OLE-DB, unless the environment requires direct access to OLE-DB for full OLE-DB functionality. Converting SQL Server clients from DB-Library to ODBC 3.0 makes the client compatible with future versions of SQL Server. Both DB-Library and ODBC clients require client-based connection strings to connect to SQL Server. If you change the SQL Server name or networking addresses, you must modify all client configurations accordingly. If SQL Server 6.5 installations inherit the previous computer's network address and machine name, you do not need to reconfigure clients.

Conduct a Pilot Test

To make sure that deployment was successful, conduct a pilot test to verify all application and system processes against a test upgrade and the initial upgrade of SQL Server databases. A good test charts the deployment process for the scope of the target audience, and determines design validity, deployment success, and data completeness. The complete pilot test procedure includes selecting the pilot sites, planning and running the pilot test, and evaluating test results.

Select the Pilot Site

Consider the test's focus and objectives, and how visible the pilot site is to other groups and management. Limit the size of the pilot group to approximately one hundred users at the same physical location. Use these criteria:

- Proximity to the project team.

- Ability to provide meaningful feedback.

- Positive attitude towards the project.

- Willingness to talk positively about the experience.

Evaluate Test Results

Define the pilot closure point—the point at which the team and the pilot group can decide whether to continue converting SQL Server databases or to revert to the previous system at the pilot site. Document all issues, problems, concerns, and risks. Include user surveys, lists of technical problems, contact names and numbers, suggestions, time frames, and application performance.

Deploy SQL Server 6.5 on the System

Carry out the deployment processes and procedures developed and validated during the pilot. Work with various business units, database application areas, and sites to deploy SQL Server 6.5 in stages. During deployment, continue to validate implementation scripts, training materials, and certification documents for the existing deployment and future versions of SQL Server.

Survey users after the deployment to find out what they liked or didn't like. Use this information to improve future installations, or to fine-tune the system. Gather requirements for system enhancements from a variety of perspectives:

- **Users** work with the system on a daily basis and can identify future functional requirements.

- **Administrators** perform administrative tasks and can point out ways to automate processes to reduce operational costs.

- **Operations personnel** manage database performance and capacity; they can suggest ways to automate error detection, resolution, and tracking processes too reduce system costs.

- **Technical support personnel** provide information on the topics users call about most frequently, which can be used to fine-tune the system or improve user training.

More Information

List of resources.

Resource	Location
Overview	
Description of Microsoft Solutions Framework	"A Quick Tour of the Solutions Framework Model" on TechNet or http://www.microsoft.com/msf/
Microsoft Developer Network (MSDN): tools and product information	http://msdn/.microsoft.com/developer/
Microsoft TechNet: Technical information, including recent sample application information on Microsoft Exchange	http://www.microsoft.com/technet/
Premier Support Services (PSS) and Technical Assistance Manager (TAM)	http://www.microsoft.com/enterprise/ "Services for the Enterprise—Premier Technical Account Manager" on TechNet
SQL Server training	"Premier Support" on TechNet
	Product Information and Sales: (800) 426-9400
	Consult your MCS liaison or TAM for additional information.
Microsoft BackOffice Resource Kit: Tools and white papers on deployment and management; especially useful when designing the directory synchronization process	http://www.backoffice.microsoft.com
Microsoft SQL Server home page	http://www.microsoft.com/sql/
Channel Training and Certification: Training for network administrators and others	http://www.microsoft.com/directacces/partnering http://www.microsoft.com/train_cert/ Product Information and Sales: (800) 426-9400
Microsoft Solution Providers	http://www.microsoft.com/mcsp/
Microsoft Product Support: updated product information and technical support offerings	http://www.microsoft.com/support/
Personal Support Center: Search or browse for technical support information about Microsoft products and technologies	http://support.microsoft.com/support
Microsoft Press	1-800-MSPRESS (677-7377) http://mspress.microsoft.com/
Windows NT Magazine	http://www.winntmag.com/comm
Planning	
"Choosing a Backup and Restore Strategy"	*MS SQL Server Administrator's Companion* found on TechNet
"MS SQL Server Architectural Planning and Design"	TechNet

Resource	Location
"Planning and Implementing Your SQL Server Solution"	Part 2 of the BackOffice Resource Kit, Second Edition found on TechNet
Software necessary to build a test environment: Windows NT Server 4.0 SQL Server 6.5	http://www.microsoft.com/ntserver estweb/SQL65 Microsoft Sales Information Center (800) 426-9400
Windows NT white papers and related topics	http://www.microsoft.com/ntserver/
SQL Server white papers and related topics	http://www.microsoft.com/sql/
BackOffice Resource Kit. Includes tools and white papers that assist with SQL Server deployment and management.	http://www.microsoft.com/backoffice/
TechNet: technical information, including recent application information on SQL Server	http://www.microsoft.com/technet/
Microsoft Certified Professional (MCP) training	http://www.microsoft.com/mcp/
Development	
"MS SQL Server Support and Troubleshooting"	TechNet
"Planning an Installation or Upgrade"	TechNet
"Migrating Sybase Applications to Microsoft SQL Server"	TechNet
See "Staging" in *SQL Server 6.5 Resource Guide*	TechNet
Q135684, Title: INF: Frequently Asked Questions About Microsoft SQL Server	http://support.microsoft.com/support/kb/articles/ q135/6/84.asp
Q133177, Title: INF: Changes to SQL Server 6.0 That May Affect 4.2x Apps	http://support.microsoft.com/support/kb/articles/ q133/1/77.asp
Q152032, Title: INF: Changes to SQL Server 6.5 that Affect 6.0 Apps	http:://support.microsoft.com/support/kb/articles/ q152/0/32.asp
Q149650, Title: Bug: Upgrade Fails if Not Enough Space on Master for Tempdb	http://support.microsoft.com/support/kb/articles/ q149/6/50.asp
Q149566, Title: BUG: Upgrade/Install Fails if Model DB is Larger Than Msdb	http://support.microsoft.com/support/kb/articles/ q149/5/66.asp
Q150020, Title: BUG: MSDTC Fails to Start if Different Drives/Paths Are Chosen	http://support.microsoft.com/support/kb/articles/ q150/0/20.asp
Q110983, Title: INF: Recommended SQL Server for WIN NT Memory Configurations	http://support.microsoft.com/support/kb/articles/ q110/9/83.asp
Q115050, Title: INF: When to Use Tempdb In RAM	http://support.microsoft.com/support/kb/articles/ q115/0/50.asp
Q152247, Title: INF: Backup Strategies and Tips Before Upgrading SQL Server	http://support.microsoft.com/support/kb/articles/ q152/2/47.asp
Q151050, Title: BUG: 6.5 Upgrade Requires Domain Login for SQL Executive	http://support.microsoft.com/support/kb/articles/ q151/0/50.asp

(continued)

Resource	Location
Q146018, Title: BUG: Database Upgrade May Generate Error #159	http://support.microsoft.com/support/kb/articles/ q146/0/18.asp
Q140895, Title: INF: Diagnostic Tips for the Microsoft SQL Server ODBC Driver	http://support.microsoft.com/support/kb/articles/ q140/8/95.asp
Q138541, Title: INF: ODBCPING.EXE to Verify ODBC Connectivity to SQL Server	http://support.microsoft.com/support/kb/articles/ q138/5/41.asp
"Open Database Connectivity Frequently Asked Questions"	http://support.microsoft.com/support/odbc/faq/ faq3663.asp
"INF: ODBC SQL Server Connection Parameters" (Q137635)	http://support.microsoft.com/support/kb/articles/ q137/6/35.asp
Q166967, Title: INF: Proper SQL Server Configuration Settings	http://support.microsoft.com/support/kb/articles/ q166/9/67.asp
Q166244, Title: SMS: SQL Server Tuning Parameters for Systems Management Server	http://support.microsoft.com/support/kb/articles/ q166/2/44.asp
Q134937, Title: INF: Running SQL Versions 6.0 and 4.21 Side-by-Side	http://support.microsoft.com/support/kb/articles/ q134/9/37.asp
Q119401, Title: INF: Rebuilding SQL Server Entries After Reinstalling Win NT	http://support.microsoft.com/support/kb/articles/ q119/4/01.asp
Q155283, Title: INF: Troubleshooting SQL Executive and Task Scheduling	http://support.microsoft.com/support/kb/articles/ q155/2/83.asp
Q146116, Title: BUG: Load Master DB Can Fail After Master.Dat is Rebuilt	http://support.microsoft.com/support/kb/articles/ q146/1/16.asp
Q140697, Title: INF: Win16 ODBC Applications in a Win32 Environment	http://support.microsoft.com/support/kb/articles/ q140/6/97.asp
Q155697, Title: BUG: SQL Setup Fails If Non-NIC Hardware Profile Is Used	http://support.microsoft.com/support/kb/articles/ q155/6/97.asp
Q134749, Title: PRB: Procedures May Fail w/ MSG 2821 After v.6.0 Upgrade	http://support.microsoft.com/support/kb/articles/ q134/7/49.asp
Deployment	
"Planning and Implementing Your SQL Server Solution"	*BackOffice Resource Kit*, Part 3 on TechNet
"Maintaining Your SQL Server Solution"	*BackOffice Resource Kit*, Part 4 on TechNet
See "Staging" in *SQL Server 6.5 Resource Guide*	TechNet
Microsoft SQL Server 6.5 Deployment Guide	TechNet

Index

Register Today!

Return this
Deploying Microsoft® SQL Server™ 7.0 Notes from the Field
registration card today

OWNER REGISTRATION CARD

0-7356-0726-5

Deploying Microsoft® SQL Server™ 7.0 Notes from the Field

FIRST NAME   MIDDLE INITIAL   LAST NAME

INSTITUTION OR COMPANY NAME

ADDRESS

CITY   STATE   ZIP

(   )

E-MAIL ADDRESS   PHONE NUMBER

U.S. and Canada addresses only. Fill in information above and mail postage-free.
Please mail only the bottom half of this page.

For information about Microsoft Press®
products, visit our Web site at
mspress.microsoft.com

Microsoft®*Press*